Economic Cooperation, Bilateral and Regional Trade Agreements and Investments for Improved International Relations

Anita Medhekar
https://orcid.org/0000-0002-6791-4056
Central Queensland University, Australia

Anisul M. Islam
University of Houston, USA

S. Jobayear Ahmed
https://orcid.org/0000-0001-6356-2666
Bangladesh Foreign Trade Institute, Bangladesh

IGI Global
Scientific Publishing
Publishing Tomorrow's Research Today

Vice President of Editorial — Melissa Wagner
Director of Acquisitions — Mikaela Felty
Director of Book Development — Jocelynn Hessler
Production Manager — Mike Brehm
Cover Design — Jose Rosado

Published in the United States of America by
IGI Global Scientific Publishing
701 East Chocolate Avenue
Hershey, PA, 17033, USA
Tel: 717-533-8845 | Fax: 717-533-7115
Website: https://www.igi-global.com E-mail: cust@igi-global.com

Library of Congress Cataloging-in-Publication Data

Names: Medhekar, Anita, 1962- editor | Islam, Anisul M., 1952- editor | Ahmed, S. Jobayear, 1988- editor
Title: Economic cooperation, bilateral and regional trade agreements and investments for improved international relations / [edited by] Anita Medhekar, Anisul M. Islam, S. Jobayear Ahmed.
Description: Hershey, PA : IGI Global Scientific Publishing, [2026] | Includes bibliographical references and index. | Summary: "The book aims to thoroughly explore prospects of trade and investment opportunities and challenges for sustainable development between nations by improving international relationships"-- Provided by publisher.
Identifiers: LCCN 2025021298 (print) | LCCN 2025021299 (ebook) | ISBN 9798337317823 hardcover | ISBN 9798337317830 paperback | ISBN 9798337317847 ebook
Subjects: LCSH: International economic relations | International trade | Sustainable development--International cooperation
Classification: LCC HF1359 .E248 2026 (print) | LCC HF1359 (ebook) | DDC 337--dc23/eng/20260126
LC record available at https://lccn.loc.gov/2025021298
LC ebook record available at https://lccn.loc.gov/2025021299

British Cataloguing in Publication Data
A Cataloguing in Publication record for this book is available from the British Library.

We dedicate this book "Economic Cooperation, Bilateral and Regional Trade Agreements and Investments for Improved International Relations", in the loving memory of our parents; late Mrs. Shaila Chitnis-Medhekar & Mr. Sharad Medhekar, late Mrs. Momena Akthar, Mrs. Shaheena Goni & late Mr. S. Osman Goni, and late S. Jobayear Ahmed who tragically left for heavenly abode in January 2026.

Editorial Advisory Board and List of Reviewers

Table of Contents

Detailed Table of Contents

trade agreements, developing infrastructure, promoting sustainable economic practices, and embracing digital trade. It also discusses the role of foreign direct investment (FDI) and external trade partnerships. The chapter concludes with policy recommendations to enhance economic integration and foster long-term growth in South Asia.

Incorporating environmental protections in bilateral and regional trade agreements is crucial for fostering sustainable economic development. Early trade agreements focused on economic liberalization, whereas contemporary frameworks increasingly integrate environmental obligations to tackle climate change, resource depletion, and ecological degradation. This paper examines the development of environmental provisions in trade agreements, enforcement mechanisms, and optimal practices for sustainability-oriented trade policy. Prominent case studies such as the CPTPP, EU-Mercosur, and ACFTA, underscore both achievements and obstacles in the execution of environmental requirements. Moreover, market incentives like carbon pricing, border tax adjustments, and green subsidies are essential for harmonizing economic and environmental goals. The research offers policy suggestions for enhancing environmental protections, assuring adherence, and promoting international collaboration. The incorporation of comprehensive sustainability measures in trade agreements will be essential for attaining enduring environmental and economic resilience.

The EU-27, a key economic bloc, operates within an integrated trade framework emphasizing free movement, regulatory harmonization, and global trade agreements. This study analyzes its internal trade mechanisms, external partnerships, and sectoral impacts. The EU's intra-trade structure fosters cross-border commerce, with evolving trends in industry integration. Bilateral and multilateral agreements enhance trade ties, shaping relations post-Brexit. Agriculture benefits from the

Common Agricultural Policy, while manufacturing relies on innovation and global value chains. Green energy policies drive sustainability, with renewable targets and trade incentives. Regulatory frameworks ensure high standards and competitiveness, amid emerging digitalization and sustainability challenges. This study explores EU-27's trade agreements, sector-specific effects, and evolving policies, using qualitative analysis and case studies from WTO and EU trade reports. Insights will guide policymakers and industry leaders in navigating the complexitics of EU trade in a dynamic global landscape.

This chapter discusses how digital trade and investment have reshaped global economic dynamics in the twenty-first century. It investigates the increasing increase of digital trade and investment, stressing their role in expanding market access, stimulating innovation, and supporting inclusive development. The discussion stresses the revolutionary impact of technologies such as artificial intelligence and cloud computing on trade efficiency and transparency. Regional frameworks are also studied for their role in harmonizing digital legislation. The chapter also addresses important challenges, such as digital inequalities, regulatory fragmentation, protectionism, and cybersecurity risks, while relating digital transformation to Sustainable Development Goals. Policy recommendations stress digital infrastructure investment, FDI facilitation, public-private partnerships, and international cooperation. Ultimately, the chapter demonstrates that digital commerce and investment are vital to attaining sustainable, inclusive, and resilient global economic growth.

This chapter explores the integration of digital technologies into trade policies for advancing the Blue and Circular Economy (BCE) in emerging economies. It examines how bilateral, multilateral, and regional agreements can enable digital

Foreword

The importance of Bilateral and Regional Trade Agreements cannot be overemphasised for improved international relations and economic cooperation. In an era, which has been marked by liberalisation, supply chain realignments, strategic competition and shifting development priorities, bilateral and regional trade agreements have emerged as central instruments of statecraft and diplomacy. This fact has been very well explained in different chapters of the book. By integrating empirical analysis with conceptual framework and regional case studies, the volume highlights the multi-faced role of economic cooperation in an increasingly multipolar and interdependent world. It explores as to how asymmetries in bargaining power shape outcomes and how developing economies navigate complex landscapes and how regionalism both complements and competes with multilateralism. Economic cooperation has emerged as a defining pillar of international relations in the 21st century which has been shaped by globalization, international geopolitical reassignments, technical changes, and pre-determined sustainable challenges.

The book discusses the latest developments and their impact on trade, supply chains, economic cooperation at the international level like de-dollarization, Russia Ukraine conflict, Arab-Israel conflict, The Red Sea Shipping crisis, South Asia tensions, and Trump Tariff policy. There is a significant move by countries to reduce reliance on the U. S. dollar in global trade, finance and reserves driven by concerns over U S sanctions, high debt, and geopolitical fragmentation. The ongoing U S tariff policy interests the policy makers at the international level because it affects not only trade but also the trade agreements, economic cooperation, and international relations. The book discusses the dynamics, agreements, and impact of trade in goods within the EU 27 countries. It will encourage the researchers to study the opportunities and challenges of EU- India Free Trade Agreement concluded in January 2026. This is officially referred to as the Broad-based Trade Agreement and represents an ambitious attempt to deepen bilateral integration, known as the '*Mother of all Trades.*'

The strong merit of the book lies in the fact that it not only discusses the impact of its economic relation on trade but also the role of the trade blocks in climate action, biodiversity, preservation of environment and clean energy transitions. The volume discusses the importance of green finance to promote environmental sustainability, reduce pollution and climate change. Thus, Green Finance is important for achieving environmental goals, promoting initiatives that protect environment, help in clean transport, sustainable waste management, and biodiversity conservation. In this regard, the role of BRICKS has been discussed. So, it will interest the environmentalists and policy makers to craft trade policy that aligns economic progress with conservation of environment.

A distinguishing strength of this book lies in its integration of formal quantitative methodologies including Gravity Model, Engel Curve estimation and structured correlation and regression analysis into the study of regional and bilateral trade agreements. The Gravity Model, foundational to empirical international trade analysis enables the systematic estimation of bilateral trade flows between Portugal and its 15 partners. By integrating Engel Curve analysis, the book moves beyond aggregate trade volume analysis and addresses micro economic welfare implications, thereby strengthening the developmental and policy relevance. Regression Model has been used to stress the importance of gender sensitive policies to promote equality and meet the United Nations' Sustainable Development Goals. This study has been made with reference to G20 countries. Thus, the book advances beyond descriptive regionalism and is a great contribution to the cumulative scientific study of international trade governance.

The book commands global relevance by systematically examining the evolution and functioning of major regional and bilateral trade architecture across different continents. It discusses the institutional sophistication of the European Union to the emerging dynamism of the African Continental Free Trade Area and the expansive reach of the Regional Comprehensive Partnership and the diversity of BIMSTEC in contemporary trade governance. It does not concentrate on a single region or bloc, it offers a comparative and comprehensive analysis of trade agreements across continents – examining their institutional design, navigation dynamics, and strategic implications of diverse regional framework.

However, these blocks work within the broader framework of the multilateral trading system under the WTO. The novelty of the study lies in a strategic framework placing Bangladesh in a regional model for circular space economy transition and examines the convergence and divergence of India and Bangladesh in pursuing a circular space economy through BIMSTEC framework. It also elaborates how regionalism has become primary driver of rule-making in international commerce thus making the work indispensable for scholars, policy makers and practitioners engaged in the future of global integration. By combining theoretical insight with empirical depth, this work bridges scholarship and policy. Given its global scope and analytical rigour, this book will resonate with scholars, policy makers, and students across regions.

Shashi Jain
Dev Samaj College for Women, Chandigarh, India

Foreword

In an era defined by profound geopolitical shifts, technological transformation, and mounting sustainability challenges, economic cooperation has become more than a policy choice—it is a global imperative. The book, *Economic Cooperation, Bilateral and Regional Trade Agreements and Investments for Improved International Relations,* arrives at an important time in world's economic history, offering timely and rigorous insights into how nations can harness trade, investment, and connectivity to foster peace, prosperity, and resilience.

The 21st century has witnessed a recalibration of global economic governance. Though institutions such as the World Trade Organization continue to provide multilateral foundations, the momentum has increasingly shifted toward dynamic bilateral and regional frameworks. Alliances like G-20, European Union, BRICS, Association of Southeast Asian Nations (ASEAN), South Asian Association for Regional Cooperation (SAARC) reflect both opportunity and urgency: opportunity to deepen integration and innovation, and urgency to respond to trade fragmentation, protectionist pressures, supply chain vulnerabilities, and strategic competition among major powers.

The recent Free Trade Agreement between the European Union and India in January 2026 symbolizes a broader shift toward strategic economic partnerships grounded in dialogue, trust, and shared vision. At the same time, rising tariffs, sanctions, and regional conflicts remind us that economic interdependence, if not managed equitably and responsibly, can generate tension as readily as cooperation. The February 2026 India-US trade deal, structured as an Interim Agreement is a pragmatic step forward towards "managed trade" approach. This volume makes a significant scholarly contribution by examining economic cooperation not merely as a commercial arrangement, but as a multidimensional instrument of diplomacy and development. The chapters demonstrate how trade agreements and investment frameworks shape development trajectories, influence global power relations, and support—or hinder—the realization of the United Nations Sustainable Development Goals (SDGs). By integrating empirical research, theoretical analysis, and regional case studies, the contributors highlight the pathways through which connectivity, foreign direct investment, digital transformation, environmental safeguards, gender equality, and inclusive policy design can strengthen international relations.

What distinguishes this book is its balanced and forward-looking perspective. It does not overlook the realities of geopolitical rivalry, economic nationalism, or asymmetries in bargaining power. It confronts these complexities while highlighting practical strategies for cooperation grounded in sustainability, inclusivity, and shared prosperity. The emphasis on export-led growth, digital trade, environmental integration, energy partnerships, and gender-sensitive social protection underscores that economic cooperation must be comprehensive and human-centered, to meet the United Nations 17-SDGs, for the welfare of the global population. For policymakers, diplomats, scholars, students, business leaders, and international organizations, this volume offers both conceptual clarity and actionable insight. It encourages nations: large and small, to view economic engagement as a bridge toward mutual trust and long-term resilience. This book stands as a thoughtful and timely contribution to the global discourse on economic cooperations for trade, investment, and enhanced international relations. It reminds us that despite the uncertainties of our time, co-operation remains possible, and is indeed essential for shaping a more inclusive, stable, peaceful, and prosperous world.

Preeti Sudan
Union Public Service Commission, India

Foreword

Following years of move towards liberal trade policies promoting multilateral trade, aid and economic cooperation, the world is facing increasing challenges from forces of nationalism, self -interest and geo-political domination. The world's largest military and economic powerhouse, the USA, has challenged the wisdom of multilateral/bilateral trade and economic and social cooperation agreements arguing that these have amounted to exploitative relationships against the interests of the USA and have tended to tilt heavily in favor of the other parties to the agreements. This perception has unfortunately led to US withdrawal from several multilateral cooperation agreements relating to health and the natural environment, weakened US support for the UN and the NATO, and led to the imposition of steep and discriminatory bilateral tariffs aimed at improving the trade balance in favor of the USA while also serving as a major source of revenues.

The US move has fanned a simmering debate in several other countries where a segment of the intellectual and political leadership has been questioning the benefits of liberal trade and economic cooperation policies believing that these instruments of globalization benefit only the rich few at the expense of the working class. Consequently, there is now a growing pressure in these countries to abandon liberal trade, aid and economic cooperation policies that promote globalization and move towards greater self-reliant and autarkic policies using trade protection and capital controls.

Against this backdrop, this book titled, *Economic Cooperation, Bilateral and Regional Trade Agreements and Investments for Improved International Relations*, is a bold attempt to preserve and foster greater global progress with trade, aid and economic cooperation based on liberal economic policies that minimizes trade protection and supports global cooperation on capital flows and investments. This collected volume brings together diverse scholarly perspectives to examine how economic cooperation functions as a tool for fostering stability, prosperity, and trust among nations. The book makes a strong case for promoting connectivity, international trade, foreign direct investment, and tourism to facilitate trade and cooperation as a means for promoting global shared economic prosperity. It seeks to dispel the notion that trade and economic cooperation is a zero-sum game where winning countries gain at the expense of countries that lose out.

The book does recognize that there are potential tradeoffs that need to be carefully managed. Among the challenges include power imbalances, supply chain disruptions, digitalization, Artificial Intelligence, tariffs and non-tariff barriers, sanctions, war/conflicts, and the need for equitable distribution of benefits among participating nations. The book argues that these tradeoffs can be better managed through negotiations based on a cooperative solution. The alternative approach based on high tariffs, trade wars, autarky, and preservation of self- interest can lead to slowdown of progress towards national and global economic prosperity, hurt the achievement of SDGs, cause greater damage to the natural environment, and push global conflicts.

This book is an important contribution to enhance the understanding of how better trade and economic cooperation can be a positive force for promoting global welfare. The book's central hypothesis that there need not be a conflict between national and global interests in pursuing better trade and cooperation agreements and that such cooperation can play a major role in lowering global conflict is a powerful message that ought to be supported and promoted. By integrating conceptual frameworks, empirical analysis, and regional case studies, I believe the book will be an excellent resource and valuable reference tool for government officials, policymakers, economists, business owners, academicians, researchers, think tanks and international organisations.

Sadiq Ahmed

Policy Research Institute, Bangladesh & World Bank, Bangladesh

Preface

The book titled, *Economic Cooperation, Bilateral and Regional Trade Agreements and Investments for Improved International Relations*, discusses and explores the prospects of trade, investment, and tourism opportunities and challenges for sustainable development. In a connected global economy, economic cooperation through regional trade agreements fosters international relations and promotes sustainable economic growth. These agreements facilitate the free flow of goods, services, and investments while serving at the same time as strategic instruments for enhancing political, diplomatic, and cultural ties among nations. By reducing trade and other barriers, and encouraging mutual investment, countries can achieve greater economic integration and resilience with a shared vision. However, the pursuit of such cooperation also brings challenges, including power imbalances, supply chain disruptions, digitalization, Artificial Intelligence, tariffs and non-tariff barriers, sanctions, war/conflicts, and the need for equitable distribution of benefits among participating nations.

Economic cooperation has re-emerged as a defining pillar of international relations in the twenty-first century, shaped by globalization, geopolitical realignments, technological change, and pressing sustainability challenges. Against this backdrop, nations are increasingly recalibrating multilateral trade agreements and investment frameworks such as AfCFTA, ASEAN, BRICS, BIMSTEC, G-20, QUAD, EU and SAARC, among others, within the framework of WTO rules and regulations, not only to promote economic growth, but also to secure and build resilience, innovation, cooperation, for long-term sustainable inclusive economic development, peace, progress and prosperity for all. The most recent historic Free Trade Agreement (FTA) deal was signed between 27-European Union (EU) countries and India on the 27th of January 2026, with a market of 2 billion people, representing 25% of the global GDP. The aim to have a strategic economic partnership between the 27-EU countries and India with constructive dialogue, trust, openness, people-to-people contact, and friendship, to promote peace, prosperity, and progress.

This edited reference book brings together diverse scholarly perspectives to examine how economic cooperation functions as a tool for fostering stability, prosperity, and trust among nations. The chapters collectively explore how trade agreements, investment flows, and institutional frameworks shape power relations, development trajectories, and global governance. By integrating empirical analysis, conceptual frameworks, and regional case studies, the volume highlights the multifaceted role of economic cooperation in an increasingly multipolar and interdependent world. This book provides relevant theoretical framework and valuable insights and guidance by examples and case studies for promoting connectivity, international trade, foreign direct investment, and tourism to facilitate trade and cooperation, amidst the 21st century challenges. The book covers topics such as global business, trade, financial investment, and partnerships for growth, among others. This book is expected to be an excellent resource and valuable reference tool for government officials, policymakers, economists, business owners, researchers, think tanks and international organizations.

The book has several main goals:

- Discusses and explores the prospects of how bilateral and multilateral regional trade agreements for trade, investment, tourism opportunities, for improve international relations and the challenges for sustainable development. Amidst the uncertainty in the New Year of 2026, in the face of changing global power-dynamics, geo-political power shifts around trade, tariffs, security, de-dollarization, wars/conflicts and territorial claims and competence for dominance among superpowers like the US, China and Russia. The book aims to foster an in-depth understanding of emerging bilateral and multilateral trade and investment partnership between nations with a shared vision for enhancing connectivity, commerce, trade, tourism, and collaboration for peace, progress and prosperity for economic, social, and human development, in a context of a sustainable future.
- Analysis of how the economic cooperation, bilateral and regional trade agreements and investment opportunities to improved international relations and partnerships can contribute towards export-led inclusive economic growth for societies and economies, supporting the achievement of UN's Sustainable Development Goals (SDGs).
- Given the current geopolitical power shifts, global US trade tariffs, sanctions, and conflicts; this book provides an in-depth analysis of strategies and initiatives to increase connectivity by various countries for economic cooperation, and engaging in bilateral and regional trade agreements and investments for shared vision of peace, economic growth, and meeting the sustainable development goals (SDGs).

- Exploration of the role of government and countries to encourage partnerships for the development of innovative strategies in diplomacy, trade strategies and practical solutions to challenges for promoting connectivity, commerce, trade, investment, and tourism through increased cooperation, build trust and friendships in an environmentally responsible manner for shared prosperity; amidst the random US tariffs, sanctions, geopolitical power shifts, conflicts, control over strategic resources and territorial claims by super-powers.

ORGANISATION OF THE BOOK

The book presents a collection of book chapters covering key topics around "Economic Cooperation, Bilateral and Regional Trade Agreements and Investments for Improved International Relations" by different researchers from different countries around the globe. A brief summary of each chapter is given below:

Chapter 1: "The Importance of Bilateral and Multilateral Regional Trade Agreements and Cooperation in the 21st Century" (by Anita Medhekar and Anisul Islam)

The introductory chapter establishes the conceptual foundation by examining the importance of increased International cooperation among nations in the twenty-first century and argues that all countries need to prioritise to bring peace, stability, prosperity, progress, and inclusive and sustainable economic development and growth for the world population. In the post-pandemic and the current geo-political situation, there is rise in cross-border conflicts and tensions between Russia-Ukraine, Middle-East and South Asian countries, US tariffs, de-dollarization efforts, rise of BRICS, QUAD and regional free trade agreements are shaping the global environment. All countries must recognise the importance of a shared vision of economic cooperation, collaboration, partnerships, peace, mutual respect, friendship, and trust required between bordering neighbours, trading partners across land locked countries or nations across the oceans; in order to promote bilateral, regional, or multilateral trade, tourism, investment opportunities for sustainable economic development, inclusive growth, prosperity, and to achieve United Nations Sustainable Development Goals for all global citizens.

Chapter 2: "Leveraging Afghanistan's Geopolitical Position for Regional Connectivity and Trade Integration" (by Hamayun Khan)

This chapter is based on qualitative empirical data, explores Afghanistan's strategic geographical location along the ancient trade silk-route that makes it a natural link between energy-rich Central Asia and energy-deficient South Asia. Historically, people of Afghanistan have suffered for decades due to foreign interference such as under the British colonial rule, followed by the invasion of Russia, and subsequently by the US. These resulted in political instability, economic collapse and humanitarian crisis. This chapter also explores the socio-economic advantages and opportunities that Afghanistan can benefit from given its strategic geographical location between central Asia and south Asia to foster domestic growth and regional integration through three major initiatives: the Turkmenistan–Afghanistan–Pakistan–India (TAPI) gas pipeline, the Lapis Lazuli Corridor, and the Chabahar Port. It further evaluates the potential economic and social benefits from these initiatives alongside governance constraints, security risks, and the impact of international sanctions, and concludes that Afghanistan can facilitate trade, attract foreign direct investment, build institutional capacity and reforms, improve diplomatic engagement with cross-border countries and promote regional trade, cooperation, and partnerships to transform the country and have peace, progress, and inclusive economic growth for Afghanistan.

Chapter 3: "The Effects of Regional Trade Agreements on Portuguese Trade" (by Nuno Carlos Leitão)

This empirical chapter examines the importance of the gravity model in explaining bilateral trade between Portugal and its fifteen trading partners for three decades 1990-2023. It applies econometric models (Quantile Regressions, Poisson Pseudo Maximum Likelihood- PPML, and Random Effects) to test the effects of common religion, regional trade agreements, tariff rates, economies of scale, borders and geographical distance. The findings show that economies of scale and trade agreements are positively correlated with bilateral trade. Further, predictive negative relationship between geographical distance and bilateral trades transport logistics costs is confirmed with increased bilateral trade between Portugal and Spain. However, imposition of tariffs reduces bilateral trade between countries.

Chapter 4: "Enhancing Economic Cooperation and Trade Integration in SAARC countries" (by Mallika Roy and Khaleda Maiful)

This chapter emphasises that economic cooperation plays a vital role in fostering sustainable development and growth, promoting trade, and enhancing mutual prosperity among nations within a region. This chapter explores economic cooperation within the South Asian Association for Regional Cooperation (SAARC), focusing on trade agreements, investments, and regional integration. Established in 1985, SAARC aimed to promote economic integration through initiatives like the South Asian Free Trade Area (SAFTA). Despite efforts to reduce tariffs and boost intra-regional trade, challenges such as geopolitical tensions, infrastructure deficiencies, and regulatory barriers have impeded progress. The chapter highlights opportunities to strengthen regional cooperation by improving trade agreements, developing infrastructure, promoting sustainable economic practices, and embracing digital trade. It also discusses the role of foreign direct investment (FDI) and external trade partnerships and provides policy recommendations to enhance economic integration and foster long-term growth in South Asia.

Chapter 5: "Integrating Environmental Safeguards Into Bilateral and Regional Trade Agreements" (by Rismawati Rismawati, Eko Ganis Sukoharsono, Monika Handayani, and Javaid Ahmad Wagay)

Sustainable economic growth requires environmental protections in bilateral and regional trade agreements. Early trade agreements focused on economic liberalization, whereas modern one's address climate change, resource depletion, and ecological damage. Environmental provisions, enforcement methods, and sustainability-focused trade policy best practices are examined in this article. CPTPP, EU-Mercosur, and AfCFTA case studies show environmental improvements and problems. Market-based methods including carbon pricing, border tax adjustments, and green subsidies help connect economic and environmental goals. The research recommends policies to improve environmental preservation, compliance, and worldwide cooperation. Trade agreements must include comprehensive sustainability measures for long-term environmental and economic resilience.

Chapter 6: "Dynamics, Agreements, and Industry Impacts of Trade in Goods within the EU-27" (by Mallika Roy and Bablu Biswas)

The 27-European Union countries, a key economic trading bloc, operates within an integrated trade framework emphasizing free movement, regulatory harmonization, and global trade agreements. This study analyses EU-27 internal trade mechanisms, external partnerships, and sectoral impacts. The EU's Agriculture benefits from the Common Agricultural Policy, while manufacturing relies on innovation and global value chains. Regulatory frameworks ensure high standards and competitiveness, amid emerging digitalization and sustainability challenges. This study explores EU-27's trade agreements, sector-specific effects, and evolving policies, using qualitative analysis and case studies from WTO and EU trade reports. Insights will guide policymakers and industry leaders in navigating the complexities of EU trade in a dynamic global landscape.

Chapter 7: "Digital Trade and Investment in the 21st Century: Opportunities, Challenges, and Policy Implications for Sustainable Development" (by Saizal Pinjaman)

This chapter discusses how digital trade and investment have reshaped global economic dynamics in the twenty-first century. It investigates the role of increased digital trade and investment, stressing their role in expanding market access, stimulating innovation, and supporting inclusive development. The discussion stresses the revolutionary impact of technologies such as artificial intelligence and cloud computing on trade efficiency and transparency. This chapter also addresses important challenges such as digital inequalities, regulatory fragmentation, protectionism, and cybersecurity risks, while relating digital transformation to Sustainable Development Goals. Policy recommendations stress digital infrastructure investment, FDI facilitation, public-private partnerships, and international cooperation. The chapter demonstrates that digital commerce and investment are vital to attaining sustainable, inclusive, and resilient global economic growth.

Chapter 8: "Divergence and Convergence in the Bay of Bengal: India, Bangladesh, and the Pursuit of a Circular Space Economy through BIMSTEC" (by Mohammad Rashed Hasan Polas, Mohammad Ekramol Islam, Abu Saleh Md. Sohel-Uz-Zaman, Abdullah Al Fahad, Md. Masud Rana, and S. Jobayear Ahmed)

The chapter explores the growing emphasis on sustainability in the global space sector, which has opened new pathways for emerging economies to integrate into the evolving circular space economy. The study's novelty is a strategic framework placing Bangladesh in a regional model for circular space economy transition and examines the convergence and divergence of India and Bangladesh in pursuing a circular space economy through the BIMSTEC framework. Using a comparative case-based analysis supported by secondary data, policy documents, and conceptual modelling, the study explores how technological innovation, governance, and regional collaboration shape circularity strategies, by embedding circular principles into its development goals. Policymakers should invest in dual-use technologies, foster partnerships, and build capacity to align with global sustainability goals.

Chapter 9: "The Role of Bilateral, Regional, and Multilateral Trade Agreements: Facilitating Sustainable Economic Development Through Agriculture, Manufacturing and Services" (by Mallika Roy, Saha Runa, and Mohammad Mamun Bhuyan)

In today's interconnected global economy, trade agreements are vital instruments shaping development in agriculture, manufacturing, and services. While bilateral, regional, and multilateral agreements aim to enhance growth, their role in promoting sustainable development remains uneven and underexplored. Although trade liberalization has been widely studied, there is limited understanding of how different trade frameworks impact sustainability across sectors and countries. This study fills that gap through a comprehensive review of literature from diverse economies, examining how trade agreements influence environmental, social, and economic outcomes. The findings reveal that trade can foster technology transfer, resource efficiency, and inclusive growth, but these benefits depend on strong governance, enforcement, and the inclusion of sustainability provisions. By synthesizing global evidence, this research offers actionable insights for policymakers to craft trade policies that align economic progress with long-term sustainability.

We are living in challenging times in 2026 and beyond, given the geo-politics impacting international trade, foreign investments, tourism, and overall global cooperation. Current tariff and protectionist policies, geopolitical conflicts, competition for global dominance are resulting in a world with deteriorating trust, goodwill, and diplomatic relations between/among countries. Further in January 2026, various bilateral and multilateral free trade agreements for economic partnership with Arab nations is on the table, triggered by geo-political economic crisis, by India, besides the India and EU -27countries FTA, which is an incredibly significant development in global trade agreements. This book is timely and aims to be a leading source of information for establishing connectivity and improving bilateral and multilateral trade relationships and cooperation between/among nations and regions to face the future global challenges. In the midst of these challenges, it is still possible to foster relationships and cooperation to find opportunities to take advantage of and to find solutions to the shared global problems. The chapters in this book will provide valuable insights and guidance by examples for international economic cooperation necessary for peace and improved relationships in promoting bilateral and multilateral trade, tourism, and investment between countries. It is also imperative to integrate with the UN-SDG's in contributing towards a more sustainable and resilient shared future vision between nations, through a neighbourly collaborative effort for peace, progress, and economic prosperity.

By catering to this diverse audience, this book aims to provides valuable insights, research findings, and practical guidance to academic, scholars, research students, international organizations, businesses and practitioners of international trade relations, diplomats, and international organizations for exploring economic cooperation, bilateral and multilateral trade, peace, economic development and trade routes and related supply chain logistics for economic growth and sustainable development. Further, for enhancing sustainability in bilateral and multilateral trade in goods and services and facilitating investment and tourism opportunities, thereby contributing to the broader goals of peace, prosperity, and sustainable and inclusive economic and social development of nations and the globe.

We acknowledge the valuable contributions made by all the authors; without their support and contributions the book would not have been completed. We would also like to thank the blind reviewers of the book chapters, who provided valuable feedback to the authors, to ensure that work is based on quality and provide honest, critical, and constructive feedback.

Finally, we would like to thank the IGI Global Publishing, Acquisition and Development Team, Cassandra Martin (Assistant Acquisitions Editor), Evan Attivo (Assistant Development Editor), Elizabeth Barrantes (Managing Editor of Book Development), Melissa Wagner (Vice President of Content Strategy & Research Integrity), Editorial Advisory Board, and the IGI Global Book Development Team for their regular help and support during the various stages of editorial process and developmental stages of the book.

Anita Medhekar
Central Queensland University, Australia

Anisul M. Islam
University of Houston, USA

S. Jobayear Ahmed
Bangladesh Foreign Trade Institute, Bangladesh

Acknowledgment

We appreciate and acknowledge the efforts of everyone towards the development of this book titled: *Economic Cooperation, Bilateral and Regional Trade Agreements and Investments for Improved International Relations*. We wish to sincerely thank all authors for their invaluable contributions.

We are deeply grateful to all the Authors, to their responses for the call for chapter proposals, revisions involved and chapter submissions for this book on Economic Cooperation, Bilateral and Regional Trade Agreements and Investments for Improved International Relations

Without their valuable contributions in a timely manner, adhering to the IGI Global' Before You Write' Guidelines, we would not have been able to complete this book successfully.

We are also thankful to the blind reviewers of the chapters, who made their contribution by providing invaluable suggestions and feedback, which were implemented by the authors. All the chapter authors made valuable contribution making many revisions to the chapters for presenting their research, and improvements in the process of chapter development.

The work progressed in highly coordinated manner despite the contributors belonging to different parts of the world. This work carries, behind it, the encouragement, support and good wishes of family members and colleagues.

We would also like to thank and acknowledge members of the IGI-Global Publishers' team, Director of Intellectual Property & Contracts for their continuing guidance, coordination, suggestions, and support during the development stage of this book.

Finally, we would like to thank IGI Global publishers book project development team Elizabeth Barrantes (Managing Editor of Book Development), Melissa Wagner (Vice-President of Content Strategy & Research Integrity), and Cassandra Martin

(Assistant Acquisitions Editor) for their commitment to international research and publish on current topics impacting the changing geo-politics of global dynamics of international trade and economic relations.

Anita Medhekar
Central Queensland University, Australia

Anisul M. Islam
University of Houston, USA

S. Jobayear Ahmed
Bangladesh Foreign Trade Institute, Bangladesh

Chapter 1
The Importance of Bilateral and Multilateral Regional Trade Agreements and Cooperation in the 21st Century

Anita Medhekar
http://orcid.org/0000-0002-6791-4056
Central Queensland University, Australia

Anisul M. Islam
University of Houston-Downtown, USA

ABSTRACT

International economic cooperation is particularly important and must be a priority for all countries in the world to bring peace, prosperity, progress, and inclusive economic development and growth for the world population. All countries must recognise the importance and share a vision of economic cooperation, collaboration, partnerships, peace, mutual respect, friendship, and trust required between bordering neighbours, trading partners across land locked countries or nations across the oceans; in order to promote bilateral, regional, or multilateral trade, tourism, investment opportunities for sustainable economic development, inclusive growth, prosperity, and growth in gross domestic product (GDP) and achieve United Nations Sustainable Development Goals for all global citizens.

DOI: 10.4018/979-8-3373-1782-3.ch001

1. INTRODUCTION

International economic cooperation is particularly important and should be a priority for all countries to bring peace, prosperity, progress, inclusive economic development and growth for the world population. All countries must recognise the importance of and a shared vision of economic cooperation, collaboration, partnerships, peace, mutual respect, friendship, dignity, and trust required between/amongst bordering neighbours, trading partners across land locked countries or nations across the oceans; in order to promote bilateral, regional, or multilateral trade, tourism, and investment opportunities for economic development, inclusive growth, prosperity, resulting in gross domestic product (GDP) growth and per-capital income growth of all its citizens.

Regional trade agreements and systems are shaping global businesses. With the ending of World War-2. formation of General Agreement on Tariffs and Trade (GATT) was formed in 1948; a multilateral trade agreements came into effect with 23 member countries providing tariff concessions and regulating international trade. Since January-1-1995, regional trade agreements were preferential and were regulated by World Trade Organisation (WTO). Whereas in the 21st century, the regional trade agreement are focussing on larger trading blocs facilitating trade and integration of countries in global value chains (Elliott, 2018; Grossman, 2016; Pomfret, 2020).

Examples of multilateral regional trade agreements in the 21st century is group of 12 *member* countries (*Australia, Brunei Darussalam, Canada, Chile, Japan, Malaysia, Mexico, New Zealand, Peru, Singapore, the United Kingdom, and Vietnam)*– forming *Comprehensive and Progressive Agreement for Trans-Pacific Partnership* (CPTPP), for trade in goods, services, and investment opportunities, reducing tariffs and non-tariff barriers and promoting economic integration in the Asia-Pacific region. Further, the Regional Comprehensive Economic Partnership (RCEP) is one of the largest trading blocks of 15- Asia-Pacific member countries (Austarlian Government, 2025; Richard, 2014; Singapore Ministry of Trade & International Economic Relations, 2025). Thrasher and Gallagher (2008) emphasized that effective trade policy for comparative advantage is required for long-run diversification and economic development so that there is global and regional convergence of such trade policies that benefit the partner nations.

However, recent years cooperation and collaboration for trade, investment, economic development, and inclusive growth between countries has been in decline, with trade wars, protectionism and raising nationalism. Countrics should proactively have a committed shared vision for peace, prosperity, economic development and growth of its neighbours and the entire region, driven by connectivity, commerce and collaboration, trade, and tourism to overcome these challenges. A transformative bilateral or multilateral international policy of cooperation and collaborative partnership for the future is important to build upon shared values of trust, respect, and understanding for mutual benefits, peace, and prosperity that international cooperation can bring to all the world's population and meet the United Nations Sustainable Development Goals.

The Global Financial Crisis of 2008-09, saw the cooperation between group of 20 countries and formed G-20 leadership to promote trade, investment, and inclusive economic growth and development. Similarly, Global Pandemic is another excellent example as to how scientists from different countries came together and cooperated with public-private-partnerships (PPPs), to invent the vaccines within one year and took collaborative measures of closing borders and grounded airlines to stop the spread of the virus and follow all pandemic-related World Health Organisations (WHO) regulations (Islam, 2021a). However, in recent years, we are seeing not only increasing bilateral and multilateral partnerships formed across borders and oceans but also escalating trade frictions, tariff and non-tariff barriers disruptions initiated by the USA, and armed conflicts between neighbours in the world, with increasing war expenditure, destruction, death, and displacement of people from various countries as refugees, shaping the geo-politics around the world (Josephs, 2026).

Quarter of the 21st century is almost around the corner, and rather than engaging in peaceful dialogue and negotiations, there is increasing geo-political pressure in 2026, with rising tensions between the USA and Venezuela, Mexico, and Denmark over Greenland (Yussuf, 2026). Further BRICS economies (Brazil, Russia, India, China and South Africa) formed in 2005 are also actively using their own currencies for bilateral-trade settlements amongst the member nations, develop BRICS+ digital trade currency unit backed by gold payment system. BRICS economies have taken this decision in order to have more economic and financial independence to reduce dependence on the currency of a single country=US dollar for international trade and circumvent USA trade sanctions and further as stated by IMF due to Trump's-Tariff shocks, global GDP economic growth is expected to show down in to 3.1% in 2026 (BRICS, 2026; Global Business Outlook, 2025, International Monetary Fund, 2025).

Therefore, there is an urgency to increase development expenditures which requires cooperation and peace dialogue for improved bilateral and multilateral international relationships for economic development and promoting trade and investment opportunities in various sectors of the economy, technology transfers, sustainable and climate-resilient development, environmental conservation, and green energy across the world. Furthermore, safe and reliable rail, road, air, ocean transport infrastructure as well as information and communication technology (ICT) infrastructure are needed to smooth the international supply chains of the world and improve connectivity and enhance commerce and trade to bring about inclusive economic growth and regional prosperity for the world's population.

All over the world, with the increase in demand, there is an urgency to increase development expenditures which requires cooperation and peace dialogue for improved bilateral and multilateral international relationships for economic development and promoting trade and investment opportunities in various sectors of the economy, technology transfers, sustainable and climate-resilient development, environmental conservation, and green energy across the world. Furthermore, safe and reliable rail, road, air, ocean transport infrastructure as well as information and communication technology (ICT) infrastructure with increasing use of Artificial Intelligence (AI) are needed to smooth the international supply chains of the world and improve connectivity and enhance commerce and trade to bring about inclusive economic growth and regional prosperity for the world's population.

Moreover, the leaders of the countries with their shared values and vision need to be proactive in focusing on collaboration and cooperation to bring about peace, prosperity and improve relationships with neighbouring countries. to improve bilateral and multilateral international relations for building trust and promoting economic cooperation and collaboration for growth. Therefore, having a multiplier effect on other sectors of the economy and bringing prosperity to the lives of the millions of people living in emerging and developing countries, war torn zones, refugee camps who are deprived of benefits of economic growth. It is imperative that the countries need to set new standards for bilateral, regional, and multilateral cooperation and collaboration for a peaceful and prosperous world.

This chapter is structured as follows: The introductory section of the chapter introduces the growing economic importance and significance of Economic Cooperation, Bilateral and Regional Trade Agreements and Investments for Improved International Relations. Section-2 provides a literature review on international trade, along with bilateral and multilateral trade agreements, and cross-border investments, trade, and tourism. Section-3 provides a discussion with examples of economic cooperation and bilateral and multilateral trade and investment agreements. Section-4 discusses the challenges and opportunities faced by countries in the current times and need for economic cooperation, bilateral and multilateral trade agreements for improved international relations in the 21st century, amidst the geo-political dynamics, wars, and USA tariffs, followed by the concluding section.

2. LITERATURE REVIEW

International Trade

The 'Father of Economics' Adam Smith's (1723-1790), *Theory of Absolute Advantage,* where an individual, firm or a country produced goods and services more efficiently than other individual, firm or a country given the same number of resources. Adam Smith's theory is followed by Economist David Ricardo's (1772-1823), *Neo-Classical Trade Theory* emphasises that all countries who engage in free trade, benefit from trade and are better-off, based on comparative advantage (Ricardo, 2004). *Neo-classical Trade Theory* explains that countries have different opportunity costs to produce the same good. Therefore, if each country specialises and produced those goods in which it has lowest opportunity costs compared to others and exports the surplus has comparative advantage in the production of that good. Thus, all counties will benefit from trade based on comparative advantage (Watson, 2017).

Further, Ricardo's trade theory is illustrated by '*Heckscher-Ohlin*" model, which assumes that there is no market failure, all countries have perfect competition, given constant technology and similar mix of goods and services between nations and different factors of production in different countries producing different goods (Krugman et al., 2018; Todaro & Smith, 2020). Further, Samuelsons theorem on comparative advantage concludes that international trade can gain higher welfare by obtaining higher price for the product if the countries engage in trade based on comparative advantage, with increasing foreign direct investment, in human capital and technology casing an increase in employment and overall gains from trade liberalisation, achieving pareto optimal situation (FDI) (Krugman et al., 2018; Watson, 2017).

Trade means exchange of good and services. Such trade happens with the domestic economy (called domestic trade) or between nations (called international trade). If such trade is voluntary, both parties engaged in the trade is likely to benefit irrespective of trade being domestic or international. As such, economics do not view trade as a zero-sum game (meaning one party gains at the expense of the other). Trade is then viewed as a mutually beneficial (non-zero-sum game, both parties are expected to benefit).

It is a well-established principle in economics that open trade with little or no barriers, both domestic and international, is expected to be mutually beneficial to parties engaged in trade, provided it is done voluntarily without coercion and no fraud involved. A country can engage with the world by opening up its economy to the rest of thew world for cross-border trade flows, cross-border investment flows, technology and skills transfers, human resource flows (migration, tourism, talents and skills). Such moves lead country towards more openness and integration with the global economy. A country may integrate with other nations through bilateral agreements (between two countries), regional agreements (several countries within a geographic region), and multilateral agreements (involving many nations).

International Regional Trade Agreements

World economies in the 21st century have become more connected due to Regional Trade Agreements (RTAs) at bilateral or multilateral levels, resulting in free global trade in goods, services, capital flows and foreign direct investments. There are many underlying driving forces - historical, economic, strategic, security, and political reasons/factors that lead to these trade accords agreements between two nations or group of nations. Trade is a catalyst to drive economic development and growth, by gaining access to global markets and enhanced international competitiveness and increased consumption and economic growth (Huchet-Bourdon et al., 2018; Medhekar, 2022; Oppong-Baah et al., 2022; Romer, 2021; Todaro & Smith, 2020). Martin et al. (2012) study based on date between 1950-2000, note that besides the gains from trade, regional trade agreements between countries post wars, can promote and encourage peaceful relations as the opportunity costs of conflict is too high.

At international level, Bilateral and Multilateral, FTAs between countries aims to reduce or eliminate tariff and non-tariff barriers such as import quotas and sanctions, and promote free trade and investment opportunities. FTAs provides various benefits in terms of business access to international markets, reduce costs, increase international business competitiveness, strengthen commercial ties between countries and business partners, and provide variety of goods at affordable prices to the consumer. Despite its benefits, it also incurs costs such as domestic business have to compete with low costs foreign goods from China, increased unemployment, relocation of industries to countries with cheap labour and production costs, and lack f or less regulated labour and environmental regulations and trade dependencies for the receiving counties and cause supply shocks.

Institutions of the World Trade Organization (WTO, 2025), General Agreement on Tariffs and Trade (GATT) and preferential trade agreements (PTAs) are established to promote international cooperation through the granting of non-reciprocal and or unilateral tariff preferences by developed countries to developing countries. However, these international agreements have generated critical trade dependencies for the receiving countries, and so developing countries have resorted to negotiate and convert PTAs to FTAs with developed countries (Baena-Rojas & Herrero-Olarte, 2020).

For example, Australia, has bilateral-FTA with 15 counties (Chile, China, Hong Kong, India, Indonesia, Japan, Korea, Malaysia, New Zealand, Peru, Singapore, Thailand, the United Arab Emirates, the United Kingdom and the United States). Further, four *'Plurilateral Trade Agreements'*. (Australian Government, 2025). **(a)** ASEAN-Australia-New Zealand Free Trade Area (AANZFTA), **(b)** Comprehensive and Progressive Agreement for Trans-Pacific Partnership (CPTPP), **(c)** the Pacific Agreement on Closer Economic Relations (PACER) Plus, and **(d)** the Regional Comprehensive Economic Partnership (RCEP). Under these agreements, parties enter legally binding commitments to open access to each other's markets for goods, services and investment opportunities. Furthermore, Australia has two comprehensive FTA under negotiation with India and European Union Countries (Australian Government, 2025; Singapore Ministry of Trade & International Economic Relations [SMTIER], 2025).

Bilateral and multilateral trade agreements for example between any two countries such as Australia and Indonesia (bilateral), four countries (USA, Japan, Australia and India (QUAD) or more countries (multilateral) such as Association of Southeast Asian Nation (ASEAN), ASEAN Free Trade Agreement (AFTA), African Continental Free Trade Area (AfCFTA) Brazil, Russia, India, China, and South Africa (BRICS), South Asian Association for Regional Cooperation (SAARC), North American Free Trade Agreement (NAFTA), and European Union-Free Trade Agreement (EUFTA) (Morozkina & Skryabina, 2021; Southgate, 2025; WTO, 2025).

All these bilateral, multilatearl agreements and FTAs negotiations create a single market, increase free flow of goods and services, encourage trade, harmonise investment and intellectual policies and create regional value chains between countries in a geographical area with impact in generating employment, FDI opportunities and meeting few of the UN-SDGs such as no poverty, zero hunger, and employment creation (WTO, 2025).

Empirical studies show a positive relationship between free trade liberalization and an increased GDP growth and development (Hasan, 2021; Huchet-Bourdon et al., 2018). However, the benefits generated from liberalized trade have not been evenly distributed across all sectors, as developing countries continue to encounter challenges stemming from poor infrastructure and restricted access to international markets (Krugman et al., 2018). As a result, supportive policy measures are essential to enable every sector and population to fully benefit from the opportunities and prospects brought about by FTA, trade liberalization and foreign direct investments.

United Nations Trade and Development (2024) analysed the trade data between 2007- 2023 concluding that merchandise trade between the developing countries in Global South (regional and intra-regional) doubled from US$2.3 Trillion to US$5.6 trillion, outpacing growth in the global trade. Exports grew in the initial years, leveled off, and then declined during the pandemic years. This impacted on the developing countries, which relied on export-led-growth strategies. Given the rise of protectionist policies in developed countries, supply chain disruptions, Trump's Tariffs, and increasing technological advancement could have a negative impact on developing countries productivity level and economic growth.

Tariff and Non-Tariff Barriers

Tariffs and Non-Tariff barriers determine political, economic trade policies and relationships between countries, and shaping geo-political global trade dynamics as countries are experiencing since the US Trump government came to power in 2025. If a country does not want to engage in openness or wants to engage partially in openness, they can use various means or tools to create barriers to restrict trade. Creating barriers to trade is also known as trade protection. A country can use tariff as means to protect the domestic economy from trade with other nations. This is known as tariff barriers. Tariff is a kind of discriminatory tax that is imposed only on imported goods but not on domestically produced goods. This is intended to create an artificial advantage in favour of the domestic goods against imported goods.

Tariffs are the traditionally the oldest form of trade policy, used as a source of governments revenue/income. It is a fixed tax imposed on each unit of imported good, for example $5 on imported one tonne of wheat, making it more expensive and less competitive compared to domestically produced goods. Whereas Ad-volurem Tariff is a tax levied as a fraction of the values of the imported goods. For example, if US levies 35% tariff on imported electronic goods. The overall effect of tariff in both cases is to raise the cost of shipping goods to a country. These barriers on one hand reduces consumers surplus and the burden is passed on to consumers in terms of higher prices. On the other hand, the main purpose has been to raise revenue for the government and to protect the domestic strategic and infant industries such as agriculture and defence (Krugman et al., 2018; Todaro & Smith 2020).

Besides tariff barrier, a country can use many other tools to protect its economy against imports and thereby shield the domestic industry from foreign competition. These may include quota restrictions, subsidies given only to producers of domestic goods, creating relatively higher health and safety standards, technical specifications, quality standards, environmental standards, labour standards compared to other countries. In addition, a country can also use very non-transparent or less visible tools such as cultural barriers, nationalistic and patriotic sentiments against foreign goods, and finally to the extreme case of imposing outright ban on any international trade (known as embargo). These tools are commonly known as non-tariff barriers.

Non-Tariff Barriers (NTBs) are hidden in regulation, unclear and unevenly applied administrative hurdles which can block competition and restrict international trade. For example, quotas, import -licenses, subsidies, technical standards, sanitary, health and safety quality standards (eg for automobile and food safety, packaging, and labelling standards and regulations, anti-dumping rules, pollical embargoes and sanctions (e.g. South African Apartheid), restricting the quantity, quality, or banning the goods entering a country through imports (Krugman et al., 2018). Therefore, NTBs raises compliance costs of licencing, bands and delays, thus making trade difficult and a bureaucratic political issue for developing countries in particular and countries involved in general (Chakraborty & Dey, 2024; Krugman et al., 2018; Lupan, 2018).

Thus, when a country uses tariff as a tool or various non-tariff barriers as tools, or a combination of different tools, the result is expected to be similar. For example, any type of barrier will result in less trade flows, higher prices, less competition, lower product quality, less product varieties available to consumers, among others. Ultimately, the country will experience less than potential growth and development due to the above effects.

Bilateral and Multilateral Tade Agreements

Trade agreements are generally negotiated between nations to reduce barriers to trade and thereby to increase openness to trade, tourism and investment opportunities. The negotiations can be done on a bilateral basis, between two countries on cultural, social, economic environmental, tourism and other capacity building projects for peace, progress and prosperity mutually beneficial to the two countries involved (Medhekar & Haq, 2020). Examples may include Australia-U.S., South Korea- U.S. Israel-U.S, Bangladesh-India, and India-Pakistan amongst others (Medhekar & Ali, 2012; Medhekar, 2019).

Trade agreements are also negotiated among several countries in a specific geographic region known as regional agreements such as the former NAFTA (North American Free Trade Agreement) or its recent version U.S-MCA Agreement (U.S., Mexico and Canada Agreement), ay of Bengal Initiative for Multi-Sectoral Technical and Economic Cooperation BIMSTEC (Bangladesh, Bhutan, India, Myanmar, Nepal, Srilanka, and Thailand) or SAARC (South Asian Agreement for Regional Cooperation), Asia Pacific Economic Cooperation (APEC) to name a few (Aggarwal & Urata, 2006; Ali & Medhekar, 2016; Konwer & Hazarika, 2025; Medhekar & Kaur, 2022; Uddin et al., 2025). There are many such agreements involving countries in a specific region to promote cooperation for economic development and growth in technology transfer, trade, energy, security and disaster management, having a direct impact on economic integration and crating pathways for sustainable long-term growth. Finally, trade agreements can be multilateral involving many countries in the world such as the 27-memebr EU (European Union), or the GATT (General Agreement on Trade and Tariff) in the post-WWII period, or the eventual WTO rules governing multilateral trade among many nations. The multilateral agreements may include countries even located in different regions of the world.

3. EXAMPLES OF ECONOMIC COOPERATION-BILATERAL AND MULTILATERAL REGIONAL TRADE AND INVESTMENT AGREEMENTS

The following sections discusses the various bilateral and multi-lateral regional trade and investment agreements.

a) **Comprehensive and Progressive Agreement for Trans-Pacific Partnership (CPTPP):** Australian Government's Department of Foreign Affairs and Trade (2025)- theme for *CPTPP- 2025* was *Delivering Sustainable Trade and Resilient Growth*, by focusing on three overarching priorities for the group of 12 member countries (*Australia, Brunei Darussalam, Canada, Chile, Japan, Malaysia, Mexico, New Zealand, Peru, Singapore, the United Kingdom, and Vietnam)*:
   - *Increasing trade* between member nations and generating economic gains to communities.
   - *Facilitating trade* by improving processes and making it easy for members to trade with each other.
   - *Commitment to spread the benefits from trade* by ensuring that CPTPP supports sustainable trade practices and inclusive trade growth, where all member countries and their population benefits from trade (Australian Government, DFAT- 2025).

b) **Regional Comprehensive Economic Partnership (RCEP):** Regional Comprehensive Economic Partnership is the largest global trading block in covering 30% of the world's population (approximately 2.3 billion) and Gross Domestic Product (GDP) in the Indo-Pacific region. RCEP includes *15 Asia-Pacific countries*: consisting of *10 ASEAN member countries* and *(Brunei, Cambodia, Indonesia, Laos, Malaysia, Myanmar, Philippines, Singapore, Thailand, Vietnam)* and their *five non-ASEAN* free-trade partners *(Australia, New Zealand, Japan, South Korea, and China)*. Further, India was original member to RECP, but withdrew its membership in 2019 (Austarlian Border Force, 2020). RECP has unlimited potential for Small and Medium Enterprises (SMEs) business cooperation in the Asia-Pacific region and deliver socio-economic mutual benefits to its population for inclusive economic growth of ASEAN and Free Trade Agreement (FTA) non-ASAEN partners.

c) **European Union Trade Agreement:** European Union (EU) was launched in 1995. It has bilateral and regional trade agreements with numerous developed and developing countries outside the EU nations such as EU-Australia, EU-China, EU-India, EU-Mexico, EU-South Africa EU-ASEAN, agreement based on various issues related to trade, security, investment partnership for economic cooperation. The aim is to cooperatively negotiate and effectively apply the

European Union FTAs between EU member states at a bilateral and multilateral level. There are currently 33 European Union-FTAs with 44 countries outside the EU member states and constantly under review and negotiations (European Union, 2025) The aim is to benefit the countries mutually, and provide better market access for companies to export and import goods with competitive advantage in terms of lower preferential import duties through negotiations. Further, EU has 62-trade agreement with the third countries, demonstrating a preferential trade agreements with varying degree of intra-EU trade rules and regulations with the EU members. For examples on trade in goods, intellectual property rights, organic agriculture and sustainable development (Dür, 2025).

d) **African Continental Free Trade Agreement (AfCFTA)** was originally formed in 1991 by Abuja treaty and formally became effective in 2019 to facilitate intra-African trade and reduce tariffs and NTBs between 55 member countries of the African continent, in a single market to boost intra-African trade in African made goods and services, fostering cooperation, economic integration and promoting socio-economic development and growth in the African continent and reducing dependency of imported goods and making Africa more competitive (Debrah, et al., 2024). Formation of AfCFTA has driven structural transformation in the member countries of the African continent to reduce dependency on overseas imports, African continental integration and cooperation to be a self-reliant African continent, diversity its production, promote intra- African trade and socio-economic cooperation, to achieve the seventeen United Nations Sustainable Development Goals with a focus on poverty alleviation, zero hunger, good health and wellbeing for all, and gender equality besides climate change (Songwe et al., 2021).

e) **BRICS –** Group of five major countries was formed in 2005 (Brazil, Russia, India, China and South Africa) besides new member countries Egypt, Ethiopia, United Arab Emirates and Iran have also joined to develop partnership and benefit form multilateral agreements for capacity building technical assistance for development projects and meet the sustainable development goals. In 2026, BRICS meeting will be Chaired by India. The official opening of the BRICS website was launched on the 13- January-2026 by the external Affairs Miniter Dr Jai Shankar. The theme and vision of 2026 BRICS under the Indian leadership as quoted by Dr Jai Shankar is: *"Building for Resilience, Innovation, Cooperation and Sustainability". It draws inspiration from Prime Minister's "Humanity First and People-centric"...this reflects our belief that cooperation among BRICS members can help address shared challenges in a balanced and in an inclusive manner. The theme underscores the importance of strengthening capacities, promoting innovation, and ensuring sustainable development for the benefit of all. (BRICS, 2026).* Given the current unstable and changing geo-political environment, BRICS is a voice and platform for the countries in the Global South for cooperation and peaceful dialogue among emerging markets in the developing economies to build resilience and meet the sustainable development goals. The aim of BRICS in 2026 for the future will be to is to work together in a multilateral partnership and focus on the vision of- Resilience to face public health emergencies, food security, agriculture, disaster and supply chain shocks. Further, BRICS will be a constructive platform to for driving innovation as the key engine for technological development and emerging technologies to address socio-economic, energy, and environmental challenges facing developing countries and adopting a people-to-people dialogue and exchange, to have a people-centric approach, for inclusive development through multilateral cooperation and sustainability to build an equitable, peaceful and prosperous world. Finaly BRICS- New Development Bank is a financially credible sustainable institution and an instrument for economic cooperation between the member countries for supporting development projects in infrastructure, health, education, agriculture and innovative technologies which are people-centric for inclusive sustainable development (BRICS, 2026).

4. CURRENT GLOBAL INTERNATIONAL TRADE AND TARIFF SCENARIO

In the post-WWII era, the U.S. emerged as the dominant economic, political, technological and military power. But the Cold War began in the aftermath of the WWII between the U.S. as leading the Western (or capitalist) alliance on one side and the former U.S.S.R as leading the Eastern (or Communist) alliance. This time-period is characterized as the bipolar era in global affairs as the two countries the U.S. and the USSR became the two dominant global powers challenging each other (Islam, 2021b). During this bipolar world, most other countries were aligned with one of the two blocks or some countries tried to stay as independent. During this time, the world economy was characterized by massive tariff and non-tariff barriers, restrictions on tourism and cross-border investments, currency restrictions and controls, massive arms buildups, high government interventions to manage and control the economy, among others. The result was much less trade flows in goods and services, cross-border investments, tourism, technology transfers, skill transfers, cross-border migration, and cultural interaction (Islam, 2021b). The countries as well as the global economy suffered due to low levels of all the above productive and welfare-enhancing activities. As a result, the potential for growth and development remained subdued and less than potential.

The above closed-economy regime changed dramatically with the Fall of the Berlin Wall in 1989 and the collapse of the former USSR, paving the way for a more open and integrated world economy, The world economy started to change in the direction of more openness, greater and deeper integration towards a more globalized world. The pace of integration accelerated since 1990's with many countries in the world kept moving away from old regime of closed economy model to the direction of a more open economy model of development. Countries began to integrate with the world by adopting and implementing various internal and external reforms to integrate in the global economy. The list of countries includes even the highly closed former Eastern European nations and most other developing and emerging economies. This increased openness and globalization led to greater volume of trade, investments, technology transfers, skills transfers, tourism flows, people-to-people contacts that led to prosperity in many countries including major emerging countries like China, India, Brazil, to name a few (Islam, 2021b).

However, the expectation that a rising tide will lift all boats did not happen unfortunately. Some countries did prosper very rapidly, notably China, India, Bangladesh, Malaysia, South Kores, Singapore, Hong Kong, Taiwan, Vietnam, Brazil, and South Africa, to name a few. However, some very poor countries, some land locked countries, and some countries in Africa and Latin America and in Asia did not receive the expected benefits from the march of globalization(Islam, 2021b). Obviously, these countries became disillusioned and disappointed as their economies struggled to maintain the economic status quo and some countries experienced declines. Similar frustration began to simmer even in some of the rich industrialized countries in the West as some industries began to disappear (moving overseas through outsourcing) causing loss of jobs and income accompanied by rising poverty and increased inequality. The disillusionment occurred in both the right and the left of the ideological spectrum in these countries, albeit with some similar and some dissimilar concerns.

On the ideological right, the concerns grew due to immigration and the associated cultural and religious integration concerns, openness leading to job and income losses due to open trade and outsourcing, deindustrialization of some regions of the country due to decline in manufacturing bases, rural areas not experiencing any benefits of open trade, among others. On this side of the equation were the powerful domestic industry-interest groups such as trade and professional associations, politicians and pollical parties on the right, antiimmigrant groups, to name a few. On the left of the ideological spectrum, concerns against globalization arose from labor unions due to job and income losses, stagnant wages, competition with low-wage and lax labor-standard in foreign countries (such as child-labor issue or slave-labor issue), and environmental degradation, these ills presumably being blamed on globalization. Labor unions and environmental groups or interests were in the forefront of this side of the equation. From the above background discussion, it is very clear that current globalization trend is under severe stress and backlashes in different countries including the western countries who actively promoted globalization and openness over the years since the post-WWII (Altman & Bastian, 2024; Contractor, 2017a; Ghemawat & Altman, 2016; Islam, 2021a,).

The anti-globalization trend in the West have gathered increased momentum such as the Brexit movement in the U.K led by right wing politician Nigel Farage and the rise of Donald Trump to the Presidency of the U.S. During his first term as the U.S. President (Jan 2017 to January 2021), and invoked many anti-globalization measures such as travel ban on some Muslim countries, tariff increase on some critical products such as cement, aluminium and steel on other countries who are presumed to be friends and foes alike, and started a trade war against its presumed main adversary China. US-President even called China as the currency manipulator. He doubled down on this policy during his 2nd term in office beginning in January 2025 (Contractor, 2017a; Contractor, 2017b). US-Administration imposed massive tariffs on many foreign countries and imports from them, friends and foe alike in the name of America First or Make America Great Again (MAGA) movement.

In addition, he started massive campaign at home to deport many undocumented immigrants at a massive scale using even military power. To add fuel to the fire, there is a strong rise of nationalistic and anti-globalization sentiments in many western countries as they see job losses, increased inequality and poverty among some segments of the population, greater immigration of foreign nationals viewed as taking their jobs away and importing foreign cultures and religions. Examples include movement for Brexit, inward-looking home-country focus movements, rise of Trump and his promoting anti-immigration and anti-globalization agenda. Trump began a trade and currency war against China in his first term in office. Now in his second term in office, he has expanded those anti-immigration and anti-globalization policies with anti-immigration raids and deportations, massive tariff raises against all countries in the world, friends and foes alike.

These are causing adverse effects on trade flows, financial and investment flows, migration and tourism flows, transfer of technology flows, among others. The result is predicted to be a world with less openness and reduced globalization, with increasing geo-political tensions and conflicts in 2026 and future years. Economic theories predict that such forces will have many adverse consequences on the world economy as well as many individual countries. If these trends continue, the result is predicted to be loss of jobs and income, less social mobility, more poverty, greater environmental degradation, and overall slower economic growth and development.

5 CHALLENGES AND OPPORTUNITIES

Over the last three decades events such as the end of the cold war, 1997 Asian financial crisis, rise of China and its violation of maritime sovereignty in the South Chian Sea, the 2020 pandemic public health emergency and supply chain disruptions, climate change impact, ongoing conflict between Russian Ukraine 2023 and Isreal-Arab since 2024, internal conflicts and fall of governments in various SAARC countries and with the coming to power in 2025, the painful US Trump government' Tariffs, the global geopolitics has changed forever. Further with the election of the US government to power in 2025, the painful US Trump government' Tariffs, Venezuela political and economic crisis linked to drug trafficking and corruption (Buschschliuter, 2026) and the US -administration push to buy Greenland for US national security and dominate the western hemisphere has further created global uncertainties and lack of trust in US-administration and geopolitics has changed forever (Yussuf, 2025).

There is a challenge of establishing regional grouping and relationships with appropriate economic strategies for implementing policies for the mutual benefit given the changing geo-political environment, security tensions in the South China Seas and the Indo-Pacific region, US random tariffs and sanctions, trade and travel restrictions and their impact on the nations. Further exploration may reveal new strategies to improve international bilateral and multilateral relations and economic agreements among nations. Some of these countries have formed various bilateral, regional, and multilateral grouping such as AfCFTA, ASEAN, BRICS, BIMSTEC, G-20, QUAD, EU and SAARC, among others, within the framework of WTO rules and regulations.

For example, the concerns of tariffs and non-tariff barriers, cross-border regional conflicts and wars, geopolitical-power shifts, food security, public health emergencies, cyber security, climate change, unemployment, infrastructure development, technological innovation, and border and maritime security concerns besides trying to meet the greater public and global good and UN-SDGs. With the onset of the current anti-globalization and anti-immigration movements in different western countries, the world is facing serious challenges to cope with this phenomenon. Different countries, particularly in the South may now has to carefully navigate through big power rivalry between the U.S. and China on one hand and the U.S. and Russia on the other. The emerging and developing countries in the South would have to face the push and pull factors from the major economic, political, and military powers. The following are some of the potential major challenges that would be encountered by many countries in the world.

Challenges

a. Dealing with current trade war situation between/among the U.S. and China, U.S. and Russia, U.S. and other countries
b. Dealing with the rise of nationalistic ideology and growing patriotic sentiments within many nation states
c. Dealing with potential future global pandemic
d. Dealing with potential global economic and financial crises
e. Dealing with US-dollar dominance versus rise of other rival currencies
f. Grab for resources such as gold, oil, gas, and critical minerals/rare-earth elements
g. Dealing with global warming and climate change
h. Dealing with the emerging multipolar world and possibly new cold war rivalry
i. Threat to globalization, global order, lack of trust, and militarisation across the globe

Opportunities for Cooperation

As we know, crisis and challenges can open up door for opportunities to explore for mutual benefit and promote peace and prosperity and progress of nations. There are still ample opportunities at the global stage to cooperate with each other and among willing nations to address many global challenges. These challenges can open up opportunities to explore by industries and country leaders for the benefit of the countries and the world at large. Some of these challenges faced by all countries in the world are to explore opportunities for cooperation for enhance economic development and growth:

a. Explore the bilateral and/or multilateral trade and investment opportunities between/among emerging countries in the south
b. Peaceful negotiation and cooperation within BRICS countries and their expanding relationship with other nations
c. Peaceful negotiation and cooperation between Eastern and Western European countries
d. Peaceful bilateral cooperation with neighbouring countries for trade, travel and investment opportunities
e. Peaceful bilateral and multilateral cooperation across different continents such as between Central Asia, South Asia, East Asian Economies, and Africa, Latin America, Eastern Europe, Western Europe and Pacific Island Economies
f. Peacefully negotiate and cooperate with each other to urgently address global environmental crisis such as global warming and climate change

g. Cooperate to develop technology and transfer of technology to build resilience and address global warming, climate change and global health emergencies
h. Peacefully negotiate and cooperate to tackle the global migration, terrorism, drug and human trafficking problems across borders.

DISCUSSION

The significance of bilateral and multilateral regional trade agreements and cooperation for economic development cannot be undermined given the global trade dynamics and geopolitics powershifts, conflict and war (Russia-Ukraine, USA-Isreal and Iran in the Middle East) driven disruptions to global supply chains, rise in the price of oil, and emerging trade blocs tensions, must be a priority for all countries in the world to bring peace, prosperity, progress, and inclusive economic development and growth for the world population. All countries must recognise the importance and share a vision of economic cooperation, collaboration, partnerships, peace, mutual respect, friendship, and trust required between bordering neighbours, trading partners across land locked countries or nations across the oceans; in order to promote bilateral, regional, or multilateral trade, tourism, investment opportunities for sustainable economic development, and meet United Nations Sustainable Development Goals (UN-SDG, 2025). The ministerial QUAD meeting held in September 2019, between the four democratic nations of Australia, India, USA, and Japan was held in September 2019, to find a concrete solution to mutual and global problems, through QUAD strategic cooperation, partnership and coronavirus vaccination alliance for investment, production, and distribution to keep the nations safe, stable, and secure Further cooperate under QUAD to solve climate change, cyber security, and pandemic related issues and have a free and open Indo-Pacific region (Medhekar & Kaur, 2022; Ngaibiakching & Pande, 2020).

Other contributing chapters in this edited book provide valuable insights and guidance for promoting bilateral and multilateral trade agreements, connectivity, international trade, and global investment opportunities with case study examples and reviews. Covering topics such as global business, trade, tourism, tariffs, and financial investment flows. Economists, scholars, large multinational companies, strategic industries, government, and policymakers need to understand the implications of the current geo-political scenarios related to tariff and non-tariff impact on the economy.

CONCLUSION

This introductory chapter provides the background to the international trade theory literature from historical perspective, bilateral and multilateral trade agreements, to current anti-globalisation, international trade and tariff barriers, de-dollarization, militarization, USA-Isreal and Iran conflict and war, Venezuelan and Greenland issues. Therefore, there is an ever-growing need to build trust, respect and peaceful dialogue for economic cooperation, peaceful negotiations for promoting bilateral cooperation and collaboration for regional trade agreements. The future looks bleak with slow global GDP growth rate, amidst the geo-political dynamics, mistrust created by the current situation due to regional cross-border wars, internal country conflicts, rise of nationalism, Trump-administration's tyranny of tariffs, sanctions, Venezuela and Greenland issues. In the remaining of the 21st century, generations and multilateral agreements for cross-border investments, trade and tourism for improved international relations is important to face various global challenges together, and reap the benefits from cooperative opportunities to improve wellbeing of humans and bring peace, progress and prosperity for sustainable inclusive people-centric economic development and disarmament and growth for our future generations, and save the planet earth at every front from human destruction and war and move towards, for sustainable peace, progress, and prosperity for all the people on this planet.

REFERENCES

Aggarwal, V. K., & Urata, S. (2006). *Bilateral Tade Agreements in the Asia-Pacific: Origins Evolutions, and Implications* (1st ed.). Routledge., DOI: 10.4324/9781315020976

Ali, M. M., & Medhekar, A. (2016). Bilateral Trade through official channel between India and Bangladesh: An analysis with the use of Time Series forecasting models. *Journal of Economic Cooperation and Development, 37*(3), 135–170.

Austarlian Border Force. (2020). RECEP -Free Trade Agreements. https://www.abf.gov.au/importing-exporting-and-manufacturing/fta/free-trade-agreements/regional-comprehensive-economic-partnership-agreement

Austarlian Government DFAT. (2025). Comprehensive and Progressive Agreement for Trans-Pacific Partnership (CPTPP). https://www.dfat.gov.au/trade/agreements/in-force/cptpp/comprehensive-and-progressive-agreement-for-trans-pacific-partnership

Australian Government. (2025). Free Trade Agreements https://business.gov.au/products-and-services/exporting/free-trade-agreements

Baena-Rojas, J. J., & Herrero-Olarte, S. (2020). From Preferential Trade Arrangements to Free Trade Agreements: One of the Downturns of Cooperation in International Relations? *Social Sciences (Basel, Switzerland), 9*(8), 139. DOI: 10.3390/socsci9080139

BRICS. (2026). Launch of BRICS India 2026 Logo, Theme and Website by the External Affairs Minister. https://www.mea.gov.in/press-releases.htm?dtl/40585/Launch_of_BRICS_India_2026_Logo_Theme_and_Website_by_the_External_Affairs_Minister

Chakraborty, D., & Dey, O. (2024). Non-tariff Barriers and Trade Flows. In *Influence of WTO and Global Dynamics on Trade Flows: A Machine-Generated Literature Overview* (pp. 245–287). Springer Nature Singapore. DOI: 10.1007/978-981-99-7375-0_3

Contractor, F. J. (2017a). What is globalization? How to measure it and why many oppose it (part 1). GlobalBusiness.blog, May 8. Accessed from: https://globalbusiness.blog/2017/05/08/what-is-globalization-part-1-how-to-measure-it-and-why-many-oppose-it/.

Contractor, F. J. (2017b). What is Globalization Part 2: Global Leadership in an Era of Growing Nationalism, Protectionism, and Anti-Globalization (Part 1 & Part 2), accessed from: https://globalbusiness.blog/2017/06/02/global-leadership-in-an-era-of-growing-nationalism-protectionism-and-anti-globalization-part-2

Debrah, Y. A., Olabode, O. E., Olan, E., & Nyuur, R. B. (2024). The African continental free trade area (AfCFTA): Taking stock and looking ahead for international business research. *Journal of International Management*, *30*(2), 101120. Advance online publication. DOI: 10.1016/j.intman.2024.101120

Dür, A. (2025). EU trade agreements and external differentiation: A large language model approach. *West European Politics*, *48*(5), 1059–1085. DOI: 10.1080/01402382.2024.2425549

Elliot, K. A. (2018). *The WTO and Regional/Bilateral Trade Agreements. The Handbook of International Trade Agreements. Edn. (1).* Routledge.

European Union. (2025). Trade and Economic Security. https://policy.trade.ec.europa.eu/eu-trade-relationships-country-and-region/negotiations-and-agreements_en

Ghemawat, P., & Altman, S. A. (2016). *DHL Global Connectedness Index 2016: The State of Globalization in an Age of Ambiguity*. Deutsche Post DHL Group.

Global Business Outlook. (2025, June 27). Why BRICS+ backs local currency trade? https://globalbusinessoutlook.com/magazine/banking-and-finance-magazine/why-brics-backs-local-currency-trade/

Grossman, G. M. (2016). The Purpose of Trade Agreements. Chapter 7. *Handbook of Commercial Policy*, 1(Part-A), 379-434. DOI: 10.3386/w22070

Hasan, M. D. (2021). The relationship between trade openness and economic growth in Bangladesh: An empirical analysis. *Journal of Economic Studies (Glasgow, Scotland)*, *48*(3), 456–472.

Huchet-Bourdon, M., Le Mouël, C., & Vijil, M. (2018). The relationship between trade openness and economic growth: Some new insights on the openness measurement issue. *World Economy*, *41*(1), 59–76. DOI: 10.1111/twec.12586

Islam, A. M. (2021a). Impact of Covid-19 Pandemic on Global Output, Employment and Prices-An Assessment. *Transnational Corporations Review*, *13*(2), 189–201. DOI: 10.1080/19186444.2021.1936852

Islam, A.M. (2021b). Is Economic Globalization Under Strain? *Management and Economics Research Journal*, 7(1),1-4, Article ID 9900039. DOI: DOI: 10.18639/MERJ.2021.9900039

Josephs, J. (2026- Jan). How tariff disruption will continue reshaping the global economy in 2026. https://www.bbc.com/news/articles/czejp3gep63o

Konwer, , SHazarika, , O.B. (2025). India and the BIMSTEC- regionalism, multilateral frameworks and a changing global order. Australian *Journal of International Affairs, 79*(6), 969-987. https://doi.org/10.1080/10357718.2025.2548934

Krugman, P. R., Obstfeld, M., & Melitz, M. (2018). *International Economics* (11th ed.). Pearson.

Lupan, R. (2018). Non-tariff barriers and deepening economic integration within the European Union. In *Simpozion Ştiinţific Internaţional al Tinerilor Cercetători* (pp. 18-21).

Martin, P., Mayer, T., & Thoenig, M. (2012). The Geography of Conflicts and Regional Trade Agreements.*American Economic Journal. Macroeconomics*,*4*(4), 1–35. https://www.aeaweb.org/articles?id=10.1257/mac.4.4.1. DOI: 10.1257/mac.4.4.1

Medhekar, A. (2019). Trade in healthcare services and Economic Development: case of Kenya & South Africa. In Evelyn, F. W., & Peter, J. N. (Eds.), *The Service Sector and Economic Development in Africa. Studies in Development Economics* (pp. 181–195). Routledge.

Medhekar, A. (2021). Australia- India: Bilateral Trade Opportunities and Challenges. In Hooke, (Eds.), *Emerging Business and Trade Opportunities Between Oceania and Asia* (pp. 57–86). IGI Global., DOI: 10.4018/978-1-7998-4126-5.ch004

Medhekar, A. (2022). Australia's Bilateral and Multilateral Health Sector Partnership with South Asian Nations: Opportunities and Challenges. In Medhekar, (Eds.), *Strategic Cooperation and Partnerships Between Australia and South Asia: Economic Development, Trade, and Investment Opportunities Post-COVID-19* (pp. 1–21). IGI Global., DOI: 10.4018/978-1-7998-8657-0.ch001

Medhekar, A., & Ali, M. M. (2012). A Cross-Border Trade in Healthcare services: Bangladesh to India. *The Business and Management Review*, *2*(1), 1–13.

Medhekar, A., & Haq, F. (2020). Cross-Border Cooperation for Bilateral Trade, Travel and Tourism: A Challenge for India and Pakistan. In Castanho, R. A. (Ed.), *Cross-Border Cooperation (CBC) Strategies for Sustainable Development* (pp. 168–191). IGI Global., DOI: 10.4018/978-1-7998-2513-5.ch010

Medhekar, A., & Kaur, H. (2022). Look-East Act-East Policy: India and Southeast Asian Economic Cooperation. In Medhekar, A., & Kaur, H. (Eds.), "*Evaluating Trade and Economic Relations Between India and Southeast Asia*," (Ch1, pp.1-22). USA: IGI Global Publishing. DOI: DOI: 10.4018/978-1-7998-5774-7.ch001

Morozkina., & Skryabina, V. (2021). BRICS and Partnerships for Sustainable Development: Prospects for Trade with Least Developed Countries. *International Organisations Research Journal, 16*(1). https://doi.org/DOI: 10.17323/1996-7845-2021-01-04

Ngaibiakching, N., & Pande, A. (2020). India's Act East Policy and ASEAN: Building a Regional Order Through Partnership in the Indo-Pacific. *International Studies*, *57*(1), 67–78. DOI: 10.1177/0020881719885526

Oppong-Baah, T., Bo, Y., Twi-Brempong, C., Amoah, E. O., Prempeh, N. A., & Addai, M. (2022). The Impact of trade openness on economic growth: The case of Ghana and Nigeria. *Journal of Human Resource and Sustainability Studies*, *10*(1), 142–160. DOI: 10.4236/jhrss.2022.101010

Pomfret, R. (2020). *Regionalism" and The Global Trade System. Discussion Paper Jean Monnet Chair in the Economics of European Integration*. University of Adelaide., https://iit.adelaide.edu.au/ua/media/2066/2020-05-regionalism-rp-final.pdf

Ricardo, D. (2004). *(1817/1821). On the Principles of Political Economy and Taxation, Collated Text of all Three Editions*. Liberty Fund Press.

Richard, B. E. (2014). Multilateralising 21st Century Regionalism, OECD *Report (46 pages)*, International Economic Department. OECD: Paris. https://repository .graduateinstitute.ch/record/286980/references?v=pdf

Romer, P. (2021). Growth Theory. *Endogenous Growth in Historical Perspective: From Adam Smith to Paul Romer*, 251.

Singapore Ministry of Trade & International Economic Relations. {SMTIER} (2025). Regional Comprehensive Economic Partnership. https://www.mti.gov.sg/trade-international-economic-relations/agreements/free-trade-agreements-fta/rcep/

Smith, A. (1776/1784). *An Inquiry into the Nature and Causes of the Wealth of Nations*. Liberty Fund Press.

Songwe, V., MacLeod, J. M., & Karingi, S. (2021). The African Continental Free Trade Area: A Historical Moment for Development in Africa. *Journal of African Trade*, *8*(2), 9. Advance online publication. DOI: 10.2991/jat.k.211208.001

Southgate, L. (2025). Explaining ASEAN institutional balancing success and failure. *Asian Security*, *21*(2), 149–167. DOI: 10.1080/14799855.2025.2527885

Thrasher, R.D., & Gallagher, K.P. (2008). 21st century trade agreements: implications for long-run development policy. The Frederick S. Pardee Centre for the Study of Longer-Range Future. Boston University. Paper No-2

Todaro, M. P., & Smith, S. C. (2020). *Economic Development*. Pearson.

Uddin, M. R., Sadik, N., & Rahman, M. M. (2025). Globalization, physical capital, and human capital nexus with economic growth: Evidence from BIMSTEC. *Research in Globalisation, 10*, 100284. DOI: 10.1016/j.resglo.2025.100284

United Nations Trade and Development (UNCTAD). (2024). The reshaping of global trade: How developing countries can strategize. https://unctad.org/news/reshaping-global-trade-how-developing-countries-can-strategize#:~:text

Varghese, P. (2018). Indian Economic Strategy 2035. Department of Foreign Affairs and Trade. Retrieved from https://dfat.gov.au/geo/india/ies/index.html

Watson, M. (2017). Historicising Ricardo's comparative advantage theory, challenging the normative foundations of liberal International Political Economy. *New Political Economy, 22*(3), 257–272. DOI: 10.1080/13563467.2016.1216535

World Bank. (2023). https://blogs.worldbank.org/en/trade/africa-pursues-free-trade-amid-global-fragmentation

World Tade Organisation. (2025). Regional Trade Agreements and the WTO. https://www.wto.org/english/tratop_e/region_e/scope_rta_e.htm

Yussuf, A. (2026-Jan-7). Why does Trump want Greenland and why it is so important?.https://www.abc.net.au/news/2026-01-07/why-does-trump-want-greenland-and-why-is-it-so-important/106203650

ADDITIONAL READING

Buckley, R. P. Voi, Io Lo., & Boutle, L.L.(Eds.). (2008). *Challenges to Multilateral Trade: The impact of Bilateral Preferential and Regional Agreements*. Netherlands: Kluwer Law International.

Daniel, M. (2020). Trade Unions and Trade in Africa: African Continental Free Trade Area. https://tradeunionsinafcfta.org/the-development-of-the-afcfta-where-did-it-start/

Ornelas, E., & Freund, C. (2010). *Regional Trade Agreements*. Policy Research working paper; no. WPS 5314. World Bank. http://hdl.handle.net/10986/3799 License: CC BY 3.0 IGO."

Rashid, M. K., Basit, A., Qazi, T. F., & Niazi, A. K. (2021). Comprehensive Analysis of Tariff Barriers Worldwide: A Composite Assessment Approach. *Journal of Accounting and Finance in Emerging Economies*, *7*(1), 205–215. DOI: 10.26710/jafee.v7i1.1583

Shibli, A., Islam A.M., & Ahmed, S. (2013). Global Opportunities and Challenges for Bangladesh: A Preliminary Analysis", *Southwest review of International Business Research*, 24(1). 85-89.

Siddiqui, K. (2018). David Ricardo's comparative advantage and developing countries: Myth and reality. *International Critical Thought*, *8*(3), 426–452. DOI: 10.1080/21598282.2018.1506264

World Trade Organization {WTO} (2025). *World Trade Report*. https://www.wto.org/english/thewto_e/thewto_e.htm

KEY TERMS AND DEFINITIONS:

Bilateral Relations: Bilateral relation is between two countries, such as USA and Australia . this can be for trade, investment, defence and security for mutually benefit.

Free Trade Agreements (FTAs): Free Trade Agreements is between two or more countries to reduce or eliminate quotas, tariff and non-tariff barriers to trade and investment in certain goods and services. These FTAs mutually benefits countries producers, investors, exporters, and importers. For example, 1983- Australia-New Zealand Closer Economic Relationship Trade Agreement, Singapore-Australia-FTA 2003, China-Australia-FTA- 2015), Australia-India Economic Cooperation and Trade Agreement (AI-ECTA)-2022, Australia-UAE Comprehensive Economic Partnership Agreement- 2025, North American-FTA and US-Canada-FTA of 1988 with Mexico included in 1993.

Geo-Politics: In the 21st century global political- power dynamics and various geo-political factors like climate topography, geographical location and natural resources of countries (e.g. oil, gas, critical minerals, nations border-territories, military power, powerful countries- USA, China, Russia, sanctions, control over payment systems, interference in foreign policy etc.) are shaping the international relations and influencing domestic and international politics, foreign policy, interaction between countries, political leaders, multinational corporations, strategic industries, non-state actors like pressure groups and terrorist groups, and other stakeholders for their political advantage.

Multilateral Relations: Multilateral relations are between more than two countries for trade, tourism, investment, cultural, economic, scholarship and scientific collaboration, Agriculture policy, water resources, defence and security which is of mutual benefit. For example, ASEAN, AFTA, AFCFTA, SAARC, EU etc.

QUAD: The Quadrilateral Security Dialogue - Group of four major trading nations form strategic forum to cooperate to work on shared challenges and opportunities such as free and open trade, maritime security, immigration, climate change, technology-AI, natural disaster response growth of military powers and other regional challenges within their region. For example (EU, Japan, USA and Canada) and QUAD between (USA, Australia, Japan and India)

Regional Trade Agreements (RTA): Regional trade agreements are reciprocal economic or preferential trade agreements between more than two countries to eliminate trade quotas, tariff and non-tariff barriers. For example, APEC, ASEAN, EU, and RCEP to have trade liberalisation and access to each other markets, to increase competition and expand investment, trade, and travel opportunities and capacity building needs initiatives through projects in developing countries on social, intellectual, economic, environmental and technology transfer.

Sustainable Development: Sustainable development is defined as an inclusive development activity that uses the scarce social, economic, and environmental resources in a sustainable manner to meet the needs of the present generation and to achieve the United Nations 17- SDGs, without compromising the ability of the future generations to meet their needs.

Tariff and Non-Tariff Barriers: Tariff is a tax on imported goods and it is a more transparent way to create trade barriers; Non-tariff barriers are many other forms of trade restrictions such as quota restrictions, subsidies, health standards, technical specifications, national security clauses, cultural preferences for home goods, buy home goods campaigns, embargos, among others.

Chapter 2
Leveraging Afghanistan's Geopolitical Position for Regional Connectivity and Trade Integration

Hamayun Khan
http://orcid.org/0000-0002-8711-7652
SolaTeach Inc., USA

ABSTRACT

Afghanistan's location at the crossroads of Central, West, and South Asia makes it a natural link between energy-rich Central Asia and energy-deficient South Asia. This chapter examines how that position can foster domestic growth and regional integration through three major initiatives: the Turkmenistan–Afghanistan–Pakistan–India (TAPI) gas pipeline, the Lapis Lazuli Corridor, and the Chabahar Port. It evaluates their economic and social potential alongside governance constraints, security risks, and the impact of international sanctions. Drawing on qualitative analysis and recent empirical data, the chapter explores how Afghanistan can improve trade facilitation, attract investment, and strengthen institutional capacity for regional partnerships. The findings suggest that targeted investment, sustained diplomatic engagement, and credible institutional reforms could transform Afghanistan into a viable trade and transit hub, promoting long-term stability and inclusive, broad-based growth.

INTRODUCTION

The world is consistently undergoing enormous tectonics changing order, particularly in globalization and industrialization (World Economic Forum [WEF],

DOI: 10.4018/979-8-3373-1782-3.ch002

2025). These dynamics, while disruptive, present opportunities for both national and regional economic development (Bertelsmann Stiftung, 2024). Afghanistan, given its geostrategic location, stands both as a potential beneficiary and contributor to this evolving global order (UNCTAD, 2019).

As Masomy (2021) and Noorzi (2021) note, Afghanistan's enduring role as a land bridge between Central and South Asia persists into today's corridor plans. Despite decades of conflicts and political instability, the country is strategically positioned, linking regional markets and facilitating access to natural resources (Sanchez Cacicedo, 2022). Landlocked and located at the crossroads of Central, West, and South Asia (National Intelligence Council, 2002), Afghanistan connects energy-rich nations in the north—such as Turkmenistan, Kazakhstan, and Uzbekistan—with energy-deficient and struggling economies like Pakistan and India (Safi & Alizada, 2018). Afghanistan is also a South Asian Association for Regional Cooperation (SAARC) member, but the bloc's prolonged dysfunction has shifted practical connectivity toward sub-regional corridors and bilateral arrangements (Aryal, 2022). This positioning imbues Afghanistan with distinct geopolitical, geo-economic, and geostrategic significance, making it a critical node in regional connectivity and trade initiatives.

However, realizing this potential remains, to some extent, challenging. Persistent barriers include security concerns, fragile governance, and underdeveloped infrastructure (International Crisis Group, 2022; Small, 2015), compounded by structural issues such as reliance on the parallel opium economy (United Nations Office on Drugs and Crime [UNODC], 2011). Nonetheless, signs of resilience are emerging, such as the revival of rail routes between China and northern Afghanistan (Yawar & Rasooli, 2024) and participation in regional frameworks like the Economic Cooperation Organization (ECO) and the Ashgabat Agreement (European Union Institute for Security Studies [EUISS], 2023).

Recent geopolitical realignments, particularly sanctions on regional powers like Russia, have shifted trade dynamics toward alternative routes traversing Afghanistan (Center for Strategic and International Studies [CSIS], 2024). Strategic transit points such as Iran's Bandar Abbas and Chabahar ports, and Pakistan's Gwadar Port, are gaining prominence in inter-regional trade networks (Hussain & Nawaz, 2021). These routes intersect with major initiatives like the International North-South Transport Corridor (INSTC), China's Belt and Road Initiative (BRI), and the European Union's Global Gateway (Sanchez Cacicedo, 2022). Zaki (2023) highlights that the BRI's targeted infrastructure investments could deepen Afghanistan's integration with Eurasian markets, provided that governance and security conditions align with regional investment norms. Institutional frameworks such as the Afghanistan—Pakistan Transit Trade Agreement (APTTA) also influence corridor viability, with Rlung (2024) finding that tariff parity and procedural reforms could substantially reduce trade costs.

Regional powers—including China, Iran, Russia, Türkiye, and India—are increasingly engaging in Afghanistan from a geo-economic standpoint (Caspian Policy Center, 2023). The evolution of sanctions regimes has fragmented global trade into competing blocks, elevating the strategic value of intermediary corridors through Central Asia and the Global Majority states (Aiyar et al., 2023). In this context, Afghanistan's location at the crossroads of these blocs raises its value as a practical overland connector within Eurasia (Carnegie Endowment for International Peace, 2025).

Following Russia's 2022 invasion of Ukraine, EU exports to Russia fell by 58% and imports by 86%, with even sharper declines for sanctioned goods (Council of the European Union, 2024; Eurostat, 2024). UK imports from Russia dropped by 94% and exports by 74% (Savic, 2025). In response, Moscow pivoted toward developing economies—especially China—pushing bilateral trade to $245 billion in 2024 (UK Parliament, 2024), a shift analysts see hardening Russia's long-term eastward orientation (Center for Strategic and International Studies [CSIS], 2024; Luck, 2025). This reorientation elevates the strategic value of overland corridors across Central Asia, with Afghan routes offering critical terrestrial links among China, Russia, and South Asia.

Afghanistan's active participation in multilateral organizations such as the SAARC, the Shanghai Cooperation Organization (SCO), and the ECO further highlights its potential to foster regional trade frameworks. As nations seek to leverage connectivity for economic growth and progress toward the United Nations Sustainable Development Goals (SDGs)—particularly SDG 8 (Decent Work and Economic Growth)—Afghanistan's integration into regional supply chains could contribute significantly to stability and prosperity.

This chapter examines how Afghanistan can move from a conflict-affected state to a regional economic hub by leveraging its geographic and economic potential. It analyzes key infrastructure projects, geopolitical dynamics, and trade agreements, highlights constraints such as political instability and rivalries, and, in line with the book's focus on actionable cooperation, reviews trade frameworks, governance institutions, and policy tools to operationalize Afghanistan's connectivity potential.

By examining key bilateral and multilateral frameworks—such as South Asian Free Trade Agreement (SAFTA), ECO, and World Trade Organization (WTO) commitments—and the legal and institutional conditions for corridor success, this chapter offers policymakers, academics, and practitioners' evidence-based strategies to turn infrastructure into sustained economic gains. As Ijirshar (2022) demonstrates, improvements in trade facilitation and logistics efficiency can significantly accelerate economic growth, reinforcing the importance of aligning corridor development with institutional reforms. It also addresses a key gap: most studies stress Afghanistan's security fragility, but few examine its geographic role in trade-led development amid BRICS expansion, China's BRI, and Russia's eastward pivot. This chapter adds an economic lens, highlighting regional corridors and multilateral integration as pathways to more durable development.

Objectives of the Chapter

This chapter aims to:

- Show how Afghanistan's location at the crossroads of Central, South, and West Asia gives it geostrategic importance and potential to become a key Eurasian trade and connectivity hub.
- Examine major infrastructure projects, trade routes, and multilateral frameworks—including Turkmenistan-Afghanistan-Pakistan-India (TAPI), Central Asia–South Asia power project (CASA-1000), Chabahar Port, the Lapis Lazuli Corridor, and China's BRI—as major gateways of regional integration through Afghanistan.
- Analyze opportunities and structural constraints—political instability, security volatility, weak institutions, and poor infrastructure—shaping Afghanistan's integration into regional and global trade.
- Propose policy-oriented recommendations for national leaders, regional actors, and international institutions to unlock Afghanistan's trade potential and promote shared regional development goals.

These objectives address gaps in the literature, which highlight Afghanistan's geostrategic potential but overlook institutional capacity, governance reform, and coordinated infrastructure. Using cases like TAPI and CASA-1000, the chapter links regional connectivity goals to national policy priorities and outlines practical strategies for multilateral cooperation.

Rationale

Afghanistan's landlocked location and its proximity to key trade routes place the country at the core of several regional trade and connectivity initiatives. The country holds the potential to serve as a corridor connecting resource-rich Central Asia with the consumer markets of South Asia and vice versa. Major projects like the TAPI pipeline, the Lapis Lazuli Corridor, and the Chabahar Port initiative underscore Afghanistan's untapped potential as a transit hub (Javaid, 2024). Over the past two decades, Afghanistan's integration into regional economic organizations such as SAARC, SCO, and ECO highlights its strategic significance in fostering regional trade and economic development (Farasoo, 2016).

However, political instability, socio-economic crisis, weak infrastructure, and trade barriers have severely constrained Afghanistan's capacity to harness these opportunities (World Bank, 2024). Sedra (2014) argues that ongoing insecurity, a fragmented security sector, and uneven state-building undermine investor confidence and regional cooperation, requiring coordinated action by neighbors, international financial institutions (IFIs) i.e. the World Bank, and Asian Development Bank (ADB), and multilateral bodies such as the UN and WTO. Afghan policymakers—especially the Finance and Industry & Commerce ministries and transport/trade bodies—must lead in creating an enabling environment for trade and investment. Afghanistan can leverage its location and targeted policies to become a regional trade hub for South and Central Asia.

LITERATURE REVIEW: THEMATIC GAPS AND THEORETICAL ANCHORS

This section synthesizes academic literature to ground Afghanistan's trade and connectivity potential in theory frameworks.

- **Geoeconomics of Landlocked States:** Landlocked Developing Countries (LLDCs) typically absorb higher logistics costs and depend on neighbors' infrastructure and border procedures, which can erode competitiveness unless offset by policy and corridor design (Faye et al., 2004; Arvis et al., 2010). Afghanistan shares these constraints but also possesses unique geopolitical relevance that can mitigate some disadvantages when paired with strategic policy.
- **Political Economy of Trade Corridors:** Studies on transnational infrastructure such as BRI, TAPI, and CASA-1000 highlight the interplay between diplomacy, economic dependence, and regional power asymmetries (Summers, 2016; Sidaway et al., 2020). These corridors are not just economic projects—they are political instruments shaped by trust, governance, and negotiation.
- **Regional Integration and the SDGs:** Literature emphasizes the role of infrastructure in achieving SDG- 9(industry, innovation, and infrastructure) and SDG-8 (decent work and economic growth), particularly for post-conflict and fragile states (UNCTAD, 2019). Afghanistan's strategic location aligns with these goals but requires governance frameworks that ensure inclusivity and sustainability.

- **Risk and Fragility in Infrastructure Development:** Fragile states face elevated risks in project implementation—ranging from conflict spillovers and corruption to weak land rights and legal enforcement (Collier, 2009). Scholars stress the need for phased implementation, community engagement, and donor coordination in fragile contexts.

AFGHANISTAN'S ECONOMIC CONTEXT

A. Historical Role as a Trade Hub

Afghanistan has historically sat at the crossroads of South Asia, Central Asia, and the Middle East, serving as a key roundabout for trans-regional trade and cultural exchange (Omarkhail & Zahid, 2025). Its cities—such as Balkh, Herat, and Kandahar—were important nodes along the ancient Silk Road, which linked China, Central Asia, Persia, the Mediterranean, and later the Islamic world (Kurin, 2002; National Geographic Education, n.d.; Roos, 2021; Lü et al., 2021). While the term "Silk Road" itself dates from the 19th century, the underlying routes enabled the movement of goods such as silk, spices, and metals, as well as the circulation of religious ideas, artistic traditions, and scientific knowledge (Kurin, 2002; Roos, 2021). Control over these routes translated into both economic and political influence, reinforcing Afghanistan's role as an intermediary between empires.

Figure 1. Map of the Silk Road (300 B.C.–A.D. 100), illustrating the historical trade routes and cities through which Afghanistan served as a central corridor between East and West. Source: UNESCO

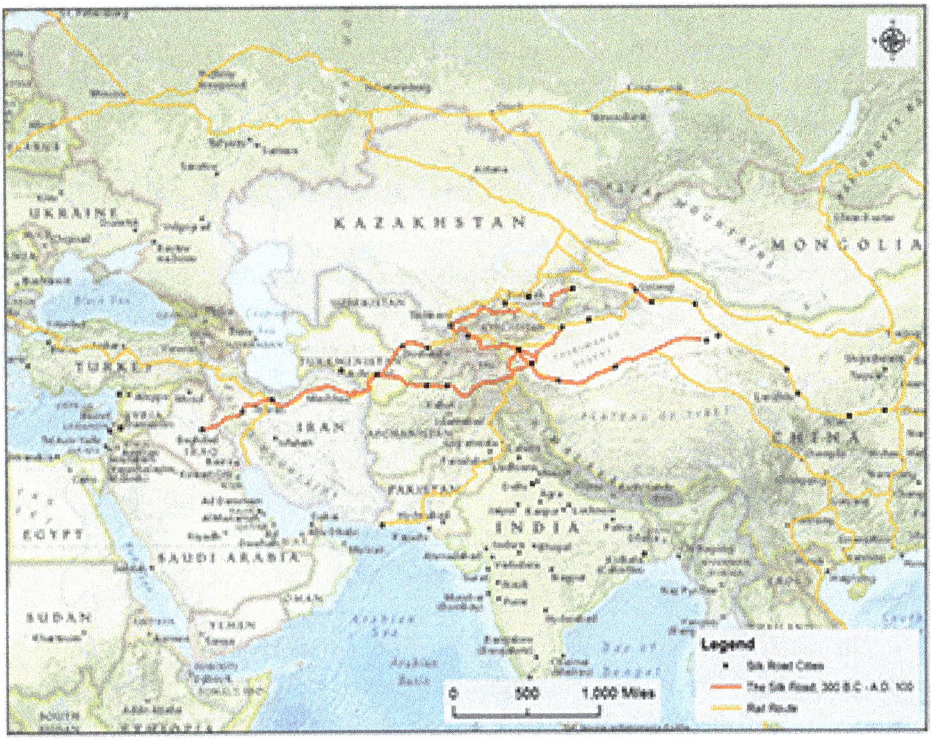

This facilitated a structured trade route between China and the West (Skylence, n.d.). Contemporary initiatives such as BRI and the Lapis Lazuli Corridor revive aspects of this legacy. They aim to reconnect regions once linked by caravan routes, now through modern highways, railways, and energy networks (Safi & Alizada, 2018; Rahim, 2019; Alekberli-Museyibova, 2023). Afghanistan's historical function as a bridge between civilizations is therefore directly relevant to current efforts to build Eurasian corridors.

B. Economic Significance

Afghanistan's geographic positioning gives it exceptional potential as a transit and trade hub at the junction of Central and South Asia and the wider Eurasian space (Aziz, 2016; Noorzi, 2021). Major regional initiatives—TAPI, CASA-1000, the Lapis Lazuli Corridor, and the Chabahar Corridor—can generate transit revenue, diversify trade, and expand energy access (Farasoo [EFSAS], 2019; Javaid, 2024).

- Afghanistan is already part of several multimodal trade corridors, including:
- The Lapis Lazuli Corridor via Turkmenistan, Azerbaijan, Georgia, and Türkiye to Black Sea ports.
- Rail corridors connecting Afghanistan to Pakistan's Karachi Port.
- The Kazakhstan–Turkmenistan–Afghanistan–Iran (KTAI) Corridor, linking Central Asia to Iranian ports such as Bandar Abbas (Ahmadov, 2021; IRU, 2020; ECO, 2020).

i. Strategic Trade Routes

Serving as a land bridge, Afghanistan connects energy-rich Central Asia with South Asian markets and ports in the Arabian Sea. Projects such as the Lapis Lazuli Corridor, Five Nations Railway, Chabahar-linked routes, TAPI, and CASA-1000 echo the Silk Road's former role of linking economies and societies (Alekberli-Museyibova, 2023; Rahim, 2019). In practice, trade flows still depend heavily on key crossings such as Torkham and Chaman, underlining both the opportunities and vulnerabilities of Afghanistan's transit position (Rahim, 2018; Intellinews, 2024).

ii. Transit Potential and Revenue Generation

Afghanistan's regional trade integration offers major opportunities through transit fees, customs revenues, and logistics industries. As a node in international corridors, it could develop free trade zones, industrial parks, and dry ports in border provinces, boosting jobs, investment, and fiscal income. Rail initiatives backed by Uzbekistan, Kazakhstan, Turkmenistan, Tajikistan, India, and China underscore its transit potential, as Central Asian states seek shorter routes to the Indian Ocean and key partners like Pakistan, India, and Tajikistan already account for over 60% of Afghan exports (Pleis, Lliteras, Wood, Bain, & Hendrickson, 2015). As Kazakhstan's Foreign Minister Yerzhan Kazykhanov once remarked, "We must look beyond 2014 and help Afghans help themselves." a sentiment that echoes broader calls for more effective and mutually beneficial international partnerships in post-conflict contexts (Gormley, 2009).

iii. Natural Resources

Afghanistan holds vast untapped mineral wealth—lithium, copper, iron ore, rare earths, and natural gas—vital for the global green transition and high-tech manufacturing. This endowment places it at the center of a "great extractives race," as major powers and firms compete for access to these strategic resources (Hunter & Ginn, 2025). If managed transparently and effectively, these resources could anchor

Afghanistan's economic development, drive exports and supporting domestic value-added industries. Khan (2024) cautions that the race for Afghanistan's lithium and other critical minerals could undermine sovereignty if dominated by foreign actors without fair Afghan ownership or benefit-sharing. Afghanistan's future thus depends on strong institutions, transparent contracts, and safeguards against exploitation so that, with the right infrastructure and regional cooperation, it can join the global clean energy value chain while securing sustainable, inclusive gains at home.

iv. Economic Interdependence and Integration

As BRI, ECO, and SCO prioritize connectivity, Afghanistan's hub role grows: integration into multilateral trade networks can cut transport costs, expand market access, deepen cross-border cooperation, and help stabilize a fragile region. Particularly the BRI has demonstrated potential to reduce trade restrictions and enhance Afghanistan's connectivity through targeted infrastructure investments and diplomatic engagement. Zaki (2023) argues that BRI can deepen Afghanistan's integration with Eurasian markets through infrastructure and geo-economic partnerships, if domestic governance aligns with regional norms. Evidence shows BRI can boost trade, lower barriers, and support sustainable development when coupled with proactive diplomacy and regional cooperation (Tian, Zaki, & Haihua, 2024). These strategic alliances are not only facilitating trade routes but also helping to shape a more stable economic environment across the broader region. Afghanistan's future hinges on serving as a regional connector: lowering transport costs, expanding market access, and deepening interdependence through corridors like Lapis Lazuli and BRI-backed, security-supported infrastructure.

ROLE OF THE GOVERNMENT IN ADVANCING REGIONAL CONNECTIVITY

Afghanistan's government is crucial to realizing regional connectivity plans: despite external support, weak coordination, limited capacity, and corruption in domestic institutions have slowed projects like TAPI and CASA-1000 (Transparency International, 2024). The chapter shows that stronger governance is vital for infrastructure delivery, cross-border agreements, and policy continuity. Key ministries should coordinate via a National Connectivity Task Force, with more responsibility delegated to local hubs like Herat and Balkh. Investments in digital customs and anti-corruption reforms are needed to build trust so Afghanistan can shift from a passive corridor to an active coordinator of regional connectivity.

Geopolitical Significance

Afghanistan's geopolitical relevance extends far beyond its borders. Afghanistan's position gives outside powers incentives to compete or cooperate there, not for its domestic market size alone, but because access *through* it affects wider regional strategies. Over centuries, great powers have vied for control or influence in Afghanistan—not merely for its internal value, but because of its position as a critical gateway to broader regional ambitions. In the contemporary era, as geopolitical rivalries intensify and connectivity becomes a strategic asset, Afghanistan's location has once again placed it at the center of a high-stakes geopolitical chessboard (Aziz, 2016; Salahi, 2022; Caspian Policy Center, 2024; Weinbaum & Ali, 2025). Its future, therefore, is not only a matter of domestic governance but of regional balance and international alignment.

i. Geostrategic Location

Afghanistan's landlocked but central geography gives it unparalleled geostrategic importance: at the intersection of South Asia, Central Asia, the Middle East, and China, it serves as a vital corridor for goods, energy, and influence and, as a historic Silk Road crossroads, now sits at the heart of modern initiatives such as BRI, the China-Pakistan Economic Corridor (CPEC), and the INSTC (Institute for the Study of Ancient Cultures, University of Chicago, n.d.). Bordering Pakistan, Iran, Turkmenistan, Uzbekistan, Tajikistan, and China, it lies beside some of the world's most contested geopolitical zones, offering landlocked Central Asian republics the shortest routes to seaports in South Asia and the Middle East (Brkić, 2025) and alternative overland links westward to Iran and eastward to South Asia and Indo-Pacific markets (Carll, 2021). For China, Afghanistan is a crucial link in westward integration with Europe, and influence over it directly or indirectly shapes access to projects like the TAPI pipeline, emerging rail networks, and transit corridors connecting Eurasia to the Indian Ocean (Afzal, 2025). As China, Russia, India, Iran, and Türkiye advance their agendas across the heart of Asia, Afghanistan remains a pivotal arena where strategic ambitions converge, compete, and sometimes collide (Caspian Policy Center, 2024).

ii. Influence of Global and Regional Powers

Major global and regional powers have long vied for influence in Afghanistan as a transit zone for energy, military logistics, and political leverage, with the United States and NATO spending two decades there to counter terrorism and limit rival powers' access (North Atlantic Treaty Organization [NATO], n.d.). Since 2021, new dynamics have emerged, with China and Russia increasingly seeking engagement with the Taliban (Khan & Sayed, 2025), leveraging economic and diplomatic channels to secure political and economic interests (OilPricc.com, 2024). China sees Afghanistan as vital to extending the BRI westward and buffering instability in Xinjiang, while Russia views it as part of its "Greater Eurasian Partnership," shaping both security and trade dynamics (Sangar, 2017).

Iran, India, Pakistan, and the Gulf states follow differing Afghanistan policies shaped by security, economic, and ideological interests (Shah, Ahmad, & Alam, 2023). Pakistan sees Afghanistan as central to its strategic depth, while India views access via Iran's Chabahar Port as a counterweight to Pakistani influence (SAIS Review of International Affairs, 2024). Iran, meanwhile, continues to assert its relevance through trade corridors and shared ethnic and religious ties in western Afghanistan (Gohel, 2010). Afghanistan can either enable or obstruct regional cooperation, serving as both a arena for power rivalry and, with inclusive governance and coordination, a platform for shared security and economic integration.

iii. Security Dynamics

After the withdrawal of American and allied forces followed by the Taliban's regain of power in August 2021, Afghanistan's security situation has become a key factor for regional stability, influencing both internal dynamics and foreign relations (Weinbaum & Ali, 2025). Afghanistan's rugged terrain and porous borders continue to provide strategic cover for non-state actors, positioning the country as a key arena for proxy conflicts and transnational terrorism. (Mir, 2023). Instability inside Afghanistan often spills into neighboring countries, increasing tensions along the borders, interrupting trade, and pushing people to flee their homes (Center for Preventive Action, 2025). For countries like Pakistan, Iran, and China, Afghanistan is both a buffer and a risk—demanding careful engagement to manage security concerns without getting too deeply involved (Salahi, 2022). Regional actors, therefore, are now adjusting their policies, trying to secure their borders while staying cautious of a possible return of extremist hideouts.

iv. Diplomatic Leverage

Control over Afghanistan has long been a lever in wider geopolitical rivalries, and today it remains central to power contests—from China–India competition and U.S.–Russia tensions to strategic struggles among Gulf states (Congressional Research Service, 2018). Control over Afghanistan has long been a lever in wider geopolitical rivalries, and today it remains central to power contests—from China–India competition and U.S.–Russia tensions to strategic struggles among Gulf states

(Garlick, 2025). These platforms not only promote cooperation but also serve as tools for projecting power—allowing member states to strengthen their regional standing under the banner of stability and development.

V. Great Power Competition

Afghanistan holds a pivotal position in the region particularly signified by the shifting global order. With the retreat of Western influence—marked clearly by the U.S. withdrawal in 2021—countries like China and Russia have stepped in to fill the vacuum, seeking to expand their presence through infrastructure projects, diplomatic outreach, and security partnerships (Kim, Aydıntaşbaş, Stent, & Varma, 2024). For Beijing, Afghanistan represents a crucial link in BRI; key to stabilizing its western frontier and connecting Central Asia with South Asia (Omarkhail & Zahid, 2025). At the same time, Moscow aims to reassert its traditional role in the region through defense cooperation and multilateral coordination (Qiang & Jia, 2025).

Meanwhile, global sanctions regimes and the rise of alternative supply chain blocs are narrowing Afghanistan's economic options (Runde, Pforzheimer, Bryja, & Smutny, 2024). Countries such as Iran, China, and Russia—each under Western pressure—are increasingly integrating Afghanistan into broader realignment strategies (Wishnick, 2021). In this new context, Afghanistan is not only a fragile state but also a strategic chess piece—one that could tilt the balance in Eurasia's emerging Great Power Competition.

REGIONAL CONNECTIVITY INITIATIVES

Afghanistan has historically served as a pivotal economic corridor for traders moving goods between the Middle East and India, from West to East and vice versa (Noorzi, 2021). Today, its potential is defined by concrete energy and transport initiatives that rewire trade across Central and South Asia, the Middle East, and beyond. Access to Afghanistan's transit corridors is a key instrument in geo-economic rivalry. Such connectivity routes now shaping regional competition over market access, energy flows, and supply chains—from China–India trade dynamics and U.S.–Russia sanctions-busting routes to the Gulf states.

i. TAPI Pipeline: Energy as Diplomacy

The TAPI pipeline, often referred to as the Trans-Afghanistan Pipeline, is a $10 billion regional energy initiative aimed at transporting 33 billion cubic meters of natural gas annually along a 1,814-kilometer route—from the Galkynysh gas fields in Turkmenistan, through Afghanistan and Pakistan, to India (Afzal, 2025). For Afghanistan, the project offers both economic opportunity and diplomatic leverage. It is expected to generate around $400 million per year in transit fees, and by its third decade of operation, could supply up to 1.5 billion cubic meters of natural gas for domestic use (Kaleji, 2025). TAPI also has the potential to stimulate job creation and infrastructure development in underserved regions, offering a pathway to internal stabilization (Mehrzai, 2019).

Portions of TAPI-related enabling works have advanced in Turkmenistan and Pakistan, but the cross-border pipeline itself remains delayed due to financing and security constraints (Salimova-Tekay, 2022). Despite its promise, the project has faced years of delays due to financing constraints and insecurity, underscoring regional stability as a precondition for lasting connectivity. (Indeo, 2025). For Turkmenistan, TAPI represents a strategic effort to diversify export routes and reduce its dependence on China and Russia (Lemon & Norov, 2025). For Pakistan and India—often adversaries in regional politics—the pipeline creates a rare avenue for constructive engagement based on mutual economic benefit (Patro, 2024). TAPI is expected to create thousands of jobs, improve energy access in gas-deficient areas, spur industrial growth, and support Turkmenistan's diversification while anchoring South–Central Asia's evolving energy network (Fazl-e-Haider, 2023).

ii. CASA-1000: Transmitting Power and Trust

The CASA-1000 project, a $1.2 billion regional energy initiative, envisions a 1,300-kilometer transmission line capable of delivering 1,300 megawatts of surplus hydroelectric power from Kyrgyzstan and Tajikistan to Afghanistan and Pakistan (Harvard Kennedy School, 2025). The system comprises 484 km of High-voltage Alternating Current (HVAC) transmission line from Datka in Kyrgyzstan to Sugd in Tajikistan to facilitate Kyrgyz exports; 114 km of additional HVAC lines between Regar and Sangtuda substations in Tajikistan; and 789 km of high-voltage direct current (HVDC) line linking Sangtuda to Nowshera in Pakistan—passing directly through Afghan territory (International Secretariat for CASA-1000, n.d.). By aligning seasonal power needs, the project strengthens regional energy cooperation, with Afghanistan's segment essential for grid stability, cheaper clean energy, and linking upstream and downstream states. (World Bank, 2024).

Without progress in Afghanistan, CASA-1000 risks stranding over $1 billion in assets and becomes a test of regional trust, with success hinging on Afghanistan's stability, institutional capacity, and backing from donors like the World Bank (including $2.2B during 2010—2021 and a further $300M approved in Feb 2024), whose role has been pivotal in funding and coordination (World Bank, 2024). Notably, the World Bank has reaffirmed its commitment to development in Afghanistan by approving $300 million in new funding as of February 2024—underscoring its pivotal role in sustaining momentum for critical infrastructure and energy projects like CASA-1000 (France24, 2024).

iii. Chabahar Port: A Maritime Gateway

Located in southeastern Iran, the India—Iran-developed Chabahar Port offers landlocked Afghanistan direct maritime access to the Arabian Sea, providing a more reliable, cost-effective gateway to regional and global markets (EFSAS, 2019; NDTV, 2024). Equally important, Chabahar provides a policy and logistics counterweight to reliance on Karachi and Gwadar, adding redundancy when politics disrupt overland flows (Maritime Gateway, 2025). Pakistan's control over these routes is a key vulnerability for Afghan exporters, as tensions or disputes can trigger unilateral trade disruptions (Jadoon, 2025). The India–Afghanistan–Iran transit agreement makes Chabahar a key asset, enabling India–Afghanistan–Central Asia trade without Pakistan and giving Kabul greater economic and geopolitical flexibility (Shukla, 2024).

The Chabahar–Zahedan railway strengthens the corridor, while Chabahar helps Afghanistan expand exports of dry fruits, saffron, and minerals, diversifying markets and reducing dependence on a few crossings. (Hayes, 2025). Geopolitically, Chabahar is a counterbalance to China's investment in Pakistan's Gwadar Port under the CPEC, while reinforcing India's strategic footprint in Afghanistan and Central Asia (Wani, 2024).

iv. Lapis Lazuli Corridor: Reawakening Ancient Trade Routes

Launched in 2017, the Lapis Lazuli Corridor links Afghanistan to Europe through Turkmenistan, Azerbaijan, Georgia, and Türkiye (Rahim, 2019). Named after Afghanistan's historic lapis lazuli trade, this 2,000+ km multimodal corridor of roads, rail, and ports revives parts of the Silk Road, linking Afghan producers to European markets via the Caspian and Black Seas. (TRACECA, n.d.). The Lapis Lazuli corridor carries not only economic but also civilizational significance, as it mirrors historic exchanges between eastern and western societies through the Silk Road (Tariq, 2023). Strategically, the corridor can reduce transit time by 30—40% and lower shipping costs versus traditional routes through Pakistan or Iran (Alekberli-Museyibova, 2023).

By linking to the Trans-Caspian International Transport Route and Middle Corridor, Lapis Lazuli expands Afghanistan's Eurasian links and supports customs harmonization, digital documentation, and streamlined borders (United Nations Office for South-South Cooperation [UNOSSC], 2022). The project embodies regional cooperation and shared ownership. For Afghanistan, Lapis Lazuli is both a trade artery and geopolitical asset, positioning it as a hub between Central/South Asia and Europe while reducing dependence on Pakistani ports (Wafa & Mazloum Yar, 2023). Alekberli-Museyibova (2023) argues that The Lapis Lazuli Corridor revives ancient trade routes, restoring Afghanistan's role as a bridge between civilizations and a hub of regional economic integration.

Comparative Analysis of Key Regional Connectivity Initiatives

Table 1 compares the scope, nature, and benefits of four major initiatives—TAPI, CASA-1000, Chabahar Port, and the Lapis Lazuli Corridor—to show how energy projects deliver economic dividends while trade corridors provide market access and geopolitical alternatives, together illustrating how Afghanistan's geography can drive growth and regional interdependence.

Table 1. Comparative Overview of Key Regional Connectivity Initiatives Involving Afghanistan

Project Name	Project Type	Countries Involved	Estimated Cost	Benefits to Afghanistan	Sources
TAPI Pipeline	Energy (Gas)	Turkmenistan, Afghanistan, Pakistan, India	$10 billion, later it was cut by 30% to US$7 billion	$400-$500mn transit fees,1.5 bcm gas use	(Global Energy Monitor, n.d.)
CASA-1000	Energy (Electricity)	Kyrgyzstan, Tajikistan, Afghanistan, Pakistan	$1.2 billion	Energy access, $45mn annual revenue	(International Secretariat for CASA-1000, n.d.) & (Center for Strategic & Regional Studies [CSRS], n.d.)
Chabahar Port	Maritime Trade	India, Iran, Afghanistan	$500 million+	Diversified sea access, avoids Karachi	(Reuters, 2024)
Lapis Lazuli Corridor	Multimodal Trade	Afghanistan, Turkmenistan, Azerbaijan, Georgia, Türkiye	$2 billion+	Export to Europe via 5 countries	(Kucera, 2017)

THE ROLE OF REGIONAL ORGANIZATIONS IN SHAPING AFGHANISTAN'S REGIONAL CONNECTIVITY

Regional organizations can advance Afghanistan's connectivity by providing cooperation platforms, facilitating trade agreements, and supporting infrastructure development. (Ministry of Foreign Affairs of Afghanistan, 2022). Because Afghanistan lies at a strategic Eurasian crossroads as a land bridge between Central and South Asia, it can significantly deepen trade integration and shape emerging regional dynamics (Salahi, 2022). Advancing Afghanistan's infrastructure is vital for regional connectivity and South–Central Asian trade complementarities, but its impact hinges on geopolitics, institutional capacity, and political will (Bertelsmann Stiftung, 2024). Compared to alternative routes, Afghanistan offers more direct and cost-efficient corridors for moving goods via roads, railways, pipelines, and energy transmission lines (Yar, Zahid, & Miakhil, 2023).

i. South Asian Association for Regional Cooperation (SAARC)

Since its establishment in 1985, SAARC has viewed expansion from regional economic connectivity viewpoint as a key part of its agenda (Foreign Policy Association, n.d.) —similar to the growth trajectories of the European Union and Association of Southeast Asian Nations (ASEAN) (Asian Development Bank, 2009). Afghanistan's accession to SAARC in 2007, in particular, was a pivotal step that opened new pathways for the country's regional integration (European External Action Service, 2021). SAARC provides Afghanistan a platform to boost regional connectivity in trade, energy, and infrastructure by enabling multilateral trade deals, cross-border energy projects, and aligned transport networks with South Asian economies (Ibrahimi, 2007).

SAARC's influence has waned amid India–Pakistan tensions, while SAFTA (2006) has taken on a more practical role in advancing regional trade liberalization (UN LDC Portal, n.d.). Although Afghanistan joined SAFTA in 2011, conflict has limited its use of this tariff-cutting, market-integration framework, which—alongside SAARC's connectivity initiatives—could still support its connectivity goals if regional political will, especially between India and Pakistan, is revived (Kumar, n.d.). Afghanistan's inclusion in SAARC signals regional acceptance and ties it to long-term plans for infrastructure, economic cooperation, and energy-sharing. If SAARC is strengthened, Afghanistan can use it to bolster trade corridors, deepen links with South Asian supply chains, and reinforce its regional integration role (Khushboo, 2025).

Afghanistan also offers unique advantages to SAARC that can complement South Asia's economic and security landscape (Ahmad & Wani, 2018). With vast minerals, a young workforce, and a gateway location, Afghanistan can bridge South and Central Asia; stable SAARC integration could enhance energy security, diversify trade, and make SAARC a stronger north–south link between Central Asia's resources and South Asia's markets (Usanas Foundation, 2024).

ii. Shanghai Cooperation Organization (SCO)

The SCO has become a key platform for Afghanistan's engagement with neighbors and major powers like China and Russia. As an observer, it can join security dialogues and regional planning—especially after the 2021 U.S. withdrawal—keeping its security and economic concerns on the agenda with nearby and interested states (Saboor, Ahmed, & Shabbir, 2021).

Alimov (2017) discusses the SCO evolving role in promoting regional security and its growing cooperation with the United Nations. Although the SCO is best known for countering terrorism, separatism, and extremism, it also promotes economic cooperation and infrastructure, aligning closely with Afghanistan's goal of becoming a Central–South Asian transit hub. Stronger ties with SCO members can open new trade corridors, attract transport and energy investment, and support regional integration, while providing Afghanistan a political forum to voice priorities, avoid isolation, and benefit from joint projects, easier borders, and increased regional investment. (Alimov, 2017). Afghanistan's location offers strategic value: Uzbekistan and Tajikistan could use its territory to reach Pakistani markets and Iranian ports, and with greater stability it could become a key link in regional supply chains, with the SCO helping to coordinate this transition (Borangaziev, 2024).

iii. Economic Cooperation Organization (ECO)

The ECO plays a practical role in enhancing Afghanistan's regional connectivity. The United Nations Economic and Social Commission for Asia and the Pacific [UNESCAP] (2014) Under the ECO framework, Afghanistan, Iran, Pakistan, and Central Asian states are developing key routes such as the Islamabad–Tehran–Istanbul (ITI) railway and the Kazakhstan–Turkmenistan–Afghanistan–Iran (KTAI) corridor, backed by the Ashgabat Agreement (2016) and the ECO Transit Transport Framework Agreement (TTFA) to streamline trade, harmonize customs, and support infrastructure development.

The KTAI corridor is a multimodal trade route designed to strengthen economic linkages between Central and South Asia. This aligns with long-standing goals for cross-regional integration (Asian Development Bank, 2005). Its operational efficiency improved after the Transports Internationaux Routiers (TIR) system was adopted in November 2019, allowing goods to move across borders under a unified customs document without repeated inspections. Officially launched in July 2020, the KTAI-TIR route connects Bandar Abbas in Iran to Central Asia via Afghanistan, offering a shorter, faster, and more cost-effective alternative to traditional trade paths.

The International Road Transport Union [IRU] (2020) and the ECO (2020), The KTAI corridor cuts transit times by up to five days and significantly lowers transport costs, giving landlocked Afghanistan better access to regional and maritime markets via Iranian ports and connecting it to a 128-million-strong, nearly $500 billion regional market—strengthening its role as a transit hub in an integrating economic bloc. The International Road Transport Union [IRU] (2020) highlights the KTAI corridor's importance for regional transit, with Afghanistan's participation helping it integrate into ECO-led networks, benefit from harmonized rules, attract investment (e.g., Khaf–Herat rail), and access technical and donor support.

CHALLENGES TO CONNECTIVITY

Despite its strategic location, Afghanistan's emergence as a connectivity hub is constrained by political instability, weak institutions, fiscal limits, and geopolitical tensions that deter investment and raise trade costs. Effective connectivity also depends on transparent customs, harmonized transit rules, credible dispute resolution, and alignment with international norms, yet heavy reliance on Pakistan's routes, limited diversification, and poor enforcement of agreements weaken its bargaining power and keep costs high (see Table 2).

Gaps in customs modernization, unpredictable tax regimes, and weak investor protections further deter regional trade. Integrating tools such as the WTO's Trade Facilitation Agreement (TFA), the UN's Legal Guide on Transit, and bilateral investment treaties can help build the institutional backbone for sustainable corridors. Analysis of the APTTA and slow implementation of SAFTA and the TFA highlight the need for tariff parity, harmonized customs codes, and transparent tariff schedules. Table 2 summarizes key challenges, associated indicators, and their impacts on Afghanistan's role as a regional trade and transit corridor.

Table 2. Challenges to Afghanistan's Regional Connectivity: Indicators and Impacts

Challenges	Indicators	Impact on Regional Connectivity	Sources
Political Instability & Security	**Fragile States Index 2024:** Score 103.9 (rank 7th most fragile of 179 countries) — reflecting chronic conflict and violence.	Insecurity deters investors, disrupts trade routes, and delays infrastructure development.	(The Fund for Peace, 2024)
Institutional Capacity & Governance Limitations	**Corruption Perceptions Index 2024:** Score 17/100 (rank 165/180, a decline from 24/100 in 2022) indicating severe governance deficits.	Weak institutions and corruption lead to project delays and erode international trust.	(Transparency International, 2024)
Financial Constraints and Sanctions	**Aid Dependency (pre-2021):** Foreign aid comprised ~40% of GDP and financed ~75% of public spending (2019)—support largely halted after 2021.	Loss of aid and sanctions limit infrastructure funding and isolate Afghanistan from global finance.	(Runde, Pforzheimer, Bryja, & Smutny, 2024)
Trust Deficit with Neighboring Countries	**Diverted Transit Trade:** ~59% of Pakistan—Afghanistan transit cargo shifted to Iranian routes by 2024 due to border frictions.	Border frictions and low confidence lead to trade diversion and underuse of Afghan transit corridors.	(intellinews, 2024)
Geopolitical Rivalries and Regional Tensions	**Low Regional Trade Integration:** Intra-South Asia trade is <5% of total trade (vs ~35% in East Asia), reflecting political barriers.	Regional tensions exclude Afghanistan from projects and reroute trade through rival-backed alternatives.	(Nawaz, 2020).
Missed Opportunities & Delayed Projects	**TAPI Gas Pipeline:** 33 billion m³/year, $8—10 billion project launched in 2018 — still not operational as of 2024 due to security/political delays.	Key projects remain unfinished due to conflict, resulting in lost economic and transit benefits.	(Patro, 2024)
Physical Infrastructure Gaps	**Limited Infrastructure:** Only ~35% of the population has access to grid electricity (2019 estimate); the country has only ~100—200 km of railway lines.	Poor roads, limited rail, and energy shortages reduce trade volume and efficiency.	(International Crisis Group, 2022)

OPPORTUNITIES FOR CONNECTIVITY

Despite ongoing instability, Afghanistan retains significant potential to become a regional transit hub (see Table 3). Projects like Chabahar Port and the Lapis Lazuli Corridor offer alternatives to Pakistan-based routes, widening access to Europe, South

Asia, and the Middle East, while regional bodies such as ECO and SCO provide cooperation platforms in trade, energy, and transport where SAARC has fallen short. Multilateral support is a critical driver. The Asian Development Bank's (ADB) US $5 billion Central Asia Regional Economic Cooperation (CAREC) initiative and over US $2.2 billion in World Bank development financing signal renewed interest in regional integration. Practical tools such as the TIR system on the KTAI route have already reduced transit times by about five days, while large projects like TAPI and CASA-1000 could generate more than US $400 million in annual benefits and attract employment and private investment if effectively governed.

Comparative evidence from LLDCs such as Uzbekistan, Rwanda, and Laos shows that corridor gains require not just infrastructure but policy reform, trade facilitation, and social safeguards. Digital customs, environmental impact assessments, and targeted Small and Medium-sized Enterprise (SME) support help localize benefits, while UNESCAP and ADB modelling suggests that full corridor integration could cut transit times by up to 40%, raise export revenues by 30–35%, and create over 100,000 jobs when governance, environmental, and inclusion measures are in place.

Afghanistan scores low on the World Bank's Logistics Performance Index, but investing in digital trade platforms, e-manifests, warehousing, and intermodal hubs could cut delays and spoilage while improving real-time tracking and customs co-ordination. Experiences from Rwanda, Nepal, and Uzbekistan show that geography need not be destiny: simplified transit agreements, predictable dispute resolution, and active regional diplomacy—guided by UN Office of the High Representative for LDCs/LLDCs/SIDS (UN-OHRLLS) and WTO's LLDC frameworks—can help Afghanistan convert its location into a durable connectivity asset.

Table 3. Key Opportunities to Enhance Afghanistan's Regional Connectivity

Opportunities	Indicators	Impact on Regional Connectivity	Sources
Diversifying Trade Routes	Chabahar Port: 8.5M tons/year capacity (India Ports Global, 2023); Lapis Lazuli Corridor: links 6 countries via road-rail	Offers alternatives to Pakistan routes; improves access to Europe, South Asia, and the Middle East.	(Ministry of External Affairs Government of India [MEA], 2024)
Institutional Reforms & Capacity Building	World Bank funded >$300M for customs, education & trade reform (2015—2020)	Building skilled human capital and trade governance enhances Afghanistan's project management capacity.	(World Bank, 2025)
Role of Regional Organizations (ECO, SCO)	ECO membership includes 10 countries with combined GDP >$1.9 trillion (Economic Cooperation Organization [ECO], 2024)	ECO and SCO provide neutral platforms for trade, energy, and transport cooperation amid SAARC gridlocks.	(Economic Cooperation Organization [ECO], 2024) & (Asian Development Bank, n.d.)
Multilateral Financial & Diplomatic Support	ADB pledged $5B+ to regional connectivity under CAREC; WB contributed $2.2B to Afghan development (2010—2021)	Financing and technical assistance from IFIs can reintegrate Afghanistan into regional trade systems.	(World Bank, 2024)
Confidence-Building & Regional Diplomacy	TIR system reduces transit time by 5 days via KTAI route (IRU, 2020); joint customs initiatives piloted with Iran	Cross-border coordination and simplification of customs procedures can ease political tensions and trade flow.	(International Road Transport Union [IRU], 2022)
Spillover Effects of Connectivity	TAPI projected to generate 12,000+ jobs in Afghanistan; CASA-1000 to boost energy revenues by $45M/year	Regional projects can create employment, increase exports, and support investment in logistics and services.	(Sadat, 2015)

Potential Economic Gains from Regional Integration

Table 4 shows how regional integration could transform Afghanistan's trade performance: Karachi-based transit currently takes 3–18 days and is politically fragile, whereas routes via Iran's Chabahar Port can cut delivery times to 5–7 days and make shipping up to 60% cheaper and 50% faster, sharply boosting export competitiveness. ADB estimates show that better corridors could raise Afghanistan's exports by at least 15%, with full integration scenarios exceeding 200%; even moderate upgrades point to 30–40% growth. Once fully operational, TAPI and CASA-1000 could generate about $400–500 million and $60 million annually, while digital trade facilitation could boost SME export participation by 20%. Together, these figures underscore why connectivity should be a core pillar of Afghanistan's economic strategy.

Table 4. Potential Economic Gains from Regional Integration Scenarios for Afghanistan

Metrics	Current Baseline	Post-Integration Estimate	Source
Average transit time (to India via Pakistan)	Karachi—Kandahar: 913 km (3—4 days); Karachi—Mazar-e-Sharif: 2,500 km (16—18 days); Karachi—Jalalabad: 1,640 km (7—8 days); Karachi—Kabul: 1,843 km (8—10 days)	5—7 days via Chabahar (5 by sea, 4 by road)	(Rahim, 2017) & (International Road Transport Union [IRU], 2020)
Afghanistan's export volume (2022)	$2.66 billion US dollars, a 30.29% increase from 2021	Up to 15% increase (conservative projection based on ADB modeling)*; 202% increase (aggressive scenario with full corridor build-out and trade facilitation); 30—40% increase (modeled estimate, see note)	(Aziz,2005) & (Cidob Foundation, 2024)
Potential TAPI annual revenue	$400—500 million	Unlocked after full implementation	(Ministry of Mines and Petroleum [MoMP], 2025)
CASA-1000 energy revenue	$45 million/year	Up to $60 million with extended grid use	(Center for Strategic & Regional Studies [CSRS], n.d.)
SME export participation (current)	Not explicitly quantified; SMEs constitute ~80 % of Afghan businesses, 50 % of GDP, and employ over one-third of the labor force.	+20% increase via e-commerce and digital trade support (modeled scenario)	(Abdullah, 2021)
Reduction in shipping costs (Chabahar vs Karachi route)	—	60% lower shipping costs and 50% shorter shipment time	Hellenic Shipping News (2022)

ROLE OF INTERNATIONAL ORGANIZATIONS IN FACILITATING REGIONAL COOPERATION

Multilateral institutions such as the United Nations (UN), World Bank, and WTO underpin regional cooperation in fragile, landlocked states like Afghanistan (see Table 5): the UN enables dialogue on security and resource governance, the World Bank finances corridors like CASA-1000 (US $1.17 billion) and TAPI while strengthening institutions, and the WTO reduces tariffs, supports trade agreements, and offers dispute settlement, complemented by ECO, SCO, and KTAI's TIR-based system that cut transit times and coordinate cross-border projects. At the same time, Afghan entrepreneurs, SMEs, diaspora networks, and women-led businesses are crucial for turning connectivity into inclusive growth, so regional initiatives should embed gender-sensitive measures—such as support for women-led SMEs via digital trade, e-commerce, and targeted capacity-building—to ensure that gains from trade reach local communities.

Table 5. Key Multilateral and Regional Actors Facilitating Trade, Connectivity, and Development in Afghanistan

Organizations	Function	Impact	Sources
United Nations (UN)	• Peace and security through diplomatic frameworks and missions • Development coordination via UNDP & UNESCAP supporting trade facilitation and environmental governance	UN platforms support water-sharing and cross-border energy dialogue in Central and South Asia	(United Nations Economic and Social Commission for Asia and the Pacific [UNESCAP], n.d.)
World Bank	• Infrastructure financing: CASA-1000 (US $1.17B), TAPI (US $450-$500M Afghan transit revenue) • Technical assistance for harmonizing trade, energy, and transport policies	Approach 3.0 enables basic services in Afghanistan via third parties while funding trade infrastructure	(World Bank, 2018) & (International Secretariat for CASA-1000, n.d.)
World Trade Organization (WTO)	• Trade facilitation through transit and tariff reduction • Capacity building and dispute resolution mechanisms for trade compliance	WTO guided Afghanistan's 2016 accession, aligning national laws with global trade norms	(World Trade Organization [WTO], 2015)
Regional Partnerships	• Joint customs and TIR systems (e.g., KTAI Corridor) reducing transit time by up to 5 days • Regional coordination via ECO and SCO on energy, transport, and counterterrorism	Bilateral projects have generated hundreds of millions in trade revenue; routes shortened by 30—40%	(Arel USAM & Bingöl, 2022)

IMPLICATIONS FOR POLICY AND MANAGERIAL PRACTICE

For Afghan agencies: create a National Connectivity Task Force to coordinate corridor security, customs digitalization, SEZ/dry-port governance, and PPP standards, with public KPI dashboards. For regional partners: embed TIR and paperless-trade pilots in binding MOUs with tariff-parity clauses and joint border incident-response playbooks. For donors/IFIs: use ring-fenced, results-based financing tied to milestones (e.g., CASA-1000 energization, TAPI ROW clearances, e-customs interoperability, SME export onboarding). For private logistics/SMEs: co-invest in dry ports and cold-chain nodes near Herat/Balkh under one-stop clearance and predictable fee schedules.

Directions for Future Research

Future research should estimate corridor spillovers on local labor markets and women-led SMEs under different security scenarios; micro-measure shipment time/

cost for Karachi vs. Chabahar/Lapis Lazuli and alternative routings during future Pakistan–Afghanistan border closures; stress-test governance conditions that keep CASA-1000/TAPI viable through political shocks; and model environmental and social safeguards for critical-minerals spurs linked to export corridors.

CONCLUSION AND VISION FOR AFGHANISTAN'S INTEGRATION

Afghanistan stands at a critical inflection point: its position at the junction of South and Central Asia gives it a unique chance to convert geography into growth through well-governed trade and energy corridors. Realizing this vision, however, depends on the country's ability to stabilize, implement reforms, and forge durable partnerships. Afghanistan's integration into regional trade networks is not only its own priority but a regional necessity: in an era of geopolitical fragmentation and climate risk, corridors like TAPI, CASA-1000, Chabahar, and Lapis Lazuli can stabilize the region by building interdependence and diversifying access to key markets. International organizations such as the World Bank, WTO, UNESCAP, ECO, and SCO can provide finance, technical support, and policy frameworks, but durable integration ultimately depends on Afghan-led governance—strong oversight, modern customs, and coherent institutions. In this sense, connectivity is inseparable from governance reform: only a capable Afghan state can convert infrastructure into lasting regional bridge-building.

Policy Recommendations

Afghanistan's potential as a key node in Eurasian trade and energy networks is real but depends on coordinated policy action and robust bilateral/multilateral agreements, with corridors aligned to SDG 8 (Decent Work and Economic Growth), SDG-9 (Industry, Innovation, and Infrastructure), and SDG 17 (Partnerships for the Goals) using SDG-based metrics. External support helps, but progress ultimately hinges on Afghan institutions and partners improving governance, institutional coherence, and locally grounded implementation.

1. *Prioritize security and political stability.* Lasting connectivity depends on inclusive governance, conflict resolution, and disarmament, supported by neutral, non-interventionist regional engagement.
2. *Strengthening institutions and governance.* With support from the World Bank, ADB, and others, Afghanistan should modernize customs, digitize trade, and build capacity in trade, transport, and infrastructure ministries.

3. *Expand and safeguard key corridors.* Projects like TAPI, CASA-1000, Lapis Lazuli, and Chabahar need ring-fenced multilateral financing and an intergovernmental monitoring body to withstand political shocks and ensure transparency.
4. *Use regional platforms for trust-building.* ECO and SCO should coordinate infrastructure and provide structured dialogue on border security, energy sharing, and trade harmonization.
5. *Promote facilitation, local benefits, and resource governance.* Common transit standards, digital and TIR-based trade, local jobs, SME participation, and transparent, environmentally sound mineral contracts are essential to ensure inclusive, sustainable gains.

Expected Contributions

This chapter offers a grounded analysis of Afghanistan's potential as a regional trade and connectivity hub (drawing on cases like TAPI, CASA-1000, and Lapis Lazuli), identifies strategies for trust-building, infrastructure, and trade facilitation in fragile contexts, and provides policymakers, IFIs, and multilaterals with practical recommendations to advance connectivity and integrate Afghanistan into regional and global trade.

REFERENCES

Afzal, S. (2025). Unlocking economic potential: The TAPI pipeline's role in regional integration. *The Diplomatic Herald Journal.* https://tdhj.org/blog/post/tapi-pipeline-role-integration/

Ahmad, S. S., & Wani, N. U. H. (2018). Trade potential of Afghanistan against SAARC: An application of Gravity Model Approach. *Kardan Journal of Economics and Management Sciences, 1*(4), 1–19. DOI: 10.31841/KJEMS.2021.66

Ahmadov, N. (2021). Azerbaijan, Afghanistan, and Turkmenistan sign trilateral roadmap for cooperation on Eurasian connectivity. *Eurasia Daily Monitor, 18*(23). The Jamestown Foundation. https://jamestown.org/program/azerbaijan-afghanistan-and-turkmenistan-sign-trilateral-roadmap-for-cooperation-on-eurasian-connectivity/

Aiyar, S., Chen, J., Ebeke, C. H., Garcia-Saltos, R., Gudmundsson, T., Ilyina, A., . . . Trevino, J. P. (2023). Geo-economic fragmentation and the future of multilateralism. *International Monetary Fund.* https://www.imf.org/en/Publications/WP/Issues/2023/01/13/Geo-Economic-Fragmentation-and-the-Future-of-Multilateralism-528208

Alekberli-Museyibova, N. (2023). Revitalization of the Lapis Lazuli Corridor: From Afghanistan to Europe. *Eurasia Daily Monitor, 20*(110). The Jamestown Foundation. https://jamestown.org/program/revitalization-of-the-lapis-lazuli-corridor-from-afghanistan-to-europe/

Alimov, R. (2017). The role of the Shanghai Cooperation Organization in counteracting threats to peace and security. *UN Chronicle.* https://www.un.org/en/chronicle/article/role-shanghai-cooperation-organization-counteracting-threats-peace-and-security

Arvis, J.-F., Raballand, G., & Marteau, J.-F. (2010) The cost of being landlocked. The World Bank. Pages, Washington DC. DOI: 10.1596/978-0-8213-8408-4

Aryal, S. K. (2022). *State of regional integration in South Asia: Does post-Sri Lanka crisis have positive impact?* The Geopolitics. https://thegeopolitics.com/state-of-regional-integration-in-south-asia-does-post-sri-lanka-crisis-have-positive-impact/

Asian Development Bank. (2005). *Opening transport corridors between Central Asia and South Asia* (Regional Business Roundtable, Bishkek, Kyrgyz Republic, 3—4 November 2005). Central Asia Regional Economic Cooperation (CAREC) Program. https://www.carecprogram.org/uploads/Paper-Opening-Transport-Corridors-Central-and-South-Asia.pdf

Asian Development Bank. (2009). *Study on intraregional trade and investment in South Asia.* https://www.adb.org/sites/default/files/publication/28658/intraregional-trade-investment.pdf

Aziz, M. (2016). Afghanistan: The geopolitics of regional economic integration. The emergence of China as the new facilitator. CIDOB. https://www.cidob.org/sites/default/files/2024-11/313-342_afghanistan_the_geopolitics_of_regional_economic_integration_the_emergence_of_china_as_the_new_facilitator.pdf

Bertelsmann Stiftung. (2024). *BTI 2024 Country Report — Afghanistan.* https://bti-project.org/en/reports/country-report/AFG

Borangaziev, A. (2024). *Is Afghanistan ready for dialogue with Central Asia on water issues?* Times of Central Asia. https://timesca.com/is-afghanistan-ready-for-dialogue-with-central-asia-on-water-issues/

Brkić, B. (2025). Central Asian countries push for regional development at Termez Dialogue. *Euronews.* https://www.euronews.com/2025/05/21/central-asian-countries-push-for-regional-development-at-termez-dialogue

Carll, E. (2021). An Afghanistan at peace could connect South and Central Asia. *Atlantic Council — New Atlanticist.* https://www.atlanticcouncil.org/blogs/new-atlanticist/an-afghanistan-at-peace-could-connect-south-and-central-asia/

Carnegie Endowment for International Peace. (2025). *BRICS expansion and the future of world order: Perspectives from member states, partners, and aspirants.* https://carnegieendowment.org/research/2025/03/brics-expansion-and-the-future-of-world-order-perspectives-from-member-states-partners-and-aspirants

Caspian Policy Center. (2023). China, Russia, and great power politics in Afghanistan and Central Asia. https://www.caspianpolicy.org/research/guest-contributions/china-russia-and-great-power-politics-in-afghanistan-and-central-asia

Caspian Policy Center. (2024). China, Russia, and great power politics in Afghanistan and Central Asia. https://www.caspianpolicy.org/research/central-asia/china-russia-and-great-power-politics-in-afghanistan-and-central-asia

Center for Preventive Action. (2025). Instability in Afghanistan. Council on Foreign Relations. https://www.cfr.org/global-conflict-tracker/conflict/war-afghanistan

Center for Strategic and International Studies [CSIS]. (2024). How sanctions have reshaped Russia's future. https://www.csis.org/analysis/how-sanctions-have-reshaped-russias-future

Collier, S. J. (2009). Topologies of power: Foucault's analysis of political government beyond "governmentality.". *Theory, Culture & Society*, *26*(6), 78–108. DOI: 10.1177/0263276409347694

Congressional Research Service. (2018). *China-India great power competition in the Indian Ocean region: Issues for Congress* (CRS Report R45194). https://www.crs.gov/

Council of the European Union. (2024). Sanctions against Russia explained. https://www.consilium.europa.eu/en/policies/sanctions-against-russia-explained

Cross-border Paperless Trade in Asia and the Pacific [UNESCAP]. (2014). *ECO: Rail-based intermodal transport corridors.* https://www.unescap.org/sites/default/files/ECO.pdf

Economic Cooperation Organization [ECO]. (2020). ECO—KTAI Road Corridor Test Run Kicks Off from Iran. https://eco.int/eco-ktai-road-corridor-test-run-kicks-off-from-iran

European External Action Service. (2021). South Asian Association for Regional Cooperation (SAARC). https://www.eeas.europa.eu/eeas/south-asian-association-regional-cooperation-saarc_en

European Union Institute for Security Studies [EUISS]. (2023). *Annual report 2023* (EUISS-DIR-CA(2024)1). https://www.iss.europa.eu/sites/default/files/Annual_report_2023.pdf

Eurostat. (2024). Russia-EU — international trade of main product groups. European Commission. https://ec.europa.eu/eurostat/statistics-explained/index.php?title=Russia-EU_-_international_trade_of_main_product_groups&oldid=558089

Farasoo, A. (2016). Afghanistan's quest for regional cooperation. *Fair Observer — Central & South Asia.* https://www.fairobserver.com/region/central_south_asia/afghanistan-pakistan-south-asia-economy-terrorism-news-67132/

Farasoo [EFSAS]. (2019). *The Chabahar Port: A potential game changer for Afghanistan.* https://www.efsas.org/commentaries/the-chabahar-port-a-potential-game-changer-for-afghanistan/

Faye, M. L., Mcarthur, J., Sachs, J. D., & Snow, T. (2004). The Challenges Facing Landlocked Developing Countries. *Journal of Human Development*, *5*(1), 31–68. DOI: 10.1080/14649880310001660201

Fazl-e-Haider, S. (2023). *Revival of TAPI pipeline project brings serious geopolitical implications for Russia. Eurasia Daily Monitor, 20(91).* The Jamestown Foundation.

France24. (2024). World Bank approves $300 mn in new funding for Afghanistan. https://www.france24.com/en/live-news/20240215-world-bank-approves-300-mn-in-new-funding-for-afghanistan

Garlick, J. (2025). Beyond Central Asia: The ever-expanding influence of the Shanghai Cooperation Organization. *European Hub for Security Studies.* https://eh4s.eu/publication/beyond-central-asia-the-ever-expanding-influence-of-the-shanghai-cooperation-organization

Gohel, S. M. (2010). Iran's ambiguous role in Afghanistan. *CTC Sentinel, 3*(3). https://ctc.westpoint.edu/irans-ambiguous-role-in-afghanistan/

Gormley, D. (2009). Getting more from international partnerships. Naval Postgraduate School Center for Contemporary Conflict. https://www.academia.edu/12734832/Getting_More_from_International_Partnerships

Harvard Kennedy School. (2025). *Development diplomacy in action: The CASA-1000 electricity grid* (HKS Case Program). https://case.hks.harvard.edu/development-diplomacy-in-action-the-casa-1000-electricity-grid/

Hayes, C. (2025). India-Afghanistan thaw: A geopolitical pivot to regional trade dominance. *A Invest.* https://www.ainvest.com/news/india-afghanistan-thaw-geopolitical-pivot-regional-trade-dominance-2505/

Hunter, M., & Ginn, P. (2025). Treasure hunt: Why is Afghanistan part of the great extractives race? *Global Initiative Against Transnational Organized Crime.* https://globalinitiative.net/analysis/why-is-afghanistan-part-of-the-great-extractives-race/

Hussain, F., & Nawaz, S. (2021). Geostrategic imperatives for Pakistan of Gwadar Port. *Asian Journal of Peacebuilding*, *9*(2), 427–441. DOI: 10.18588/202111.00a205

Ibrahimi, S. Y. (2007). Afghans divided on regional integration. *Institute for War & Peace Reporting.* https://iwpr.net/global-voices/afghans-divided-regional-integrationiwpr.net

Ijirshar, V. U. (2022). Trade facilitation and economic growth among middle-income countries. *arXiv.* https://arxiv.org/pdf/2204.11088

Indeo, F. (2025). TAPI gas pipeline: A paradigm of the Central Asian pragmatic approach toward Taliban. *Trends Research and Advisory.* https://trendsresearch.org/insight/tapi-gas-pipeline-a-paradigm-of-the-central-asian-pragmatic-approach-toward-taliban/

Institute for the Study of Ancient Cultures, University of Chicago. (n.d.). Afghanistan. https://isac.uchicago.edu/explore-oi/afghanistan

Intellinews. (2024). Pakistan-Afghanistan transit trade drops 59% in FY2023/24. https://www.intellinews.com/pakistan-afghanistan-transit-trade-drops-59-in-fy2023-24-340687/

International Crisis Group. (2022). Afghanistan's security challenges under the Taliban. https://www.crisisgroup.org/asia/south-asia/afghanistan/afghanistans-security-challenges-under-taliban

International Crisis Group. (2022). *The Taliban's neighborhood: Regional diplomacy in Afghanistan* (Report No. 337). https://www.crisisgroup.org/asia/south-asia/afghanistan/337-talibans-neighbourhood-regional-diplomacy-afghanistan

International Road Transport Union [IRU]. (2020). *Final report: Project for development of Kyrgyz-Tajikistan-Afghanistan-Iran (KTAI) road transport corridor.* https://www.iru.org/system/files/Final%20report%20-%20Project%20for%20development%20of%20Kyrgyz-Tajikistan-%20Afghanistan-Iran%20%28KTAI%29%20road%20transport%20corridor.pdf

International Road Transport Union [IRU]. (2020). *TIR helps open India—Iran—Afghanistan intermodal trade*. IRU. https://www.iru.org/news-resources/newsroom/tir-helps-open-india-iran-afghanistan-intermodal-trade

International Secretariat for CASA-1000. (n.d.). *About CASA-1000*. Retrieved June 12, 2025, from https://www.casa-1000.org/about-casa-1000/

Jadoon, A. (2025). Decoding Pakistan's 2024 airstrikes in Afghanistan. *War on the Rocks.* https://warontherocks.com/2025/03/decoding-pakistans-2024-airstrikes-in-afghanistan/

Javaid, F. (2024). Challenges and opportunities for regional connectivity: Afghanistan's role between Pakistan and the Central Asian region. In Pietrzak, P. (Ed.), *Analyzing global responses to contemporary regional conflicts* (pp. 275–297). IGI Global., DOI: 10.4018/979-8-3693-2837-8.ch013

Kaleji, V. (2025). *The first phase of the TAPI gas pipeline: From Serhetabat, Turkmenistan to Herat*. Central Asia-Caucasus Analyst.

Khan, H. (2024). Afghanistan's lithium: Sovereignty vs. foreign exploitation. *The Diplomat.* https://thediplomat.com/2024/08/afghanistans-lithium-sovereignty-vs-foreign-exploitation/

Khan, H. (2024). Charting Afghanistan's economic future: Recommendations for reform. *Stimson Center.* https://www.stimson.org/2024/charting-afghanistans-economic-future-recommendations-for-reform/

Khan, H., & Sayed, N. (2025). *How Afghanistan can benefit from China's investments.* The Diplomat. https://thediplomat.com/2025/02/how-afghanistan-can-benefit-from-chinas-investments/

Khushboo, D. (2025). The challenges of SAARC as a regional organization: A special reference to the Indo-Pak conflict. *International Journal for Research Trends and Innovation, 10*(4). https://www.ijrti.org

Kim, P. M., Aydıntaşbaş, A., Stent, A., & Varma, T. (2024). The China-Russia relationship and threats to vital US interests. *Brookings Institution.* https://www.brookings.edu/articles/the-china-russia-relationship-and-threats-to-vital-us-interests/

Kumar, R. (n.d.). SAARC: Changing realities, opportunities, and challenges. Paper presented at the DIE Conference on Regional Economic Integration Beyond Europe, Bonn. https://www.idos-research.de/fileadmin/_migrated/content_uploads/SAARC_changingrealities.pdf

Kurin, R. (2002). The Silk Road: Connecting people and cultures. In *The Silk Road: Connecting peoples and cultures* [Program Book]. Smithsonian Center for Folklife & Cultural Heritage. https://festival.si.edu/2002/the-silk-road/the-silk-road-connecting-peoples-and-cultures/smithsonian

Lemon, E., & Norov, R. (2025). *How China is adapting to Tajikistan's demand for security cooperation.* Carnegie Endowment for International Peace. https://carnegieendowment.org/posts/2025/03/how-china-is-adapting-to-tajikistans-demand-for-security-cooperation?lang=en

Lü, Q. Q., Henderson, J., Wang, Y., & Wang, B. (2021). Natron glass beads reveal the proto-Silk Road between the Mediterranean and China in the 1st millennium BCE. *Scientific Reports, 11*(1), 3537. DOI: 10.1038/s41598-021-82245-w PMID: 33574376

Luck, P. (2025). How sanctions have reshaped Russia's future. *Center for Strategic and International Studies.* https://www.csis.org/analysis/how-sanctions-have-reshaped-russias-future

Maritime Gateway. (2025). Taliban looks to develop Chabahar Port to cut Pakistani port dependency. https://www.maritimegateway.com/taliban-looks-to-develop-chabahar-port-to-cut-pakistani-port-dependency/

Masomy, M. J. (2021). Afghanistan as a land bridge between Central Asia and South Asia. *Electronic Journal of Social and Strategic Studies, 2*(1), 77–91. DOI: 10.47362/EJSSS.2021.2113

Mehrzai, M. E. (2019). Economic benefits and importance of TAPI Project. *IJRDO —. Journal of Historical Geography*, *1*(1). https://ijrdo.org/index.php/history/article/view/3095

Ministry of External Affairs. Government of India [MEA]. (2024). Rajya Sabha: Question No. 44 — Chabahar Port Project. https://www.mea.gov.in/rajya-sabha.htm?dtl/38631/QUESTION+NO+44+CHABAHAR+PORT+PROJECT

Ministry of Foreign Affairs of Afghanistan. (2022). *RECCA Brief Policy Series — Issue 1: How can regional economic cooperation be accelerated within the RECCA region?* https://recca.mfa.gov.af/wp-content/uploads/2022/11/RECCA-BPS-ISSUE-1.pdf

Ministry of Mines and Petroleum [MoMP]. (2025). TAPI Project. Government of the Islamic Emirate of Afghanistan. Retrieved August 10, 2025, from https://momp.gov.af/tapi-project

Mir, A. (2023). No good choices: The counterterrorism dilemmas in Afghanistan and Pakistan. *CTC Sentinel, 16*(10). https://ctc.westpoint.edu/commentary-no-good-choices-the-counterterrorism-dilemmas-in-afghanistan-and-pakistan/

National Geographic Education. (n.d.). The Silk Road. https://education.nationalgeographic.org/resource/silk-road/

National Intelligence Council. (2002). *Afghanistan and regional geopolitical dynamics after 11 September: Conference proceedings, 18—19 April 2002* (CR 2002-02). Office of the Director of Central Intelligence. https://www.dni.gov/files/documents/afghanistan_2002.pdf

Nawaz, S. (2020). Institutions, Regional Integration and Bilateral Trade in South Asia: PPML-based evidence. *Pakistan Development Review*, *59*(2), 221–241. https://www.jstor.org/stable/27184732. DOI: 10.30541/v59i2pp.221-242

NDTV. (2024). Chabahar Port would benefit landlocked Afghanistan, Central Asia: India. https://www.ndtv.com/india-news/chabahar-port-would-benefit-landlocked-afghanistan-central-asia-india-5688770

Noorzi, M. Y. (2021). Afghanistan: Regional connectivity hub. *Eastern Studies*, *15*, 287–300. DOI: 10.4467/20827695WSC.21.014.14721

North Atlantic Treaty Organization. (n.d.). NATO and Afghanistan. https://www.nato.int/cps/en/natohq/topics_8189.htm

OilPrice.com. (2024). Why Russia and China are vying for influence in Afghanistan. https://oilprice.com/Geopolitics/International/Why-Russia-and-China-are-Vying-For-Influence-in-Afghanistan.html

Omarkhail, I., & Zahid, A. (2025). Afghanistan's perspectives on the Belt and Road Initiative: Strengths, weaknesses, opportunities, and threats. *Asian Journal of Political Science, 33*(3), 481–505. Advance online publication. DOI: 10.1080/02185377.2025.2473887

Parliament, U. K. (2024). Russia: Overseas Trade. Written question and answer — UIN 15290. https://questions-statements.parliament.uk/written-questions/detail/2024-02-22/15290

Patro, B. (2024). India should take a proactive interest in the TAPI pipeline. *Stimson Center.* https://www.stimson.org/2024/india-should-take-a-proactive-interest-in-the-tapi-pipeline/

Pleis, L. J., Lliteras, R., Wood, D. A., Bain, M. D., & Hendrickson, S. J. (2015). The Afghanistan National Railway: A plan of opportunity. *Joint Force Quarterly.* https://ndupress.ndu.edu/Media/News/News-Article-View/Article/577556/the-afghanistan-national-railway-a-plan-of-opportunity/

Qiang, X., & Jia, L. (2025). Russia's new Eurasian security architecture: Implications for the Eurasian region. *Horizons, 29.* https://www.cirsd.org/en/horizons/horizons-winter-2025-issue-no-29/russias-new-eurasian-security-architecture

Rahim, S. A. (2018). Afghanistan's dependence on Pakistan: Transit trade and the cost of being landlocked. *Kardan Journal of Economics & Management Sciences, 1*(4), 68—79. https://kardan.edu.af/data/public/files/KJEMS-4th-3.pdf

Rahim, S. A. (2019). Lapis Lazuli Corridor: Meeting the economic aspirations of Afghanistan and member countries. *Kardan Journal of Economics and Management Sciences, 2*(3), 67-78. https://kardan.edu.af/Research/CurrentIssue.aspx?j=KJEMS

Reuters. (2024). India signs 10-year deal with Iran to operate Chabahar port. https://www.reuters.com/world/india/india-sign-10-year-pact-with-iran-chabahar-port-management-et-reports-2024-05-13/

Rlung, A. S. (2024). Effect of Afghanistan—Pakistan Transit Trade Agreement on trade cost parity. *MPRA Paper.* https://mpra.ub.uni-muenchen.de/123183/

Roos, D. (2021). *The Silk Road: 8 goods traded along the ancient network.* History. A&E Television Networks. (Last updated May 28, 2025.) https://www.history.com/articles/silk-road-trade-goods

Runde, D. F., Pforzheimer, A., Bryja, T., & Smutny, C. (2024). *The future of assistance to Afghanistan: A dilemma.* Center for Strategic and International Studies. https://www.csis.org/analysis/future-assistance-afghanistan-dilemma

Saboor, A., Ahmed, S., & Shabbir, T. (2021). Post-withdrawal situation of US troops from Afghanistan: Role of Shanghai Cooperation Organization (SCO). *Global International Relations Review*, *4*(4), 43–54. Advance online publication. DOI: 10.31703/girr.2021(IV-IV).05

Sadat, S. M. (2015). *TAPI and CASA-1000: Win-win trade between Central Asia and South Asia* (Policy Brief No. 25). OSCE Academy in Bishkek. https://osce-academy.net/upload/file/Policy_Brief_25.pdf

Safi, M., & Alizada, B. (2018). *Integrating Afghanistan into the Belt and Road Initiative: Review, analysis, and prospects.* Friedrich Ebert Stiftung. https://library.fes.de/pdf-files/bueros/kabul/15587.pdf

SAIS Review of International Affairs. (2024). From Balochistan to beyond: How Iran emerged as a senior partner to Pakistan. https://saisreview.sais.jhu.edu/from-balochistan-to-beyond-how-iran-emerged-as-a-senior-partner-to-pakistan/

Salahi, Z. (2022). Afghanistan: A Junction of Asia's Connectivity. *The National Bureau of Asian Research.* https://www.nbr.org/publication/afghanistan-a-junction-of-asias-connectivity/

Salimova-Tekay, J. (2022). Infrastructure financing in Kyrgyzstan (PER Series Working Paper). Macroeconomic Policy & Financing for Development Division.

Sanchez Cacicedo, A. (2022). Unlocking Afghanistan's connectivity potential: Opportunities for the EU. *EUISS Brief No. 15.* https://www.iss.europa.eu/publications/briefs/unlocking-afghanistans-connectivity-potential-opportunities-eu

Sangar, K. (2017). *Russia and China in the age of grand Eurasian projects: Prospects for integration between the Silk Road Economic Belt and the Eurasian Economic Union.* Cambridge Journal of Eurasian Studies., DOI: 10.22261/YDG5KF

Savic, B. (2025). Sanctions and the geopolitics of trade. *Geopolitical Intelligence Services.* https://www.gisreportsonline.com/r/sanctions-trade-routes

Sedra, M. (2014). An uncertain future for Afghanistan's security sector. *Stability*, *3*(1), 35. Advance online publication. DOI: 10.5334/sta.ei

Shah, Z., Ahmad, B., & Alam, A. (2023). Understanding Convergence and Divergence in Pak-Iran Relations. *Journal of Development and Social Sciences*, *4*(3), 1265–1276. DOI: 10.47205/jdss.2023(4-III)117

Shukla, A. (2024). The Chabahar Port and India-Iran Agreement. *International Council for Policy Studies.* https://www.icpsnet.org/issuebrief/The-Chabahar-Port-and-India-Iran-Agreement

Sidaway, J. D., Rowedder, S. C., Woon, C. Y., Lin, S., & Pholsena, V. (2020). *Introduction: Research agendas raised by the Belt and Road Initiative.* Environment and Planning C. *Politics and Space*, *38*(5), 795–802. DOI: 10.1177/2399654420911410

Skylence. (n.d.). The Silk Road of China. https://www.skylence.com/blogs/journal/the-silk-road-of-china

Small, A. (2015). *The China—Pakistan Axis: Asia's New Geopolitics.* London: Hurst; New York: Oxford University Press.

Summers, T. (2016). China's 'new silk roads': Sub-national regions and networks of global political economy. *Third World Quarterly*, *37*(9), 1628–1643. DOI: 10.1080/01436597.2016.1153415

Tariq, M. T. (2023). The Importance of Lapis Lazuli Corridor for Afghanistan. *International Journal of Research in Academic Humanities*, *3*(5), 276–280. Advance online publication. DOI: 10.55544/ijrah.3.5.28

The Fund for Peace. (2024). *Fragile States Index 2024: Global data.* https://fragilestatesindex.org/global-data/

Tian, G., Zaki, Z., & Haihua, Y. (2024). Strategic Alliance: The Contribution of the "Belt and Road Initiative "to Easing Trade Restrictions for Afghanistan. *Research in Business & Social Science*, *13*(7), 326–342. DOI: 10.20525/ijrbs.v13i7.3658

TRACECA. (n.d.). *Lapis Lazuli Corridor.* Retrieved November 10, 2025, from https://traceca.ge/en/route/silk-road/lapislazulicorridor

Transparency International. (2024). *Corruption Perceptions Index 2024: Afghanistan.* https://www.transparency.org/en/cpi/2024/index/afg

UNCTAD. (2019). *Islamic Republic of Afghanistan: Rapid eTrade readiness assessment* (UNCTAD/DTL/STICT/2019/5). *United Nations Conference on Trade and Development.*

United Nations Economic and Social Commission for Asia and the Pacific [UN-ESCAP]. (n.d.). *Framework Agreement on Facilitation of Cross-border Paperless Trade in Asia and the Pacific (CPTA).* https://www.unescap.org/projects/cpta

United Nations Office for South-South Cooperation [UNOSSC]. (2022). *Digital trade integration: Role of South-South and triangular cooperation* (South-South Ideas Paper). https://southsouth-galaxy.org/wp-content/uploads/2023/08/South-South-Ideas-Digital-Trade-Integration-Role-of-South-South-and-Triangular-Cooperation.pdf

United Nations Office on Drugs and Crime [UNODC]. (2011). *The global Afghan opium trade: A threat assessment.* https://www.unodc.org/documents/data-and-analysis/Studies/Global_Afghan_Opium_Trade_2011-web.pdf

Usanas Foundation. (2024). Why South Asia is needed in Afghanistan. https://usanasfoundation.com/why-south-asia-is-needed-in%20Afghanistan

Wafa, N., & Mazloum Yar, F. G. (2023). Geopolitical influence of Afghanistan's neighbors on the country's domestic and foreign policies. *Devotion: Journal of Research and Community Service.*

Wani, A. (2024). The Chabahar gambit: India's play for influence in Central Asia. https://www.orfonline.org/research/the-chabahar-gambit-india-s-play-for-influence-in-central-asia

Weinbaum, M. G., & Ali, N. (2025). US disengagement and new regional security dynamics in Afghanistan's neighborhood. *Middle East Institute.* https://www.mei.edu/publications/us-disengagement-and-new-regional-security-dynamics-afghanistans-neighborhood

Wishnick, E. (2021). Prospects for Sino-Russian coordination in Afghanistan. *War on the Rocks.* https://warontherocks.com/2021/11/prospects-for-sino-russian-coordination-in-afghanistan/

World Bank. (2018). *Project appraisal document on a proposed loan…* (P145010). https://documents1.worldbank.org/curated/en/283351468170975849/pdf/83250 0PAD0P145010Box382156B00OUO090.pdf

World Bank. (2024). Afghanistan overview. https://www.worldbank.org/en/country/afghanistan/overview

World Bank. (2024). World Bank Group announces next phase of support for people of Afghanistan. https://www.worldbank.org/en/news/press-release/2024/02/15/world-bank-group-announces-next-phase-of-support-for-people-of-afghanistan

World Bank. (2024). *The World Bank in Afghanistan: Overview.* https://www.worldbank.org/en/country/afghanistan/overview

World Bank. (2024). Q&A: CASA-1000 Resumption in Afghanistan. https://www.worldbank.org/en/news/statement/2024/02/23/casa1000resumptionafghanistan

World Bank. (2025). *Afghanistan development update: Unlocking youth potential for resilience and economic recovery.* https://thedocs.worldbank.org/en/doc/71dd45bbb425564ee41e22e1dc2c2f57-0310012025/original/Afghanistan-Development-Update-April-2025-Final.pdf

World Economic Forum. [WEF]. (2025). Global trade is changing — and these cities are seizing the opportunity. https://www.weforum.org/stories/2025/03/cities-global-trade-changing-seize-moment/

World Trade Organization [WTO]. (2015). *World Trade Report 2015: Speeding up trade — Benefits and challenges of implementing the WTO Trade Facilitation Agreement.* https://www.wto.org/english/res_e/booksp_e/world_trade_report15_e.pdf

Yar, F. G. M., Zahid, S., & Miakhil, J. M. (2023). Afghanistan's geopolitical and geo-economic significance in regional connectivity and development. *Journal of Political and Legal Sovereignty*, *1*(2), 78–86. DOI: 10.38142/jpls.v1i2.86

Yawar, M. E., & Rasooli, M. (2024). *Examining the position of Afghanistan in the new plan of China's Belt and Road Initiative (with emphasis on media strategies).* Law and Humanities Quarterly Reviews, 3(1). Available at *SSRN*: https://ssrn.com/abstract=4687249

Zaki, Z. (2023). Strategic alliance: The contribution of the Belt and Road Initiative to Afghanistan's trade integration. *International Journal of Research in Business and Social Science*, *13*(7), 239–251. DOI: 10.20525/ijrbs.v13i7.3658

ADDITIONAL READINGS

Faye, M. L., McArthur, J., Sachs, J. D., & Snow, T. (2004). The challenges facing landlocked developing countries. In Lomborg, B. (Ed.), *Global crises, global solutions* (pp. 269–286). Cambridge University Press.

Javaid, F. (2024). Challenges and opportunities for regional connectivity: Afghanistan's role between Pakistan and the Central Asian region. In P. Pietrzak (Ed.), *Analyzing global responses to contemporary regional conflicts* (pp. 275–297). IGI Global. Aziz, M. (2016). Afghanistan: The geopolitics of regional economic integration—The emergence of China as the new facilitator. In Arel USAM & O. Bingöl (Eds.), *Future dynamics in Asia: Full papers book* (pp. 313–342). İstanbul Arel University.

Small, A. (2015). *The China–Pakistan axis: Asia's new geopolitics.* Hurst. DOI: 10.1093/acprof:oso/9780190210755.001.0001

Summers, T. (2016). China's "new silk roads": Sub-national regions and networks of global political economy. In P. A. Haslam, J. Schafer, & P. Beaudet (Eds.), *Introduction to international development* (3rd ed., pp. 410–420). Oxford University Press. Collier, P. (2009). Post-conflict recovery: How should policies be distinctive? In B. Lomborg (Ed.), *Global crises, global solutions* (2nd ed., pp. 417–450). Cambridge University Press.

UNCTAD. (2019). *Islamic Republic of Afghanistan: Rapid eTrade readiness assessment.* United Nations.

World Bank. (2018). *Project appraisal document for CASA-1000* (Report No. 83250-PK). World Bank.

KEY TERMS & DEFINITIONS

Chabahar Corridor: An India—Iran—Afghanistan route leveraging Iran's Chabahar Port to access the Indian Ocean while bypassing Pakistan's overland chokepoints.

Dry Port: Inland terminal with customs, warehousing, and intermodal transfer directly linked to a seaport.

KPI (Time Release, Dwell, On-time Energy Flow): Operational metrics tracking border/customs and network reliability for corridors.

Paperless Trade: UNESCAP framework enabling mutual recognition of electronic trade documents and data exchange.

PPP: Contractual arrangement that allocates risks and performance obligations between public authorities and private investors/operators.

Practical overland connector: a piece of land such as a country or region that people can realistically use to move goods and travel between other places by road or rail.

Rules of Origin: Criteria that assign the "economic nationality" of a product for tariff preferences and safeguards.

Sanctions Compliance: Screening and controls to lawfully trade/finance under sanctions regimes (goods, end-users, vessels, banks).

SEZ / Dry-Port Governance: Regulatory model for zones/terminals (land use, fees, one-stop desks) that anchors corridor spillovers locally.

TAPI Pipeline: A proposed natural gas pipeline linking Turkmenistan—Afghanistan—Pakistan—India aimed at regional energy trade and interdependence.

TIR System: A standardized, bonded transit regime allowing sealed cargo to cross multiple borders with a single guarantee and minimal inspections.

Trade Facilitation: Process, legal, and digital reforms (risk-based inspections, e-manifests, single windows) that cut time/cost variability in cross-border trade.

Transit Trade: Movement of goods across one or more intermediary states under treaty-based rights and obligations (e.g., APTTA), with simplified customs and time-bound clearance.

APPENDIX

Abbreviations

ADB Asian Development Bank
APTTA Afghanistan–Pakistan Transit Trade Agreement
BRI Belt and Road Initiative
BRICS Brazil, Russia, India, China, South Africa (expanded bloc)
CASA-1000 Central Asia–South Asia Electricity Transmission and Trade Project
CPEC China–Pakistan Economic Corridor
CSIS Center for Strategic & International Studies
ECO Economic Cooperation Organization
EUISS European Union Institute for Security Studies
HVAC/HVDC High-Voltage Alternating/Direct Current
IFI(s) International Financial Institution(s)
INSTC International North–South Transport Corridor
IRU International Road Transport Union
KPI(s) Key Performance Indicator(s)
KTAI Kazakhstan–Turkmenistan–Afghanistan–Iran Corridor
LLDC(s) Landlocked Developing Country(ies)
NCTF National Connectivity Task Force (proposed)
PPP(s) Public–Private Partnership(s)
SAARC South Asian Association for Regional Cooperation
SAFTA South Asian Free Trade Agreement
SCO Shanghai Cooperation Organization
SDG(s) Sustainable Development Goal(s)
SEZ(s) Special Economic Zone(s)
SME(s) Small and Medium-sized Enterprise(s)
TAPI Turkmenistan–Afghanistan–Pakistan–India Gas Pipeline
TFA Trade Facilitation Agreement
TIR Transports Internationaux Routiers (International Road Transport)
TTFA Transit Transport Framework Agreement
UNESCAP UN Economic & Social Commission for Asia and the Pacific
UN-OHRLLS UN Office of the High Representative for LDCs/LLDCs/SIDS
WEF World Economic Forum
WTO World Trade Organization

Chapter 3
The Effects of Regional Trade Agreements on Portuguese Trade

Nuno Carlos Leitão
Polytechnic Institute of Santarém, Portugal & CEFAGE, University of Évora, Portugal & CEsA, Lisbon University, Portugal

ABSTRACT

The main objective of this research is to demonstrate the importance of the gravity model in explaining bilateral trade between Portugal and its fifteen main partners. The selected countries provide an idea of the international economic relations between Portugal and its main trading partners for the period 1990-2023. In this context, we formulate econometric models (Quantile Regressions, Poisson Pseudo Maximum Likelihood- PPML, and Random Effects) to test the effects of common religion, regional trade agreements, tariff rates, economies of scale, borders and geographical distance. The economies of scale and trade agreements are positively correlated with bilateral trade. Moreover, geographical distance indicates that the transport and logistics costs decrease, verifying a negative relationship between geographical distance and bilateral trade. The general border revealed that it stimulated the bilateral trade between Portugal and Spain. Subsequently, the tariff rates and their applications show decreased bilateral trade.

INTRODUCTION

This chapter investigates the determinants of Portuguese trade and fifteen main trading partners using the arguments of the gravity model. The selected countries listed in the methodology section provide an overall idea of the international eco-

DOI: 10.4018/979-8-3373-1782-3.ch003

nomic relations of the Portuguese economy. The data are organized in panel form for the period 1990-2023.

In recent decades, the gravity model applied to international trade has been the object of study from a theoretical and empirical point of view (Capoani, 2024; Leitão, 2024; Jadhav & Ghosh, 2024; Sharma et al., 2022).

As can be seen in the next section, the classical models of international trade (Smith's (1776) absolute advantage, Ricardo's (1817) comparative advantage, and Heckscher-Ohlin's (1933) neoclassical model) enable us to explain the gravity model. Furthermore, the models of monopolistic competition associated with intra-industry trade (e.g., Krugman 1979; Lancaster 1980) are established considering the assumptions of the gravity equation.

Another area introduced in the gravity model, but not so frequently, is the impact of tariffs, as analyzed by Hayakawa & Yoshimi (2023), namely tariff rates. However, developing some databases, such as CEPII (Centre d'Informations Internationales), the World Bank Indicators, and the Macrotends dataset, allows researchers to introduce this variable in the gravity equation.

In this line, this research seeks to answer the following questions: i) How does the size of economies stimulate bilateral trade? ii) To what extent do geographical proximity and common religion promote international trade? iii) Do geographical distance and standard trade agreements positively impact Portuguese bilateral trade? iv) To what extent do tariffs affect Portuguese bilateral trade?

The studies by Santos Silva and Tenreyro (2006) and Santos Silva and Tenreyro (2011) demonstrated that the use of the OLS estimator should not be applied since some variables used in the gravity equation, namely the dummy variables, assume the value zero, suggesting the use of the Poisson Pseudo Maximum Likelihood (PPML) estimator. Recent studies have followed this recommendation or used alternative methodologies with Random Effects, or as Egger and Staub (2015) suggest through GLM estimators (Poisson, Gamma, or Gaussian). More recent works, such as Geldner (2024) and Bergstrand and Clance (2023), suggest alternative Quantile Regressions since the sign of the coefficients obtained by PPML is challenging to interpret and sometimes contrary to the underlying hypotheses of the gravity model.

The following section presents the background and the literature review, where we present and discuss the literature that supports our investigation. The methodology and econometric strategy are considered in section 3, where we show the hypotheses to be tested in the empirical study. The empirical results appear in section 4, where the econometric results are discussed and finally, we present the conclusions and recommendations for economic policy in section 5.

BACKGROUND AND LITERATURE REVIEW

This section presents a series of empirical studies that analyse the relationship between the gravity model and international trade. The arguments of the gravity model explain the factors of bilateral trade. In this context, is it essential to understand what impact common language and geographical distance have on bilateral trade?

We begin this section using bibliometric analysis as a framework. The Scopus database was used, and the research was conducted between February 8 and February 11, 2025; the words "gravity and trade and cost" were used as criteria and it was observed that there were 132 articles and 4 book chapters on the research topic. Regarding thematic areas, Scopus indicates that Economics, Econometrics and Finance have 98 documents, Social Sciences have 44 documents, Business, Management and Accounting have 29 documents and Engineering has 28.

The main keywords can be seen in Figure 1, through the analysis conducted by the VOSviewer software (version 1.6.20), where the following words stand out: "international trade; trade costs; gravity model; trade flow; cost analysis".

The gravity model's assumptions explain the keywords and their frequency of occurrence. Typically, economic size and geographical distance are essential determinants for explaining international trade flows (export-import, trade intensity, or intra-industry trade).

Thus, the importance of the economic dimensions of the countries of origin and destination, as well as their similarities, allows for a reduction in trade costs. In other words, the economic dimension is positively correlated with trade volume.

Figure 1. Co-occurrence of Keywords.

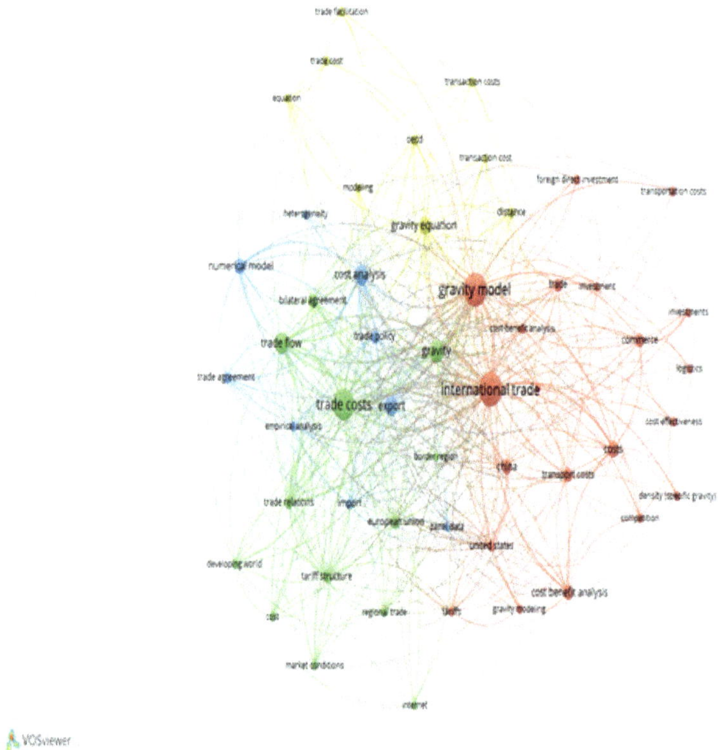

Source: Scopus database and VOSviewer.

Using the co-occurrence criterion through the VOSviewer software, it is possible to observe the essential words through the strength of their link and the connections between the different clusters in Table 1.

Moreover, it is also essential to test the effect of the scale of economies and understand if bilateral trade is associated with similar types of demand or, if on the contrary, is explained by different types of demand.

The empirical studies of gravity models (e.g., Tinbergen 1962; Isard 1969; Anderson & van Wincoop, 2003) support the questions presented. Then, the studies demonstrate a positive relationship between economic scales and bilateral trade.

Table 1. Keywords organized by link strength

Keywords	Total link strength
International Trade	265
Trade Costs	212
Gravity Model	206
Trade Flow	159
Cost Analysis	137
Export	129
Gravity	122
Numerical Model	90
Gravity Equation	89
Bilateral Agreements	75
Tariff Structure	71
Trade Relations	70
Costs	67
European Union	60
Import	53
Trade Agreement	53
Trade Policy	53
Unites Sates	51
China	50

Source: Scopus database and VOSviewer.

A meta-analysis on the topic of the gravity model demonstrates that it was imported from physics law and has been used most frequently in economics and geography. As several studies demonstrated (e.g., Tinbergen 1962; Isard, 1969; Anderson & van Wincoop, 2003; Capoani, 2024; Leitão, 2024), trade or foreign direct investment flows are studied based on the foundations of Newton's law of gravitation. Economic geography (e.g. Krugman 1991; Venables, 2006) demonstrates that per capita income assesses the size and scope of economies, showing that this variable positively influences the flows of an economy. On the other hand, geographical distance is inversely related to international trade and investment flows.

The empirical studies state that geographical proximity or cultural and linguistic encourage bilateral trade relations (e.g., Capoani, 2024; Reina et al., 2024; Leitão 2024; Kunroo & Ahmad, 2023). These variables are essential to studying the internationalization process via international trade. In this context, the common religion, trade agreements, and borders encourage bilateral trade, as Pöyhönen (1963), Gould (1994), Breton (1999), and Balogh & Leitão (2019) referred.

Furthermore, it is essential to consider the fragmentation process or outsourcing of international trade (e.g., Leitão 2024; Greaney & Kiyota, 2020; Fertő et al., 2022). The practice of outsourcing international production, or fragmentation, also known as offshoring or supply chain, was introduced into international economics by Jones and Kierzkowski (1990)s. With globalization, economists of international trade and spatial and regional economics began to study the relationship between intermediate products and the final products. Thus, the classical and neo-classical theories of international trade (Ricardo and the Heckscher-Ohlin model) explain the specialization associated with the theory of comparative advantages between economies, where the main objective will be the reduction of marginal costs, allowing them to maximize profit (Jones & Kierzkowski, 1990).

The empirical studies also demonstrate the relevance of economic scales and the diverse types of demand to explain the gravity model (Chen et al., 2024; Egger et al., 2024; Doanh & Heo, 2018; Jámbor et al., 2016).

Conceptually, Smith's (1776) theory of absolute advantages does not explain trade flows in which one country has an absolute advantage in the production costs of both goods. Ricardo's (1817) introduction of comparative advantage explained the assumptions of international trade, based on relative costs, relative prices, and opportunity costs. However, the introduction of two productive factors in trade (capital-K, labour-L) was considered by the Heckscher-Ohlin model (1933), where abundance and factor intensity allow explaining trade flows. However, monopolistic competition and new trade theories allow us to explain intra-industry trade, considering not only the size of economies, but also innovation, price differentiation, and geographical distance (e.g., Krugman 1979, Lancaster 1980).

Regarding the association between the gravity model and Portuguese bilateral trade, we have observed abundant empirical studies in recent years (e.g., Leitão 2023; Pacheco & Matos, 2022; Fernandes &Forte, 2022; Gouveia et al., 2018).

Moreover, it is essential to mention that there exist fresh articles that analyse the bibliometric systematic literature review between bilateral trade and gravity model (e.g., Leitão 2024; Jadhav & Ghosh, 2024; Sharma et al., 2022). Below, we present some recent contributions that are also in line with the contributions of Portuguese bilateral trade.

The recent article of Capoani (2024) discusses the concept and the arguments of the gravity model and their interaction with perfect competition (Ricardian model, Heckscher-Ohlin model) and monopolistic competition (duopoly and oligopoly structure). The author revisits the relationship between geo, cultural and economic variables, and international trade.

Another interesting contribution is the article of Reina et al., (2024) that evaluates the impact of economic and geographical variables on immigration between Germany and Portugal. The econometric model validates the arguments of the gravity model.

Over the last few years, empirical studies (e.g., Leitão 2023; Pacheco & Matos 2022) demonstrate that a common language promotes bilateral commercial relations between economies, usually associated with reduced transaction and transport costs. From this perspective, the introduction of the geographical distance variable as a factor in understanding the extent to which geographical proximity between partners allows for an increase in bilateral trade (e.g., Martin-Mayoral et al., 2016; Reina et al., 2024; Balogh & Leitão 2019).

Population variables between domestic and foreign countries and income per capita between partners have been used to evaluate economies of scale between trading partners. Empirical studies demonstrate that the potential market stimulates trade flows between two economies (e.g., Chen et al., 2024, Abdi et al., 2023).

Gandou and Sönmez (2023) consider the determinants of international trade on ECOWAS, and they found that income per capita positively correlates with bilateral trade. According to previous studies, this result shows again that scales of economies are essential to promote bilateral trade. The costs of transport analysed by geographical distance are negatively associated with bilateral trade. This result is according to the previous studies presented in this literature review. Finally, the results of Gandou & Sönmez (2023) also showed that colony positively affects bilateral trade of ECOWAS.

The empirical study by Thu et al., (2019) evaluated Vietnam's handicraft exports and their determinants. The econometric results presented by the authors demonstrated that foreign income per capita positively affects exports. The variables of home and host population are positively associated with exports. Thu et al., (2019) also showed that geographical distance negatively correlates with exports, and similar language and trade agreements are directly associated with Vietnam trade.

The potential Indonesian exports of the agriculture sector and ASEAN countries were investigated by Malu et al., (2024). The authors demonstrate that exporter income per capita and importer trade income per capita positively correlate with exports, indicating that supply and demand are essential to stimulating Indonesia's exports. The coefficient of geographical distance presents an expected sign, i.e., geographical distance is negatively correlated with bilateral trade. Finally, the dummy variable of the border is not according to the expected sign, i.e., based on the results of Malu et al., (2024), the border is not an important variable to explain the determinants of Indonesian exports.

The experience of Pakistan trade and South Asian countries was investigated by Masood et al., (2023), and they found a positive association between income per capita and bilateral trade. Besides, the trade agreements and economic size (income per capita) positively affect bilateral trade. These results are according to previous studies. The study also showed that tariffs discourage trade between Pakistan and

South Asian countries. However, common language showed a negative correlation with Pakistan trade, and this result doesn't have support in this literature.

The study of Balogh and Aguiar (2022) considered the gravity model in Latin America and the Caribbean. The authors formulated two equations that considered the dependent variables of the agricultural sector exports. The variables of economic scales (income per capita and partner income per capita) positively affect exports, as well as a common language and colonies. The variable of trade agreements, namely the dummy variable of MERCOSUR, exhibited a positive relationship with bilateral trade, reflecting the importance of regional trade agreements within the countries of the same regional block. Moreover, the geographical distance negatively affects exports, indicating that similar characteristics and proximity are essential to promote trade.

Considering the Random Effects estimator, the study of Khati and Kim (2022) evaluated the gravity model in India and ASEAN countries. The researchers used the total bilateral trade as a dependent variable, and they found that income per capita by India and trade partners positively affect bilateral trade between India and ASEAN countries, and the common language positively correlates with total bilateral trade.

From the analysis, the size of the economies, the common language, the common religion, the common border, and the trade agreements promote trade relations between trading partners with identical characteristics. Relative to geographical distance, studies demonstrate that geographical proximity promotes bilateral trade.

METHOD: DATA AND ECONOMETRIC STRATEGY

This section presents the hypotheses to be tested in an empirical study. Furthermore, we formulated the econometric models and justified the signs expected from the literature.

Recent empirical studies (e.g., Chernozhukov et al., 2024; Geldner, 2024; Leitão, 2023; Zapata et al., 2023) indicate that the OLS estimator should not be applied to gravity models since some variables commonly used assume the value zero and cannot be used since there are problems with bias and endogeneity. In this context, many studies have applied the suggestion of Santos Silva & Tenreyro (2006), Santos Silva & Tenreyro (2011) Poisson Pseudo Maximum Likelihood (PPML), or Egger & Staub (2016) through GLM estimators (Poisson, Gamma, or Gaussian). More recently, Chernozhukov et al., (2024) and Geldner (2024) presented another solution, the quantile regressions. The authors consider this estimator more efficient. Our research uses this methodology in the central body of the text.

This investigation evaluates Portuguese bilateral trade with the fifteen main partners of the Portuguese economy for the period 1990-2023. Bilateral international trade between Portugal and the fifteen main partners (Angola, Brazil, China, Czech Republic, Spain, the US, France, Germany, Italy, Japan, Netherlands, England, Switzerland, Poland, and Mozambique) for 1990-2023 is formulated. International trade data, total exports and imports in millions of euros were collected from the Portuguese National Statistics Institute - INE. This selection aims to study the significant trade Portuguese partners and ex-colonies, i.e. Portuguese-speaking countries and countries with different stages of development. This research also introduces the effect of common religion (Christianism) and tariff rates on bilateral Portuguese trade. The data is organized in the form of a panel.

Independent Variable and Hypothesis Development

Next, we present the hypotheses according to the literature review in the last section.

H1: The economic dimension stimulates bilateral trade.

The economic size of economies aims to consider the economics of scales. Therefore, the economics of scales are essential to differentiated products, promoting bilateral trade in general. The empirical studies of Egger et al., (2024) and Kunroo and Ahmad (2023) found a positive sign of economic size on bilateral trade. Portuguese trade studies such as Leitão (2023), Pacheco & Matos (2022), Fernandes & Forte (2022), and Gouveia et al., (2018) also found a positive impact on Portuguese bilateral trade. The economic dimensions were collected from the World Bank - Development Indicators.

For this hypothesis, we consider the following variables:

GDPT- Portuguese income per capita in US dollars from World Bank, World Development Indicators (2024).

GDPK- Trade partner income per capita in US dollars.

DIM: GDPT + GDPK

H2: Border countries, common religions, and trade agreements promote bilateral trade between two economies.

BORDER- the dummy variable that varies between 1 and 0. We attribute the value 1 to Spain and zero to other trade partners. The studies of Martin-Mayoral et al., (2015) and Reina et al., (2024) support this hypothesis.

RELIGION- This is also a dummy variable that varies between 1 and 0. The value 1 corresponds to common religion (Christianism) and zero to those that do not. Balog & Leitão (2019), Nadal & Gallego (2022), and Bergstrand & Clance (2023) found a positive correlation between common religion and bilateral trade.

EU- The Dummy variable takes the value 1 if the partner country is a member of the European Union and zero for those not.

H3: The geographical distance aims to determine the logistic costs between the bilateral trade.

DISTANCE- is the distance between the capitals in km2. In this case, the distance between Lisbon and each of the capitals of the trade partners is under analysis. This variable has been collected from CEPII. Studies by Leitão (2023), Pacheco & Matos (2022), and Balogh & Leitão (2019) found a negative correlation between geographic distance and bilateral trade.

H4: Tariffs are negatively correlated with Portuguese trade flows.

Tariff- Portuguese tariff rates, historical data from Macrotrends database. There are some studies like Hayakawa & Yoshimi (2023), Jack et al., (2008), Masku et al., (2001), Beghin & Bureau (2001) and Disdier et al., (2015) also found a negative relationship between tariffs and trade. Macrotrends collects this variable. This database is an online platform that covers commercial policy, financial and economic datasets.

In the following equation we present the variables taken into consideration in this study:

$$LogTRADE_{it}=\beta_0+\beta_1 LogGDP_{Tit}+\beta_2 LogGDP_{Kit}+\beta_3 LogDIM_{it}+\beta_4 RELIGION_{it}+\beta_5 LogDISTANCE_{it}+\beta_6\, LogTARIFF+\beta_7\, BORDER+\beta_8 EU+\mu it \quad (1)$$

In the general equation, the variable dependent is Portuguese total bilateral trade, and the independent variables are Portuguese income per capita ($LogGDP_{Tit}$), trade partners ($LogGDP_{kit}$), Portuguese income per capita plus trade partners (LogDIM), common religion (RELIGION), geographical distance (LogDISTANCE), border (BORDER), European country member (EU) and µit is a random disturbance. Then, the expected signs are $\beta_1>0$, $\beta_2>0$, $\beta_3>0$, $\beta_4>0$, $\beta_7>0$, $\beta_8>0$, and $\beta_5<0$, $\beta_6<0$.

The French Centre for the World Economy, CEPII, provides access to geo-economic variables, including geographic distance, border, and economic integration processes.

Once the general equation and the respective independent variables are presented, it is possible to formulate the following models:

Model [1]:

$$LogTRADE_{it}=\beta_0+\beta_1 LogGDP_{Tit}+\beta_2 LogDIM_{it}+\beta_3 RELIGION_{it}+\beta_4 LogDISTANCE_{it} +\mu it \quad (2)$$

Model [2]:

$$LogTRADE_{it}=\beta_0+\beta_1 LogGDP_{Tit}+\beta_2 LogGDP_{Kit}+\beta_3 BORDER_{it}+\beta_4 EU_{it} +\mu it \quad (3)$$

Model [3]:

$$LogTRADE_{it}=\beta_0+\beta_1 LogGDP_{Tit}+\beta_2 LogGDP_{Kit}+\beta_3 LogDISTANCE_{itit}+\beta_4 LogRELIGION_{it} +\mu it \quad (4)$$

Model [4]:

$$LogTRADE_{it}=\beta_0+\beta_1 LogTARIFF_{it}+\beta_2 LogGDP_{Tit}+\beta_3 LogGDP_{Ktit}+\beta_4 LogDISTANCE_{it} +\mu it \quad (5)$$

Table 2 summarizes the description of variables used in this research and their sources.

Table 2. Description of variables used in this research.

Variables	Description	Expected Sings	Source
LogTRADE	Bilateral total exports plus imports by each country.	Dependent Variable	INE-Portuguese National Institute of Statistics
LogTARIFF	Portuguese tariff rates	[-]	Macrotrends database
$LogGDP_t$	Portuguese income per capita in US dollars.	[+]	World Bank Indicators
$LogGDP_k$	Trade partner income per capita in US dollars.	[+]	World Bank Indicators
LogDIM	GDP_t+GDP_k.	[+]	World Bank Indicators
BORDER	Dummy variable, takes 1 to Spain and zero to other countries.	[+]	CEPII
RELEGION	Dummy variable takes 1 to Christian religion and zero to other religion.	[+]	Own composition
LogDISTANCE	Geographical distance between capital partners.	[+]	CEPII
EU	European Member Countries	[+]	CEPII

Source: Author's elaboration.

EMPRIRICAL RESULTS AND DISCUSSION

This section evaluates the properties of the variables used in the models and their determinants, considering the arguments of the gravity model. Thus, we present the descriptive statistics of the variables used, followed by the multicollinearity test. Then, we used the Quantile Regression estimators (e.g., Geldner, 2024, Bergstrand & Clance 2023, Leitão 2023) and we tested the validity of the slope of coefficients across quantiles, considering the arguments of Koenker and Basset (1982). Therefore, if the coefficients are different across quantiles, the conditional quantiles are not equal, and the results of Chi-Square statistics are statistically significant. We also present Poisson Pseudo Maximum Likelihood (PPML) and their interpretation for each model in the body of the text.

The descriptive statistics of the variables used in model 1 are considered in Table 3.

Table 3. Descriptive variables in Model 1

Statistics	LogTRADE	LogGDP$_T$	LogDIM	RELIGION	LogDISTANCE
Mean	3.259	4.224	4.883	0.733	3.548
Median	3.315	4.236	4.706	1.000	3.476
Maximum	4.745	4.303	6.653	1.000	4.048
Minimum	1.107	4.119	4.2884	0.000	2.699
Std. Dev.	0.662	0.048	0.528	0.443	0.379
Skewness	-0.429	-0.685	2.362	-1.055	-0.460
Kurtosis	3.205	2.598	7.789	2.114	2.342
Probability	0.000	0.000	0.000	0.000	0.000
Observations	510	510	510	510	510

Source: Own elaboration.

The variables of incomes per capita (LogDIM) and bilateral trade (LogTRADE) show the highest maximum values. Moreover, we observe that kurtosis presents a positive trend for all variables and asymmetric negative values for the variables by bilateral trade (LogTRADE), Portuguese income per capita (LogGDP$_T$), common religion (RELIGION) and geographical distance (LogDISTANCE).

The variance inflation test for model 1 is presented in Table 4. The variables used in the first equation demonstrated that Portuguese income per capita (LogGDP$_T$), economic dimension (LogDIM), the common religion (RELIGION), and geographical distance (LogDISTANCE) don't present the problem of multicollinearity.

Table 4. The variance inflation test for Model 1

Variables	VIF	1/VIF
$LogGDP_T$	1.02	0.980
LogDIM	1.26	0.793
RELIGION	1.28	0.784
LogDISTANCE	1.24	0.805
Mean VIF	1.20	

Source: Own elaboration.

Table 5 reports the model 1 using Quantile regressions. The economic dimension (Portuguese income per capita) positively affects Portuguese bilateral trade.

Table 5. Portuguese Gravity model for Model 1 by Quantile Regressions

	Quantile	Coefficient	Std. Error	t-Statistic	Prob.
$LogGDP_T$	0.10	3.343***	0.576	5.804	(0.000)
	0.20	2.962***	0.616	4.810	(0.000)
	0.30	4.228***	0.558	7.574	(0.000)
	0.40	4.047***	0.459	8.803	(0.000)
	0.50	3.643***	0.448	8.1403	(0.000)
	0.60	3.558***	0.476	7.476	(0.000)
	0.70	3.043***	0.489	6.213	(0.000)
	0.80	3.508***	0.526	6.668	(0.000)
	0.90	4.335***	0.405	10.707	(0.000)
LogDIM	0.10	0.194***	0.030	6.464	(0.000)
	0.20	0.094**	0.037	2.542	(0.011)
	0.30	0.006	0.038	0.1705	(0.864)
	0.40	-0.021	0.041	-0.506	(0.613)
	0.50	-0.006	0.044	-0.1341	(0.894)
	0.60	0.010	0.052	0.203	(0.839)
	0.70	0.020	0.053	0.380	(0.704)
	0.80	0.034	0.0501	0.681	(0.496)
	0.90	-0.022	0.052	-0.424	(0.672)
RELIGION	0.10	-0.364***	0.043	-8.467	(0.000)
	0.20	-0.339***	0.046	-7.412	(0.000)
	0.30	-0.1632***	0.053	-3.085	(0.002)
	0.40	-0.0323	0.049	-0.666	(0.506)

continued on following page

Table 5. Continued

	Quantile	Coefficient	Std. Error	t-Statistic	Prob.
	0.50	0.0253	0.045	0.556	(0.578)
	0.60	0.093**	0.045	2.046	(0.041)
	0.70	0.127**	0.053	2.413	(0.016)
	0.80	0.158***	0.058	2.712	(0.006)
	0.90	0.171***	0.058	2.932	(0.003)
LogDISTANCE	0.10	-1.6301***	0.0649	-25.123	(0.000)
	0.20	-1.533***	0.075	-20.461	(0.000)
	0.30	-1.3791***	0.065	-21.079	(0.000)
	0.40	-1.2698***	0.0610	-20.809	(0.000)
	0.50	-1.206***	0.0565	-21.374	(0.000)
	0.60	-1.1273***	0.0517	-21.788	(0.000)
	0.70	-1.017***	0.0505	-20.130	(0.000)
	0.80	-0.928***	0.047	-19.466	(0.000)
	0.90	-0.779***	0.064	-12.176	(0.000)
C	0.10	-6.2636***	2.377	-2.635	(0.008)
	0.20	-4.362*	2.453	-1.778	(0.076)
	0.30	-9.784***	2.328	-4.203	(0.000)
	0.40	-9.244***	1.939	-4.767	(0.000)
	0.50	-7.807***	1.867	-4.181	(0.000)
	0.60	-7.762***	1.9324	-4.0170	(0.000)
	0.70	-5.935***	2.0428	-2.9054	(0.003)
	0.80	-8.206***	2.256	-3.637	(0.000)
	0.90	-11.809***	1.7469	-6.761	(0.000)
Wald Test	112.019*** (0.000)				

Source: Own elaboration.

Notes: ***- the variable has statistical significance at 1%, **- the variable has statistical significance at 5%, and *- the variable has statistical significance at 10%.

From Table 5 the variable ($LogGDP_T$) is statistically significant at 1%. According to the hypothesis formulated, this result shows the importance of economic scales in bilateral trade. The empirical studies of Martin-Mayoral (2016), Kunroo and Ahmad (2023), and Capoani (2024) also support this tendency. However, the other coefficient of economic scales (LogDIM) is statistically significant only in quartiles 0.1 and 0.2.

The coefficient for common religion (RELIGION) positively affects bilateral Portuguese trade. The variable presents statistically significant at a 1% level. This result showed that the common religion stimulates bilateral trade (Balog and Leitão 2019; Nadal and Gallego 2022; Bergstrand and Clance, 2023) between the quantiles 0.6. 0.7, 0.8, and 0.9.

Regarding geographical distance (LogDISTANCE), we observe a negative effect on Portuguese trade, showing that geographical proximity encourages the relationship between trade partners across quantile regressions (e.g. Chen et al., 2024; Capoani, 2023; Martín-Mayoral et al., 2016).

Besides, the slope equality test shows that Chi-Square statistics are statistically significant across quantiles.

In table 6, it is possible to observe the econometric results for model 1 using the Pseudo Maximum Likelihood estimator.

Table 6. Model 1 with Poisson Pseudo Maximum Likelihood

Variable	Coefficient	Std. Error	t-Statistic	Prob.
$LogGDP_T$	1.448***	0.153	9.480	(0.000)
LogDIM	0.011	0.013	1.040	(0.299)
RELIGION	-0.034***	0.012	-2.780	(0.005)
LogDISTANCE	-0.373***	0.012	-25.240	(0.000)
C	-3.650***	0.648	-5.630	(0.000)
Adjusted R-squared	0.59			
Observations	510			

Source: Own elaboration.

Notes***- the variable has statistical significance at 1%.

The descriptive statistics for model 2 are presented in Table 7. The variable of per capita income of trading partners ($LogGDP_K$) presents the highest maximum value, followed by the total bilateral trade (LogTRADE) variable. Regarding kurtosois, it is observed that all variables used in the model present a positive distribution. Reflecting the skewness statistic, observing asymmetry between the variables is possible. The variables total trade (LogTRADE) and Portuguese per capita income ($LogGDP_T$) have negative signs. In contrast, the remaining variables of income from trading partners ($LogGD_K$), BORDER and trade agreements (EU) have a positive sign.

Table 7. Descriptive variables in Model 2

Statistics	LogTRADE	$LogGDP_T$	LogGDPK	BORDER	EU
Mean	3.259	4.224	4.714	0.066	0.468
Median	3.315	4.236	4.514	0.000	0.000
Maximum	4.745	4.303	6.651	1.000	1.000
Minimum	1.107	4.119	3.798	0.000	2.699
Std. Dev.	0.662	0.048	0.603	0.249	0.499
Skewness	-0.429	-0.685	2.090	3.474	0.126
Kurtosis	3.205	2.598	6.825	13.071	1.0158
Probability	0.000	0.000	0.000	0.000	0.000
Observations	510	510	510	510	510

Source: Own elaboration.

The variance inflation test for model 2 is presented in Table 8. The variables used in the second equation demonstrated that Portuguese income per capita ($LogGDP_T$), trade partner income per capita ($LogGDP_k$), the common border (BORDER) and trade agreement (EU) don't present the problem of multicollinearity.

Table 8. The variance inflation test for Model 2

Variables	VIF	1/VIF
$LogGDP_T$	1.02	0.982
$LogGDP_k$	1.05	0.950
BORDER	1.11	0.901
EU	1.09	0.915
Mean VIF	1.07	

Source: Own elaboration.

Next, we present in Table 9 the estimates obtained for the determinants of the gravity model (model 2). In general, the coefficients are according to the expected signs.

The economic dimensions or economic scales ($LogGDP_T$) are positively correlated with bilateral trade, demonstrating that the economic dimension is essential to international trade. The coefficient is statistically significant at 1% across all quantiles. Gandou & Sönmez (2023), Malu et al., (2024) and Masood et al., (2023) found a positive sign of economic size on bilateral trade. However, the trade partner income per capita ($LogGDP_K$) presents an unexpected sign.

The dummy variable of BORDER demonstrates that Spain is an essential partner of Portugal. Abundant literature indicates that a common border encourages bilateral trade (e.g., Zapata et al., 2023, Bergstrand & Clance 2023, Balogh & Leitão 2019). The variable is statistically significant at 1% across the whole quantile.

The studies of Pöyhönen (1963), Gould (1994), and Breton (1999) referred to the fact that trade agreements are essential to promote bilateral trade. Then, the studies demonstrated a positive relationship between trade agreements and bilateral trade. The results illustrate that the dummy variable of European countries' members (EU) positively correlates with bilateral Portuguese trade. The variable is statistically significant at 1% by all quantile regressions. Balogh &Aguiar (2022), Capoani (2024), and Stavytskyy et al., (2019) also found a positive relationship between trade agreements and bilateral trade.

The slope of coefficients across quantiles demonstrated that the variables are different across the quantiles. The result of Chi-Square statistics is statistically significant (Wald test).

Table 9. Portuguese Gravity model for Model 2 by Quantile Regressions

	Quantile	Coefficient	Std. Error	t-Statistic	Prob.
$LogGDP_T$	0.10	5.021***	0.8053	6.236	(0.000)
	0.20	5.536***	1.005	5.5087	(0.000)
	0.30	4.768***	0.752	6.339	(0.000)
	0.40	5.1592***	0.589	8.7505	(0.000)
	0.50	4.199***	0.614	6.839	(0.000)
	0.60	4.171***	0.588	7.085	(0.000)
	0.70	3.650***	0.602	6.059	(0.000)
	0.80	3.390***	0.527	6.428	(0.000)
	0.90	3.074***	0.394	7.803	(0.000)
$LogGDP_K$	0.10	0.183***	0.035	5.261	(0.000)
	0.20	-0.032	0.043	-0.758	(0.448)
	0.30	-0.120**	0.049	-2.453	(0.014)
	0.40	-0.1804***	0.038	-4.744	(0.000)
	0.50	-0.1931***	0.044	-4.436	(0.000)
	0.60	-0.239***	0.051	-4.690	(0.000)
	0.70	-0.268***	0.052	-5.1300	(0.000)
	0.80	-0.224****	0.051	-4.386	(0.000)
	0.90	-0.2701***	0.037	-7.314	(0.000)
BORDER	0.10	1.584***	0.0691	22.916	(0.000)
	0.20	1.271***	0.091	13.931	(0.000)

continued on following page

Table 9. Continued

	Quantile	Coefficient	Std. Error	t-Statistic	Prob.
	0.30	1.005***	0.120	8.362	(0.000)
	0.40	0.731***	0.056	13.123	(0.000)
	0.50	0.702***	0.060	11.729	(0.000)
	0.60	0.650***	0.057	11.354	(0.000)
	0.70	0.487***	0.059	8.190	(0.000)
	0.80	0.456***	0.054	8.443	(0.000)
	0.90	0.385***	0.040	9.5393	(0.000)
EU	0.10	0.499****	0.068	7.353	(0.000)
	0.20	0.3418***	0.075	4.570	(0.000)
	0.30	0.4130***	0.097	4.2496	(0.000)
	0.40	0.5915***	0.060	9.784	(0.000)
	0.50	0.545***	0.070	7.800	(0.000)
	0.60	0.406***	0.071	5.719	(0.000)
	0.70	0.4645***	0.064	7.234	(0.000)
	0.80	0.454****	0.054	8.381	(0.000)
	0.90	0.396***	0.042	9.5093	(0.000)
C	0.10	-19.873***	3.337	-5.955	(0.000)
	0.20	-20.624***	4.1803	-4.933	(0.000)
	0.30	-16.797***	3.109	-5.401	(0.000)
	0.40	-18.052***	2.478	-7.283	(0.000)
	0.50	-13.811***	2.579	-5.354	(0.000)
	0.60	-13.274***	2.5191	-5.269	(0.000)
	0.70	-10.797***	2.5920	-4.1654	(0.000)
	0.80	-9.7964***	2.3907	-4.0977	(0.000)
	0.90	-8.119***	1.7634	-4.6047	(0.000)
Wald Test	77.196*** (0.000)				

Source: Own elaboration.

Notes: ***- the variable has statistical significance at 1%, **- the variable has statistical significance at 5%

In table 10, we can observe the estimates for model 2 considering the Poisson Pseudo Maximum Likelihood.

Table 10. Model 2 with Poisson Pseudo Maximum Likelihood

Variable	Coefficient	Std. Error	t-Statistic	Prob.
$LogGDP_T$	1.504***	0.176	8.570	(0.000)
$LogGDP_K$	-0.0.32***	0.009	-3.280	(0.000)
BORDER	0.209***	0.013	16.270	(0.000)
EU	0.144***	0.0153	9.430	(0.000)
C	-5.111***	0.755	-6.770	(0.000)
Adjusted R-squared	0.412			
Observations	510			

Source: Own elaboration.
Notes***- the variable has statistical significance at 1%.

The descriptive statistics for Model 3 are shown in Table 11. The variables of per capita income of trading partners ($LogGDP_K$) and bilateral trade (LogTRADE) present the highest maximum value. Observing kurtosis is monitored that all variables used in the model show a positive distribution.

Regarding the skewness statistic, a negative sign was observed for total trade (LogTRADE), Portuguese per capita income ($LogGDP_T$), and geographical distance (LogDISTANCE). Nevertheless, trade partners' income per capita ($LogGDP_K$) is positive.

Table 11. Descriptive variables in Model 3

Statistics	LogTRADE	$LogGDP_T$	LogGDPK	LogDISTANCE	RELIGION
Mean	3.259	4.224	4.714	3.548	0.733
Median	3.315	4.236	4.514	3.476	1.000
Maximum	4.745	4.303	6.651	4.048	1.000
Minimum	1.107	4.119	3.798	2.699	0.000
Std. Dev.	0.662	0.048	0.603	0.379	0.443
Skewness	-0.429	-0.685	2.090	-0.460	-1.055
Kurtosis	3.205	2.598	6.825	2.342	2.114
Probability	0.000	0.000	0.000	0.000	0.000
Observations	510	510	510	510	510

Source: Own elaboration.

The variance inflation test for model 3 is presented in Table 12. The variables used in the third equation demonstrated that Portuguese income per capita ($LogGDP_T$), trade partner income per capita ($LogGDP_k$), the geographical distance (LogDISTANCE) and common religion (RELIGION) don't present the problem of multicollinearity.

Table 12. The variance inflation test for Model 3

Variables	VIF	1/VIF
$LogGDP_T$	1.02	0.978
$LogGDP_k$	1.24	0.804
LogDISTANCE	1.24	0.806
RELIGION	1.27	0.789
Mean VIF	1.19	

Source: Own elaboration.

Table 13 shows the gravity regression results for Portuguese trade in model 3. Considering the estimations, the Portuguese income per capita ($LogGDP_T$) positively affects bilateral trade across quantile regressions and the income per capita ($LogGDP_T$) is statistically significant at a 1% level.

Table 13. Portuguese Gravity model for Model 3 by Quantile Regressions

	Quantile	Coefficient	Std. Error	t-Statistic	Prob.
$LogGDP_T$	0.10	3.1926***	0.555	5.749	(0.000)
	0.20	3.018***	0.618	4.885	(0.000)
	0.30	4.281***	0.566	7.563	(0.000)
	0.40	4.079***	0.464	8.784	(0.000)
	0.50	3.637***	0.449	8.107	(0.000)
	0.60	3.567***	0.476	7.501	(0.000)
	0.70	2.950***	0.460	6.418	(0.000)
	0.80	3.530***	0.527	6.693	(0.000)
	0.90	4.3970***	0.418	10.526	(0.000)
$LogGDP_K$	0.10	0.171***	0.024	7.145	(0.000)
	0.20	0.085***	0.031	2.695	(0.007)
	0.30	0.021	0.034	0.608	(0.543)
	0.40	-0.012	0.047	-0.324	(0.746)
	0.50	-0.002	0.040	-0.056	(0.955)
	0.60	0.017	0.048	0.343	(0.732)
	0.70	0.038	0.047	0.822	(0.411)
	0.80	0.034	0.049	0.699	(0.485)
	0.90	0.012	0.056	0.2063	(0.836)
LogDISTANCE	0.10	-1.609***	0.063	-25.452	(0.000)
	0.20	-1.526***	0.073	-20.889	(0.000)

continued on following page

Table 13. Continued

	Quantile	Coefficient	Std. Error	t-Statistic	Prob.
	0.30	-1.387***	0.067	-20.771	(0.000)
	0.40	-1.274***	0.062	-20.608	(0.000)
	0.50	-1.206***	0.057	-21.285	(0.000)
	0.60	-1.126***	0.052	-21.701	(0.000)
	0.70	-1.0235***	0.052	-20.037	(0.000)
	0.80	-0.928***	0.051	-18.245	(0.000)
	0.90	-0.828***	0.070	-11.829	(0.000)
RELIGION	0.10	-0.371***	0.042	-8.896	(0.000)
	0.20	-0.346***	0.046	-7.525	(0.000)
	0.30	-0.151***	0.054	-2.773	(0.005)
	0.40	-0.034	0.048	-0.706	(0.480)
	0.50	0.031	0.046	0.671	(0.503)
	0.60	0.099**	0.046	2.189	(0.032)
	0.70	0.146***	0.048	3.030	(0.003)
	0.80	0.160***	0.057	2.765	(0.005)
	0.90	0.167***	0.057	2.943	(0.003)
C	0.10	-5.542**	2.297	-2.414	(0.016)
	0.20	-4.561*	2.460	-1.854	(0.064)
	0.30	-10.052***	2.3804	-4.2227	(0.000)
	0.40	-9.406***	1.9666	-4.783	(0.000)
	0.50	-7.8014***	1.883	-4.143	(0.000)
	0.60	-7.838***	1.947	-4.026	(0.000)
	0.70	-5.622***	1.957	-2.872	(0.004)
	0.80	-8.295***	2.266	-3.660	(0.000)
	0.90	-12.057***	1.794	-6.721	(0.000)
Wald Test	77.196*** (0.000)				

Source: Own elaboration.

Notes***- the variable has statistical significance at 1%, **- the variable has statistical significance at 5%, and *- the variable has statistical significance at 10%.

The empirical studies of Leitão (2023), Pacheco & Matos (2022), Fernandes & Forte (2022), and Gouveia et al., (2018) also found the same tendency for the Portuguese economy. Again, the results demonstrate the importance of economies of scale to differentiated products and consequently promote the bilateral Portuguese trade. Considering the trade partner income per capita ($LogGDP_K$), the coefficient presents statistical significance at a 1% level with the excepted sign only in quartiles 0.1 and 0.20.

The coefficient of geographical distance (LogDISTANCE) is according to the hypothesis formulated, demonstrating that geographical proximity is essential between commercial partners and the Portuguese economy (e.g. Martin-Mayoral et al., 2015, Reina et al., 2024, Balogh & Leitão 2019).

Considering common religion (dummy variable), we observe that in the quantiles between 0.60 and 0.90, the variable presents a positive effect on trade and is significant at a 1% level. According to the results obtained, common religion promotes an increase in trade flows, reinforcing and increasing similarities between trading partners. The empirical studies of Balog & Leitão (2019), Nadal & Gallego (2022), and Bergstrand & Clance (2023) give support to our result.

In Table 14, we can observe the estimates for model 3 using the Poisson Pseudo Maximum Likelihood estimator. All independent variables used in the equation are statistically significant. In more detail, we can state that Portuguese per capita income ($LogGDP_T$), geographical distance (LogDISTANCE) and common religion (RELIGION) present statistical significance at a 1% level.

Regarding the income of business partners, it is observed that the coefficient has statistical significance at the 10% level.

Thus, our results validate the hypotheses formulated about economies of scale measured by per capita income ($LogGDP_T$, $LogGDP_K$). The studies by Malu et al., (2024), Gandou & Sönmez (2023), and Massod et al., (2023) find an impact of economies on bilateral trade.

The coefficient of geographical distance (LogDISTANCE) shows that the reduction in transport costs increases bilateral trade by (0.376%). For instance, the studies of Caponi (2024), Leitão (2023), Pacheco & Matos (2022) find a negative effect between geographical distance and bilateral trade.

Finally, the result found for the common religion (RELIGION) does not see the signal of the dominant hypothesis.

Table 14. Model 3 with Poisson Pseudo Maximum Likelihood

Variable	Coefficient	Std. Error	t-Statistic	Prob.
$LogGDP_T$	1.434***	0.152	9.470	(0.000)
$LogGDP_K$	0.016*	0.094	1.730	(0.083)
LogDISTANCE	-0.376***	0.015	-25.280	(0.000)
RELIGION	-0.032***	0.012	-2.620	(0.009)
C	-3.618***	0.644	-5.610	(0.000)

continued on following page

Table 14. Continued

Variable	Coefficient	Std. Error	t-Statistic	Prob.
Adjusted R-squared	0.59			
Observations	510			

Source: Own elaboration.

Notes***- the variable has statistical significance at 1; *- the variable has statistical significance at 10%.

In the following tables, we present the descriptive statistics and econometric results obtained for model 4, emphasizing the impact of tariffs on bilateral trade. Thus, in Table 15, we present the descriptive statistics. Like the previous model, the per capita income of trading partners (LogGDP$_K$) and bilateral trade (LogTRADE) variables show the highest maximum value. Furthermore, kurtosis demonstrates that the variables used in the model have a positive distribution.

As in the previous model, the skewness statistic presents a negative sign by the total trade (LogTRADE), Portuguese per capita income (LogGDP$_T$) and geographical distance. Nevertheless, the tariff rates (LogTARIFF) and trade partners' income per capita (LogGDP$_K$) are positive.

The VIF test for model 4 is shown in Table 16. The variables used in the equation demonstrated that the tariff rates (LogTARIFF), Portuguese income per capita (LogGDP$_T$) trade partner income per capita (LogGDPk), and geographical distance (LogDISTANCE) don't present the problem of multicollinearity.

Table 15. Descriptive variables in Model 4

Statistics	LogTRADE	LogTARIFF	LogGDP$_T$	LogGDPK	LogDISTANCE
Mean	3.235	0.397	4.219	4.706	3.548
Median	3.297	0.350	4.235	4.514	3.476
Maximum	4.647	0.798	4.289	6.641	4.048
Minimum	1.107	0.143	4.119	3.798	2.699
Std. Dev.	0.659	0.175	0.046	0.603	0.379
Skewness	-0.436	0.409	-0.834	2.096	-0.460
Kurtosis	3.197	2.129	2.530	6.845	2.342
Probability	0.000	0.000	0.000	0.000	0.000
Observations	480	480	480	480	480

Source: Author's elaboration.

Table 16. The variance inflation test for Model 4

Variables	VIF	1/VIF
LogTARIFF	3.66	0.273
$LogGDP_T$	3.66	0.273
$LogGDP_k$	1.14	0.875
LogDISTANCE	1.14	0.876
Mean VIF	2.40	

Source: Own elaboration.

In Table 17, it is possible to observe the econometric results for model 4 through quantile regressions.

The tariff rates variable (LogTARIFF) finds statistical significance for all quantiles and sees the sign advanced by the literature, demonstrating that tariffs hurt bilateral trade. The results are in line with the studies of Hayakawa & Yoshimi (2023), Jack et al., (2008), Masku et al., (2001), Beghin & Bureau (2001) and Disdier et al., (2015).

Regarding the economies of scale variable, only the size of the Portuguese economy ($LogGDP_T$) has statistical significance on bilateral trade throughout the quantile regressions. As empirical studies (Leitão 2023; Pacheco & Matos 2022, Fernandes & Forte 2022; Gouveia et al., 2018) conducted within the scope of the Portuguese economy have demonstrated, the size of countries' economies is essential for differentiating products and gaining competitiveness for the exporting country.

The coefficient of geographical distance (LogDISTANCE) has statistical significance throughout quantile regression. The results are according to theoretical predictions, i.e., there is a negative relationship between geographical distance and bilateral trade. The studies by Martin-Mayoral et al., (2015), Reina et al., (2024), Balogh & Leitão (2019), Caponi (2024), Leitão (2023), and Pacheco & Matos (2022) also found a negative effect between geographic distance and bilateral trade.

In Table 18, the results for model 4 using the Poisson Pseudo Maximum Likelihood estimator (PPML) can be observed; the econometric results are by the theoretical predictions. Thus, it is confirmed that tariff rates reduce bilateral trade flows between trading partners. However, the size of the economies, which assesses economies of scale, shows that Portuguese income per capita and that of trading partners promote Portuguese bilateral trade.

Geographical distance (LogDISTANCE) shows that the reduction of transport and logistics costs explains Portuguese bilateral trade.

Table 17. Portuguese Gravity model for Model 4 by Quantile Regressions

	Quantile	Coefficient	Std. Error	t-Statistic	Prob.
LogTARIFF	0.10	-0.340	0.407	-0.836	(0.404)
	0.20	-0.581*	0.320	-1.816	(0.070)
	0.30	-0.391**	0.197	-1.984	(0.047)
	0.40	-0.451**	0.201	-2.242	(0.025)
	0.50	-0.270	0.208	-1.295	(0.196)
	0.60	-0.565**	0.246	-2.301	(0.022)
	0.70	-0.692***	0.212	-3.256	(0.001)
	0.80	-0.498**	0.203	-2.458	(0.014)
	0.90	-0.580**	0.234	-2.474	(0.013)
$LogGDP_T$	0.10	3.324**	1.5241	2.181	(0.029)
	0.20	2.134	1.370	1.558	(0.119)
	0.30	3.387***	0.830	4.079	(0.000)
	0.40	2.528***	0.767	3.295	(0.001)
	0.50	2.655***	0.759	3.497	(0.000)
	0.60	1.9207**	0.921	2.086	(0.038)
	0.70	1.301	0.814	1.599	(0.111)
	0.80	2.062**	0.805	2.563	(0.010)
	0.90	2.020**	0.888	2.275	(0.023)
$LogGDP_K$	0.10	0.109	0.089	1.226104	(0.221)
	0.20	0.057	0.083	0.687267	(0.492)
	0.30	-0.003	0.035	-0.083795	(0.933)
	0.40	-0.020	0.040	-0.487005	(0.627)
	0.50	-0.016	0.045	-0.364347	(0.716)
	0.60	-0.029	0.058	-0.485965	(0.627)
	0.70	0.048	0.047	1.029288	(0.304)
	0.80	0.024	0.048	0.495595	(0.620)
	0.90	-0.050	0.063	-0.800015	(0.424)
LogDIST	0.10	-1.639***	0.123	-13.322	(0.000)
	0.20	-1.533***	0.092	-16.649	(0.000)
	0.30	-1.299***	0.046	-28.186	(0.000)
	0.40	-1.258***	0.048	-26.012	(0.000)
	0.50	-1.238***	0.054	-22.935	(0.000)
	0.60	-1.098***	0.051	-21.625	(0.000)
	0.70	-1.048***	0.045	-23.073	(0.000)

continued on following page

Table 17. Continued

	Quantile	Coefficient	Std. Error	t-Statistic	Prob.
	0.80	-0.973***	0.049	-20.011	(0.000)
	0.90	-0.987***	0.154	-6.413	(0.000)
C	0.10	-5.896	6.185	-0.953	(0.341)
	0.20	-0.662	5.947	-0.111	(0.911)
	0.30	-6.385	3.582	-1.782	(0.075)
	0.40	-2.731	3.311	-0.825	(0.410)
	0.50	-3.358	3.273	-1.026	(0.305)
	0.60	-0.4727	3.950	-0.109	(0.905)
	0.70	1.762	3.550	0.4964	(0.619)
	0.80	-1.596	3.503	-0.456	(0.649)
	0.90	-0.826	3.814	-0.217	(0.829)
Wald Test	83.423*** (0.000)				

Source: Own elaboration.

Notes***- the variable has statistical significance at 1%, **- the variable has statistical significance at 5%, and *- the variable has statistical significance at 10%.

Table 18. Model 4 with Poisson Pseudo Maximum Likelihood

Variable	Coefficient	Std. Error	t-Statistic	Prob.
LogTARIFF	-0.155**	0.065	-2.390	(0.017)
LogGDP$_T$	0.907***	0.276	3.290	(0.001)
LogGDP$_K$	0.025**	0.010	2.470	(0.014)
LogDISTANCE	-0.372***	0.018	-26.880	(0.000)
C	-1.404	1.189	-1.180	(0.238)
Adjusted R-squared	0.581			
Observations	480			

Source: Own elaboration.

Notes***- the variable has statistical significance at 1; *- the variable has statistical significance at 10%.

FUTHER RESEARCH

In terms of perspectives for future work, it will be interesting to test the effect of the gravity model on Portuguese revealed comparative advantages, using, for example, the index of Balassa (1965, 1966) and the index of Grubel and Lloyd

(1975) to consider the intra-industry trade and disaggregate intra-industry trade into horizontal intra-industry trade (HIIT) and vertical intra-industry (VIIT), as in previous studies by Crespo & Fontoura (2004), Faustino & Leitão (2007), Leitão et al., (2010) and Faustino & Leitão (2011). The theme of differentiation of similar quality products, referred to by HIIT as different types of quality (VIIT) continues to have an impact on the study of economic integration processes, international trade and the international economy, namely the effect not only of standard trade agreements on exports or imports, but also on total bilateral trade, or intra-industry trade. However, as these studies demonstrate, the methodology of Greenaway et al., (1995) inflates intra-industry trade, namely vertical differentiation. One solution could be to evaluate the global supply chain trade and the gravity model, as this allows us to evaluate parts and components and final products, thus allowing us to analyse fragmentation or outsourcing (e.g., Greaney & Kiyota 2020; Fertő et al., 2022). Furthermore, most empirical studies that use gravity model arguments do not frequently use the impact of tariffs on international trade in econometric models. However, as mentioned in this research, some databases such as CEPII (Centre d'Informations Internationales), the World Bank Indicators, and Macrotrends allow this variable's use in the gravity equation.

Another interesting and emerging area is the study of digital trade (e.g., Mirzaye & Mohiuddin, 2025; Li & Wang, 2024). Indeed, digital trade enables reduced transaction and transportation costs, thereby maximising profits through digital services and transactions. However, published secondary data on digital trade remains fragile, i.e., few international organisations, such as the World Trade Organisation (WTO) or the OECD, publish this information in the form of a digital trade index. In this context, it may be worthwhile to examine this topic considering the concepts of production fragmentation and global value chains, particularly within the context of tariff and non-tariff barriers.

CONCLUSION AND POLICY RECOMMENDATIONS

As we referred, this research sought to formulate four equations with different objectives. In the first equation, we develop a model focusing on bilateral trade and the arguments of the gravity model, where the assumptions of the Ricardo and Heckscher-Ohlin model are presented. The following equations consider the effects of scale economies, common borders, geographical distance, standard trade agreements, common religion, geographical distance, and tariff rates.

The arguments of historical and cultural aspects are determinants of international trade. The literature (Gould, 1994; Geldner, 2024; Leitão, 2023; Zapata et al., 2023) demonstrates that borders, geographical proximity, trade agreements, and common religion are agents that promote international trade. Trade agreements and a common religion stimulate bilateral relations between countries, reducing transaction and transport costs. The bibliometric analysis demonstrated that the keywords most used in this study are international trade, trade costs, gravity model, trade flow, and cost analysis. The variables used, such as economies of scale, common borders and trade agreements aim to evaluate comparative advantages compared to other nations.

The study of Feruni & Hysa (2020) used the gravity model by Albania's experience and their fifteen trade partners. The authors applied the Random Effects estimator to the equation for exports and imports and showed that economic size positively impacts trade. Besides, the geographical distance demonstrated that it is negatively correlated with trade.

The literature considers them agents that reduce asymmetries between the member countries of that geographical space. As can be seen, cultural affinities cannot be dissociated from globalization, internationalization, and the process of regionalization on a global scale. As can be seen, this reality is intrinsically associated with several areas of knowledge, namely economics, geography, political science, law and issues of sovereignty and culture. Hence, in most empirical studies on the gravity model, the problems of colonies or former colonies are part of the econometric model. Thus, trade flows are associated with cultural, political, and social aspects, which, as already mentioned, translate into phenomena of acculturation and the reduction of regional asymmetries, which have implications for the international order.

Regarding the tariff rates, the empirical studies by Hayakawa & Yoshimi (2023), Jack et al., (2008), and Masku et al., (2001) showed that the use of tariffs and commercial instruments decreases bilateral trade.

In the results discussion section, we seek to discuss the impact of economies of scale, adjacency costs, geographical distance, common religion, and tariff rates on Portuguese international trade.

The results are also based on empirical studies using different estimators (quantile regressions and Poisson Pseudo Maximum Likelihood PPML). Furthermore, the variables used in the different models do not present multicollinearity, as demonstrated in the empirical study.

This study identified that the most recent studies for the Portuguese economy have focused more on the potential of exports (e.g., Leitão 2023; Pacheco & Matos, 2022; Fernandes & Forte, 2022; Gouveia et al., 2018), that is, it was identified the need to seek to analyze total bilateral trade.

The econometric results found by total trade have some implications for economic policy and can be helpful to policymakers. Below, we present some implications that may be useful for the government and for Portuguese trade policy.

The economy of scales is an important strategic instrument for promoting international trade. This assumption should deal with the internalization process via international trade. As referred, the empirical studies of Leitão (2023), Pacheco & Matos (20222) and Fernandes & Forte (2022) give support to our results. A Border, namely Spain, shows that it is an important partner in Portuguese total bilateral trade. The studies of Martin-Mayoral et al., (2015) and Reina et al., (2024) argue that border is directly associated with bilateral trade. Thus, it is clear that geographical and cultural proximity promote international trade.

The variable of geographical distance is negatively correlated with total bilateral trade; this result reflects once again the importance of the geographical proximity of markets to decrease transport and transaction costs. The monopolistic models such as Krugman (1979) and Lancaster (1980) support this result. Transportation and transaction costs affect trade flows and may result in a decrease in bilateral trade between trading partners.

The common religion can be an agent of the reduction of logistical and communication costs. Our results have support for studies of Balog & Leitão (2019), Nadal & Gallego (2022) and Bergstrand & Clance (2023). The common religion also helps to stimulate Portuguese commercial trade, reducing transport costs.

As well as the studies of Hayakawa & Yoshimi (2023), Jack et al., (2008), Masku et al., (2001), Beghin & Bureau (2001) and Disdier et al., (2015), our research demonstrates that commercial instruments, namely tariff rates decrease the bilateral trade between trade partners.

From the results presented, it is possible to infer some impacts on economic policy, society, and economic diplomacy. Therefore, Portuguese-speaking member countries must continue to develop cooperation agreements to reduce transport costs and promote similar policies and interests.

REFERENCES

Abdi, H. A., Zaidi, M. A. S., & Karim, Z. A. (2023). Economic complexity and trade flows in selected COMESA and Asia countries. *Technological and Economic Development of Economy*, *29*(3), 188–205. DOI: 10.3846/tede.2023.18682

Anderson, J. E., & van Wincoop, E. (2003). Gravity with Gravitas: A Solution to the Border Puzzle. *The American Economic Review*, *93*(1), 170–192. DOI: 10.1257/000282803321455214

Balassa, B. (1965). Trade Liberalization and Revealed Comparative Advantage. *Manchester School*, *33*(2), 99–123. DOI: 10.1111/j.1467-9957.1965.tb00050.x

Balassa, B. (1966). Tariff Reductions and Trade in Manufactures Among Industrial Countries. *The American Economic Review*, *56*, 466–473.

Balogh, J. M., & Aguiar, M. B. (2022). Determinants of Latin American and the Caribbean Agricultural Trade: A Gravity Model Approach. *Zemedelská Ekonomika*, *68*(4), 127–136. DOI: 10.17221/405/2021-AGRICECON

Balogh, J. M., & Leitão, N. C. (2019). A Gravity Approach of Agricultural Trade: The Nexus of the EU and African, Caribbean and Pacific Countries. *Zemedelská Ekonomika*, *65*(11), 509–519. DOI: 10.17221/131/2019-AGRICECON

Beghin, J., & Bureau, J. C. (2001). Quantification of Sanitary, Phytosanitary, and Technical Barriers To Trade for Trade Policy Analysis. Iowa State University, Center for Agricultural and Rural Development *Working Paper 01-WP-291*.

Bergstrand, J. H., & Clance, M. W. (2023). and Matthew W. Clance, Quantile Gravity: Economic Integration Agreements, Least Traded Goods, and Least Developed Economies, September 2023, *Working Papers*.

Breton, A. (1999). *Exploring the Economics of Language*. New Canadian Perspectives, Canadian Heritage.

Capoani, L. (2023). Review of the Gravity Model: Origins and Critical Analysis of its Theoretical Development. *SN Business & Economics*, *3*(5), 95. DOI: 10.1007/s43546-023-00461-0

Capoani, L. (2024). The Gravity Equation in International Trade: An Overview of the Introduction of Gravity to the Study of Economics and Its Systematic Barriers. *European Journal of the History of Economic Thought*, *31*(3), 487–520. DOI: 10.1080/09672567.2024.2329064

CEPII. (*Centre d'Informations Internationales) GeoDist* Database. Notes on CEPII's distances measures: The GeoDist database Thierry Mayer & Soledad Zignago (2011). No 2011- 25 December DOCUMENT DE TRAVAIL. Available at: https://www.cepii.fr/cepii/en/bdd_modele/bdd_modele_item.asp?id=6

Chen, Y., Ma, Q., & Tao, R. (2024). Addressing the fixed effects in gravity model based on higher-order origin destination pairs. *International Journal of Geographical Information Science*. Advance online publication. DOI: 10.1080/13658816.2024.2343763

Chernozhukov, V., Fernández-Val, I., & Weidner, M. (2024). Network and Panel Quantile Effects via Distribution Regression. *Journal of Econometrics*, *240*(2), 105009. DOI: 10.1016/j.jeconom.2020.08.009

Crespo, N., & Fontoura, M. (2004). Intra-industry Trade by Types: What Can We Learn from Portuguese data? *Review of World Economics*, *140*(1), 53–79. DOI: 10.1007/BF02659710

Disdier, A. C., Fontagné, L., & Mimouni, M. (2015). Tariff Liberalization and Trade Integration of Emerging Countries. *Review of International Economics*, *23*(5), 946–971. DOI: 10.1111/roie.12198

Doanh, N. K., & Heo, Y. (2018). Horizontal Intra-industry Trade in Korea: A Dynamic Panel Data Analysis. *Journal of International Logistics and Trade*, *16*(1), 1–10. DOI: 10.24006/jilt.2018.16.1.1

Egger, P. H., Li, J., & Ouyang, J. (2024). Taking Grubel and Lloyd to Dance in the City: Domestic Intra-Industry Trade in China. *Economics Letters*, *244*, 111925. DOI: 10.1016/j.econlet.2024.111925

Egger, P. H., & Staub, K. E. (2016). GLM Estimation of Trade Gravity Models with Fixed Effects. *Empirical Economics*, *50*(1), 137–175. DOI: 10.1007/s00181-015-0935-x

Faustino, H. C., & Leitão, N. C. (2007). Intra-Industry-Trade: A Static and Dynamic Panel Data Analysis. *International Advances in Economic Research*, *13*(3), 313–333. DOI: 10.1007/s11294-007-9097-8

Faustino, H. C., & Leitão, N. C. (2011). Fragmentation in the Automobile Manufacturing Industry: Evidence from Portugal. *Journal of Economic Studies (Glasgow, Scotland)*, *38*(3), 287–300. DOI: 10.1108/01443581111152409

Fernandes, A., & Forte, R. (2022). The Impact of Economic Diplomacy on Exports: The Portuguese Case. *International Journal (Toronto, Ont.)*, *77*(2), 216–247. DOI: 10.1177/00207020221135382

Fertő, I., Kheyirkhabarli, M., & Sass, M. (2022). Gravity Models with TiVA Data: Do They Bring New Results? *Applied Economics Letters*, *31*(8), 702–705. DOI: 10.1080/13504851.2022.2145010

Feruni, N., & Hysa, E. (2020). Free Trade and Gravity Model: Albania as Part of Central European Free Trade Agreement (CEFTA). In Christiansen, B., & Shuwaikh, F. (Eds.), *Theoretical and Applied Mathematics in International Business* (pp. 60–90). IGI Global Scientific Publishing., DOI: 10.4018/978-1-5225-8458-2.ch004

Gandou, A., K., S. & Sönmez, A. (2023). The Role of Industrialization in Trade: A Panel Data Gravity Model Analysis on ECOWAS Countries (1995-2020*). Jass Studies-The Journal of Academic Social Science Studies*, 16(98), 395 414. DOI: 10.29228/JASSS.72786

Geldner, T. (2024). Exchange Rates and Trade Balance Dynamics: A Quantile Regression Analysis. *Applied Economics.* Advance online publication. DOI: 10.1080/00036846.2024.2311067

Gould, D. (1994). Immigrant Links to The Home Country: Empirical Implications for U.S. Bilateral Trade Flows. *The Review of Economics and Statistics*, *76*(2), 302–316. DOI: 10.2307/2109884

Gouveia, S., Rebelo, J., & Lourenço-Gomes, L. (2018). Port Wine Exports: A Gravity Model Approach. *International Journal of Wine Business Research*, *30*(2), 218–242. DOI: 10.1108/IJWBR-02-2017-0008

Greaney, T. M., & Kiyota, K. (2020). The Gravity Model and Trade in Intermediate Inputs. *World Economy*, *43*(8), 2034–2049. DOI: 10.1111/twec.12947

Greenaway, D., Hine, R., & Milner, C. (1995). Vertical and horizontal intra-industry trade: A Cross Industry Analysis for the United Kingdom. *Economic Journal (London)*, *105*(433), 1505–1518. DOI: 10.2307/2235113

Grubel, H. G., & Lloyd, P. J. (1975). *Intra-Industry Trade: The Theory and Measurement of International Trade in Differentiated Products*. Macmillan Press.

Hayakawa, K., & Yoshimi, T. (2023). Tariff Rates in Gravity. *The Journal of International Trade & Economic Development*, *33*(8), 1477–1494. DOI: 10.1080/09638199.2023.2277779

Heckscher, E., & Ohlin, B. (1933). *International and Inter-Regional Trade*. Harvard University Press.

Isard, W. (1969). Some Notes on the Linkage of the Ecologic and Economic Systems. *Papers in Regional Science*, *22*(1), 85–96. DOI: 10.1111/j.1435-5597.1969.tb01455.x

Jadhav, S., & Ghosh, I. (2024). Future Prospects of the Gravity Model of Trade: A Bibliometric Review (1993–2021). *Foreign Trade Review, 59*(1), 26–61. DOI: 10.1177/00157325221140154

Jámbor, A., Balogh, J., & Kucsera, P. (2016). Country and Industry Specific Determinants of Intra-Industry Agri-Food Trade in the Baltic Countries. *Agricultural Economic Czech*, 62, 2016 (6): 280–291. DOI: 10.17221/153/2015-AGRICECON

Jones, R., & Kierzkowski, H. (1990). The role of services in production and international trade: A theoretical framework. In Jones, R., & Krueger, A. (Eds.), *The political economy of international trade: Festschrift in Honor of Robert Baldwin*. Basil Blackwell.

Khati, P., & Kim, C. (2022). Impact of India's free trade agreement with ASEAN on its goods exports: A gravity model analysis. *Economies, 11*(1), 1–19. DOI: 10.3390/economies11010008

Krugman, P. (1979). Increasing Returns, Monopolistic Competition, and International Trade. *Journal of International Economics, 9*(4), 469–479. DOI: 10.1016/0022-1996(79)90017-5

Krugman, P. (1991). Increasing Returns and Economic Geography. *Journal of Political Economy, 99*(3), 483–499. DOI: 10.1086/261763

Kunroo, M. A., & Ahmad, I. (2023). Heckscher-Ohlin Theory or the Modern Trade Theory: How the Overall Trade Characterizes at the Global Level? *Journal of Quantitative Economics, 21*(1), 151–174. DOI: 10.1007/s40953-022-00330-x

Lancaster, K. (1980). Intra-Industry Trade under Perfect Monopolistic Competition. *Journal of International Economics, 10*(2), 151–175. DOI: 10.1016/0022-1996(80)90052-5

Leitão, N. C. (2023). The Impact of Geopolitical Risk on Portuguese Exports. *Economies, 11*(12), 291. DOI: 10.3390/economies11120291

Leitão, N. C. (2024). Gravity Model and International Trade: A Survey of Literature. *Administrative Sciences, 14*(9), 219. DOI: 10.3390/admsci14090219

Leitão, N. C., Faustino, H., & Yoshida, Y. (2010). Fragmentation, Vertical Intra-industry Trade, and Automobile Components. *Economic Bulletin, 30*, 1006–1015.

Li, J., & Wang, F. (2024). A Study on the Competitiveness and Influencing Factors of the Digital Service Trade. *Sustainability (Basel), 16*(8), 3116. DOI: 10.3390/su16083116

Macrotrends (2025). Portugal Tariff Rates 1988-2025. Available at: https://www.macrotrends.net/global-metrics/countries/PRT/portugal/tariff-rates

Martin-Mayoral, F., Carofilis, G. M., & Guijarro, J. C. (2016). The Effects of Integration Agreements in Western Hemisphere trade, 1970–2014. *The Journal of International Trade & Economic Development*, *25*(5), 724–756. DOI: 10.1080/09638199.2015.1125519

Masood, S., Khurshid, N., Haider, M., Khurshid, J., & Khokhar, A. M. (2023). Trade Potential of Pakistan with the South Asian Countries: A Gravity Model Approach. *Asia Pacific Management Review*, *28*(1), 45–51. DOI: 10.1016/j.apmrv.2022.02.001

Mirzaye, S., & Mohiuddin, M. (2025). Digital Transformation in International Trade: Opportunities, Challenges, and Policy Implications. *Journal of Risk and Financial Management*, *18*(8), 421. DOI: 10.3390/jrfm18080421

Nadal, J. R., & Gallego, M. S. (2022). Gravity Models for Tourism Demand Modeling: Empirical Review and Outlook. *Journal of Economic Surveys*, *36*(5), 1358–1409. https://wileyonlinelibrary.com/journal/joes. DOI: 10.1111/joes.12502

Pacheco, L. M., & Matos, A. P. (2022). Foreign Presence and Export Performance: The Role of Portuguese Commercial Diplomacy. *The International Trade Journal*, *36*(2), 147–169. DOI: 10.1080/08853908.2021.1907262

Pöyhönen, P. (1963). A Tentative Model for the Volume of Trade between Countries. *Weltwirtschaftliches Archiv*, *90*, 93–100. https://www.jstor.org/stable/40436776

Reina, J. C., Cuaresma, J. C., Fenz, K., Zellmann, J., Yankov, T., & Taha, A. (2024). Gravity Models for Global Migration Flows: A Predictive Evaluation. *Population Research and Policy Review*, *43*(2), 29. DOI: 10.1007/s11113-024-09867-6

Ricardo, D. (1817) *The Theory of Comparative Advantage*. In: Ricardo, D., Vol. 1 Ed. By Pierro Sraffa with Collaboration of M.H. Dobb, Principles of Political Economy and Taxation, Cambridge University Press, Cambridge, London.

Santos-Silva, J. M. C., & Tenreyro, S. (2006). The Log of Gravity. *The Review of Economics and Statistics*, *88*(4), 641–658. DOI: 10.1162/rest.88.4.641

Santos Silva, J. M. C., & Tenreyro, S. (2011). Further Simulation Evidence on the Performance of the Poisson Pseudo-Maximum Likelihood Estimator. *Economics Letters*, *112*(2), 220–222. DOI: 10.1016/j.econlet.2011.05.008

Sharma, P., Rohatgi, S., & Jasuja, D. (2022). Scientific Mapping of Gravity Model of International Trade Literature: A Bibliometric Analysis. *Journal of Scientometric Research*, *11*(3), 447–457. DOI: 10.5530/jscires.11.3.48

Smith, A. (1776). *The Wealth of Nations*. W. strahan and T. Cadell, London.

Statistical Portugal (2024). Instituto Nacional de Estatística (INE), and PORDATA-International Trade in Goods Statistics.

Stavytskyy, A., Kharlamova, G., Giedraitis, V., & Sengul, E. C. (2019). Gravity model analysis of globalization process in transition economies. *Journal of International Students*, *12*(2), 322–341. DOI: 10.14254/2071-8330.2019/12-2/21

Thu, L. A., Fang, S., & Kessani, S. S. (2019). Factors influencing Vietnam's handicraft export with the gravity model. *Journal of Economic Development*, *21*(2), 156–171. DOI: 10.1108/JED-08-2019-0021

Tinbergen, J. (1962). *Shaping the world economy; Suggestions for an international economic policy*. Twentieth Century Fund.

Venables, A. J. (2006). Shifts in Economic Geography and their Causes. CEP Discussion Paper No 767. 1-21.

World Bank. (2024). World Development Indicators (WDI). Available at: https://data.worldbank.org/indicator

Zapata, A. N., Vacas, M. A., & Payá, J. H. (2023). Drivers of Technological Export Performance in Spain: A Regional Approach, 2000–2016. *Regional Statistics*, *13*(6), 997–1025. DOI: 10.15196/RS130601

ADDITIONAL READING

Saxena, R., Pant, D. K., Singh, A., Sharma, P., & Pant, S. C. (2024). How Far India has Succeeded in Harnessing its Export Potential in Rice? *Evidence Using Stochastic Frontier Gravity Model. The Journal of International Trade & Economic Development*, •••, 1–21. DOI: 10.1080/09638199.2024.2381790

Song, J. C., & Ekoula, H. (2024, October 28). W., M., A. (2024). Does Financial Integration Contribute to Bilateral Trade in Africa: An Empirical Investigation by the Augmented Gravity Model. *Journal of the Knowledge Economy*, *16*(3), 12078–12117. Advance online publication. DOI: 10.1007/s13132-024-02309-w

Tang, C., Rosland, A., Li, J., & Yasmeen, R. (2023). The Comparison of Bilateral Trade between China and ASEAN, China and EU: From the Aspect of Trade Structure, Trade Complementarity and Structural Gravity Model of Trade. *Applied Economics*, *56*(9), 1077–1089. DOI: 10.1080/00036846.2023.2174940

Taralashvili, T. (2024). How Interstate soft Conflicts Affect Bilateral Migration: Results from a Structural Gravity Model. *Inter Economics*, *179*, 100522. DOI: 10.1016/j.inteco.2024.100522

KEY TERMS AND DEFINITIONS

Comparative Advantages: The Heckscher-Ohlin model introduced the concept and was later disseminated by the various indicators of revealed comparative advantages, the best known being that of Bela Balassa. Although its theoretical construction is based on a structure of markets in perfect competition, the concept continues to be helpful in international economics in explaining the specialization of economies.

Fragmentation: Fragmentation, also known as outsourcing, allows us to explain the importance of specialization in economies and the relationship between the parts and components of products and the final products that have developed an interest in the academic community. Fragmentation adapted classical and neoclassical international trade theories to explain vertical product differentiation.

Gravity Model: The assumptions of Newton's laws of physics were introduced the gravity model into the Economics and Economic Geography models. Generally, geographical distance is negatively impacted by trade flows.

Intra-Industry Trade: The various definitions of intra-industry trade all state that the coexistence of exports and imports of the sector or product explains this type of trade. This type of trade is explained by monopolistic competition, price differentiation and economies of scale.

Chapter 4
Enhancing Economic Cooperation and Trade Integration in SAARC Countries

Mallika Roy
http://orcid.org/0000-0002-5854-5084
Central Queensland University, Australia & University of Chittagong, Bangladesh

Khaleda Begum Maiful
http://orcid.org/0009-0007-8685-6393
University of Chittagong, Bangladesh

ABSTRACT

Economic cooperation plays a vital role in fostering sustainable growth, promoting trade, and enhancing mutual prosperity among nations within a region. This chapter explores economic cooperation within the South Asian Association for Regional Cooperation (SAARC), focusing on trade agreements, investments, and regional integration. Established in 1985, SAARC aimed to promote economic integration through initiatives like the South Asian Free Trade Area (SAFTA). Despite efforts to reduce tariffs and boost intra-regional trade, challenges such as geopolitical tensions, infrastructure deficiencies, and regulatory barriers have impeded progress. The chapter highlights opportunities to strengthen regional cooperation by improving trade agreements, developing infrastructure, promoting sustainable economic practices, and embracing digital trade. It also discusses the role of foreign

DOI: 10.4018/979-8-3373-1782-3.ch004

direct investment (FDI) and external trade partnerships. The chapter concludes with policy recommendations to enhance economic integration and foster long-term growth in South Asia.

1. INTRODUCTION

1.1 Background

The South Asian Association for Regional Cooperation (SAARC) was established in 1985 to promote economic and regional integration among its eight member states: Afghanistan, Bangladesh, Bhutan, India, Maldives, Nepal, Pakistan, and Sri Lanka. One of the key initiatives aimed at fostering trade cooperation among SAARC nations was the South Asian Free Trade Area (SAFTA) agreement. The South Asian Free Trade Area (SAFTA) agreement, signed in 2004 by SAARC nations, aimed to create a free trade area of 1.8 billion people and reduce customs duties to zero by 2016 (Akram et al., 2014). It was designed to reduce tariffs and promote cross-border trade, yet its implementation has been hindered by political tensions, non-tariff barriers (NTBs), and inadequate infrastructure (Hertel & Mirza, 2009). While SAFTA was expected to promote intra-regional trade through tariff reductions and dismantling of non-tariff barriers (Hirantha, 2004), recent studies suggest that neither SAFTA nor its predecessor SAPTA have significantly increased intra-regional trade (Gaurav & Bharti, 2019). South Asia remains one of the least integrated regions globally, with trade at less than one-third of its potential (Ali & Mufti, 2020). Intra-regional trade within SAARC remains significantly lower than that of other regional blocs, accounting for only about 5% of the total trade volume, compared to 25% in Association of Southeast Asian Nations-ASEAN and over 60% in the European Union-EU (Kathuria, 2018).

Foreign direct investment (FDI) in the SAARC region has been unevenly distributed, with India receiving a significant portion of inflows (Sahoo et al., 2014). Macroeconomic and institutional factors play crucial roles in attracting FDI to SAARC countries, including Gross Domestic Product-GDP, financial development, infrastructure, and political stability (Kumar et al., 2025). Despite the potential benefits of FDI for economic development, the experience among SAARC countries has been mixed (Erum et al., 2016). Inward FDI stock has been found to have a negative and statistically significant impact on income inequality in selected SAARC countries (Mushtaq et al., 2014). Regional integration arrangements can reduce trade costs and stimulate FDI flow among partner countries (Alam & Zubayer, 2010). However, intra-regional FDI flow within SAARC remains low compared to outward flow, despite the potential for increased intra-regional investment (Alam & Zubayer, 2010).

Challenges include irrational sensitive lists, non-tariff and para-tariff barriers, weak infrastructure, and lack of political will (Ali & Mufti, 2020). To enhance intra-regional trade, SAARC countries should accelerate tariff cuts, reduce items in sensitive lists, eliminate non-tariff barriers, and facilitate cross-border movement of people and goods (Ali & Mufti, 2020; Gaurav & Bharti, 2019).

1.2 Significance of Economic Cooperation and Trade Integration

Economic cooperation and trade integration within SAARC are crucial for enhancing regional stability, economic growth, and poverty reduction. Despite the geographical proximity and shared cultural heritage, intra-regional trade remains significantly low compared to other regional blocs. Strengthening trade and investment ties can reduce economic disparities, improve market efficiency, and create employment opportunities. Moreover, overcoming political and regulatory barriers can facilitate seamless trade flows, reduce transaction costs, and attract foreign direct investment (FDI), ultimately contributing to sustainable economic development. Digital and financial integration also play a vital role in fostering cross-border transactions and enhancing financial accessibility across SAARC nations.

1.3 Research Objective and Key Questions

The main objective of this study is to analyse the barriers, opportunities, and policy measures needed for enhancing economic cooperation and trade integration in SAARC countries. To address this the following research questions have been considered:

- What are the primary barriers hindering intra-regional trade and investment among SAARC nations?
- How can trade facilitation measures and policy reforms improve economic integration in the SAARC region?
- What role does financial and digital integration play in enhancing economic cooperation among SAARC countries?

2. THEORETICAL FOUNDATION

Economic cooperation and trade integration in SAARC countries can be analysed through two key theoretical frameworks: Regional Integration Theory and

Gravity Model of Trade. These theories provide a foundation for understanding the challenges and opportunities associated with economic collaboration in South Asia.

2.1 Regional Integration Theory

Regional Integration Theory explains how and why countries form regional economic alliances to enhance trade, investment, and overall economic growth. According to Balassa (1961), regional integration follows a hierarchical process, progressing from a preferential trade agreement to a full economic and political union. In the context of SAARC, this theory helps explain the objectives of agreements like the South Asian Free Trade Area (SAFTA) and the role of institutions like the SAARC Development Fund (SDF) in fostering cooperation. However, political tensions, regulatory disparities, and trust deficits among SAARC nations have hindered deeper integration, limiting the success of SAFTA. This theory highlights the importance of reducing trade barriers, harmonizing policies, and fostering political activity will for successful economic integration.

2.2 Gravity Model of Trade

The Gravity Model of Trade (Tinbergen, 1962) posits that trade flows between two countries are directly proportional to their economic size (GDP) and inversely proportional to the distance between them. This model has been widely used to assess trade potential and the impact of trade agreements, including SAFTA. In the SAARC region, studies using this model (e.g., Rodríguez-Delgado, 2007; Gaurav & Bharti, 2019) indicate that intra-regional trade remains significantly below its potential due to high trade costs, non-tariff barriers, and infrastructural challenges. The model suggests that improving trade facilitation measures, reducing sensitive lists, and investing in regional infrastructure could enhance trade flows among SAARC countries. Additionally, the Gravity Model emphasizes the role of cross-border investment and financial integration in strengthening economic cooperation.

Figure 1. Theoretical foundation of this study

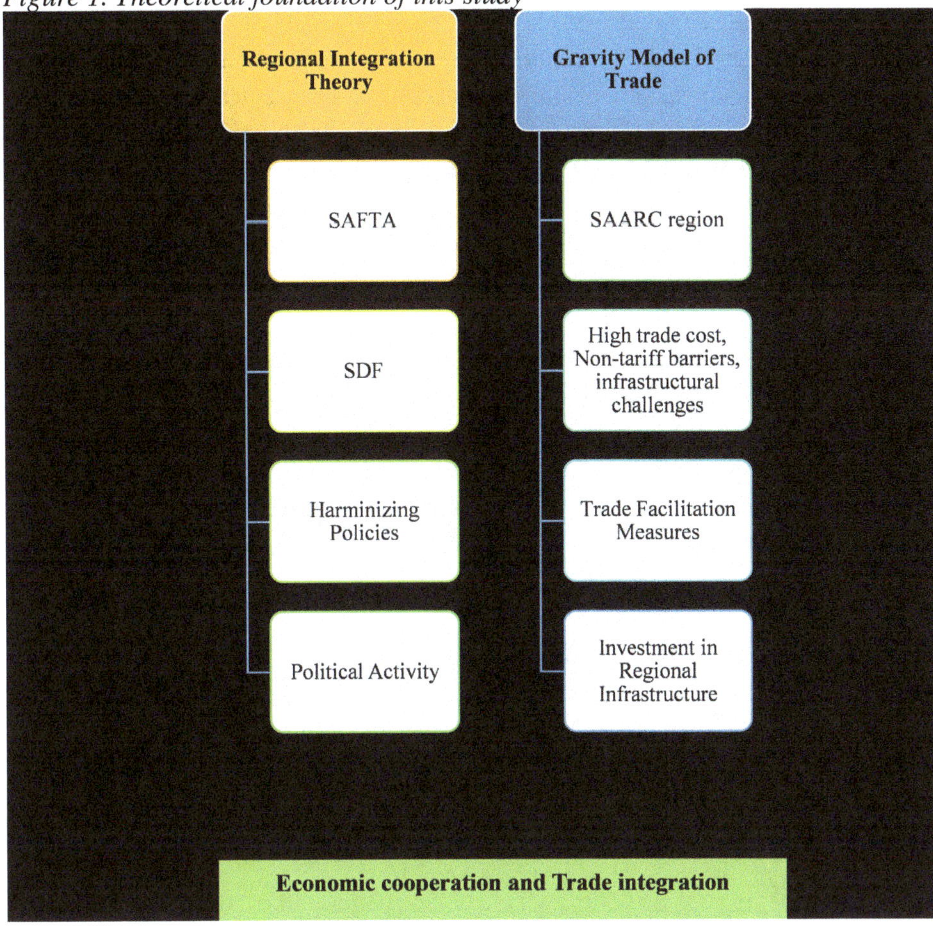

Theories of Regional Integration and the Gravity Model of Trade provide a robust conceptual foundation for the study (Figure 1). Regional Integration Theory explains the structural stages through which countries collaborate economically, offering insight into SAARC's efforts such as SAFTA and the SAARC Development Fund. It underscores the need for policy harmonization, trust-building, and political commitment to overcome persistent barriers to deeper integration. Complementing this, the Gravity Model of Trade offers an empirical lens to assess trade performance and potential within the region, highlighting how economic size and proximity should naturally foster greater trade—yet remain underutilized due to trade costs, infrastructural deficits, and non-tariff barriers. Together, these theories inform the study's framework by illustrating both the aspirational and practical pathways to enhance regional trade and economic cooperation in South Asia.

3. METHODOLOGY

To analyse the key themes and trends in economic cooperation and trade integration in SAARC countries, a systematic literature review was conducted in multiple stages.

3.1 Stage 1: Initial Search in Scopus

The first step involved searching for relevant literature in Scopus, using the following Boolean search query:

("SAARC" OR "South Asia") AND ("trade integration" OR "economic cooperation")

This search yielded a total of 183 documents. Among them, 3 were in Chinese, 2 in Russian, and 1 in Spanish, which were excluded to maintain consistency in language. After limiting the selection to English-language studies, the final dataset comprised 177 documents. The publication range for these studies spanned from 1981 to 2025, covering more than four decades of research on regional economic integration.

3.2 Stage 2: Keyword Co-Occurrence Analysis Using VOSviewer

To identify the dominant themes and research trends, a co-occurrence analysis was performed using VOSviewer, a bibliometric mapping tool. This analysis helped cluster key concepts and terms frequently used in the literature, revealing major themes such as:

- Trade agreements and regional cooperation
- Geopolitical influences on trade
- Sustainability and renewable energy
- Foreign direct investment and economic development
- Comparative regionalism (SAARC vs. BIMSTEC (Bay of Bengal Initiative for Multi-Sectoral Technical and Economic Cooperation), EU, etc.)

3.3 Stage 3: Systematic Review and Extended Search

Building upon the findings from VOSviewer, a systematic review was designed to refine the search further and include high-quality studies. Additional searches were conducted in the following databases:

- Scopus

- ScienceDirect
- Web of Science
- Google Scholar

This extended search aimed to capture relevant studies that were not included in the initial Scopus dataset. A total of 145 studies were identified as relevant to the review, providing deeper insights into economic cooperation and trade integration in the SAARC region.

By integrating bibliometric analysis and systematic review methodologies, this study offers a comprehensive understanding of existing research and highlights key policy and economic implications for regional trade.

3.4 PRISMA Diagram

This study will employ a systematic review approach using the PRISMA (Preferred Reporting Items for Systematic Reviews and Meta-Analyses) framework. The research will involve a comprehensive analysis of academic literature from databases such as Scopus, Web of Science, and Google Scholar, focusing on peer-reviewed articles, policy papers, and government reports. The inclusion criteria will be studies related to SAARC trade, economic integration, FDI, and regional agreements. Data extraction and synthesis will follow PRISMA guidelines to ensure methodological rigor, transparency, and replicability.

A total of 2653 records were identified through database searching. After removing duplicates, 2308 records remained and were screened for relevance (See Figure 2). Of these, 2152 records were excluded based on title and abstract screening. The full texts of 156 articles were assessed for eligibility, resulting in 123 articles being excluded with reasons such as irrelevance to the research objectives, insufficient data, or not meeting inclusion criteria. Ultimately, 33 studies were included in the qualitative synthesis.

Figure 2. PRISMA diagram

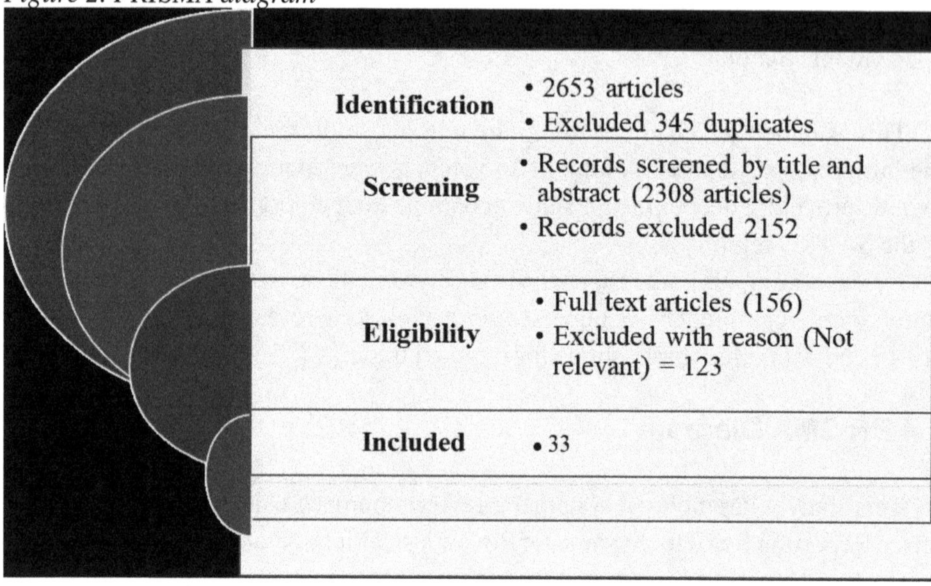

4. FINDINGS AND ANALYSIS

4.1 Bibliometric Analysis

4.1.1 Evolution of the Studies

The following figure explores the temporal trends in the dataset, aiming to uncover patterns and shifts in occurrences over the years, which may shed light on underlying influences or changing dynamics in the subject under investigation.

The data represents the distribution of occurrences across different years, showing fluctuations in frequency over time (Figure 3). The results indicate that the highest number of occurrences occurred in 2020, 2024, and 2021, each with 13 instances.

Figure 3. Evolution of the studies

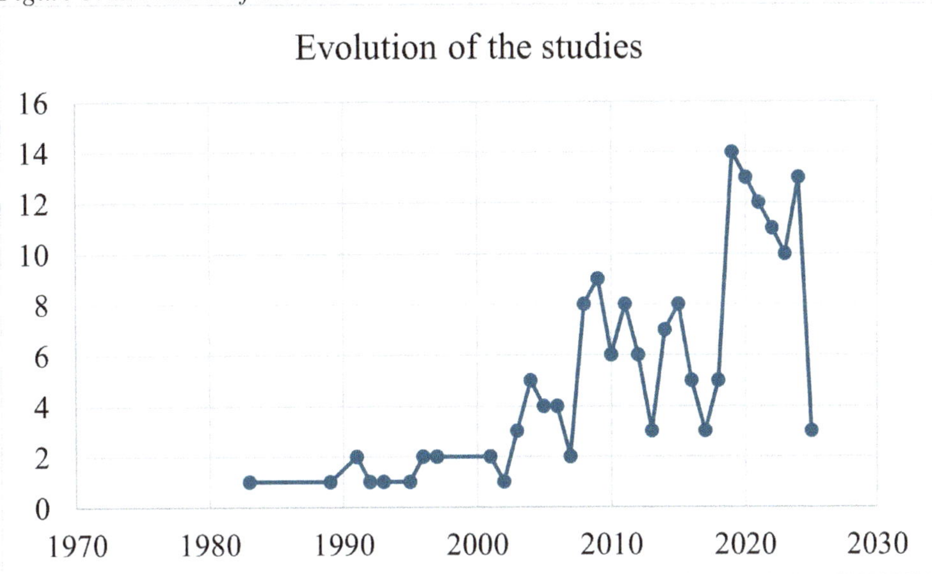

The lowest frequencies were observed in 1992, 1993, 1995, and 2002, each with a single occurrence. The analysis reveals a general pattern of increasing frequencies in more recent years, particularly in the 2010s and 2020s, suggesting an upward trend or changing dynamics over time. Such trends can offer valuable insights into the temporal shifts in the area of focus, potentially reflecting evolving societal, technological, or environmental factors.

4.1.2 Influential Keywords

All Keywords

The co-occurrence network visualization highlights key themes related to economic cooperation and trade integration in SAARC countries through different keyword clusters. The analysis can be categorized into distinct thematic areas, each represented by a cluster of interrelated concepts (Figure 4).

Figure 4. Mapping Research Themes through Keyword Co-occurrences

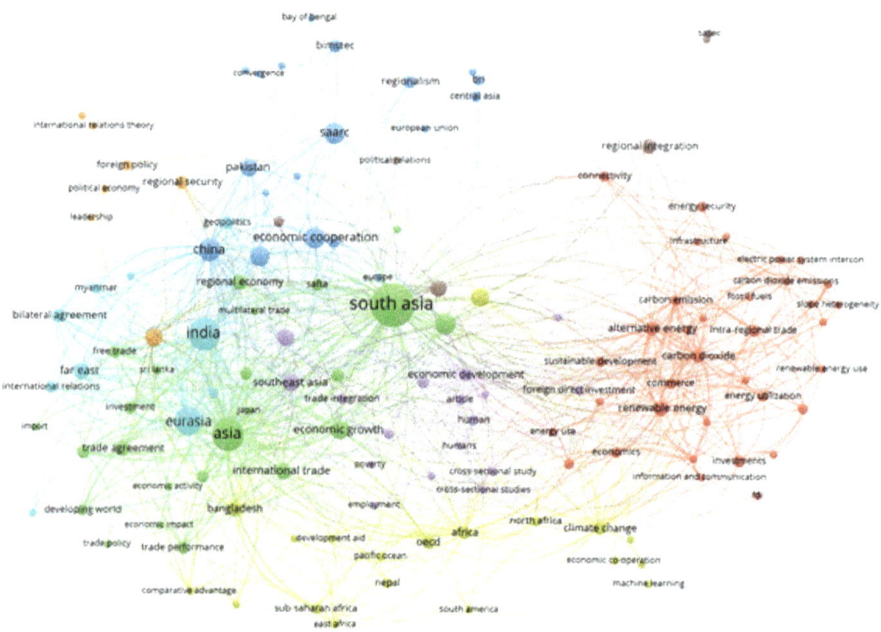

The green cluster is centred around South Asia, India, Eurasia, trade agreements, and investment. This cluster highlights the importance of regional trade policies, economic impact, and investment strategies in shaping trade dynamics. India and Bangladesh emerge as key players in promoting trade agreements and strengthening economic ties across the region. The focus here is on market-driven growth, trade performance, and the comparative advantages of different nations within South Asia.

The blue cluster represents SAARC, economic cooperation, Pakistan, China, geopolitics, and regional security. This cluster suggests that political economy and security issues play a crucial role in shaping economic integration. Keywords such as bilateral agreements, SAFTA, and geopolitical concerns indicate that while economic cooperation is a goal, factors like security concerns and international diplomacy significantly influence trade relationships between South Asian nations. Pakistan and China are prominently linked, suggesting China's growing influence in the region's trade policies.

The red cluster revolves around renewable energy, carbon emissions, commerce, infrastructure, and energy security. This theme highlights the increasing role of sustainability in regional economic integration. The focus is on alternative energy sources, intra-regional trade in renewable energy, and the impact of carbon emissions on economic cooperation. While no specific SAARC country is directly mentioned, the theme suggests that energy security is becoming an essential factor in regional trade discussions.

The yellow cluster focuses on climate change, economic development, OECD, Nepal, and Africa. This cluster underscores the broader international dimension of South Asian trade integration. The presence of foreign direct investment, development aid, employment, and economic cooperation suggests that Nepal is increasingly relying on external partnerships for economic growth. This cluster also connects South Asia with global development policies, showing linkages with Africa and OECD nations.

The light blue cluster emphasizes regionalism, convergence, European Union, BIMSTEC, and the Bay of Bengal. This cluster reflects a comparative approach, examining how SAARC aligns with or differs from other regional organizations like BIMSTEC and the EU. Discussions around convergence and political relations indicate that alternative trade blocs and regional collaborations may serve as complementary or competitive models for economic integration in South Asia.

Country-Specific Analysis

India plays a central role in trade agreements, investment, and economic development, positioning itself as a major economic driver in the SAARC region. Pakistan is more aligned with geopolitical concerns, foreign policy, and regional security, suggesting that non-economic factors significantly impact its trade relationships. Bangladesh is linked with trade performance, economic impact, and developing world trade policies, indicating its active participation in regional trade. Sri Lanka is associated with free trade and regional trade agreements, showing its engagement in open-market strategies. Nepal appears in discussions related to economic development, foreign aid, and employment, highlighting its dependence on external support. China emerges as an external influencer, particularly in regional economic cooperation and trade relations with South Asian nations. Myanmar is included in discussions on international trade and bilateral agreements, suggesting its growing trade ties with South Asia.

Key Takeaways

The visualization indicates that economic cooperation in South Asia is highly influenced by trade agreements, security concerns, and sustainability efforts. India and Bangladesh appear to be the strongest proponents of trade integration, while Pakistan's role is shaped by geopolitical factors. Additionally, renewable energy and climate change are emerging themes in regional economic discussions. Finally,

SAARC's trade model is often compared with BIMSTEC and the EU, highlighting potential alternative frameworks for regional integration.

Author Keywords

Figure 5. Exploring Research Trends through Author Keywords

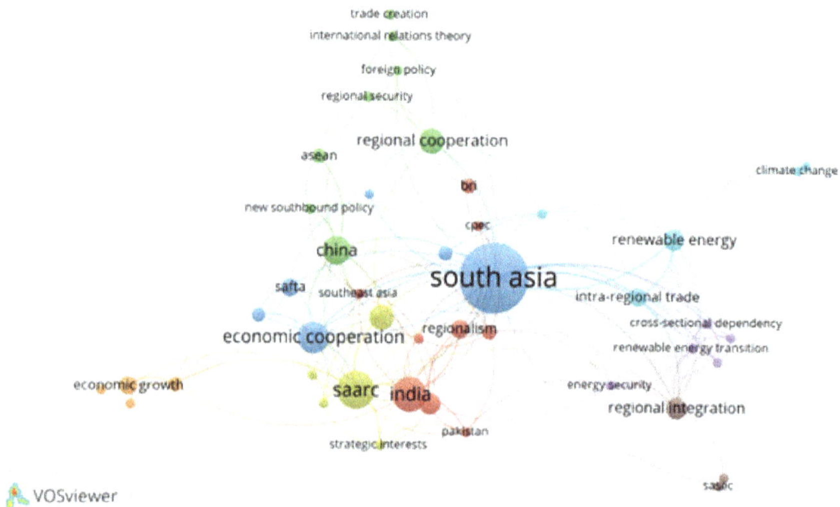

The author keyword co-occurrence network visualized using VOSviewer reveals key thematic clusters related to regional dynamics in *South Asia* (Figure 5). The central and most prominent term, *"South Asia"*, connects broadly across several clusters, highlighting its importance as a focal point. Closely linked to this are keywords such as *"regional cooperation"*, *"economic cooperation"*, *"regional integration"*, and *"intra-regional trade"*, indicating a strong scholarly interest in intergovernmental collaboration and economic interconnectedness within the region.

One major cluster involves *India*, *SAARC*, and *economic growth*, suggesting a focus on how India's strategic interests and regional institutions (like SAARC) influence economic development. A separate but related cluster centers on *China, BRI (Belt and Road Initiative)*, and *CPEC*, indicating geopolitical considerations and China's role in shaping South Asia's regional order. Terms such as *"ASEAN"* and *"new southbound policy"* extend this narrative to wider regional geopolitics, bridging South and Southeast Asia.

Another emerging cluster revolves around *renewable energy*, *climate change*, *energy security*, and *renewable energy transition*, reflecting growing academic attention on sustainable development and environmental challenges. This theme is intertwined with *regional integration* and *cross-sectional dependency*, showing a trend toward analyzing energy issues through a regional cooperation lens.

Overall, the keyword network captures a multidisciplinary intersection of *geopolitics*, *economic integration*, and *sustainable energy*, with South Asia at the nexus of regional and global discourses.

Index Keywords

Figure 6. Co-occurrence and Clustering of Author Keywords

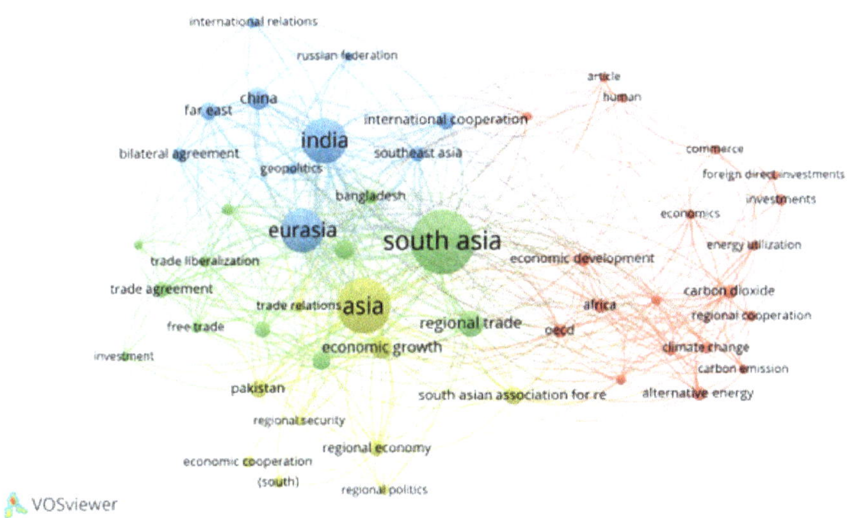

The index keywords visualization created using VOSviewer highlights the central role of *"South Asia"* in academic discourse related to trade, cooperation, and sustainability (Figure 6). The term forms the core of a highly interconnected network linking several thematic clusters. One dominant cluster surrounds *India*, *Eurasia*, *China*, and *international cooperation*, emphasizing geopolitical relations, bilateral agreements, and diplomatic interactions—especially in connection to major powers like the *Russian Federation* and *Far East*.

Another major thematic group revolves around *trade liberalization*, *free trade*, *trade agreements*, and *economic growth*, suggesting a significant scholarly focus on regional and interregional economic dynamics. Closely linked to this is *"Asia"* and *"regional trade"*, reflecting the broader regional economic integration narrative beyond South Asia.

Environmental and sustainability-related keywords form a distinct cluster, including *climate change*, *carbon emission*, *alternative energy*, *carbon dioxide*, and *energy utilization*. These terms are interlinked with *economic development, foreign direct investments*, and *regional cooperation*, indicating growing interest in the intersection between climate policy and economic planning, particularly across South-South cooperation with regions like *Africa* and *OECD* countries.

Overall, the map reveals a layered narrative encompassing geopolitical strategy, economic interdependence, and sustainable development, with *South Asia* serving as a central node in discussions on trade, diplomacy, and climate action in the broader Asian and global context.

Distinguish between Author Keywords and Index Keywords

Table 1 clearly distinguishes between *Author Keywords* and *Index Keywords* based on the two VOSviewer maps you provided:

Table 1. Difference between author keywords and index keywords in this study

Aspect	Author Keywords	Index Keywords
Central Focus	South Asia (as a focal region for cooperation, energy, and regionalism)	South Asia (as a hub for economic development, trade, and environmental policy)
Main Themes	- Regional cooperation and integration - Renewable energy and intra-regional trade - Strategic interests of India/China	- International cooperation - Trade liberalization and economic development - Climate change and carbon emission
Geopolitical Elements	India, China, Pakistan, ASEAN, SAARC, CPEC, BRI, New Southbound Policy	India, China, Russia, Eurasia, Far East, Bangladesh, Africa
Regional Organizations	SAARC, ASEAN, SASEC	South Asian Association for Regional Cooperation
Economic Focus	Economic cooperation, Economic growth, Trade creation, Intra-regional trade	Trade liberalization, Free trade, Trade agreements, Foreign direct investments, Economic growth
Energy & Environment Focus	Renewable energy, Energy security, Renewable energy transition, Climate change	Carbon emission, Carbon dioxide, Climate change, Alternative energy, Energy utilization
Theoretical/Policy Terms	Regionalism, Foreign policy, International relations theory	Geopolitics, International relations, Regional politics, Regional security
Connected Regions	South Asia, Southeast Asia	Asia, Eurasia, OECD, Africa
Research Emphasis	Emphasis on cooperation, security, and sustainable development strategies in South Asia	Broader scope including environmental economics, trade policies, and geopolitical dynamics
Visualization Density	Denser focus on South Asia's internal relations and development challenges	Broader international linkages highlighting both regional and global intersections of trade and environmental discourse

4.1.3 Identified Variable and Conceptual Model Development

Network visualization maps interconnections among keywords relating to regional cooperation, economic integration, trade, energy, and sustainability in South Asia. Table 2 demonstrates variable descriptions that we developed based on the network visualization.

Table 2. Variable Description

Variable	Role	Description
Regional Integration	Dependent Variable	The outcome variable reflecting the degree of collaboration among South Asian countries.
Economic Cooperation	Independent Variable	Formal and informal mechanisms promoting regional economic ties.
Trade Integration	Independent Variable	Level of intra- and inter-regional trade agreements and activities.
Energy Security	Independent Variable	Ensuring stable and affordable energy supply.
Renewable Energy Use	Independent Variable	Extent to which renewable sources are utilized in the region.
Foreign Direct Investment	Independent Variable	Investment from external sources into South Asian economies.
Connectivity (Infrastructure)	Independent Variable	Physical and digital infrastructure linking the region.
Climate Change	Mediating Variable	Affects both renewable energy policies and trade/investment patterns.
Sustainable Development	Mediating Variable	Channels the effects of economic cooperation and energy use toward integration.
Policy & Governance (e.g., Regional Security, Foreign Policy)	Mediating Variable	Influences the effectiveness of trade and energy strategies on integration.

The comparative analysis of author and index keywords reveals distinct yet complementary research emphases within the literature on South Asia. *Author keywords* predominantly focus on *regional cooperation, energy transitions,* and *geopolitical strategies*, reflecting the authors' intent to explore the intersection of development, diplomacy, and sustainability within South Asia. Keywords like *India*, *China*, *SAARC*, and *renewable energy* highlight a nuanced interest in internal dynamics, strategic alignments, and intra-regional collaboration. In contrast, *index keywords* present a broader, more externally oriented landscape, emphasizing *international cooperation, trade liberalization*, and *climate change*. These terms capture how databases categorize and retrieve articles based on global economic and environmental themes, as evidenced by the inclusion of regions such as *Eurasia*, *Africa*, and

OECD. While both sets underscore *South Asia* as the thematic anchor, the author keywords are more theory-driven and policy-specific (e.g., *regionalism*, *foreign policy*), whereas index keywords prioritize structured metadata on economic and environmental domains (e.g., *carbon emission*, *foreign direct investment*). Together, they illustrate a comprehensive research terrain that spans regional development goals and global integration challenges.

Conceptual Model

The following model posits that *regional integration* in South Asia is shaped by several *key independent variables*: economic cooperation, trade integration, energy security, foreign direct investment, connectivity, and renewable energy use. These effects are *mediated* by factors such as climate change, sustainable development goals, and the region's policy and governance frameworks.

Figure 7. Integrated Model of Regional Integration in South Asia

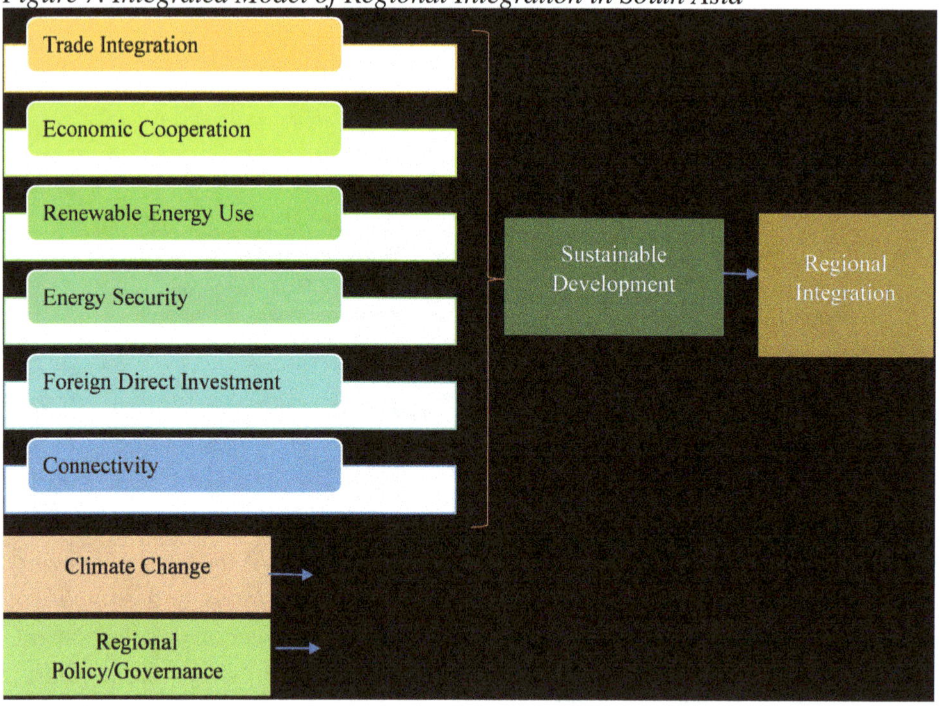

The conceptual model developed from the keyword network illustrates how regional integration in South Asia is influenced by a range of socio-economic and environmental factors (Figure 7). At the core, regional integration is the dependent variable, shaped by several independent variables including economic cooperation, trade integration, energy security, foreign direct investment (FDI), renewable energy use, and infrastructure connectivity. These independent factors foster economic ties, improve energy interdependence, and facilitate cross-border movement of goods, services, and capital. However, their influence is mediated by variables such as climate change, sustainable development, and regional governance (including policies related to foreign affairs and security). For instance, climate change pressures encourage renewable energy use and necessitate collaborative responses, which in turn contribute to sustainable development goals—acting as a pathway toward deeper regional integration. Furthermore, effective governance and policy alignment across the region moderate the effectiveness of trade and energy strategies. Together, this integrated model highlights a dynamic interplay where economic and environmental drivers, filtered through sustainability and policy frameworks, jointly determine the extent of regional integration in South Asia.

4.2 Systematic Review

4.2.1 Economic Cooperation in SAARC

Historical Context and Evolution

The South Asian Association for Regional Cooperation (SAARC) was established in 1985 with the aim of improving living standards, fostering economic growth, and enhancing regional cooperation (Kandel, 2021; Kandel, 2023). Since its inception, SAARC has made progress in various areas, including counterterrorism, telemedicine, literature, and disaster management (Kandel, 2021; Kandel, 2023). Notable achievements include the adoption of the Social Charter in 2004 and the establishment of several regional organizations (Kandel, 2021; Kandel, 2023). However, economic integration among member countries remains weak (Kandel, 2021; Kandel, 2023). The organization has faced challenges in achieving its regional goals due to a lack of trust, domestic political considerations, and concerns over sovereignty (Pattanaik, 2006). Some states have maintained an "enemy construct" against regional neighbors, hindering collective action and cooperation (Pattanaik, 2006). Despite these obstacles, the changing global environment and new security challenges underscore the importance of regional cooperation, particularly for smaller states (Pattanaik, 2006).

SAARC Regional Agreement

The South Asian Free Trade Area (SAFTA) agreement, signed in 2004 and implemented in 2006, aims to enhance regional trade integration among SAARC nations (Ratna, 2020; Sultana & Asrat, 2014). Despite its potential to create a free trade area of 1.8 billion people, SAFTA faces challenges such as non-tariff barriers, para-tariff measures, and sensitive lists that impede trade (Ratna, 2020; Ali & Mufti, 2020). Intra-regional trade in South Asia remains below its potential, with trade costs at borders being a significant factor (De, 2011). To overcome these obstacles, recommendations include strict adherence to tariff cut schedules, reduction of items in sensitive lists, and improved trade facilitation measures (Ali & Mufti, 2020). Enhancing trade facilitation could boost regional trade as effectively as tariff liberalization, particularly benefiting landlocked countries (De, 2011). Successful implementation of SAFTA is crucial for deepening market integration and addressing economic disparities in the region (Ali & Mufti, 2020).

Institutional mechanism

The SAARC region faces significant challenges in trade integration and growth, with intraregional trade at only 5.6% in 2006 (Bhattacharya & Das, 2011). Both "behind the border" and "beyond the border" constraints hinder trade potential among member countries (Bhattacharya & Das, 2014). Despite these obstacles, there is considerable potential for improving trade complementarities and achieving long-term gains (Bhattacharya & Das, 2014). The SAARC Development Fund (SDF) and SAARC Chamber of Commerce and Industry (SAARC CCI) play crucial roles in promoting trade and investment (Giri et al., 2015). To enhance regional cooperation, emphasis should be placed on technology cooperation, education, literacy, gender equality, good governance, and infrastructure development (Bhattacharya & Das, 2011; 2014). Additionally, liberalization of investment flows is essential, as there exists a close relationship between trade and FDI in the SAARC economies (Choudhury & Nayak, 2019).

4.2.2 Bilateral and Regional Trade Agreements

Key Bilateral Trade Agreement

Bilateral trade agreements, such as the India-Sri Lanka Free Trade Agreement, have shown positive effects on intraregional trade (Suhail & Sreejesh, 2011). Long-run trade complementarities exist between Pakistan and Sri Lanka, while short-run complementarities are found between India-Bangladesh and India-Sri Lanka (Kumar, 2021). Afghanistan's trade relies heavily on imports from India and Pakistan, with growing trade intensity between Afghanistan and Bangladesh, India, Pakistan, and Sri Lanka (Sadiqi & Wani, 2018). Afghanistan has a comparative advantage in agricultural commodities but lacks a strong manufacturing base (Sadiqi & Wani, 2018). To promote regional cooperation, Afghanistan must take a larger responsibility, while neighbouring governments need to respond positively to Afghan initiatives for successful regional integration (Sadiqi & Wani, 2018).

Impact of Regional Trade Agreement

The impact of regional trade agreements in South Asia, particularly SAFTA, has been limited in boosting intra-regional trade. Studies using gravity models suggest that SAFTA has had a minor effect on regional trade flows (Rodríguez-Delgado, 2007; Dembatapitiya & Weerahewa, 2015; Gaurav & Bharti, 2019). While SAFTA's impact on custom duties was found to be manageable for most members (Rodríguez-Delgado, 2007), it has not significantly increased intra-regional trade (Gaurav & Bharti, 2019). Bilateral trade agreements within South Asia have shown more positive effects on regional trade compared to broader regional agreements (Dembatapitiya & Weerahewa, 2015). To enhance trade among South Asian nations, measures such as reducing non-tariff measures, pruning sensitive lists, and resolving geo-political tensions are recommended (Gaurav & Bharti, 2019). Interestingly, potential Regional Trade Agreements-RTAs with North American Free Trade Agreement- NAFTA and the EU were found to have more significant trade effects for South Asian countries than agreements with ASEAN (Rodríguez-Delgado, 2007).

Barriers to Trade Integration

The SAARC region faces significant barriers to trade integration despite geographical and cultural proximity. Political tensions, particularly India's dominant position, create mistrust among member nations (Chaturvedi et al., 2015). Tariff and non-tariff barriers, including high Para tariffs and sensitive lists, hinder the effectiveness of free trade agreements (Kathuria, 2018). Infrastructural challenges, such as poor transport and communication networks, increase trade costs and impede connectivity (Reddy, 2019). Regulatory disparities and complicated rules further obstruct trade and movement of people (Reddy, 2019; Chanda, 2015). These factors contribute to low intra-regional trade, accounting for only 5.5% of total international trade (Reddy, 2019). To promote integration, countries must address regulatory harmonization, improve infrastructure, facilitate labour mobility, and foster a favourable policy environment (Chanda, 2015). Overcoming the trust deficit and size asymmetries is crucial for enhancing regional cooperation (Kathuria, 2018).

4.2.3 Investments and Economic Integration

Foreign Direct Investment (FDI)

Foreign Direct Investment (FDI) plays a significant role in the economic growth of SAARC countries. Studies have found that FDI positively impacts various macroeconomic factors, including GDP, inflation, government revenue, foreign reserves, and gross capital formation (Rahman & Bristy, 2015; Hasibul & John, 2017). However, the contribution of domestic private investment may be more reliable than FDI for long-term growth (Erum et al., 2016). Key determinants of FDI inflows in SAARC countries include infrastructure development, market size, economic openness, political stability, and corporate tax rates (Rai & Sharma, 2020). To attract more FDI, SAARC countries should focus on improving infrastructure, reducing corporate taxes, and implementing FDI-friendly policies (Hasibul & John, 2017; Rai & Sharma, 2020). While FDI can boost economic growth, policymakers should also consider potential adverse effects on the balance of payments due to profit repatriation (Erum et al., 2016).

Cross-Border Investment Initiatives

Cross-border investment initiatives in SAARC countries face significant challenges despite efforts to liberalize FDI policies. Intra-regional investment remains minimal compared to already low intra-regional trade levels (Ekanayake & Perera, 2015). The textiles and clothing industry, a key sector in South Asia, exemplifies this issue with less than 4% of SAARC's global exports traded within the region (Tewari, 2008). To address these challenges, a regional investment framework is crucial, alongside country-level reforms to improve individual investment climates (Ekanayake & Perera, 2015). Recommendations include reducing non-tariff barriers, expanding SAFTA to include investments and services, and focusing on key industries to demonstrate reform benefits (Thuy Van, 2011). Additionally, improving connectivity and reducing transaction costs for cross-border economic exchange are essential for regional economic integration (Roy & Banerjee, 2010). These measures could potentially stimulate intra-regional investment and trade in SAARC countries.

Digital and Financial Integration

Research on financial integration in SAARC countries reveals limited progress despite efforts towards economic cooperation. Sehgal et al. (2020) found that India has the highest perceived level of economic and financial integration with Nepal and Bhutan, while integration among other SAARC nations remains low. This is supported by Sehgal et al. (2018), who observed minimal equity market integration in the region. However, Haq (2021) demonstrated that countries with developed financial sectors benefit more from trade openness, suggesting a complementary role between financial development and trade in promoting economic growth. To enhance regional integration, Dasgupta & Maskay (2003) proposed increased financial policy cooperation and the establishment of institutions to manage trade and payments, drawing lessons from European integration. These studies collectively emphasize the need for SAARC countries to improve governance, trade linkages, and financial infrastructure to achieve higher levels of integration and economic growth.

5. CONSTRAINTS AND HURDLES IN SAARC'S DEVELOPMENT

Despite its vast economic potential and shared cultural ties, the South Asian Association for Regional Cooperation (SAARC) has failed to realize meaningful regional integration since its inception in 1985. Although it encompasses over 1.6 billion people across eight member states—Afghanistan, Bangladesh, Bhutan, India, Maldives, Nepal, Pakistan, and Sri Lanka—the organization remains hindered by a complex array of geopolitical, institutional, and structural challenges. Major initiatives such as the South Asian Free Trade Area (SAFTA) and the Motor Vehicle Agreement (MVA) have seen limited implementation, leaving SAARC's integration process in a state of inertia.

Geopolitical Tensions and Political Fragmentation

One of the primary challenges facing SAARC is the intense geopolitical tension within the region. Unlike the European Union, whose integration model inspired SAARC's formation, South Asia's political environment is deeply fragmented. The diversity of governance structures—from India's parliamentary democracy to Sri Lanka's presidential system and Nepal's monarchy-turned-federal democracy—has created institutional asymmetries that undermine cooperation (Rahman et al., 2012). The longstanding hostility between India and Pakistan, particularly over the Kashmir dispute, has been a persistent barrier to collective decision-making. This bilateral conflict has paralyzed the SAARC platform, making multilateral engagement nearly impossible (Pachori, 2019; Parihar, 2022).

Trust Deficit and Inter-State Disputes

A profound lack of trust among SAARC nations has consistently obstructed regional progress. Historical grievances, nationalistic sentiments, and mutual security concerns have contributed to persistent inter-state friction. These issues are compounded by internal conflicts and fears of economic domination, particularly from India. The colonial legacy of territorial disputes and communal violence has left unresolved tensions that continue to shape regional dynamics (Parihar, 2022). Without reconciliation of these disputes, SAARC cannot establish the stable foundations required for deeper cooperation.

Inadequacies in Regional Trade Agreements

While regional trade agreements (RTAs) are critical instruments for promoting trade liberalization, SAARC's trade frameworks—particularly SAFTA—have underperformed. The uncoordinated approach, stringent rules of origin (ROO), and long sensitive lists significantly restrict trade potential. For example, SAPTA's rigid ROO and extensive exclusion lists have historically limited intraregional trade (Baysan et al., 2006). Although bilateral FTAs, such as those between India and Sri Lanka or India and Nepal, have demonstrated some success, they remain exceptions rather than the norm (Rodríguez-Delgado, 2007). India, in particular, has pursued bilateral FTAs with most SAARC members, often bypassing the SAARC platform entirely (World Trade Organization-WTO., 2020).

Rules of Origin and Cumulative Constraints

SAFTA provides different ROO criteria for Least Developed Countries (LDCs) and non-LDCs. LDCs such as Bangladesh benefit from more lenient requirements—30% value addition plus a Change in Tariff Heading (CTH)—compared to the 40% required for non-LDCs. However, even these reduced thresholds present significant challenges for LDCs with limited manufacturing capacities. Moreover, regional cumulation rules under SAFTA are stringent and restrict the formation of efficient regional value chains (Economic and Social Commission for Asia and the Pacific-ESCAP., 2018).

Non-Tariff Barriers and Standards Harmonization

Non-tariff barriers (NTBs), particularly in the form of Sanitary and Phytosanitary (SPS) and Technical Barriers to Trade (TBTs), are some of the most pressing impediments to South Asian trade. Procedural delays, lack of testing facilities, excessive documentation, and non-recognition of national certifications all contribute to trade inefficiencies (United Nations Conference on Trade and Development- UNCTAD, 2013; ESCAP., 2018). Nepal's exports, for instance, suffer from India's refusal to accept domestic testing authorities' certifications. Similarly, inconsistencies in labelling regulations in Pakistan and Bangladesh impede processed food and cosmetics trade (Taneja et al., 2013). These fragmented regulatory frameworks reflect an urgent need for harmonization of standards and conformity assessment procedures.

Infrastructure and Customs Inefficiencies

Poor infrastructure at border points, especially at land ports, continues to hinder trade flow. Delays stem from underdeveloped road networks, limited warehousing, inefficient customs clearance, and lack of scanning and testing facilities (De & Iyengar, 2014). Electronic Data Interchange (EDI) systems often malfunction, necessitating manual processing and causing long queues and congestion. For landlocked countries like Nepal, Bhutan, and Afghanistan, transit dependency on neighbouring countries exacerbates these issues, making regional trade highly expensive and time-consuming.

Sensitive Lists and Tariff Issues

Although SAFTA has brought down the average tariff rates to 5.7% in 2024, sensitive lists remain a substantial barrier. For example, Bangladesh and Sri Lanka have included 44–45% of their imports from SAARC countries on sensitive lists (Gill, 2020). Despite WTO's push for liberalization, many SAARC countries continue to maintain long lists of protected goods. India, for instance, still maintains a considerable list of tariff lines exempted from liberalization under SAFTA. Conversely, countries like Sri Lanka and Maldives have offered preferential treatment on thousands of tariff lines, including LDC-specific concessions (WTO., 2025).

Limited Use of Trade Remedies

Most SAARC members lack institutional capacity to apply trade remedies such as anti-dumping, countervailing, and safeguard measures. While India is a leading user of such instruments—with over 250 anti-dumping measures in place by 2019—countries like Nepal, Maldives, and Bangladesh have no operational frameworks for these tools (WTO., 2020; WTO., 2022). Bangladesh, despite having relevant legislation, remains unable to conduct investigations due to institutional capacity limitations (WTO., 2019).

LDC Graduation Challenges

The imminent graduation of Bangladesh, Nepal, and Bhutan from LDC status raises concerns about the loss of special and differential treatment, preferential market access, and DFQF (duty-free quota-free) privileges. These countries will need to adjust to a more competitive trade environment without the traditional safety nets provided under WTO and regional agreements. This poses serious challenges for export diversification and resilience building (Rahman et al., 2012).

Informal Trade and Asymmetric Power Dynamics

Informal trade within the region remains substantial, particularly between India and Pakistan, with estimates exceeding $2 billion annually—nearly ten times the volume of formal trade (Rahman et al., 2012). Informal channels often compensate for the inadequacies of formal trade mechanisms. Moreover, the economic asymmetry between India and its neighbors continues to generate distrust. India contributes over 80% of SAARC's GDP and commands centrality in geography, connectivity, and trade, leading to perceptions of hegemonic dominance by smaller states (Parihar, 2022).

Inefficiencies in Trade Facilitation and Port Operations

Trade facilitation remains a major hurdle across South Asia. Manual customs procedures, lack of automation, and the absence of single-window clearance systems lead to excessive delays and documentation requirements. Traders often need more than 12 documents and 28 days to complete import procedures (Rahman et al., 2012). Certification processes (e.g., quarantine, origin, or no-objection certificates) can take up to three months, further increasing transaction costs and reducing regional competitiveness.

Transport and Logistics Bottlenecks

Transport infrastructure in South Asia suffers from chronic underinvestment. Limited port capacities, absence of large vessel handling facilities, and congested border crossings result in delayed deliveries and elevated costs. Landlocked countries face disproportionately high transit costs, affecting both import and export prices. Fragmented transport policies and lack of integrated regional networks add to the complexity (ESCAP., 2018; Rahman et al., 2012).

Currency and Payment Systems

Payment settlement mechanisms remain underdeveloped. Many countries in the region still rely heavily on the US dollar, increasing vulnerability to currency fluctuations. Initiatives like India's rupee trade arrangements and RTGS (Real Time Gross Settlement) offer promising alternatives but require broader participation and system alignment (Bangladesh Bank, 2024).

Liberalization of Trade in Services

Although the SAARC Agreement on Trade in Services (SATIS) came into effect in 2012, real progress has been slow. Only a few countries have submitted their final offer lists, and commitments remain limited in scope. Regional political tensions continue to stall service liberalization efforts, even though the services sector holds substantial promise for economic integration (WTO., 2020).

Investment and Regional Value Chains

SAARC's inability to foster intraregional investment is a missed opportunity. While there is some FDI flow between member states—such as from India, Pakistan, and Sri Lanka to Bangladesh and Nepal—comprehensive frameworks to promote regional value chains are lacking. Countries like Bangladesh have emerged as favorable FDI destinations due to global preferential market access, but regional investment strategies remain underutilized.

Food Security and Agricultural Trade

Food trade in South Asia is particularly vulnerable to SPS and TBT restrictions. Perishable goods face high spoilage risks due to inadequate storage, lack of testing facilities, and poor infrastructure at borders. Nearly 86% of the region's food trade suffers from procedural barriers that result in wastage and increased costs (CUTS International, Centre for Policy Research, Asia Foundation, 2016).

Administrative and Calendar-Related Barriers

Differences in national holidays affect trade timelines. For instance, differences between Bangladesh's Friday weekend and India's Sunday weekend can cause consignments to be delayed by several days if clearance is not completed on time (Rahman et al., 2012). This highlights the need for synchronization in administrative operations.

Lessons from ASEAN

Compared to ASEAN, SAARC has struggled to establish a functional diplomatic and economic community. ASEAN's success stems from a foundational emphasis on mutual respect for sovereignty, which fosters trust and underpins cooperation. SAARC, by contrast, has not achieved the necessary political commitment or institutional mechanisms to replicate this model (Chaudhary, 2022).

6. RECOMMENDATIONS

The South Asian region faces numerous challenges and opportunities in advancing economic integration and sustainable development. To unlock its full potential, there is an urgent need for stronger regional cooperation and institutional strengthening within frameworks such as SAARC. Addressing structural, political, and trade-related barriers through harmonized policies and improved infrastructure can enhance intra-regional trade, attract foreign direct investment, and boost competitiveness. This set of recommendations outlines key strategic actions—from trade facilitation and standards harmonization to capacity building and regional supply chain efficiency—that can help South Asia overcome its current limitations and foster inclusive growth, stability, and sustainable development across member states. The following recommendations are needed for advancing economic integration and sustainable development in South Asia:

- **Platform and Mechanism:** A regional strong formal platform and mechanism should be formed to address both its structural and political shortcomings, resolve disputes and make decisions promptly, and to reform or ensure compliance. From this perspective. SAARC needs to strengthen the institutional capacity and increase its financial resources. This leads to enable the region to implement its programs and activities more efficiently.
- **Open Trade Policy:** South Asia needs more open trade policies to enhance FDI inflow. Vietnam is open and diversified, which attracts more FDI.
- **Trade engagement:** Despite geopolitical concerns, East Asian countries such as China, South Korea, and Japan do successful business, but South Asian countries do not engage in significant trade.
- **Tariff and barriers:** Regional and bilateral FTAs can reduce import tariffs and address behind- the- border barriers that impede goods and services trade. Through removing entry barriers, FTAs can facilitate inward investment and technology transfer.
- **Intra-regional trade and economic integration:** It has been widely acknowledged that the removal of Non-Tariff Measures-NTMs, more specifically TBT, SPS and infrastructural and procedural related barriers would contribute significantly to intra-regional trade and economic integration in South Asia. The findings of the existing research also show that NTMs limit intra-regional trade in terms of agriculture and food items between South Asian member states.
- **Trade and technical standards:** Synchronization among trade and technical standards will remove the redundant procedures and practices. Emphasis has to be given on harmonization of quality standard requirements and label-

ling requirements without compromising on regulatory objectives and policy goals, strengthening standards-related capacities, establishing accreditation bodies and regional standards, developing regional conformity assessment procedures, signing Mutual Recognition Agreements (MRAs), mutual alignment of standards in various product sectors with significant trade interest for countries, to reduce the impact of existing non-tariff barriers and to facilitate trade and business. Because of the absence of MRAs in trade agreements (India-Sri Lanka FTA), bilateral trade between two states has declined in case of food products.

- **Capacity building:** Against this backdrop, coordination among member states; capacity building for the relevant authorities, officials and staff on rules and regulations (i.e. in terms of quarantine and food safety rules and regulations) to reduce information gap; improving product quality through capacity enhancements not only of exporters but also of the relevant standards and testing institutions; transparency in testing and certification procedures; adequate testing and trade standard related agencies, especially at land ports; joint accreditation of testing laboratories between all South Asian countries; adequate warehousing and storage and cold storage facilities at land ports to reduce wastage; construction of the deep-sea port; connectivity of the ports; direct shipping to reduce both time and cost; adequate border facilities with trained personnel will reduce trade costs, facilitate shipments and enhance competitiveness of the region's exports. The South Asian Regional Standards Organization (SARSO) was formed to develop regional standards and to establish uniform product standards (ESCAP., 2018).
- **Priority products and regional regulations:** The Association of Southeast Asian Nations (ASEAN) has undertaken a similar exercise by harmonizing standards for 20 priority products. Member states should work together to identify and prioritize a list of mutually beneficial products facing non-tariff barriers related to SPS and TBT measures in order to open market access (Concept Note between Bangladesh and India, 2024). In addition to that, relevant experts within region dealing with regulations could examine the hurdles and restrictions highlighted by exporters for these prioritized commodities.
- **Regional trade integration:** Strong cooperation from South Asian member states is highly needed for the developing countries, particularly for the LDCs, including those on the track of graduation to support smooth transition and sustainable graduation. Thus, regional trade integration is very important to address supply-side constraints and specially to comply with international standards.
- **Efficient regional supply chain:** There is a need for strong efforts to ensure efficient regional supply chains in South Asia.

- **Single window system:** Implementation of a single-window system at all border locations is highly required so that traders can submit all trade documents in a single platform for clearance of consignments. This will ensure transparency, predictability and reliability in whole trade procedure.
- **Cooperation versus competition:** South Asian nations would be benefitted in case of similar export product basket as the similarity improve production networks through cooperation than competition. Member states should enhance cooperation in tourism, IT, transport, health, education and professional services sectors.
- **Collaborative efforts:** Another core area of regional cooperation is to address the SDCs, which include health and wellbeing, employment and equality, ecological concerns and so on. The collaborative efforts can add value to sustainable business and trade, innovation and creative activities in this region.
- **Economic development and technological modernization:** All SAARC member states should work together for the SDCs to eradicate poverty through economic development and technological modernization. It is required more investment cooperation from member states to attain the goal. A pragmatic tax policy and a technology-driven bureaucracy can ensure investment in this region.
- **Food trade network:** A strong food trade network should be developed within the region through improving trade-related infrastructure for importing perishables efficiently. That leads to improve food security situation.
- **Regional stability:** India is well-positioned to play a key role in harnessing full potentials of the region and specifically in ensuring regional stability in South Asia.
- **Regional cooperation:** South Asia has all the components to make the region flourish, but security dynamics of the region is destroying its potentials. Strong regional cooperation in SAARC is highly required to mitigate the challenges. Despite differences on a variety of issues, ASEAN has emerged as a successful regional alliance.

7. CONCLUSION AND POLICY IMPLICATIONS

The study has examined regional trade Integration and the implications of the different trade agreements including SAFTA on the economies of different member states of the SAARC. In doing so, it has reviewed the experiences of ASEAN and EU. The study analyses the constraints faced by the member states of South Asia and the possible policies that can be taken to tackle the barriers to trade integration with its neighbor and with other Asian countries. At present, South Asian countries face numerous challenges in various aspects. Economic cooperation and deeper regional integration have worked as a powerful tool in empowering neighborhoods who are not entirely on track to harness its full potential, attain the Sustainable Development Goals, eradicate poverty and develop other indicators.

South Asia should accelerate its reforms in policies to reach the vast potential of regional trade. Intraregional trade remains mostly unexploited due to geopolitical conflict, stringent ROO, NTBs, PTBs, longer list of sensitive products, trade remedial measures (I.e. anti-dumping, countervailing and safeguard measures), lack of product and market diversification in LDCs, post LDC graduation journey of few states, lack of synchronization on standard requirements and testing certification, high proportion of informal trade, barriers in transport, high cost of doing business, lack of automation in all transaction procedures, corruption, delay in delivery, high lead time, lack of direct shipping, cumbersome clearance procedure at ports, heavy reliance on single reserve currency, low inflow of FDI etc. which impede to tap the full benefits of intraregional trade.

To address the barriers to trade in South Asia, and harness the potential of the regional trade and formation of value chains, utmost importance should be given on formation of strong formal platform at the regional level, resolving the political conflicts within the region, open trade policies, harmonization of standards and requirements throughout the trade transaction procedures, MRAs, improving compliance with international standards, elimination of NTBs, flexible RoO, improving access to finance, enhancing production capacity of the LDCs, smooth graduation of the LDCs, the creation of a robust and integrated value chain, fully automated system in all trade transactions, the efficiency of the Customs clearance, capacity building programs for officials and staff on rules and regulations, improvement in border connectivity and quality of trade infrastructures, a single-window system at all border points, coordinated efforts at the regional level and so on. Meaningful integration of South Asia is highly needed to increase the trade competitiveness of the South Asian member states.

REFERENCES

Akram, H. W., Ciddikie, M. D., & Khan, M. A. (2014). India's trade relationship with SAFTA countries: A review. *Journal of Indian Research*, *2*(1), 46–58.

Alam, M. S., & Zubayer, M. (2010). Intra regional foreign direct investment (FDI) prospect in South Asian Association of Regional Cooperation (SAARC) region. *International Journal of Economics and Finance*, *2*(3), 114–121. DOI: 10.5539/ijef.v2n3p114

Ali, I., & Mufti, A. (2020). Saarc and Safta: Dynamic of Trade Facilitation in South Asia. Available at *SSRN* 3753321. DOI: 10.2139/ssrn.3753321

Bangladesh Bank. (2024). Trading in Local Currencies: Problems and Prospects for the SAARC Countries. Bangladesh Bank. *Accessed from* https://www.bb.org.bd/pub/special/aug282024_bb_special_publication.pdf

Baysan, T., Panagariya, A., & Pitigala, N. (2006). Preferential Trading in South Asia. *World Bank Policy Research Working Paper*, (3813).

Bhattacharya, S. K., & Das, G. G. (2011). Do South-South Trade Agreements Enhance Member Countries' Trade? Evaluating Implications for Development Potentials in the Context of SAARC. *Evaluating Implications for Development Potentials in the Context of SAARC (November 1, 2011). UNU-CRIS Working Papers W-20011/2.*

Bhattacharya, S. K., & Das, G. G. (2014). Can South–South trade agreements reduce development deficits? An exploration of SAARC during 1995–2008. *Journal of South Asian Development*, *9*(3), 253–285. DOI: 10.1177/0973174114549129

Chanda, R. (2015). Challenges to regional services integration in South Asia. *South Asia Economic Journal*, *16*(2, suppl), 19S–38S. DOI: 10.1177/1391561415594730

Chaturvedi, P., Hussain, Z., & Nag, B. (2015). SAARC geopolitics and trade: Missing intra-regional connectivity a hindrance to further economic integration. *South Asian Survey*, *22*(1), 78–106. DOI: 10.1177/0971523117708963

Choudhury, R., & Nayak, D. (2019). Relationship between Trade and Investment in the SAARC Region. *World Scientific Book Chapters*, 99-135.

CUTS International. CPR, AF. (2016). Non-Tariff Measures to Food Trade in India: A Case Study of Selected Ports. CUTS International, Centre for Policy Research, Asia Foundation. *Accessed from* https://cprindia.org/wp-content/uploads/2021/12/NTB-report.pdf

Dasgupta, A., & Maskay, N. M. (2003). Financial Policy Cooperation in SAARC: A First Step Towards Greater Monetary Integration in South Asia. *South Asia Economic Journal, 4*(1), 133–143. DOI: 10.1177/139156140300400109

De, P. (2011). Why is trade at borders a costly affair in South Asia? An empirical investigation. *Contemporary South Asia, 19*(4), 441–464. DOI: 10.1080/09584935.2011.602666

De, P., & Iyengar, K. (2014). *Developing economic corridors in South Asia. Mandaluyong City, Philippines*. Asian Development Bank.

Dembatapitiya, P., & Weerahewa, J. (2015). Effects of regional trading agreements on South Asian trade: A gravity model analysis. *Tropical Agricultural Research, 26*(3).

Economic and Social Commission for Asia and the Pacific [ESCAP]. (2018). Unlocking the Potential of Regional Economic Cooperation and Integration in South Asia Potential, Challenges and the Way Forward. ESCAP, Bangkok, Thailand.

Ekanayake, R., & Perera, N. (2015). Stimulating Intra-Regional Investment in SAARC: Is a Regional Investment Agreement the Way Forward? *South Asia Economic Journal, 16*(2, suppl), 75S–101S. DOI: 10.1177/1391561415594731

Erum, N., Hussain, S., & Yousaf, A. (2016). Foreign direct investment and economic growth in SAARC countries. *The Journal of Asian Finance, Economics and Business, 3*(4), 57–66. DOI: 10.13106/jafeb.2016.vol3.no4.57

Gaurav, K., & Bharti, N. (2019). Has trade improved from SAPTA to SAFTA? Evidence from the gravity model. *International Journal of Business and Globalisation, 23*(4), 532–548. DOI: 10.1504/IJBG.2019.104832

Gill, D. M. (2020). Challenges to Regional Cooperation in South Asia: An Overview. *Journal of International Affairs, 3*(1), 42–51. DOI: 10.3126/joia.v3i1.29081

Giri, P., Karinje, P., & Verma, R., JSSATE, N., & Noida, I. J. (2015). A study and analysis of challenges, achievements and hurdles faced by SAARC nations in trade integration and growth. *International Journal of Engineering Technology. Management and Applied Sciences, 3*(1), 204–215.

Haq, M., Ahmad, I., & Jabeen, A. (2021). Financial sector development, trade openness and economic growth nexus: evidence from SAARC countries. *Forman Journal of Economic Studies, 17*(1).

Hasibul, I. R., & John, K. (2017). Impact of foreign direct investment on economic growth of the SAARC countries. *Journal of Economics and Sustainable Development, 8*, 58–66.

Hertel, T. W., & Mirza, T. (2009). The role of trade facilitation in South Asian economic integration. *Study on intraregional trade and investment in South Asia*, 12-39.

Hirantha, S. W. (2004). *From SAPTA to SAFTA: Gravity analysis of South Asian free trade. European Trade Study Group*. ETSG.

Kandel, D. I. (2021). Political and Economic Challenge of SAARC. *IOSR Journal of Humanities and Social Science*, *26*(1), 1–5.

Kandel, I. P. (2023). Political and Economic Relation in The SAARC Countries. *Researcher CAB. Journal of Research and Development (Srinagar)*, *2*(1), 129–143.

Kathuria, S. (2018). *A glass half full: The promise of regional trade in South Asia*. World Bank Publications. DOI: 10.1596/978-1-4648-1294-1

Kumar, J., Xi, C., Kumari, J., & Huang, J. (2025). Macroeconomic and Institutional Determinants of Foreign Direct Investment in SAARC Countries. *Problemy Ekorozwoju*, *20*(1), 271–287. DOI: 10.35784/preko.6747

Kumar, R. (2021). South Asia: Multilateral trade agreements and untapped regional trade integration. *International Journal of Finance & Economics*, *26*(2), 2891–2903. DOI: 10.1002/ijfe.1941

Mushtaq, M., Ahmad, K., Ahmed, S., & Nadeem, M. (2014). Impact of FDI on income distribution in selected SAARC countries. *Journal of Applied Environmental and Biological Sciences*, *4*, 1–10.

Pachori, S. (2019). Conflicts in South Asia–challenges to SAARC regionalism. *Int J Res Geogr*, *5*, 34–41.

Parihar, M. (2022). A study of South Asian Association for Regional Cooperation (SAARC) along with its role, challenges and prospects. *International Journal of Humanities and Social Science Invention*, *11*(1), 68–81.

Pattanaik, S. S. (2006). Making sense of regional cooperation: SAARC at twenty. *Strategic Analysis*, *30*(1), 139–160. DOI: 10.1080/17540054.2006.12288822

Rahman, S. H., Khatri, S., & Brunner, H. P. (2012). *Regional Integration and Economic Development in South Asia*. The Asian Development Bank and Edward Elgar Publishing., Accessed from https://www.adb.org/sites/default/files/publication/29871/regional-integration-economic-development-south-asia.pdf DOI: 10.4337/9781781005248

Rahman, S. Z., & Bristy, J. F. (2015). Macroeconomic impact of foreign direct investment: A study on SAARC countries. *European Journal of Business and Management*, *7*(34), 59–70.

Rai, K. S., & Sharma, K. A. (2020). Causal nexus between FDI inflows and its determinants in SAARC countries. *South Asia Economic Journal, 21*(2), 193–215. DOI: 10.1177/1391561420940838

Ratna, R. S. (2020). South Asian integration: Dream or reality. In *Regional and Multilateral Trade in Developing Countries* (pp. 95–105). Routledge India. DOI: 10.4324/9780367817985-7

Reddy, G. J. (2019). Regional imbalances and implications for South Asian economic integration. In *New Futures for South Asia* (pp. 161–173). Routledge India. DOI: 10.4324/9780367816827-13

Rodríguez-Delgado, J. D. (2007). SAFTA: Living in a world of regional trade agreements. *Accessed from* https://papers.ssrn.com/sol3/Delivery.cfm?abstractid=961753

Roy, J., & Banerjee, P. (2010). Connecting South Asia: The centrality of trade facilitation for regional economic integration. In *Promoting Economic Cooperation in South Asia: Beyond SAFTA* (pp. 110-138). SAGE Publications India Pvt Ltd.

Sadiqi, M. K., & Wani, N. U. H. (2018). Latency of Afghanistan-SAARC merchandise trade relation: An economic evaluation. *Kardan Journal of Economics and Management Sciences, 1*(2), 101–120. DOI: 10.31841/KJEMS.2021.82

Sahoo, P., Nataraj, G., & Dash, R. K. (2014). *Foreign direct investment in South Asia. Policy, Impact, Determinants and Challenges*. Springer. DOI: 10.1007/978-81-322-1536-3

Sehgal, S., Pandey, P., Deisting, F., & McMillan, D. (2018). Time varying integration amongst the South Asian equity markets: An empirical study. *Cogent Economics & Finance, 6*(1), 1452328. DOI: 10.1080/23322039.2018.1452328

Sehgal, S., Saini, S., & Pandey, P. (2020). Economic and financial integration in the South Asian region: A survey. In *Economic and Financial Integration in South Asia* (pp. 16–32). Routledge India. DOI: 10.4324/9781003097563-3

Suhail, P., & Sreejesh, S. (2011). The bilateral trade agreements and export performance of South Asian nations with special reference to India Sri Lanka Free Trade Agreement. *Romanian Economic Journal, 14*(42).

Sultana, S., & Asrat, J. (2014). South Asian Countries in Regional Integration Perspective: A Critical Review. *Journal of Business and Technology (Dhaka), 9*(2), 43–59. DOI: 10.3329/jbt.v9i2.26195

Taneja, N., Prakash, S., & Kalita, P. (2013). India's Role in Facilitating Trade under SAFTA. Working Paper 263. Indian Council for Research on International Economic Relations.

Tewari, M. (2008). *Deepening intraregional trade and investment in South Asia: The case of the textiles and clothing industry* (No. 213). Working Paper.

Thuy Van, L. T. (2011). *Study on Intraregional Trade and Investment in South Asia–By Thomas W.* Hertel. DOI: 10.1111/j.1943-0787.2011.01285.x

Tinbergen, J. (1962). *Shaping the world economy: suggestions for an International Economic Policy*. The Twentieth Century Fund.

WTO. (2020). Seventh Trade Policy Review: India, Report by India & Report by the WTO Secretariat, World Trade Organization, Geneva.

WTO. (2022). Fifth Trade Policy Review: Pakistan, Report by the WTO Secretariat, World Trade Organization, Geneva.

WTO. (2025). Fourth Trade Policy Review: Maldives, Report by the WTO Secretariat, World Trade Organization, Geneva.

KEY TERMS AND DEFINITIONS

ASEAN: The Association of Southeast Asian Nations (ASEAN) is a regional organization established in 1967 to promote political, economic, and social cooperation among its ten member states: Indonesia, Malaysia, the Philippines, Singapore, Thailand, Brunei, Vietnam, Laos, Myanmar, and Cambodia. ASEAN has made significant progress in regional integration through initiatives like the ASEAN Free Trade Area (AFTA) and the ASEAN Economic Community (AEC), aiming to create a single market and production base. It is often viewed as a successful model of regionalism, balancing economic growth with diplomatic neutrality. ASEAN's cooperative approach offers valuable lessons for other regions, including South Asia, in overcoming political differences to achieve shared development goals.

Cross-sectional Dependency: Cross-sectional dependency refers to the interdependence or correlation between units (such as countries or regions) in a dataset at a given point in time. In the context of regional studies, it implies that economic, political, or environmental developments in one country can significantly influence others within the same region. For example, in South Asia, trade policies, energy security, or climate impacts in one nation often affect neighboring states due to shared borders, markets, and ecosystems. Recognizing cross-sectional dependency is crucial for accurate econometric analysis and for designing effective, region-wide policy interventions.

Economic Cooperation: Economic cooperation involves collaborative efforts among countries to promote shared economic growth, stability, and development through joint policies, trade agreements, and investment initiatives. In South Asia, economic cooperation is pursued through platforms like SAARC and bilateral agreements, yet it often faces challenges due to political rivalries and uneven economic capacities. Strengthening cooperation can enhance regional connectivity, reduce poverty, and support sustainable development. It also enables countries to address common issues such as energy security, climate change, and infrastructure deficits more effectively.

Geopolitics: Geopolitics refers to the influence of geographic, political, and strategic factors on international relations and power dynamics among nations. In South Asia, geopolitics is shaped by the rivalry between major powers like India and China, the strategic interests of external actors, and regional initiatives such as the Belt and Road Initiative (BRI) and the Indo-Pacific strategy. These dynamics impact regional stability, economic cooperation, and infrastructure development. Understanding geopolitics is crucial for assessing how power competition and strategic alignments affect South Asia's integration and global positioning.

OECD: The Organisation for Economic Co-operation and Development (OECD) is an international body comprising 38 member countries, primarily high-income economies, that promotes policies to improve global economic and social well-being. It provides a platform for governments to share experiences, develop best practices, and coordinate domestic and international policies. The OECD is influential in setting global standards on economic policy, taxation, education, and development cooperation. Although South Asian countries are not members, they often engage with the OECD through partnerships and benefit from its data, policy recommendations, and development frameworks.

Regional Integration: Regional integration is the process through which neighboring countries coordinate and align their economic, political, and social policies to achieve greater unity and shared development. In South Asia, regional integration has been limited despite the presence of frameworks like SAARC and SASEC, primarily due to political mistrust and trade barriers. Successful integration can enhance economic growth, improve infrastructure connectivity, and address transboundary challenges such as energy access and climate change. Deeper integration would also strengthen the region's collective voice in global affairs and foster long-term stability.

SAARC: The South Asian Association for Regional Cooperation (SAARC) is a regional intergovernmental organization established in 1985 to promote economic growth, social progress, and regional integration among its eight member countries: Afghanistan, Bangladesh, Bhutan, India, Maldives, Nepal, Pakistan, and Sri Lanka. SAARC aims to enhance cooperation in areas such as trade, education, health, agriculture, and climate change. Despite its broad mandate, SAARC has struggled to achieve effective integration due to political tensions—particularly between India and Pakistan—and limited institutional capacity. Nevertheless, it remains a key platform for dialogue and collaboration in South Asia.

SAFTA: The South Asian Free Trade Area (SAFTA) is a regional trade agreement established in 2006 under the South Asian Association for Regional Cooperation (SAARC) to promote economic integration among its member states. Its primary goal is to reduce tariffs and trade barriers to facilitate the free flow of goods among South Asian countries, including India, Pakistan, Bangladesh, Nepal, Bhutan, Sri Lanka, Maldives, and Afghanistan. Despite its potential, SAFTA has faced limited success due to political tensions, especially between India and Pakistan, as well as non-tariff barriers and poor trade facilitation infrastructure. Strengthening SAFTA could significantly boost intra-regional trade and foster economic cooperation in one of the world's least-integrated regions.

Trade Integration: Trade integration refers to the process by which countries within a region reduce trade barriers to facilitate the free flow of goods, services, and investments. It often involves agreements on tariffs, customs procedures, and regulatory standards to promote economic cooperation. In the context of South Asia, trade integration remains limited despite regional frameworks like SAARC and SAFTA, primarily due to political tensions and infrastructural constraints. Enhancing trade integration in the region could boost economic growth, strengthen regional supply chains, and improve collective resilience to global economic shocks.

Trade Liberalization: Trade liberalization refers to the removal or reduction of trade barriers—such as tariffs, quotas, and regulations—to encourage the free exchange of goods and services across borders. It aims to boost economic efficiency, competitiveness, and access to diverse markets by allowing countries to specialize in areas of comparative advantage. In South Asia, trade liberalization efforts have been uneven due to political tensions, protectionist policies, and weak regional trade infrastructure. However, greater liberalization holds the potential to increase intra-regional trade, attract investment, and accelerate economic growth across the region.

APPENDIX

Glossary of Acronyms and Abbreviations

APTA: Asia-Pacific Trade Agreement
ASEAN: Association of Southeast Asian Nations
BIMSTEC: Bay of Bengal Initiative for Multi-Sectoral Technical and Economic Cooperation
CTH: Change of Tariff Heading
DFQF: Duty-Free Quota-Free
EDI: Electronic Data Interchange
ESCAP: Economic and Social Commission for Asia and the Pacific
EU: European Union
FDI: Foreign Direct Investment
FTAs: Free Trade Agreements
GDP: Gross Domestic Product
LDCs: Least Developed Countries
MRAs: Mutual Recognition Agreements
MVA: Motor Vehicle Agreement
NAFTA: North American Free Trade Agreement
NTBs: Non-Tariff Barriers
NTMs: Non-Tariff Measures
PTBs: Para-Tariff Barriers
ROO: Rules of Origin
RTAs: Regional Trade Agreements
RTGS: Real Time Gross Settlements
SAFTA: South Asian Free Trade Area
SAPTA: SAARC Preferential Trading Arrangement
SARSO: South Asian Regional Standards Organization
SATIS: SAARC Agreement on Trade in Services
SDGs: Sustainable Development Goals
SPS: Sanitary and Phytosanitary Measures
TBT: Technical Barriers to Trade
UNCTAD: United Nations Conference on Trade and Development
WTO: World Trade Organization

Chapter 5
Integrating Environmental Safeguards Into Bilateral and Regional Trade Agreements

Rismawati Rismawati
http://orcid.org/0000-0001-8046-6764
Universitas Muhammadiyah Palopo, Indonesia

Eko Ganis Sukoharsono
Universitas Brawijaya, Indonesia

Monika Handayani
http://orcid.org/0000-0003-4186-9864
Politeknik Negeri Banjarmasin, Indonesia

Javaid Ahmad Wagay
University of Kahsmir, India

ABSTRACT:

Incorporating environmental protections in bilateral and regional trade agreements is crucial for fostering sustainable economic development. Early trade agreements focused on economic liberalization, whereas contemporary frameworks increasingly integrate environmental obligations to tackle climate change, resource depletion, and ecological degradation. This paper examines the development of environmental provisions in trade agreements, enforcement mechanisms, and optimal practices for sustainability-oriented trade policy. Prominent case studies such as the CPTPP, EU-Mercosur, and ACFTA, underscore both achievements and obstacles in the

DOI: 10.4018/979-8-3373-1782-3.ch005

execution of environmental requirements. Moreover, market incentives like carbon pricing, border tax adjustments, and green subsidies are essential for harmonizing economic and environmental goals. The research offers policy suggestions for enhancing environmental protections, assuring adherence, and promoting international collaboration. The incorporation of comprehensive sustainability measures in trade agreements will be essential for attaining enduring environmental and economic resilience.

INTRODUCTION

Integrating Environmental Safeguards in Trade Agreements: A Sustainable Development Imperative

Trade has long been both a driver of economic growth and interdependence and an environmental threat. The growth of production, infrastructure and consumption associated with liberalised trade has put ever greater pressure on natural ecosystems resulting in losses to biodiversity; pollution; and risks to the climate. Against this global backdrop of a growing focus on sustainability, integrating environmental protection into trade agreements has become one of the key tools to reconcile economic integration with preserving nature. These safeguards are now increasingly framed not just as regulatory duties, but as critical tools for realizing climate-resilient and inclusive development.

Multilateral and regional trade regimes have increasingly incorporated environmental considerations in recent decades, meeting the call of the global agenda established by Sustainable Development Goals (SDG) numbers 12 and 13 -On sustainable Production and Consumption-; and Climate Action. Bilateral and regional trade agreements (BRTAs) from the Comprehensive and Progressive Agreement for Trans-Pacific Partnership (CPTPP), the EU–Mercosur Agreement, to the African Continental Free Trade Area (ACFTA) demonstrate development towards sustainability-oriented trade governance (Rismawati, et al., 2024). However, the extent and enforceability of these provisions are patchy around the world, inviting questions about their actual influence on ecological imperatives and global fairness.

This research explores how environmental clauses are designed, activated and monitored in modern trade agreements to assess whether these instruments can effectively balance economic- and environment-related interests. The study is carried out on the basis of qualitative synthesis of secondary literature and international trade law analysis by using SLR to identify trends, opportunities and best practices across various trade regimes. The paper adopts a legal-economic-institutional perspective and aims to achieve two objectives: the first is to provide new insights into academic discussion of sustainable trade governance while the second is to offer practical guidance for policymakers who are concerned with reconciling trade liberalization with cnvironmental protection.

1.1 Literature Review and Conceptual Background

Incorporating environmental safeguards in trade agreements has gained traction as a mechanism to align global trade with the UN's Sustainable Development Goals (SDGs). Scholars such as Esty (2001), Pauwelyn and Pelc (2022), and Jinnah and Lindsay (2016) have emphasized the dual role of trade agreements as both drivers of economic growth and potential instruments for environmental regulation (Yadav, 2023).

Research on trade–environment linkages highlights three dominant approaches:

1. Environmental Provisions in Bilateral Trade Agreements (BTAs): Studies such as Molua et al. (2023) show that over 80% of BTAs signed post-2015 include at least one enforceable environmental clause, but vary widely in scope and depth.
2. Multilateral Environmental Agreements (MEAs) and Trade Coherence: The WTO Secretariat (2021) warns of legal friction between MEA obligations and WTO principles, particularly for countries in the Global South.
3. Environmental Justice and Trade Asymmetry: Literature such as Mohy-ud-Din et al. (2025) argue that environmental safeguards, if poorly designed, may reinforce trade inequalities by acting as disguised protectionism.

Historically, trade agreements have emphasized economic liberalization by diminishing trade and investment barriers to promote economic growth. As worries over environmental deterioration have escalated, bilateral and regional trade agreements (BRTAs) have progressively integrated environmental elements. These provisions function as instruments to guarantee that economic integration does not compromise ecological sustainability (Bellmann and Bulatnikova, 2022; Yu et al., 2024)

Trade agreements frequently incorporate environmental clauses that mandate adherence to national environmental rules, prohibit the degradation of environmental standards for competitive gain, and advocate for sustainable resource management. Numerous contemporary agreements, including the Comprehensive and Progressive Agreement for Trans-Pacific Partnership (CPTPP) and the European Union's trade accords, incorporate specific environmental chapters that delineate obligations for parties to tackle climate change, deforestation, biodiversity loss, and pollution (Msigwa, et al., 2022).

The North American Free Trade Agreement (NAFTA), which subsequently transformed into the United States-Mexico-Canada Agreement (USMCA), was among the initial trade agreements to incorporate environmental protections. The accord institutes environmental collaboration structures and enhanced enforcement stipulations. The European Union has consistently integrated environmental sustainability requirements into its trade agreements, associating preferential market access with compliance to environmental and labor standards (Moshenski-Dubov, 2022).

Notwithstanding these gains, implementation and enforcement continue to pose significant obstacles. Some agreements provide binding dispute resolution methods for environmental matters, whilst others depend on voluntary collaboration, so diminishing the efficacy of the provisions. Consequently, a persistent dispute exists on the optimal balance between economic interests and ecological integrity in trade agreements.

The Transition from Trade Liberalization to Sustainability-Oriented Trade

The conventional paradigm of trade liberalization concentrated mostly on eliminating tariffs and non-tariff barriers to enhance market efficiency and stimulate economic growth (Dhingra et al., 2023) (Palmer, 2024). In recent decades, there has been a paradigm change towards sustainability-oriented trade, prompted by an increasing awareness of the environmental consequences of globalization. Climate change, deforestation, and pollution have highlighted the necessity of including environmental protections into trade policies.

Trade agreements focused on sustainability harmonize economic goals with environmental obligations, ensuring that trade facilitation does not lead to ecological degradation. Agreements like the EU-Mercosur trade accord now incorporate explicit promises to address unlawful deforestation and foster sustainable supply chains. Additionally, instruments like carbon border adjustment tariffs (CBAM) are being examined to equalize competition for nations with rigorous environmental legislation (Sotirov et al., 2022; Carodenuto & Buluran, 2021).

The evolution of global trade offers a chance to incorporate strong environmental safeguards into trade agreements, so enhancing economic cooperation for environmental protection. Nonetheless, obstacles persist in converting commitments into concrete acts, necessitating ongoing creativity in policy formulation and implementation strategies.

1.2 SDGS AND THE GLOBAL TRADE REGIME

SDGs are unanimously supported (By whom?? Sentence reads incomplete), yet trade agreements implement them unevenly. Some agreements, like the EU–CARIFORUM EPA, relate environmental chapters to SDG 12 (Responsible Consumption and Production) and SDG 13 (Climate Action), while others set no sustainability goals. This threatens coherence and enforcement, especially in low-capacity economies.

The UN Sustainable Development Goals (SDGs), adopted by all 193 United Nations member states in 2015, are a global touchstone for reconciling economic advancement, social fairness and environmental protection. Within this framework, SDG 12 (Responsible Consumption and Production) and SDG 13 (Climate Action) are most immediately connected to the environmental elements of international trading activity (Soroos, 2023). Achieving these objectives in trade policy means that liberalization itself must result in environmental safeguards and governance structures that are transparent and participatory. Yet trade deals have shown patchy adherence to them. Geneva) What is more, some regional arrangements have not even specified any required benchmarks for sustainability in their chapters addressing environmental issues, leading to regulatory fragmentation and low coherence (WTO Secretariat 2021) while the EU-CARIFORUM Economic Partnership Agreement makes explicit reference to linking its chapters on environment with SDG 12 and SDG 13.

Trade can promote or hinder sustainability depending on governance and legally binding environmental conditions. Without sufficient monitoring, dispute resolution, and capacity building, environmental language in trade contracts may be symbolic compliance. Global power dynamics also affect trade and ecology (Hassan, et al., 2024). Countries having more bargaining strength and institutional resources create environmental trade clause norms, typically neglecting poorer states' development interests. Environmental justice and differentiated responsibility must be integrated into trade governance.

Trade Agreements and the Evolution of Environmental Safeguards

Early global trade liberalization accords focused mainly on economic growth by eliminating tariffs, non-tariff obstacles, and cross-border investment. Historic trade agreements like the GATT (1947) ignored environmental concerns (Sands, 2023; Soroos, 2023). Rapid industrial expansion without environmental monitoring caused deforestation, pollution, and unsustainable resource extraction. In the 20th century, trade agreements promoted economic efficiency over environmental protection. To attract foreign investment, developing nations were pressured to lower environmental restrictions, resulting in a "race to the bottom" in ecological norms (Kumar et al., 2022).

Global awareness of environmental degradation increased after the 1972 UN Conference on the Human Environment and the 1992 Rio Earth Summit. These events changed trade policy by requiring states and international organizations to include environmental safeguards. NAFTA, 1994, was accompanied by the North American Agreement on Environmental Cooperation (NAAEC), which sought to improve environmental governance but was institutionally separate from NAFTA.

Illegal fishing, marine pollution, and air quality regulations are now part of environmental commitments in new accords like USMCA (2020). EU trade agreements include sustainability clauses demanding compliance with global environmental obligations like the Paris Agreement. The CPTPP and EU–Mercosur trade deal address deforestation, climate resilience, and sustainable resource management in a more integrated manner (Almeida, 2025). Enforcement remains a problem. Some agreements have binding dispute mechanisms, while others utilize voluntary collaboration, limiting their impact. To balance economic growth and environmental sustainability, trade agreements must strengthen their environmental provisions (Voumik et al., 2023).

1.3 JUSTIFICATION FOR THE INTEGRATION OF ENVIRONMENTAL SAFEGUARDS

Trade agreements must combine economic growth with ecological integrity and social equality; thus environmental safeguards are included. Traditional trade liberalization reduces barriers to market access, but it can also cause environmental degradation, resource exhaustion, and social inequality, hurting long-term economic resilience. Environmental provisions level the playing field by requiring enterprises to follow consistent standards, discouraging a regulatory "race to the bottom" Sustainable trade policies encourage green technology investment and innovation, enhancing long-term competitiveness. High-environmental-standards companies often benefit from consumer demand for eco-friendly items (Heyl et al., 2021). Poor environmental governance causes poor air quality, dirty water, and biodiversity loss, harming public health and livelihoods, especially vulnerable communities. Including environmental provisions in trade agreements protects human well-being. These clauses promote ethical work practices, notably in extractive and agricultural sectors, preventing exploitation. Trade agreements with strong environmental safeguards promote climate action, biodiversity conservation, and resource sustainability. Trade processes correspond with SDGs and Paris Agreement provisions on emissions, deforestation, and responsible supplier chains.

Several modern trade agreements work well. Instead of NAFTA, the USMCA includes binding provisions for air quality, marine preservation, and biodiversity commitments and compliance monitoring. An enforced environmental chapter in the CPTPP targets illegal wildlife trading and overfishing (Malingrey & Duval, 2023). The EU-Mercosur Agreement's commerce and Sustainable Development (TSD) provisions address Amazon deforestation and relate commerce to the Paris Agreement, demonstrating best practices (de et al., 2024; Matsuoka, 2025). These instances show that environmental safeguards improve economic, social, and ecological benefits. Future accords must enforce these advantages and improve trade-environmental policy coordination (Pandey, et al., 2022).

2.1 INTERACTIONS BETWEEN INTERNATIONAL ENVIRONMENTAL AND TRADE LAW

One example of positive trade–environment synergy is the EU–Vietnam Free Trade Agreement (EVFTA), which includes binding provisions on forest governance (FLEGT), labor rights, and carbon transition mechanisms. An independent EU impact report (2021) found a 17% increase in green technology investment in Vietnam's renewable energy sector within 18 months of ratification (Salem, et al., 2023). The agreement also provides structured cooperation on environmental monitoring, with EU-supported technical assistance for Vietnamese regulators.

The World Trade Organization (WTO) is crucial in formulating global trade regulations, particularly those related to environmental protection. The basic objective of WTO agreements is to diminish trade obstacles and promote liberalized commerce, while also integrating environmental factors. Article XX of the GATT (1994) explicitly allows exceptions to trade regulations for measures intended to safeguard human, animal, or plant life (Article XX(b)) and to conserve depleting natural resources (Article XX(g)), contingent upon their non-arbitrary and non-discriminatory nature.

Nonetheless, the invocation of Article XX is legally intricate. Countries must prove that such policies are environmentally justified rather than protectionist. The significant US–Shrimp case (1998) affirmed the U.S. prohibition on shrimp imports without turtle-excluder devices under Article XX(g) while condemning its biased implementation, highlighting the necessity for equitable and transparent laws (Pauwelyn & Pelc, 2022).

The WTO's Agreement on Technical Barriers to Trade (TBT) and the Sanitary and Phytosanitary Measures (SPS) Agreement provide for environmental and health-related measures, contingent upon their scientific basis and absence of unnecessary trade restrictions. These accords are especially pertinent to the management of dangerous substances, genetically modified organisms, and pesticides.

Simultaneously, Multilateral Environmental Agreements (MEAs) such as the Paris Agreement (2015), CITES, and the Basel Convention tackle global challenges including climate change, species conservation, and hazardous waste management. Certain MEA laws, however, may contradict WTO standards in instances of trade restrictions. Initiatives to align trade and environmental frameworks have intensified through debates in the WTO Committee on Trade and Environment. These initiatives seek to elucidate the alignment between trade regulations and environmental obligations, so assuring reciprocal reinforcement of global sustainability objectives.

Anticipating the future, instruments such as carbon border adjustment measures (CBAM), eco-labelling, and green subsidies are developing strategies to synchronize trade with environmental goals. Efficient collaboration between the WTO and MEA secretariats is essential for harmonizing economic and ecological priorities (Turkson et al., 2023; Mohy-ud-Din et al., 2025).

2.2. REGIONAL AND BILATERAL ENVIRONMENTAL SAFEGUARDS

Key Elements of Environmental Chapters in FTAs and RTAs

Modern bilateral and regional trade agreements (FTAs and RTAs) increasingly incorporate environmental safeguards to ensure that trade liberalization aligns with sustainability objectives. Key provisions typically include:

1. Commitment to Multilateral Environmental Agreements (MEAs) – Many agreements require parties to uphold commitments to global accords such as the Paris Agreement, the Convention on Biological Diversity, and the Montreal Protocol. These provisions ensure that trade does not undermine global environmental efforts.
2. Non-Regression and Enforcement Provisions. Environmental chapters often prohibit the weakening of environmental standards for competitive advantage. Some agreements include legally binding enforcement mechanisms and monetary penalties for noncompliance, elevating environmental obligations from rhetorical to actionable.
3. Natural Resource Sustainability. Specific clauses address the sustainable management of resources, including deforestation control, marine ecosystem

protection, and pollution mitigation especially relevant in agricultural, forestry, and extractive industries.

4. Climate-Responsive Trade Policy. New-generation FTAs increasingly link trade with climate action through provisions that promote clean energy investment, low-carbon supply chains, and technology transfer.
5. Transparency, Public Participation, and Dispute Resolution – Recent agreements encourage civil society engagement and offer structured mechanisms for environmental dispute resolution, enhancing accountability and legitimacy.

Case Illustrations: USMCA, EU Agreements, and ASEAN Commitments

USMCA (United States–Mexico–Canada Agreement). Replacing NAFTA in 2020, the USMCA marks a significant evolution by integrating enforceable environmental clauses within the main text. It addresses illegal fishing, wildlife trafficking, and mandates domestic law enforcement, thus moving beyond the non-binding provisions of the original NAAEC (Laurens et al., 2022).

The European Union has emerged as a global leader in embedding environmental and labor standards through Trade and Sustainable Development (TSD) chapters. The EU–Mercosur Agreement explicitly targets Amazon deforestation, though enforcement concerns have delayed ratification. The EU–Vietnam FTA includes binding commitments on fisheries management and climate measures (de et al., 2024).

While ASEAN lacks a unified environmental trade framework, certain agreements like RCEP contain sustainability references, though mostly non-binding (Ishikawa, 2021; Do & Burke, 2023). Regional initiatives such as the ASEAN–Japan Comprehensive Economic Partnership (AJCEP) have expanded environmental cooperation on energy efficiency, green technologies, sustainable palm oil, and marine plastic waste.

Despite this progress, challenges persist. Weak enforcement, limited political will, and inconsistent dispute mechanisms often undermine impact. As Yu et al. (2024) and Heyl et al. (2021) emphasize, preventing greenwashing and ensuring meaningful implementation remain central to aligning regional trade with environmental and climate objectives. A convergence toward binding, participatory, and SDG-aligned trade architecture is both a necessity and an emerging norm.

2.3 COMPLIANCE AND ENFORCEMENT OF ENVIRONMENTAL SAFEGUARDS

The efficacy of environmental clauses in trade agreements is significantly dependent on enforcement and dispute settlement processes. Although several FTAs and

RTAs incorporate environmental provisions, their enforceability exhibits considerable variability. Certain accords incorporate environmental issues within comprehensive trade dispute frameworks, whereas others adopt more lenient, collaborative methodologies (Heyl et al., 2021; Santeramo & Lamonaca, 2022).

The USMCA constitutes a highly enforced framework, featuring binding consequences like trade sanctions and monetary fines for environmental non-compliance. This differs from its predecessor, NAFTA, which did not possess such mechanisms. The EU's Trade and Sustainable Development (TSD) chapters include state-to-state dispute resolution, although frequently favor negotiation over punitive measures. The EU–Korea FTA established a precedent when a dispute panel required South Korea to enhance labor and environmental standards (Kübek, 2022).

Conversely, ASEAN-based agreements such as RCEP incorporate environmental provisions but lack enforceable measures, diminishing the probability of adherence. The voluntary aspect of these systems frequently diminishes their efficacy (Coenen et al., 2021; Bronckers & Gruni, 2021).

Environmental Impact Assessments (EIAs) function as a supplementary regulatory instrument. They assist in identifying and mitigating ecological concerns prior to the implementation of trade agreements. In the European Union, Sustainability Impact Assessments (SIAs) are routinely implemented, shown by the evaluation of the EU–Mercosur Agreement, which assessed effects on biodiversity and deforestation (Komkova & Habert, 2023).

The USTR performs environmental assessments throughout North America to ensure that new trade policies conform to international obligations such as the Paris Agreement. The WTO promotes EIAs among member states, although they are not obligatory (Bellmann & Bulatnikova, 2022).

Notwithstanding advancements, enforcement continues to be irregular. Future trade agreements should have more stringent binding penalties, robust monitoring mechanisms, and institutionalized Environmental Impact Assessments (EIAs) to guarantee environmental sustainability and accountability in global commerce (Heyl et al., 2021).

3.1 STRUCTURAL INEQUITIES AND CAPACITY GAPS

Environmental clauses in trade agreements often reflect the asymmetries in negotiating power between developed and developing countries. Many low- and middle-income countries lack the technical expertise, institutional capacity, and legal advisory infrastructure to engage in complex trade–environment negotiations on equal footing. As a result, they often accept boilerplate clauses without sufficient localization or implementation planning.

These disparities are particularly evident in provisions on carbon accounting, environmental impact assessments, and clean technology transfer. Countries with weak enforcement systems are at risk of signing symbolic commitments with little follow-through, thereby perpetuating greenwashing practices at the international level.

Economic Consequences of Environmental Protections in Trade Agreements

Integrating environmental safeguards into trade agreements presents both prospects and obstacles for economic advancement. Historically centered on improving market access, trade liberalization now aligns with the global necessity of sustainability. Governments and enterprises are progressively required to synchronize economic expansion with ecological accountability.

Countries that include robust environmental protections into trade agreements frequently experience sustained economic resilience and competitiveness. Green trade policies promote investments in clean technologies, energy efficiency, and sustainable resource utilization, which may reduce manufacturing costs and enhance productivity. Organizations implementing sustainable practices—such as renewable energy and low-emission supply chains—may also decrease expenses related to waste management, emissions, and regulatory compliance (Nguy n & Phan, 2025; Jameel et al., 2025).

Nonetheless, these advantages may entail immediate expenses, especially for developing economies dependent on resource-intensive sectors. Failure to achieve environmental compliance rules can increase manufacturing costs and restrict market access for exporters. Industries such as mining, agriculture, and manufacturing encounter heightened scrutiny, frequently necessitating significant investments for compliance (Cheng & Li, 2022; Qiang et al., 2021; Tan et al., 2025).

Environmental regulations may encounter opposition from the sector due to apprehensions of job displacement and financial viability. Stringent laws may result in carbon leakage; wherein polluting sectors migrate to nations with less stringent policies. To mitigate this, governments must provide financial incentives, such green subsidies and access to climate funding, to facilitate adaptation.

Trends in Green Trade and Investment

Green trade regulations are progressively impacting investment decisions as ESG factors become more significant. Investors favor sustainable markets, acknowledging the financial risks associated with environmental noncompliance. Instruments such as Carbon Border Adjustment Mechanisms (CBAMs), suggested by the EU and U.S., associate tariffs with carbon intensity, promoting cleaner production (Gu et al., 2023; Acar et al., 2022).

Current trade agreements provide preferential advantages for environmentally friendly sectors—renewable energy, sustainable agriculture, and circular manufacturing—thereby promoting sustainable investment (Bronckers & Gruni, 2021; Moshood et al., 2022). Multinational corporations are restructuring supply chains to comply with environmental standards, particularly in industries such as textiles and apparel. Ultimately, harmonizing environmental responsibilities with economic incentives will be essential to guarantee that trade fosters both sustainability and enduring success.

3.2 RISK OF PROTECTIONISM AND POLICY SPACE SHRINKAGE

There is increasing apprehension that environmental regulations, particularly when inadequately contextualized, may serve as instruments of covert protectionism. Technical standards, certification processes, and supply chain oversight requirements may impose excessive burdens on exporters from the Global South, especially smallholder growers and small to medium-sized enterprises (SMEs).

This results in the diminishment of domestic policy autonomy, compelling states to conform their environmental legislation to external expectations instead of prioritizing local interests. Reconciling environmental integrity with fair market access is a significant challenge in the formulation of contemporary trade agreements.

Divergent Environmental Regulations Among Trade Partners

A fundamental issue in implementing environmental protections in trade agreements is the inconsistency in environmental regulations and enforcement capabilities among trading partners. Countries exhibit significant disparities in their environmental policies based on their economic development, regulatory priorities, and political commitment to sustainability. Developed nations often implement rigorous environmental standards, but underdeveloped countries may struggle to adhere to them due to limited resources, inadequate infrastructure, and conflicting economic objectives (Huang et al., 2022; Mahalik et al., 2021).

The European Union (EU) has enacted stringent green trade restrictions, notably the Carbon Border Adjustment Mechanism (CBAM), which levies tariffs on imports from countries with high carbon emissions. This strategy aims to prevent carbon leakage, although it has raised concerns among developing countries that lack the financial and technological means to transition to low-carbon industries. Many emerging markets perceive these regulations as trade barriers that limit their access to international markets.

A further issue arises from the lack of harmonization in environmental regulations. Diverse trade agreements establish varying degrees of environmental protection, leading to discrepancies that obstruct compliance for multinational firms. A firm operating in multiple regions may face conflicting environmental standards, leading to increased regulatory requirements and operational costs. This dispersion underscores the need for improved international cooperation to create uniform sustainability criteria that ensure fair and consistent trading conditions.

Inconsistencies in Balancing Economic Goals and Environmental Responsibilities

The reconciliation of economic growth with ecological sustainability remains a contentious issue in international trade dialogues. Governments and industries often prioritize short-term economic gains over long-term environmental responsibilities, leading to disputes in the implementation of sustainable trade policy. Many industries, such as agriculture, mining, and manufacturing, argue that stricter environmental regulations increase production expenses, reduce global competitiveness, and threaten jobs. This has elicited resistance from business lobbyists and trade associations that influence policymaking to protect their economic interests (Rismawati, et al., 2024). Resistance from agricultural exporters has delayed the ratification of the EU-Mercosur Trade Agreement, stemming from concerns regarding deforestation and unsustainable agricultural practices in South America, juxtaposed with the EU's stringent environmental regulations (de et al. 2024).

Furthermore, political instability and changing governmental priorities can undermine environmental commitments inside trade agreements. Some nations have revoked environmental regulations to attract foreign direct investment (FDI) or boost industrial output. The United States' withdrawal from the Paris Agreement under the Trump administration (2017-2021) illustrates how shifts in political leadership can jeopardize international climate cooperation.

To address these issues, trade agreements must incorporate flexible transition procedures, capacity-building initiatives, and financial incentives for developing nations to adopt sustainable trading practices. Improving public-private partnerships, promoting international cooperation, and strengthening enforcement mechanisms can align economic interests with ecological responsibilities, ensuring that trade fosters both prosperity and sustainability.

3.3 INTERNATIONAL INSTITUTIONS AND STAKEHOLDERS: PARTICIPATION OF WTO, UN, AND REGIONAL ECONOMIC BLOCS

To rectify these disparities, academics and professionals have suggested several mechanisms, including:

- Environmental Safeguard Equalization Funds funded by high-emission nations to assist low-income counterparts.
- Specialized technical support platforms for regulatory alignment.
- Reforms in dispute resolution that incorporate equality principles and varied treatment.

Environmental safeguards can foster shared prosperity and not worsen global inequality only through redistributive and context-sensitive procedures. International institutions assist in the integration of environmental safeguards into trade agreements by establishing global norms, encouraging dialogues, and ensuring compliance. The institutions encompass the WTO, UN, and regional economic blocs, which influence trade and environmental sustainability. The World Trade Organization's Committee on Trade and Environment (CTE) examines the ways in which trade policy might protect the environment. GATT Article XX permits countries to implement environmental regulations that safeguard human health and natural resources while adhering to free trade principles. WTO decisions have faced challenges in reconciling trade liberalization with environmental objectives, encompassing conflicts about carbon border taxes, renewable energy subsidies, and eco-labeling.

The United Nations advocates for sustainable trade, chiefly via the United Nations Environment Programme (UNEP) and the United Nations Conference on Trade and Development (UNCTAD). Global enterprises are required to uphold environmental responsibility, as stipulated by Sustainable Development Goals (SDGs) 12 (Responsible Consumption and Production) and 13 (Climate Action). The UN advocates for Multilateral Environmental Agreements (MEAs) such as the Paris Agreement and the Convention on Biological Diversity, which influence environmental provisions in trade agreements. Alamoush et al. (2021)

Regional economic blocs such as the EU, ASEAN, and ACFTA are incorporating environmental stipulations into their trade policies. The EU's Green Deal and CBAM have initiated trade-climate agreements. ASEAN's sustainability initiatives tackle deforestation, marine protection, and trade resilience in response to climate change.

Contributions from the civic and private sectors

Non-governmental organizations and advocacy groups such as WWF and Greenpeace promote enhanced environmental safeguards within trade legislation. They ensure accountability of governments and corporations on environmental commitments through research, lobbying, and public campaigns. Climate litigation has compelled governments to enhance sustainability criteria in trade agreements (Reiners & Versluis, 2023; Liu & Heugens, 2024).

Regulatory constraints, consumer demand, and investment incentives compel the private sector to align corporate strategies with environmental objectives. MNC supply chains are integrating sustainability through the incorporation of Environmental, Social, and Governance (ESG) principles. Numerous companies voluntarily adhere to global sustainability standards such as ISO 14001 for environmental management and SBTi for emissions reduction.

Financial institutions and investors also appreciate green investments and sustainable trade financing, rewarding environmentally responsible firms. The Equator Principles and Green Bonds advocate for responsible investments in infrastructure, energy, and production, influencing global trade.

International institutions, regional economic blocs, civil society organizations, and the corporate sector must collaborate to incorporate environmental safeguards into trade agreements. The WTO and UN establish global trade and environmental policies, while NGOs and corporations implement and create sustainable trade practices. Trade agreements should enhance multi-stakeholder collaboration and implement binding environmental commitments to achieve global sustainability objectives and stimulate economic growth (Singh, 2024).

SOLUTIONS AND RECOMMENDATIONS: POLICY RECOMMENDATIONS AND STRATEGIC PATHWAYS

4.1 Design Principles for Inclusive Environmental Clauses

Effective environmental clauses in trade agreements must go beyond symbolic commitments. They should be grounded in four essential design principles: (1) legally binding and enforceable mechanisms, (2) adaptability to local economic and institutional contexts, (3) integrated systems for monitoring and evaluation, and (4) alignment with international environmental standards, such as the Paris Agreement and the SDGs.

Case Analyses of Trade Agreements Featuring Robust Environmental Provisions

Three key agreements CPTPP, EU-Mercosur, and ACFTA illustrate varying degrees of environmental integration. The CPTPP represents a model of binding environmental governance. It bans harmful subsidies for overfishing, addresses illegal logging, and includes enforceable dispute mechanisms. However, implementation challenges persist in countries with limited regulatory infrastructure.

The EU–Mercosur Agreement mandates commitments to halt Amazon deforestation and comply with the Paris Agreement. Though ambitious, enforcement gaps have delayed ratification. Civil society resistance has played a critical role in demanding stronger monitoring tools (de et al., 2024; Lehmen & Vidigal, 2025). The ACFTA is still in early stages regarding environmental integration. While the initial framework lacks a dedicated environmental chapter, the African Union is exploring policies for green industrialization and climate resilience, highlighting the need for sustainability amid dependence on resource exports.

Insights Gained from Previous Agreements

Key takeaways include:

1. Binding enforcement correlates with greater compliance.
2. Stakeholder engagement, especially NGOs and local communities—is vital for legitimacy.
3. Capacity-building support is essential for developing nations.
4. Transparency and accountability mechanisms, such as independent monitoring and reporting, are needed to deter greenwashing.

An analysis of the CPTPP, EU-Mercosur, and ACFTA accords yields significant insights into the development of environmental provisions inside trade agreements. Despite advancements in the integration of sustainability promises, compliance continues to be a barrier. Future agreements must prioritize enforceable environmental commitments, financial and technical assistance for developing nations, and enhanced accountability frameworks to guarantee that trade fosters both economic development and global sustainability initiatives.

4.2 Financing and Capacity Building Instruments

Adequate financing remains a major barrier for many developing countries in implementing environmental safeguards. Bilateral and multilateral funding mechanisms—such as the Global Environment Facility (GEF) or the Green Climate Fund (GCF)—should be expanded and specifically targeted to support trade-linked environmental infrastructure, especially in Least Developed Countries (LDCs).

In parallel with multilateral financing, market-based mechanisms play a critical role in incentivizing environmental compliance within trade frameworks. Market-based incentives are crucial for trade agreements with environmental safeguards. Carbon pricing, border tax adjustments, and green subsidies are efficient ways to financially motivate firms and governments to adopt sustainable practices while retaining global trade competitiveness. Market mechanisms like carbon pricing internalize the environmental costs of carbon emissions. Carbon taxes or cap-and-trade systems allow corporations to buy and sell emission allowances. Trade agreements that support carbon pricing encourage businesses to invest in low-carbon technologies to compete. Integrating carbon fees into corporate models has helped the EU ETS influence global trade partners.

Governments are using carbon border adjustment systems to avoid carbon leakage from industries moving to countries with lax environmental legislation. These tax imported goods depending on their carbon footprint to ensure foreign corporations meet domestic environmental standards. The EU's CBAM policy, which applies to steel, cement, and aluminum, is a pioneering climate-trade strategy. However, its influence on developing nations that cannot switch to greener production methods is still a problem. Green subsidies help companies invest in green technologies and processes. Renewable energy grants, electric vehicle tax credits, and sustainable agriculture support are among these incentives. Trade agreements that support green subsidies can boost innovation and the low-carbon economy. To avoid trade distortions, they must be properly constructed to conform with WTO standards (Fang & Zhou, 2022; Zhang, 2024)

4.3 Recommendations for Future Trade Agreements

Strategies for Implementing Effective and Equitable Environmental Safeguards

To guarantee that environmental measures in trade agreements are both efficacious and equitable, forthcoming trade frameworks must transcend mere symbolic language and implement binding, enforceable, and inclusive processes. These systems must reconcile sustainable objectives with varying national capacities, especially for developing economies.

Future agreements must mandate enforceable environmental responsibilities, incorporating dispute resolution mechanisms that permit proportional trade sanctions, financial fines, or market limitations. Nonetheless, such enforcement must embody varied obligations, acknowledging the diverse capacities of nations to fulfill sustainable requirements (Poletti et al., 2021).

Dispute resolution procedures must be just. Incorporating mediation tools, structured compliance paths, and facilitating civil society engagement can avert punitive actions from disproportionately impacting vulnerable nations or groups. Creating regional environmental trade tribunals or panels may enhance openness and accountability while promoting inclusive government.

Autonomous entities need to consistently oversee environmental adherence, bolstered by uniform reporting frameworks. Countries and corporations must reveal emissions statistics, resource consumption, and sustainability initiatives, promoting confidence and verifiability. To mitigate escalating global inequities, trade agreements should incorporate financial aid, technical collaboration, and technology transfer initiatives, particularly aimed at Least Developed Countries (LDCs). These instruments facilitate green transitions without imposing structural downsides.

Trade agreements ought to formalize collaboration with the commercial sector, environmental non-governmental organizations, and research institutes. Public-private partnerships can expedite innovation, enhance implementation, and foster ethical supply chains. Future agreements must incorporate climate adaption solutions, including low-carbon infrastructure, resilient supply chains, and incentives for renewable energy investments. A continual concern is the absence of unified environmental standards, which facilitates regulatory arbitrage and jeopardizes global sustainability. Policymakers are required to:

1. Establish multinational benchmarks consistent with the Paris Agreement and World Trade Organization environmental regulations.
2. Align ESG and green financing frameworks across trading systems.
3. Facilitate carbon pricing mechanisms such as the EU's CBAM, guaranteeing equity for exporters from low-income nations.

An equitable, cooperative strategy anchored on enforceability, transparency, and inclusivity will convert trade into a driver for global environmental and economic justice.

FUTURE RESEARCH DIRECTIONS: PROSPECTIVE TRAJECTORIES AND CONCLUSION

5.1 Digitalization, Circular Economy, and South-South Cooperation in Sustainable Commerce

Digital revolution is redefining global commerce and facilitating more sustainable trading practices. Innovative technologies such as blockchain, artificial intelligence (AI), and big data improve transparency, traceability, and compliance in global supply chains. Blockchain guarantees unalterable records of commodity origins, assisting governments and enterprises in verifying compliance with environmental regulations. Industries such as agriculture, fisheries, and forestry have implemented blockchain technology to monitor sustainable certification, including Fair Trade and FSC (Iftekhar & Cui, 2021).

Concurrently, AI and big data analytics enable governments and corporations to pinpoint carbon-intensive nodes within trade networks, enhance routing efficiency, and foresee climate-related hazards. These instruments facilitate ESG-compliant reporting and enhance regulatory oversight (Joshi & Sharma, 2024). E-commerce platforms enhance access to eco-friendly items, broadening markets for sustainable goods. In response, contemporary trade agreements are increasingly incorporating digital sustainability provisions that target emissions from data centers and logistical networks.

Nevertheless, digitalization incurs environmental costs, such as the energy requirements of blockchain mining and data infrastructure. Future trade agreements must promote energy-efficient digital ecosystems and responsible AI governance to guarantee technological progress matches with ecological requirements.

The emergence of circular economy idea is impacting trade frameworks in conjunction with digital integration. Circular methods advocate for resource efficiency, waste reduction, and material reutilization, departing from traditional linear "take–make–dispose" approaches (Kazancoglu et al., 2021). Trade laws increasingly incorporate measures such as Extended Producer Responsibility (EPR), transnational collaboration on recycling, eco-design incentives, and prohibitions on plastic waste exports. The EU's Green Deal requires circularity in its trade agreements, whereas the USMCA has clauses for the advancement of a circular economy.

To successfully execute these approaches, South–South collaboration is essential. Developing nations encounter common obstacles—restricted green technology, inadequate institutional ability, and finance deficiencies. Improved cooperation among regional blocs such as ASEAN, MERCOSUR, and ACFTA can promote tailored environmental protections. These collaborations facilitate the aggregation of technical expertise, collective negotiations on trade-environment matters, and customized sustainability frameworks appropriate for Southern economies.

Knowledge-sharing platforms, green technology transfer, and mutual aid funds among Global South countries might enhance their collective bargaining power in international trade discussions. South–South cooperation provides a means for reasonable, egalitarian, and adaptable sustainability transitions, ensuring that environmental stipulations in trade agreements uphold both ecological integrity and inclusive growth.

5.2 Future Research Directions: The Role of Regional and Bilateral Agreements in Advancing SDGs 12 and 13

As environmental protections are integrated into regional and bilateral trade agreements, future research must rigorously assess their tangible impact on the United Nations Sustainable Development Goals (SDGs)—notably SDG 12 (Responsible Consumption and Production) and SDG 13 (Climate Action). New trade frameworks assert their intention to foster sustainable production and climate-resilient economies; nonetheless, additional empirical study is required to evaluate:

The Effectiveness of Eco-Certifications and Labeling

Future research should investigate the efficacy of environmental certifications (e.g., FSC, MSC, organic labels) integrated inside trade agreements. Do these processes significantly influence producer behavior across many sectors, or are they mainly symbolic?. Cross-Border Circular Economy Integration Research must evaluate the extent to which bilateral and regional agreements, exemplified by the EU Circular Economy Action Plan, promote the trade of recyclable commodities, repairable materials, and secondary raw resources. What legal or logistical obstacles impede the scalability of circular trade models?

There is an increasing necessity to assess the impact of carbon-related trade provisions (e.g., CBAM in EU legislation) on exporters from poor nations. Subsequent investigations may assess whether these techniques genuinely diminish emissions or generate concealed trade distortions. Researchers ought to examine the degree to which trade provisions facilitate access to renewable energy technologies and climate finance, particularly in at-risk economies. What conditions facilitate the effective execution of these clauses?

Future research should delineate the operationalization of climate risk assessments and resilience-building tools such as climate-smart agriculture and green infrastructure clauses within trade agreements like ACFTA and USMCA, as trade intersects with climate adaptation. Ultimately, studies must examine how trade policies allocate climate responsibility across North and South regions. To what degree do contemporary trade-environment models include equity, disparities in capacity, and inclusive development?

By grounding these inquiries in policy and practice, further research may rigorously evaluate the efficacy, equality, and scalability of trade-related sustainability commitments in fulfilling SDG 12 and SDG 13.

5.3 Policy Recommendations for Future Trade Agreements

Strengthening Enforcement and Compliance – Dispute Settlement Mechanisms and Regulatory Alignment

Ensuring that environmental safeguards in trade agreements are effective requires robust enforcement mechanisms and regulatory alignment. While many trade agreements include environmental provisions, weak enforcement and lack of accountability remain significant challenges. To strengthen compliance, future agreements should incorporate:

1. Binding Dispute Settlement Mechanisms. Environmental provisions must be legally enforceable, with clear penalties for non-compliance. Trade agreements such as the United States-Mexico-Canada Agreement (USMCA) set a precedent by allowing trade sanctions for violations of environmental commitments. Future agreements should adopt similar mechanisms to ensure that sustainability obligations are upheld.
2. Regulatory Alignment Across Trade Partners. Divergent environmental regulations create compliance challenges and opportunities for regulatory arbitrage (where companies relocate to countries with weaker laws). Future trade agreements should harmonize environmental standards, ensuring that sustainability requirements are consistent across all member states.
3. Transparency and Monitoring Frameworks. Establishing independent review panels, periodic environmental impact assessments (EIAs), and data-driven sustainability tracking can improve compliance. Trade partners should commit to publicly disclosing environmental performance metrics, ensuring that commitments translate into measurable actions.

Capacity Building for Developing Economies Supporting Green Transitions in Trade Partners

Many developing countries face challenges in meeting high environmental standards due to limited financial resources, inadequate technology, and lack of institutional capacity (Barsha & Munshi, 2023; Chen et al.2022). To promote equitable trade while ensuring sustainability, future agreements should include:

1. Technical Assistance and Knowledge Transfer – Developed nations should support their trade partners by sharing green technologies, providing expertise on sustainable practices, and investing in environmental education. For example, capacity-building initiatives in renewable energy, climate-smart agriculture, and circular economy practices can enable developing economies to comply with environmental commitments.
2. Financial Support for Green Transitions – Future agreements should include climate finance mechanisms, preferential loans, and investment incentives to help developing countries adopt sustainable trade practices. International financial institutions, such as the World Bank and the Green Climate Fund, should work with trade policymakers to ensure funding accessibility for green infrastructure projects.
3. Incentivizing Sustainable Investments – Trade agreements should promote sustainability-linked incentives, such as tariff reductions for eco-friendly goods and services or preferential market access for businesses with strong environmental performance.

A major challenge in implementing environmental safeguards is the lack of global consistency in sustainability regulations. While regional trade blocs like the European Union (EU) have developed strong environmental frameworks, other regions still lag behind (Emon et al.2025; Dimnwobi et al.2023). Future trade agreements should prioritize:

1. Integration of Trade Agreements with Global Climate Commitments – Agreements must align with international sustainability frameworks such as the Paris Agreement, the Convention on Biological Diversity (CBD), and the UN Sustainable Development Goals (SDGs).
2. Regional Policy Alignment for Sustainability – Regional economic blocs such as ASEAN, ACFTA, and MERCOSUR should develop coordinated sustainability policies to facilitate cross-border cooperation in green trade initiatives, emissions reduction, and biodiversity conservation.
3. Global Trade Governance Reform – Institutions such as the World Trade Organization (WTO) should work toward integrating environmental provisions into multilateral trade rules, ensuring that sustainability commitments are reinforced at the global level.

To strengthen environmental governance in trade agreements, binding enforcement mechanisms, financial and technical support for developing economies, and regional cooperation are essential. Future trade policies must ensure that sustainability is not just an aspiration but a legal and economic priority. By integrating dispute resolution systems, capacity-building initiatives, and harmonized environmental standards, trade agreements can contribute to both economic prosperity and environmental resilience in the global economy.

CONCLUSION

The incorporation of environmental protections into bilateral and regional trade agreements has emerged as an essential element of sustainable development governance. With the expansion of global commerce, the necessity to harmonize economic liberalization with environmental stewardship and climatic resilience has heightened. This chapter has illustrated that although numerous contemporary trade agreements incorporate sustainability provisions—such as environmental impact assessments, dispute resolution mechanisms, and commitments to international environmental treaties, their efficacy significantly fluctuates based on enforceability, institutional capacity, and political will.

Case studies of accords like the USMCA, CPTPP, and EU-Mercosur elucidate critical insights concerning the significance of legal enforceability, civil society engagement, and unique obligations for emerging countries. Moreover, advancements in digitization, green finance, and circular economy concepts provide novel avenues for integrating sustainability into trade frameworks, while also introducing new regulatory and technological hurdles.

The chapter emphasizes the necessity for equitable strategies, particularly for Global South nations, via capacity-building, climate finance, and South–South collaboration. Regional blocs such as ASEAN, MERCOSUR, and ACFTA are strategically positioned to develop context-specific environmental policies that promote both commerce and sustainability.

Incorporating strong and equitable environmental protections into trade policy is crucial for promoting SDG 12 and SDG 13. Future research and regulation must emphasize enforceability, transparency, inclusion, and innovation to guarantee that trade serves as a true catalyst for global ecological integrity and intergenerational fairness.

REFERENCES

Acar, S., Aşıcı, A. A., & Yeldan, A. E. (2022). Potential effects of the EU's carbon border adjustment mechanism on the Turkish economy. Environment, Development and Sustainability, 24(6), 8162-8194. springer.comDOI: 10.1007/s10668-021-01779-1

Alamoush, A. S., Ballini, F., & Ölçer, A. I. (2021). Revisiting port sustainability as a foundation for the implementation of the United Nations Sustainable Development Goals (UN SDGs). Journal of Shipping and Trade. springer.comDOI: 10.1186/s41072-021-00101-6

Almeida, T. F. (2025). Environmental Protection or Domestic Protectionism? The EU Deforestation-Free Regulation and its Shift from Exporter to Importer of Foreign Capital. In *EU External Relations Law and Sustainability: The EU, Third States and International Organizations* (pp. 167–201). TMC Asser Press. [HTML], DOI: 10.1007/978-94-6265-655-0_8

Barsha, S., & Munshi, S. A. (2023). Implementing artificial intelligence in library services: A review of current prospects and challenges of developing countries. [HTML]. *Library Hi Tech News*. Advance online publication. DOI: 10.1108/LHTN-07-2023-0126

Bellmann, C., & Bulatnikova, A. (2022). *Incorporating environmental provisions in regional trade agreements in chapters and articles dealing with trade in services.* OECD Trade and Environment. [HTML], DOI: 10.1787/6e976798-

Chen, Y., Yao, Z., & Zhong, K. (2022). Do environmental regulations of carbon emissions and air pollution foster green technology innovation: Evidence from China's prefecture-level cities. [HTML]. *Journal of Cleaner Production, 350*, 131537. Advance online publication. DOI: 10.1016/j.jclepro.2022.131537

Coenen, J., Bager, S., Meyfroidt, P., Newig, J., & Challies, E. (2021). Environmental governance of China's belt and road initiative. Environmental Policy and Governance, 31(1), 3-17. wiley.comDOI: 10.1002/eet.1901

Dhingra, S., Freeman, R., & Huang, H. (2023). The impact of non-tariff barriers on trade and welfare. Economica. wiley.comDOI: 10.1111/ecca.12450

Dimnwobi, S. K., Okere, K. I., Onuoha, F. C., Uzoechina, B. I., Ekesiobi, C., & Nwokoye, E. S. (2023). Energizing environmental sustainability in Sub-Saharan Africa: the role of governance quality in mitigating the environmental impact of energy poverty. Environmental Science and Pollution Research, 30(45), 101761-101781. https://hdl.handle.net/10419/298246 econstor.eu

Emon, M. M. H., Khan, T., Rahman, M. A., Hamid, A. B. A., & Yaakub, N. I. (2025). GreenTech revolution: Navigating challenges and seizing opportunities. In *AI and green technology applications in society* (pp. 63–90). IGI Global Scientific Publishing. [HTML], DOI: 10.4018/979-8-3693-9879-1.ch003

Fang, M. M. & Zhou, W. (2022). Greening the road: China's low-carbon energy transition and international trade regulation. Leiden Journal of International Law. cambridge.orgDOI: 10.1017/S0922156521000704

Gu, R., Guo, J., Huang, Y., & Wu, X. (2023). Impact of the EU carbon border adjustment mechanism on economic growth and resources supply in the BASIC countries. [HTML]. *Resources Policy*, *85*, 104034. Advance online publication. DOI: 10.1016/j.resourpol.2023.104034

Hassan, M. U., Rana, A. T., Khan, M., & Gillani, S. (2024). Trade agreements and CO2 emissions in Asian countries: Accounting for institutional heterogeneity. [HTML]. *Environmental Science and Pollution Research International*, *31*(6), 9197–9217. DOI: 10.1007/s11356-023-31684-1 PMID: 38191733

Heyl, K., Ekardt, F., Roos, P., Stubenrauch, J., & Garske, B. (2021). Free trade, environment, agriculture, and plurilateral treaties: the ambivalent example of Mercosur, CETA, and the EU–Vietnam free trade agreement. Sustainability. mdpi.comDOI: 10.3390/su13063153

Huang, Y., Haseeb, M., Usman, M., & Ozturk, I. (2022). … between ICT, renewable energy, economic complexity and ecological footprint: Is there any difference between E-7 (developing) and G-7 (developed) countries? [HTML]. *Technology in Society*, *68*, 101853. Advance online publication. DOI: 10.1016/j.techsoc.2021.101853

Iftekhar, A. & Cui, X. (2021). Blockchain-based traceability system that ensures food safety measures to protect consumer safety and COVID-19 free supply chains. Foods. mdpi.comDOI: 10.3390/foods10061289

Ishikawa, K. (2021). The ASEAN Economic Community and ASEAN economic integration. Journal of Contemporary East Asia Studies. tandfonline.comDOI: 10.1080/24761028.2021.1891702

Jameel, A., Imran, M., Adam, N. A., Mirzaliev, S., Khidirov, M., & Yingying, G. (2025). Safeguarding tourism economies: Managing the financial and ecological challenges of oil spills on coastal destinations. [HTML]. *Marine Pollution Bulletin*, *213*, 117668. DOI: 10.1016/j.marpolbul.2025.117668 PMID: 39970791

Joshi, S. & Sharma, M. (2024). Intelligent algorithms and methodologies for low-carbon smart manufacturing: Review on past research, recent developments and future research directions. IET Collaborative Intelligent .... wiley.comDOI: 10.1049/cim2.12094

Kazancoglu, I., Sagnak, M., Kumar Mangla, S., & Kazancoglu, Y. (2021). Circular economy and the policy: A framework for improving the corporate environmental management in supply chains. Business Strategy and the Environment, 30(1), wiley.comDOI: 10.1002/bse.2641

Komkova, A. & Habert, G. (2023). Environmental impact assessment of alkali-activated materials: Examining impacts of variability in constituent production processes and transportation. Construction and Building Materials. sciencedirect.comDOI: 10.1016/j.conbuildmat.2022.129032

Kübek, G. (2022). Sustainable development chapters in EU FTAs and dispute settlement: lessons learned from Ukraine-Wood Products and Korea-Labour Rights. Understanding the EU as a Good Global Actor. rug.nlDOI: 10.4337/9781802202984.00026

Kumar, P., Kumar, A., Patil, M., Hussain, S., Sharma, S., Singh, S., . . . Singh, A. N. (2022). Biodiversity Resources and Ecosystem Services in the Context of the Industrialized World. In Biodiversity (pp. 23-39). CRC Press. [HTML]DOI: 10.1201/9781003220398-3

Laurens, N., Dove, Z., Morin, J. F., & Jinnah, S. (2022). NAFTA and the Environment: Decades of Measured Progress. NAFTA 2.0: From the first NAFTA to the United States-Mexico-Canada Agreement, 157-180. ulaval.caDOI: 10.1007/978-3-030-81694-0_11

Lehmen, A. & Vidigal, G. (2025). Trade and Environment in EU-Mercosur Relations: Negotiating in the Shadow of Unilateralism. European Foreign Affairs Review. httpss:// [HTML]DOI: 10.54648/EERR2025004

Liu, W., & Heugens, P. P. (2024). Cross-sector collaborations in global supply chains as an opportunity structure: How NGOs promote corporate sustainability in China. [HTML]. *Journal of International Business Studies*, *55*(4), 429–449. Advance online publication. DOI: 10.1057/s41267-023-00644-9

Mahalik, M. K., Mallick, H., & Padhan, H. (2021). Do educational levels influence the environmental quality? The role of renewable and non-renewable energy demand in selected BRICS countries with a new policy.... [HTML]. *Renewable Energy*, *164*, 419–432. Advance online publication. DOI: 10.1016/j.renene.2020.09.090

Malingrey, L., & Duval, Y. (2023). Identifying a Sustainable Path for RCEP: Global Overview and Comparative Analysis of Sustainable Development Provisions in Three Mega Regional Trade Agreements. [HTML]. *Journal of Asian Economic Integration*, *5*(2), 109–128. DOI: 10.1177/26316846231184936

Mohy-ud-Din, K., Shahbaz, M., & Du, A. M. (2025). Corporate social responsibility and climate change mitigation: Discovering the interaction role of green audit and sustainability committee. [HTML]. *Corporate Social Responsibility and Environmental Management*, *32*(1), 1198–1212. DOI: 10.1002/csr.3011

Molua, E. L., Sonwa, D., Bele, Y., Foahom, B., Mate Mweru, J. P., Wa Bassa, S. M., ... & Masumbuko, E. M. (2023). Climate-smart conservation agriculture, farm values and tenure security: implications for climate change adaptation and mitigation in the Congo Basin. Tropical Conservation Science, 16, 19400829231169980. sagepub.comDOI: 10.1177/19400829231169980

Moshenski-Dubov, G. (2022). The Protection of Environmental Law under NAFTA and CUSMA: A Canadian Perspective. Can.-USLJ. https://scholarlycommons.law.case.edu/cuslj/vol46/iss1/15 case.edu

Moshood, T. D., Nawanir, G., Mahmud, F., Mohamad, F., Ahmad, M. H., & AbdulGhani, A. (2022). Biodegradable plastic applications towards sustainability: A recent innovations in the green product. Cleaner Engineering and Technology, 6, 100404. sciencedirect.comDOI: 10.1016/j.clet.2022.100404

Msigwa, G., Ighalo, J. O., & Yap, P. S. (2022). Considerations on environmental, economic, and energy impacts of wind energy generation: Projections towards sustainability initiatives. [HTML]. *The Science of the Total Environment*, *849*, 157755. Advance online publication. DOI: 10.1016/j.scitotenv.2022.157755 PMID: 35921924

Nguy n, H. V., & Phan, T. T. (2025). Impact of economic growth, international trade, and FDI on sustainable development in developing countries. [HTML]. *Environment*. Advance online publication. DOI: 10.1007/s10668-023-04060-9

Palmer, M. (2024). Beyond Tariff Reduction: A Libertarian Approach to Reducing Non-Tariff Barriers. [HTML]. *Liberty and Security in an Anarchical World*, *I*, 281–313. Advance online publication. DOI: 10.1007/978-3-031-70525-0_10

Pandey, N., de Coninck, H., & Sagar, A. D. (2022). Beyond technology transfer: Innovation cooperation to advance sustainable development in developing countries. Wiley Interdisciplinary Reviews: Energy and Environment, 11(2), e422. wiley.comDOI: 10.1002/wene.422

Pauwelyn, J. & Pelc, K. (2022). WTO Rulings and the Veil of Anonymity. European Journal of International Law. ejil.orgDOI: 10.1093/ejil/chac027

Poletti, A., Sicurelli, D., & Yildirim, A. B. (2021). Promoting sustainable development through trade? EU trade agreements and global value chains. Italian political science review/rivista italiana di scienza politica, 51(3), 339-354. cambridge.orgDOI: 10.1017/ipo.2020.33

Qiang, O., Tian-Tian, W., Ying, D., Zhu-Ping, L., & Jahanger, A. (2021). The impact of environmental regulations on export trade at provincial level in China: evidence from panel quantile regression. Environmental Science and Pollution Research, 1-14. springer.comDOI: 10.1007/s11356-021-17676-z

Reiners, K. & Versluis, E. (2023). NGOs as new Guardians of the Treaties? Analysing the effectiveness of NGOs as decentralised enforcers of EU law. Journal of European Public Policy. tandfonline.comDOI: 10.1080/13501763.2022.2084146

Rismawati, R., Darsono, T., Pujotomo, D., Tunjungsari, H., Numberi, A., Korniawan, R., & Agustiyanto, A. (2024). Exploring the relationship between sustainable supply chain and sustainable development goals on the financial performance of SMEs. *Uncertain Supply Chain Management*, *12*(3), 1911–1922. DOI: 10.5267/j.uscm.2024.2.012

Salem, H. S., Pudza, M. Y., & Yihdego, Y. (2023). … in the Arabian Gulf region, considering population, climate change impacts, ecological and carbon footprints, and United Nations' Sustainable Development Goals. Sustainable Earth Reviews. springer.comDOI: 10.1186/s42055-023-00057-4

Sands, P. (2023). Environmental protection in the twenty-first century: Sustainable development and international law. [HTML]. *Global Environment*. Advance online publication. DOI: 10.4324/9781003421368

Santeramo, F. G., & Lamonaca, E. (2022). Standards and regulatory cooperation in regional trade agreements: What the effects on trade?. Applied Economic Perspectives and Policy, 44(4), 1682-1701. wiley.comDOI: 10.1002/aepp.13276

Singh, N. (2024). Promoting Multi-stakeholder Collaboration for Nature-Based Sustainable Development. In Nature-Based Solutions in Achieving Sustainable Development Goals: Harmonizing Nature and Progress (pp. 289-316). Cham: Springer Nature Switzerland. [HTML]DOI: 10.1007/978-3-031-76128-7_10

Soroos, M. S. (2023). Global institutions and the environment: An evolutionary perspective. [HTML]. *Global Environment*. Advance online publication. DOI: 10.4324/9781003421368

Sotirov, M., Azevedo-Ramos, C., Rattis, L., & Berning, L. (2022). Policy options to regulate timber and agricultural supply-chains for legality and sustainability: The case of the EU and Brazil. [HTML]. *Forest Policy and Economics*, *144*, 102818. DOI: 10.1016/j.forpol.2022.102818

Tan, R., Hou, K., & Wu, H. (2025). The cost of biodiversity protection: National key ecological functional zone and labor demand in China. [HTML]. *Journal of Asian Economics*, *97*, 101895. Advance online publication. DOI: 10.1016/j.asieco.2025.101895

Turkson, E., Oduro, A. D., Baffour, P. T., & Quartey, P. (2023). Regional integration and non-tariff barriers to Intra-Sub-Saharan Africa trade. [HTML]. *World Economy*, *46*(2), 396–414. DOI: 10.1111/twec.13365

Turkson, E., Oduro, A. D., Baffour, P. T., & Quartey, P. (2023). Regional integration and non-tariff barriers to Intra-Sub-Saharan Africa trade. [HTML]. *World Economy*, *46*(2), 396–414. DOI: 10.1111/twec.13365

Voumik, L. C., Rahman, M. H., Rahman, M. M., Ridwan, M., Akter, S., & Raihan, A. (2023). Toward a sustainable future: Examining the interconnectedness among Foreign Direct Investment (FDI), urbanization, trade openness, economic growth, and energy usage in Australia. Regional Sustainability, 4(4), 405-415. sciencedirect.comDOI: 10.1016/j.regsus.2023.11.003

Yadav, B. K. (2023). Impact of regulation and conformity assessment procedures on global trade. In Handbook of Quality System, Accreditation and Conformity Assessment (pp. 1-21). Singapore: Springer Nature Singapore. [HTML]DOI: 10.1007/978-981-99-4637-2_14-1

Yu, H., Wang, R., & Zhang, A. (2024). Unraveling the impact of environmental provisions in preferential trade agreements on green total factor energy efficiency. [HTML]. *Journal of Environmental Management*, *362*, 121205. Advance online publication. DOI: 10.1016/j.jenvman.2024.121205 PMID: 38823299

Zhang, Y. (2024). RETRACTED ARTICLE: Promoting sustainable growth through eco-innovation, energy transition, and human capital: a comparative analysis of G-7 economies. [HTML]. *Economic Change and Restructuring*, *57*(6), 186. Advance online publication. DOI: 10.1007/s10644-024-09770-2

Zhong, J. & Pei, J. (2024). Carbon border adjustment mechanism: a systematic literature review of the latest developments. Climate Policy. iqcyg.comDOI: 10.1080/14693062.2023.2190074

Chapter 6
Dynamics, Agreements, and Industry Impacts of Trade in Goods Within the EU-27

Mallika Roy
http://orcid.org/0000-0002-5854-5084
Central Queensland University, Australia & University of Chittagong, Bangladesh

Bablo Biswas
University of Chittagong, Bangladesh

ABSTRACT

The EU-27, a key economic bloc, operates within an integrated trade framework emphasizing free movement, regulatory harmonization, and global trade agreements. This study analyzes its internal trade mechanisms, external partnerships, and sectoral impacts. The EU's intra-trade structure fosters cross-border commerce, with evolving trends in industry integration. Bilateral and multilateral agreements enhance trade ties, shaping relations post-Brexit. Agriculture benefits from the Common Agricultural Policy, while manufacturing relies on innovation and global value chains. Green energy policies drive sustainability, with renewable targets and trade incentives. Regulatory frameworks ensure high standards and competitiveness, amid emerging digitalization and sustainability challenges. This study explores EU-27's trade agreements, sector-specific effects, and evolving policies, using qualitative analysis and case studies from WTO and EU trade reports. Insights will guide policymakers and industry leaders in navigating the complexities of EU trade in a dynamic global landscape.

DOI: 10.4018/979-8-3373-1782-3.ch006

INTRODUCTION

The European Union (EU-27) occupies a central role in the global economy, not only as one of the world's largest trading blocs but also as a regulatory power shaping international trade norms (Meunier & Nicolaidis, 2023; Neto, 2024). As of 1 January 2021, the European Union (EU) had a population of approximately 447.2 million people (Eurostat, 2022). The largest share was concentrated in Germany, home to 83.2 million residents (19% of the EU total), followed by France with 67.7 million (15%), Italy with 59.2 million (13%), Spain with 47.4 million (11%), and Poland with 37.8 million (8%) (Eurostat, 2022). Together, these five countries represented about two-thirds of the entire EU population. With a population of over 447.2 million and a highly integrated single market, the EU represents a unique experiment in regional economic integration, combining the principles of free trade with a strong regulatory framework (Egan, 2014; Jovanović, 2015). Its collective trade policy, managed by the European Commission on behalf of all member states, gives the EU significant bargaining power in global trade negotiations, making it a critical actor in setting the rules that govern international commerce (Hoffmeister, 2015).

Over the past decades, the EU has developed a sophisticated internal market system that eliminates barriers to trade among member states and ensures a common external tariff toward non-members (Brenton et al., 2001; Öberg, 2020). Externally, the EU has built an extensive network of bilateral and multilateral trade agreements with major economies and emerging markets, while simultaneously championing rules-based trade under the World Trade Organization (WTO) (Elliott, 2018; Viju-Miljusevic, 2019). This dual approach allows the EU to safeguard its internal cohesion while pursuing global competitiveness.

At the same time, the EU's trade policy is closely linked to its broader strategic objectives. Through sector-specific measures such as the Common Agricultural Policy (CAP), digital single market initiatives, and sustainability commitments under the European Green Deal, the EU has sought to align trade with economic, social, and environmental goals (Sotte & Vergamini, 2025; Stefanis et al., 2024). The Union has also become a global standard-setter, exporting its regulatory models in areas such as data protection, consumer safety, and environmental regulation—a phenomenon often referred to as the "Brussels Effect" (Bradford, 2020; Christen et al., 2022). This study examines the EU-27 trade framework in a comprehensive manner, focusing on three main dimensions: the internal trade structure that underpins the single market, the external trade agreements and partnerships that shape its global engagement, and the sector-specific contributions that highlight the Union's role in agriculture, manufacturing, services, and green technologies. By exploring these dimensions, the analysis sheds light on how the EU balances economic liberalization with regulatory control, and how its trade policies influence both domestic integration and global economic governance.

This chapter is structured as follows: it begins with a background section to establish the context and key concepts, followed by an examination of internal market integration and trade governance. The chapter then explores sector-specific implications, before analysing the trade policy and regulatory framework. Next, it discusses emerging challenges and opportunities and finally concludes with a conclusion that synthesises the main insights and implications.

BACKGROUND

The European Union plays a central role in global trade, engaging with a wide range of partners across regions through both exports and imports. Its trade relationships reflect a mix of historical ties, strategic partnerships, and growing interdependence with emerging economies.

Figure 1a. Principal partners for EU exports and imports of goods

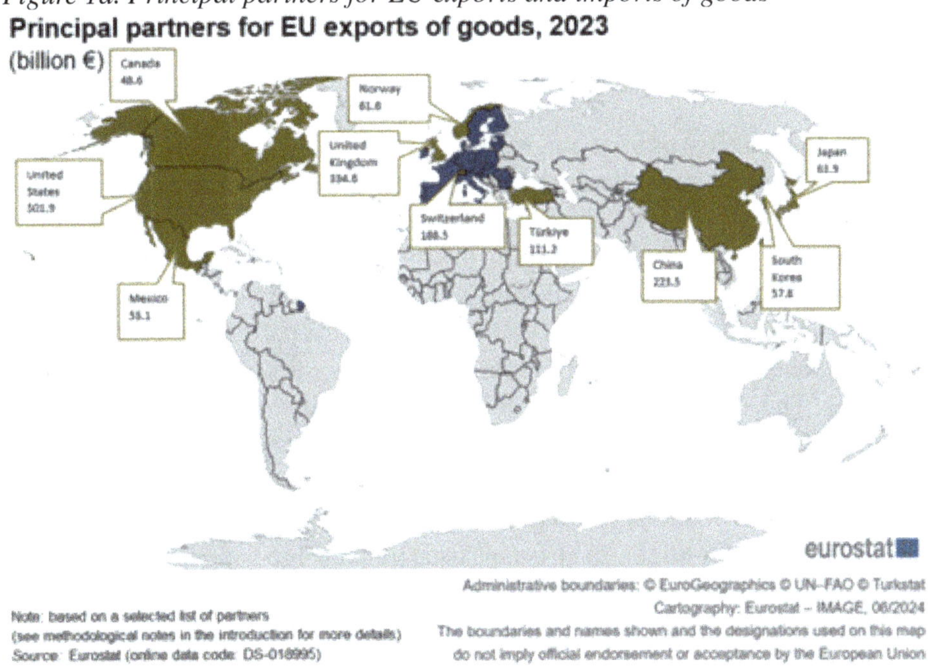

Figure 1b. Principal partners for EU exports and imports of goods

Source: Eurostat, 2023

Figure 1(a) and 1(b) provides an overview of the EU's principal trade partners in 2023 for exports and imports consequently, and they reveal important asymmetries in the EU's trade dynamics.

On the exports side, the United States (501.9 billion €) is by far the EU's largest destination, followed by the United Kingdom (394.6 billion €), Switzerland (188.5 billion €), and China (223.5 billion €). Other significant partners include Norway, Japan, and South Korea, with exports more geographically diversified across advanced economies. This highlights the EU's reliance on high-income markets for selling manufactured goods, pharmaceuticals, and high-value products. On the imports side, China dominates as the EU's largest source (516.2 billion €), followed by the United States (366.7 billion €), the United Kingdom (180 billion €), and Russia (90.7 billion €). India (65.1 billion €) also appears among the top suppliers, underlining the growing importance of emerging economies. Compared to exports, imports are more concentrated in Asia, particularly in intermediate goods, electronics, textiles, and energy products.

While the United States is the EU's most important partner for exports, China leads as the EU's largest supplier, reflecting structural trade imbalances. The EU's trade with the UK and Switzerland remains strong in both directions, illustrating enduring regional ties despite Brexit. Imports show more exposure to resource and energy suppliers such as Russia and Norway, while exports reflect Europe's strength in high-value goods. Overall, the EU runs a trade surplus with Western partners (US, UK, Switzerland) *but* a trade deficit with Asian economies (China, South Korea, India), demonstrating the dual nature of its global trade relationships.

Following the departure of the United Kingdom in 2020, the EU-27 has continued to consolidate its position as a unified market of over 447 million consumers, underpinned by a single market framework that ensures the free movement of goods, services, capital, and people (Stojkov & Warin, T., 2025). This integration allows the EU to function as both a common economic area and a collective actor in international trade negotiations, giving it substantial bargaining power in shaping global trade rules (Kamidza, 2017).

Internally, the EU's trade framework is characterized by harmonized regulations and common standards across member states, which reduce transaction costs, eliminate technical barriers to trade, and ensure fair competition within the bloc (Brenton et al., 2001; Maskus et al., 2000; Vogel, 2010). The Customs Union eliminates tariffs on intra-EU trade, while adopting a common external tariff toward non-member countries (Adedokun, 2024; Enchelmaier, 2019). The European Commission, acting on behalf of all member states, manages trade policy, ensuring coherence across diverse sectors such as agriculture, manufacturing, energy, and digital services (Carbone, 2008; Nilsson et al., 2012; Wallace, 2020). This collective approach enables small and medium-sized member states to benefit from the economic weight of the bloc, while ensuring that trade rules are applied uniformly. Externally, the EU has developed one of the most comprehensive networks of trade agreements in the world, including bilateral, regional, and multilateral frameworks (Antimiani & Salvatici, 2015; Maluck et al., 2018; Renard, 2016). As a key supporter of the World Trade Organization (WTO), the EU actively promotes rules-based global trade, while also negotiating preferential trade agreements with major economies and emerging markets (Bollyky & Mavroidis, 2017; Trommer, 2017). Partnerships such as the EU-Japan Economic Partnership Agreement, EU-South Korea FTA, and the EU-Canada Comprehensive Economic and Trade Agreement (CETA) exemplify its role as a leader in advancing liberalized yet regulated trade relations (Hladnik, 2022; Van der Vorst et al., 2022). At the same time, the EU has become a global standard-setter, exporting its regulatory models on issues such as data privacy (GDPR), environmental protection, food safety, and consumer rights—an influence often described as the "Brussels Effect" (Bradford, 2015; Jančiūtė, 2018)

Sector-specific trade impacts are also significant within the EU framework. Agriculture and food products benefit from the Common Agricultural Policy (CAP), which not only stabilizes farm incomes but also ensures a steady supply of food across the region (Kiryluk-Dryjska & Baer-Nawrocka, 2021; Westhoek et al., 2012). Industrial sectors—such as automotive, machinery, chemicals, and pharmaceuticals—are supported by harmonized production standards, enabling firms to scale production for a large unified market (Togan et al., 2005). Meanwhile, the EU is increasingly shaping global debates in digital trade, renewable energy, and green technologies, linking trade policy to its climate commitments under the European Green Deal (Leonard et al., 2021). By embedding sustainability criteria into its trade agreements and exploring mechanisms like the Carbon Border Adjustment Mechanism (CBAM), the EU positions itself as a pioneer in aligning trade with environmental and social objectives.

Overall, the EU-27 trade framework reflects a unique balance between liberalization and regulation, fostering an open internal market while using its external trade policy to promote both economic interests and global norms. This dual role not only strengthens its competitiveness but also ensures that EU trade policy remains a critical force in shaping global economic governance.

INTERNAL MARKET INTEGRATION AND TRADE GOVERNANCE

Internal Trade Structure

The EU's internal trade framework is supported by harmonized regulations that facilitate seamless cross-border movement of goods. The European Commission plays a pivotal role in ensuring uniform trade policies across member states, influencing both intra-EU trade and external trade negotiations. The internal trade structure of the EU27 has evolved significantly over time. Research shows that EU27 countries exhibit high trade diversity, exporting 78% and importing 90% of goods traded globally, with a trend towards reconcentration in recent years (Parteka, 2012). Trade restructuring during the accession process has led to increased intra-industry trade between new member states and the EU15, indicating lower welfare losses and less resistance to further integration (Fidrmuc, 2005). However, a quality-adjusted analysis reveals a persistent divide between new member states and cohesion countries compared to non-cohesion EU15 countries, particularly in terms of same-quality exports (Kaitila, 2010). These studies highlight the importance of considering both trade structure similarity and product quality when assessing the competitiveness and integration of EU countries' export markets.

Trade Agreements

The EU actively engages in bilateral free trade agreements (FTAs), regional partnerships, and multilateral frameworks, strengthening its trade ties with major economies such as the United States, China, and the United Kingdom. Agreements such as the European Economic Area (EEA) and European Free Trade Association (EFTA) enhance regional trade cooperation. The European Union (EU) has developed various trade agreements to promote European integration, maintain economic ties with former colonies, and enhance relations with developing countries (Kurzweil et al., 2003). These agreements typically cover general trade, allow phased implementation, and address sensitive agricultural products. Thc EU Commission has used bilateral trade agreements to advance integration by expanding their scope and establishing joint bodies, often overcoming member state resistance (Gastinger, 2023). The EU's trade agreements have transformed the Commission into a global political actor and increased its external action capability. Following Brexit, the UK and EU27 face challenges in negotiating new trade arrangements, particularly in the financial services sector (Rehman & Della Posta, 2018). The EU continues to pursue trade agreements with non-EU states to strengthen its international position and facilitate trade for its members (Mavroskoti, 2021). These agreements often include provisions related to intellectual property rights and other qualitative aspects (Kurzweil et al., 2003; Mavroskoti, 2021). Table 1 represents international trade structure and trade agreement of the EU-27.

Table 1. Internal Trade Structure and Trade Agreements of the EU-27

Theme	Key Features	Evidence/Findings	Sources
Internal Trade Structure	Harmonized regulations, single market policies, and Commission oversight ensure seamless intra-EU trade and cohesion.	- EU27 accounts for 78% of global exports and 90% of imports; trend toward reconcentration. - Accession boosted intra-industry trade between new members and EU15, lowering welfare losses. - Persistent quality divide between cohesion states and non-cohesion EU15 in export competitiveness.	Parteka (2012); Fidrmuc (2005); Kaitila (2010)
Trade Agreements	Bilateral FTAs, regional partnerships (EEA, EFTA), and multilateral agreements shape EU's external relations.	- Agreements cover phased integration, sensitive agriculture, and IP rights. - Bilateral deals expand Commission's role as global political actor. - Brexit created challenges in EU–UK trade (esp. financial services). - Ongoing FTAs strengthen EU's global position and external capability.	Kurzweil et al. (2003); Gastinger (2023); Rehman & Della Posta (2018); Mavroskoti (2021)

SECTOR-SPECIFIC IMPLICATIONS

Agriculture

The Common Agricultural Policy (CAP) significantly impacts agricultural trade, regulating subsidies and trade flows in commodities like dairy, meat, and grains. The EU agricultural sector has experienced significant changes due to trade liberalization and enlargement. EU membership has led to increased agricultural trade for new member states, with exports growing dynamically (Hegedüs & Kiss, 2014). However, the impact of international agricultural trade on EU economic growth is limited, primarily involving live animals, animal products, and fats/oils (Remeikienė et al., 2018). Trade openness initially negatively affects technical efficiency in EU agriculture but improves it over time, with Southern European nations showing the highest efficiency (Hart et al., 2015). The EU enlargement has resulted in increased intra-EU agri-food exports, particularly for new member states, although old member states maintain a dominant position. Approximately 70% of EU-27 agri-food exports occur within the intra-EU market, with new member states increasing exports of new varieties/products (Bojnec & Fertő, 2015). Overall, these studies highlight the complex dynamics of agricultural trade within the expanded EU.

Manufacturing

Key industries, including textiles, handicrafts, pharmaceuticals, and medical devices, are subject to stringent regulatory standards that influence trade dynamics within and beyond the EU. The manufacturing sector plays a crucial role in EU trade, with machinery and transportation products comprising 41% of total EU exports in 2016 (Chatzilazarou & Dadakas, 2024). Trade in intermediate products is significant, reflecting the multi-country nature of production processes (Ali-Yrkkö et al., 2011). Intangible assets, treated as knowledge-intensive inputs in global value chains, have shown increasing cross-country trade in EU manufacturing sectors from 2000 to 2014 (Tsakanikas et al., 2022). Innovation and technological spillovers impact the variety and quality of intra-European manufacturing trade, with innovation potentially leading to quality upgrades (Van Hove, 2010). The EU has potential to expand trade in machinery and transportation products with existing Regional Trade Agreements in the Americas, Africa, and the Middle East (Chatzilazarou & Dadakas, 2024). These findings highlight the complex nature of EU manufacturing trade and the importance of innovation, intangibles, and global value chains in shaping trade patterns and competitiveness.

Green Energy

The EU is increasingly promoting sustainable trade policies, supporting the transition to environmentally friendly industries and circular economy models. The EU has set ambitious targets for renewable energy consumption, aiming for a 20% share by 2020 and 32% by 2032 (Aune et al., 2012; Karakosta & Petropoulou, 2022). To achieve these goals, many member states have implemented Tradable Green Certificate (TGC) systems, which mandate specific percentages of renewable energy consumption (Karakosta & Petropoulou, 2022). While EU-wide trade in green certificates could potentially reduce implementation costs by up to 70%, the current system of differentiated national targets prevents fully cost-effective distribution of energy production and consumption (Aune et al., 2012). The absence of binding national targets may lead to misalignment with EU-wide welfare maximization due to cross-country externalities (Karakosta & Petropoulou, 2022). Additionally, the EU's network of preferential trade agreements (PTAs) could play a crucial role in promoting renewable energy, potentially increasing international trade in energy and contributing to the EU's energy independence as renewables become more economically viable (Leal-Arcas et al., 2015). Table 2 demonstrates the sector-specific contributions to EU trade.

Table 2. Sector-Specific Contributions to EU Trade

Sector	Key Features	Findings	Sources
Agriculture	Governed by the Common Agricultural Policy (CAP), which regulates subsidies and trade flows in dairy, meat, grains, and other commodities.	- EU membership boosts agricultural trade for new member states. - International agricultural trade contributes modestly to EU growth (mainly live animals, animal products, oils/fats). - Trade openness initially reduces but later improves technical efficiency, strongest in Southern Europe. - Enlargement increased intra-EU agri-food exports; ~70% of agri-food exports remain intra-EU.	Hegedüs & Kiss (2014); Remeikienė et al. (2018); Hart et al. (2015); Bojnec & Fertő (2015)
Manufacturing	Covers textiles, pharmaceuticals, machinery, transportation, and high-value medical devices, shaped by strict EU regulatory standards.	- Machinery and transportation products made up 41% of EU exports (2016). - Trade in intermediate products reflects multi-country production processes. - Rising role of intangible assets (2000–2014) as knowledge inputs in GVCs. - Innovation and spillovers upgrade product quality in intra-EU trade. - Potential expansion in machinery/transport trade with RTAs in Americas, Africa, Middle East.	Chatzilazarou & Dadakas (2023); Ali-Yrkkö et al. (2011); Tsakanikas et al. (2022); Van Hove (2010)
Green Energy	Focus on sustainable trade, renewable energy, and circular economy targets.	- EU targets: 20% renewable share by 2020, 32% by 2032. - Tradable Green Certificates (TGCs) used by member states; EU-wide trade could cut costs by ~70%. - Differentiated national targets hinder cost efficiency; lack of binding targets may cause misalignment. - Preferential trade agreements (PTAs) could boost renewable energy trade and EU energy independence.	Aune et al (2012); Karakosta & Petropoulou (2022); Leal-Arcas et al. (2015)

TRADE POLICY AND REGULATORY FRAMEWORK

The EU's trade regulations and their impact on the movement of goods

The EU's trade regulations significantly impact the movement of goods within the single market. The free movement of goods is a fundamental pillar of the EU's internal market, promoting trade and efficiency among member states (Varrica & Rusu, 2023). The Treaty on the Functioning of the European Union (TFEU) prohibits customs duties, quantitative restrictions, and discriminatory national taxation between member states (Homewood et al., 2022). These regulations aim to eliminate tariff and non-tariff barriers to trade, ensuring free trade in goods (Gormley, 2010). The European Commission plays a crucial role in overseeing the internal market and enforcing these provisions (Berlingher, 2018). The Community Customs Code and its associated measures govern the operation of the customs union, further facilitating the free movement of goods (Gormley, 2009). Overall, these regulations create a framework that allows goods to flow freely between EU countries without customs duties or other barriers, contributing to the EU's prosperity in a globalized world (Varrica & Rusu, 2023; Berlingher, 2018).

Harmonization of standards across member states and the impact on inter-regional trade

Research indicates that harmonization and mutual recognition of standards generally enhance trade, with mutual recognition showing a stronger positive effect due to conformity assessment recognition (Orefice et al., 2012). The harmonization of Maximum Residue Levels (MRLs) across EU member states has led to increased trade at both extensive and intensive margins, even for developing country exporters (Foletti & Shingal, 2014). Regional agreements on standards typically increase trade between participating countries, but effects on trade with non-members vary. Harmonization tends to boost exports from excluded industrial countries to the region while reducing exports from excluded developing countries. Mutual recognition agreements generally promote trade unless they contain restrictive rules of origin, which can disadvantage developing countries (Chen & Mattoo, 2008).

Customs procedures, tariffs, and non-tariff barriers to trade

The European Union (EU) customs union is incomplete due to varying trade procedures across member states, which significantly impact non-EU exports (Bourdet & Persson, 2012). Non-tariff barriers (NTBs) in the EU are governed by Articles

34, 35, and 36 of the Treaty on the Functioning of the European Union, with case law shaping their interpretation (Garnizova, 2018). Quantifying the trade effects of NTBs remains challenging, but research suggests they have significant impacts on EU trade (Dihel & Walkenhorst, 2002). NTBs have emerged as protectionist tools affecting exports from developing countries to the EU and US, particularly in agriculture (Subow, 2014). Harmonizing trade procedures within the EU could potentially increase exports from non-EU countries by 20% (Bourdet & Persson, 2012). However, data limitations and conceptual issues in estimating export potentials under free trade conditions hinder definitive conclusions on the relative restrictiveness of different NTBs (Dihel & Walkenhorst, 2002).

Table 3 represents EU trade policy and regulatory framework with key features and findings.

Table 3. EU Trade Policy and Regulatory Framework

Theme	Key Features	Findings / Impacts	Sources
EU Trade Regulations and Free Movement of Goods	Free movement of goods as a pillar of the EU single market, overseen by the European Commission.	- Customs duties, quantitative restrictions, and discriminatory taxation between member states prohibited (TFEU). - Community Customs Code governs customs union operations. - Framework eliminates tariff and non-tariff barriers, fostering efficiency and prosperity.	Varrica & Rusu (2023); Homewood et al. (2022); Gormley (2009, 2010); Berlingher (2018)
Harmonization of Standards Across Member States	Harmonization and mutual recognition of product standards and conformity assessments.	- Mutual recognition has stronger trade-boosting effects than harmonization. - Harmonized Maximum Residue Levels (MRLs) increased trade, incl. from developing countries. - Regional agreements expand trade within members, but effects differ for excluded countries (industrial vs. developing). - Restrictive rules of origin in MRAs can disadvantage developing economies.	Orefice et al. (2012); Foletti & Shingal (2014); Chen & Mattoo (2008)
Customs Procedures, Tariffs, and Non-Tariff Barriers (NTBs)	Customs union with uneven trade procedures; NTBs regulated by TFEU Articles 34–36 and shaped by case law.	- Incomplete customs union hinders non-EU exports. - NTBs significantly affect trade, especially agricultural exports from developing countries. - Harmonized trade procedures could increase non-EU exports by 20%. - Quantifying NTBs is difficult due to data and conceptual limitations.	Bourdet & Persson (2012); Garnizova (2018); Dihel & Walkenhorst (2002); Subow (2014)

CASE STUDIES

Evolving Dynamics of EU–Asia Trade Relations

The EU-Asia trade relationship has evolved significantly, with the EU becoming a leading trade partner for many Asian nations (Khandekar, 2012). However, this relationship is characterized by chronic trade deficits for the EU, particularly with East and Southeast Asian countries (Pasierbiak & Białowąs, 2024). The EU has made efforts to strengthen economic ties with Asia, including the establishment of the Asia-Europe Meeting (ASEM) and pursuing Free Trade Agreements (Smith, 2013; Kubo, 2013). Despite these efforts, the EU's approach has shifted towards defensiveness and bilateralism, potentially hindering global trade governance (Smith, 2013). Political issues, such as human rights concerns, have also impacted trade relations (Kubo, 2013). The ongoing financial crisis has further weakened the EU's position in Asia (Khandekar, 2012). Recent analyses using value-added trade statistics suggest that trade imbalances between the EU and Asian economies may be smaller than traditional gross export data indicate (Pasierbiak & Białowąs, 2024).

EU-US Trade Relations and emerging dynamics

The trade relationship between the EU and US has been a significant force in the global economy, with both entities being major trade and investment partners (Dağdemir, 2014). Their economic ties have evolved since World War II, transitioning from US dominance to a more balanced relationship (Andreescu & Sfetea, 2013). Despite the benefits of free trade, commercial disputes have strained transatlantic relations (Paukku, 2000). Efforts to resolve these conflicts through WTO mediation and negotiations have had limited success, leading to concerns about potential trade wars and protectionist measures (Paukku, 2000). The relationship has faced further challenges in recent years, with disagreements postponing negotiations on the Trans-Atlantic Free Trade Agreement (Ludwikowski, 2020). While there have been periods of improved sentiment and increased cooperation, such as US support for the European Deterrence Initiative, tensions persist, particularly regarding European military autonomy (Ludwikowski, 2020). The complex nature of EU-US trade relations continues to shape the global economic landscape.

EU–Africa Economic Partnership

The trade relationship between the EU and Africa has evolved from colonial-era arrangements to a comprehensive strategic partnership (Mangala, 2010). This long-standing relationship, formalized in the 1970s, is centered on development assistance and preferential trade cooperation (Haastrup et al., 2020). The Cotonou Agreement and Economic Partnership Agreements (EPAs) have been key in shaping EU-Africa trade relations, with a focus on creating a free trade area and aligning with WTO rules (Adetula & Osegbue, 2020; Sassi & Bernini, 2009). Agricultural trade is particularly significant, as the EU is a leading global exporter and importer of agricultural goods, while African countries rely on agricultural exports for foreign exchange (Sassi & Bernini, 2009). However, challenges remain, including limited supply potential and high EU sanitary and phytosanitary standards for African exports (Sassi & Bernini, 2009). The EU's recent Comprehensive Strategy with Africa (2020) signals a new type of engagement, reflecting the evolving nature of this crucial partnership (Haastrup et al., 2020).

Textile trade between EU and India

The textile trade between the EU and India is significant, with the EU accounting for 17-20% of Indian exports (Bywalec, 2020). However, India's share in the EU market has declined, while Bangladesh and Vietnam have gained ground (Sharma & Bharti, 2025). A proposed EU-India Free Trade Agreement (FTA) could potentially benefit India's key export sectors, particularly textiles, apparel, and leather goods (Khorana & Narayanan, 2017). Computable general equilibrium modeling suggests positive welfare effects for India under both complete and selective tariff elimination scenarios (Khorana & Narayanan, 2017). Despite lowered import tariffs, Indian firms still face various non-tariff barriers when exporting to the EU (Khorana & Soo, 2016). Firms closer to ports report lower transport costs and less corruption (Khorana & Soo, 2016). The ongoing FTA negotiations between the EU and India aim to address these trade barriers and potentially create a free trade area of 1.8 billion people (Bywalec, 2020).

EU's involvement in pharmaceutical trade

The European Union (EU) plays a significant role in the global pharmaceutical market, with its member states being major exporters and importers of pharmaceutical products (Ganslandt & Maskus, 2004). However, the EU faces challenges in balancing intellectual property rights with access to essential medicines in developing countries (Hecker, 2019). The pharmaceutical industry is crucial for many European economies, with Italy, Germany, France, and Belgium leading in production (Mossialos & Oliver, 2005). The EU's pharmaceutical policies aim to facilitate a strong, profitable industry, although it still lags behind the USA (Earl-Slater, 1997). Recent EU regulations promote R&D and drug production, supporting the industrial sector, while national regulations differ in pricing and reimbursement

(Burstall et al., 1999). The creation of a single pharmaceutical market in the EU remains a complex process, requiring careful consideration of regulatory diversity and the balance between economic factors and public health (Earl-Slater, 1997; Garattini et al., 2021).

Table 4 demonstrates EU Trade relations and sectoral engagement with key features and challenges.

Table 4. Evolving EU Trade Relations and Sectoral Engagements

Region / Sector	Key Features of Trade Relationship	Challenges / Issues	Sources
EU–Asia	EU is a major partner for Asian economies; initiatives like ASEM and FTAs pursued.	Chronic EU trade deficits with East & Southeast Asia; shift towards bilateralism; political issues (human rights); weakened EU position during financial crisis.	Khandekar (2012); Smith (2013); Kubo (2013); Pasierbiak & Białowąs (2024)
EU–US	Long-standing transatlantic partnership; major trade & investment flows; WTO mediation for disputes.	Persistent commercial disputes; stalled Transatlantic FTA talks; tensions over protectionism and EU military autonomy despite cooperation (e.g., European Deterrence Initiative).	Dağdemir (2014); Andreescu & Sfetea (2013); Paukku (2000); Ludwikowski (2020)
EU–Africa	Historic ties evolved into strategic partnership; Cotonou Agreement & EPAs shape trade; strong agricultural trade flows.	Limited African supply capacity; strict EU SPS standards restrict exports; need for WTO alignment; ongoing asymmetries.	Mangala (2010); Haastrup et al. (2020); Adetula & Osegbue (2020); Sassi & Bernini (2009)
EU–India (Textiles)	EU is a key export market for Indian textiles (17–20% of exports); proposed FTA to boost apparel, textiles, leather goods.	Declining Indian share vs. Bangladesh & Vietnam; non-tariff barriers; high transport costs and corruption inland; ongoing FTA negotiations.	Bywalec (2020); Sharma & Bharti (2025); Khorana & Narayanan (2017); Khorana & Soo (2016)
Pharmaceutical Trade	EU is a major player in global pharma; leading producers include Germany, France, Italy, Belgium; policies promote R&D and competitiveness.	Balancing IP rights with medicine access in developing countries; regulatory diversity in pricing/ reimbursement; EU lags behind US in global pharma.	Ganslandt & Maskus (2004); Mossialos & Oliver (2005); Hecker (2019); Burstall et al. (1999); Earl-Slater (1997); Garattini et al. (2021)

EMERGING CHALLENGES AND OPPORTUNITIES

The study highlights the complexities of post-Brexit trade negotiations, the role of digitalization in transforming supply chains, and the EU's growing emphasis on sustainability in trade policies. The evolving nature of the EU-27 trade framework underscores its global economic significance. As digital transformation, sustainability objectives, and geopolitical shifts continue to reshape trade dynamics, the EU must adapt its policies to maintain competitiveness and economic stability. Future research should focus on assessing the long-term effects of digital trade, the role of artificial intelligence in supply chains, and the sustainability impacts of evolving trade regulations.

The primary objective of this research is to explore the structural and functional dimensions of the EU-27's trade framework, with a focus on bilateral, regional, and multilateral trade agreements. The study also assesses the economic implications of these agreements across key industries, including agriculture, manufacturing, pharmaceuticals, and green energy. Additionally, it investigates emerging challenges such as post-Brexit trade realignments, digitalization, and sustainability-driven trade policies. This research employs a qualitative analysis of trade flows, policy documents, and case studies. Data is sourced from EU trade reports, World Trade Organization (WTO) publications, and industry-specific research. Comparative case studies are utilized to illustrate the impact of EU trade agreements on specific regions and industries. This study provides critical insights for policymakers, industry leaders, and trade analysts, offering a roadmap for navigating the complexities of EU-27 trade in an increasingly interconnected global economy.

Challenges Arising from U.S. Tariff Policy, EU–US Trade Relations, and Geopolitical Tensions

The current U.S. tariff posture, rooted in the Trump-era protectionist approach, presents significant challenges for EU–US trade relations by increasing costs on key industrial goods (such as metals, automobiles, and machinery), creating policy uncertainty, and encouraging trade diversion and delayed investment decisions; these challenges are further compounded by the EU's historical reliance on Russian gas and oil, ongoing U.S. and EU sanctions on Russia, and the prolonged Russia–Ukraine war, which together disrupt energy markets, constrain Russian exports (both energy and non-energy commodities), reduce EU exports to Russia, and indirectly weaken EU competitiveness in global markets due to higher energy and compliance costs.

Policy Recommendations for Strengthening Trade Cooperation

To address the current trade and geopolitical challenges, several policy recommendations are essential.

- Pursue tariff de-escalation and predictability through structured EU–US dialogue, transparent safeguard mechanisms, and sector-specific arrangements to reduce uncertainty for trade and investment.

- Strengthen economic cooperation beyond tariffs by promoting regulatory harmonisation, mutual recognition of standards, and digitalised customs procedures to lower non-tariff barriers.
- Reinforce bilateral, multilateral, and regional trade frameworks, particularly WTO-consistent mechanisms and EU trade and investment agreements, to support a stable, rules-based trading system.
- Enhance coordination on energy security and sanctions between the EU and the USA to mitigate disruptions from the Russia–Ukraine war, accelerate EU energy diversification, and safeguard industrial competitiveness.
- Promote sustainable investment and supply-chain resilience by encouraging strategic partnerships in clean energy, critical minerals, and advanced manufacturing to strengthen long-term international economic relations.

CONCLUSION

The EU-27 remains one of the world's most influential trading blocs, with its integrated internal market and extensive network of external trade agreements shaping global economic relations. The analysis highlights several key takeaways. First, the evolving nature of EU trade in goods reflects both its internal cohesion—through harmonized standards and regulatory frameworks—and its external engagement as a leading advocate of rules-based trade. Second, persistent challenges remain, including structural trade imbalances with Asia, supply-side limitations in Africa, and the EU's own need to adapt to geopolitical uncertainties, protectionist pressures, and rising competition from emerging economies. These obstacles underscore the importance of balancing liberalization with strategic autonomy.

Looking ahead, the future direction of EU trade policy will be strongly influenced by three interconnected forces. The first is global trade dynamics, where shifting supply chains, regional agreements, and the growing role of emerging markets will require the EU to act as both a stabilizer and an innovator. The second is the EU's sustainability goals, particularly the European Green Deal and the Carbon Border Adjustment Mechanism, which are likely to redefine trade flows by embedding environmental standards into economic relations. The third is digital transformation, which is reshaping value chains, e-commerce, data governance, and technology-driven services, areas where the EU seeks to position itself as a global standard-setter. In conclusion, the EU-27's trade framework is at a crossroads: while it faces mounting pressures, it also has the opportunity to reinforce its global influence by aligning trade with sustainability, digital innovation, and inclusive development. Its ability to integrate these priorities will determine not only its future competitiveness but also its role in shaping the evolving architecture of global trade governance.

REFERENCES

Adedokun, A. S. (2024). Improving Intra-African trade for AfCFTA and non-AfCFTA Trade flows through trade policy regime: Lessons from European Union. In *Africa-EU Relations and the African Continental Free Trade Area: Redefining the Dynamics of Power and Economic Partnership in a Complex Global Order* (pp. 53–77). Springer Nature Switzerland. DOI: 10.1007/978-3-031-57992-9_4

Adetula, V., & Osegbue, C. (2020). Trade and the Economic Partnership Agreements in EU-Africa relations. In *The Routledge Handbook of EU-Africa Relations* (pp. 211–223). Routledge. DOI: 10.4324/9781315170916-20

Ali-Yrkkö, J., Foster-McGregor, N., Hanzl-Weiss, D., Rouvinen, P., Seppälä, T., Stehrer, R., Stöllinger, R., & Ylä-Anttila, P. (2011). Trade in Intermediate Products and EU Manufacturing Supply Chains. *WIIW Research Reports.* Accessed from https://www.econstor.eu/bitstream/10419/204141/1/wiiw-research-rep-369.pdf

Andreescu, C. V., & Sfetea, R. C. (2013). EU-US Trade Relationship. *Knowledge Horizons. Economics*, *5*(4), 62.

Antimiani, A., & Salvatici, L. (2015). Regionalism versus multilateralism: The case of the European Union trade policy. *Journal of World Trade*, *49*(2).

Aune, F. R., Dalen, H. M., & Hagem, C. (2012). Implementing the EU renewable target through green certificate markets. *Energy Economics*, *34*(4), 992–1000. DOI: 10.1016/j.eneco.2011.07.006

Berlingher, R. D. (2018). Regulating free movement of goods within the european union. *Journal of Legal Studies. Vasile Goldiş*, *21*(35), 61–77.

Bojnec, Š., & Fertő, I. (2015). Does enlargement has caused intra and extra European Union agri-food trade? *Bulgarian Journal of Agricultural Science*, *21*(1), 1–15.

Bollyky, T. J., & Mavroidis, P. C. (2017). Trade, Social Preferences and Regulatory Cooperation The New WTO-Think. *Journal of International Economic Law*, *20*(1), 1–30. DOI: 10.1093/jiel/jgw076

Bourdet, Y., & Persson, M. (2012). Completing the European Union Customs Union: The effects of trade procedure harmonization. *Journal of Common Market Studies*, *50*(2), 300–314. DOI: 10.1111/j.1468-5965.2011.02203.x

Bradford, A. (2015). Exporting standards: The externalization of the EU's regulatory power via markets. *International Review of Law and Economics*, *42*, 158–173. DOI: 10.1016/j.irle.2014.09.004

Bradford, A. (2020). *The Brussels effect: How the European Union rules the world.* Oxford University Press. DOI: 10.1093/oso/9780190088583.001.0001

Brenton, P., Sheehy, J., & Vancauteren, M. (2001). Technical barriers to trade in the European Union: Importance for accession countries. *Journal of Common Market Studies, 39*(2), 265–284. DOI: 10.1111/1468-5965.00288

Burstall, M. L., Reuben, B. G., & Reuben, A. J. (1999). Pricing and reimbursement regulation in Europe: An update on the industry perspective. *Drug Information Journal, 33*(3), 669–688. DOI: 10.1177/009286159903300304

Bywalec, G. (2020). Dynamics and determinants of trade exchange between the European Union and India. *Optimum. Economic Studies, 101*(3), 123–139.

Carbone, M. (2008). Mission impossible: The European Union and policy coherence for development. *European integration, 30*(3), 323-342.

Chatzilazarou, L. A., & Dadakas, D. (2024). Trade potential in European Union manufacturing. *Journal of Economic Studies (Glasgow, Scotland), 51*(5), 1144–1163. DOI: 10.1108/JES-06-2023-0292

Chen, M. X., & Mattoo, A. (2008). Regionalism in standards: Good or bad for trade? *The Canadian Journal of Economics. Revue Canadienne d'Economique, 41*(3), 838–863. DOI: 10.1111/j.1540-5982.2008.00488.x

Christen, E., Meyer, B., Oberhofer, H., Hinz, J., Kamin, K., & Wanner, J. (2022). *The Brussels effect 2.0: How the EU sets global standards with its trade policy* (No. 2022-07). FIW-Research Reports.

Dağdemir, E. U. (2014). From Economic Protectorate to the Transatlantic Trade and Investment Partnership: A New-Age Relationship between the European Union and the United States? *Marmara Üniversitesi Avrupa Araştırmaları Enstitüsü Avrupa Araştırmaları Dergisi, 22*(1), 31–63.

Dihel, N., & Walkenhorst, P. (2002). European Union trade and non-tariff measures.

Earl-Slater, A. (1997). Recent legal and policy developments affecting the EU pharmaceutical business environment. *European Business Review, 97*(6), 267–278. DOI: 10.1108/09555349710189978

Egan, M. (2014). *Single markets: Economic integration in Europe and the United States.* OUP Oxford.

Elliott, K. A. (2018). The WTO and regional/bilateral trade agreements. In *Handbook of International Trade Agreements* (pp. 17–28). Routledge. DOI: 10.4324/9781351046954-3

Enchelmaier, S. (2019). The Foundations of the Internal Market: Free Trade Area and Customs Union under Articles 28-31 TFEU. *Erasmus L. Rev.*, *12*(3), 219–228. DOI: 10.5553/ELR.000138

Eurostat (2022). A growing population until 2020. Accessed from https://ec.europa.eu/eurostat/cache/digpub/demography_2022/bloc-1a.html?lang=en

Eurostat (2023). International trade in goods by partner. https://ec.europa.eu/eurostat/statistics-explained/index.php?title=International_trade_in_goods_by_partner

Fidrmuc, J. (2005). Trade Structure during Accession to the EU. *Post-Communist Economies*, *17*(2), 225–234. DOI: 10.1080/14631370500104943

Foletti, L., & Shingal, A. (2014). *Trade effects of MRL harmonization in the EU* (No. 720).

Ganslandt, M., & Maskus, K. E. (2004). Parallel imports and the pricing of pharmaceutical products: Evidence from the European Union. *Journal of Health Economics*, *23*(5), 1035–1057. DOI: 10.1016/j.jhealeco.2004.03.005

Garattini, S., Natsis, Y., & Banzi, R. (2021). Pharmaceutical strategy for Europe: Reflections on public health-driven drug development, regulation, and policies. *Frontiers in Pharmacology*, *12*, 685604. DOI: 10.3389/fphar.2021.685604

Garnizova, E. (2018). *The new political economy of trade: understanding the treatment of non-tariff measures in European Union trade policy* (Doctoral dissertation, London School of Economics and Political Science).

Gastinger, M. (2023). EU Trade Agreements and European Integration. Routledge. *Accessed from* https://www.taylorfrancis.com/books/mono/10.4324/9781003342427/eu-trade-agreements-european-integration-markus-gastinger

Gormley, L. W. (2009). *EU law of free movement of goods and customs union.* Oxford university press. DOI: 10.1093/oso/9780199229000.001.0001

Haastrup, T., Mah, L., & Duggan, N. (Eds.). (2020). *The Routledge handbook of EU-Africa relations.* Routledge. DOI: 10.4324/9781315170916

Hart, J., Miljkovic, D., & Shaik, S. (2015). The impact of trade openness on technical efficiency in the agricultural sector of the European Union. *Applied Economics*, *47*(12), 1230–1247. DOI: 10.1080/00036846.2014.993134

Hecker, P. (2019). EU TRADE LAW AND PHARMACEUTICALS. In *EU Law of Competition and Trade in the Pharmaceutical Sector* (pp. 377–404). Edward Elgar Publishing. DOI: 10.4337/9781785362613.00018

Hegedüs, Z., & Kiss, J. (2014). The impact of ten years of European Union membership on Hungarian agricultural trade. *Studies in Agricultural Economics (Budapest)*, *116*(2), 87–94. DOI: 10.7896/j.1407

Hladnik, A. (2022). *Comparative Analysis of Legal and Economic Aspects of the EU's Free Trade Agreements with Selected Asian Economies* (Master's thesis, ISCTE-Instituto Universitario de Lisboa (Portugal)).

Hoffmeister, F. (2015). The European Union as an international trade negotiator. In *The European Union as a diplomatic actor* (pp. 138–154). Palgrave Macmillan UK. DOI: 10.1057/9781137356857_9

Homewood, M. J., Homewood, M., & Smith, C. (2022). *EU Law Concentrate: Law Revision and Study Guide*. Oxford University Press. DOI: 10.1093/he/9780192865663.001.0001

Jančiūtė, L. (2018). *EU politics and the making of the General Data Protection Regulation: Consociationalism, policy networks and institutionalism in the process of balancing actor interests* (Doctoral dissertation, University of Westminster).

Jovanović, M. N. (2015). The economics of international integration. In *The Economics of International Integration* (2nd ed.). Edward Elgar Publishing.

Kaitila, V. (2010). *Quality-adjusted similarity of EU-countries' export structure* (No. 1227). ETLA Discussion Papers.

Kamidza, R. (2017). *From Antagonism to Re-engagement: Zimbabwes Trade Negotiations with the European Union, 2000-2016*. African Books Collective.

Karakosta, O., & Petropoulou, D. (2022). The EU electricity market: Renewables targets, Tradable Green Certificates and electricity trade. *Energy Economics*, *111*, 106034. DOI: 10.1016/j.eneco.2022.106034

Khandekar, G. (2012). The Changing Landscape of EU-Asia Relations. *Jindal Journal of International Affairs*, *2*(1), 72–89. DOI: 10.54945/jjia.v2i1.31

Khorana, S., & Narayanan, B. G. (2017). Modelling effects of tariff liberalisation on India's key export sectors: Analysis of the EU–India free trade agreement. *Margin*, *11*(1), 1–22. DOI: 10.1177/0973801016676016

Khorana, S., & Soo, K. T. (2016). Barriers to Exporting to the EU: Evidence from Textiles and Leather. *A Project Funded by the British High Commission*, 2-21.

Kiryluk-Dryjska, E., & Baer-Nawrocka, A. (2021). Regional differences in benefits from the EU Common Agricultural Policy in Poland and their policy implications. *Agriculture*, *11*(4), 288. DOI: 10.3390/agriculture11040288

Kubo, H. (2013). EU-Asia Trade Relations. In *The Palgrave Handbook of EU-Asia Relations* (pp. 247–262). Palgrave Macmillan UK. DOI: 10.1057/9780230378704_16

Kurzweil, M., Ledebur, O. V., & Salamon, P. (2003). Review of trade agreements and issues. *Accessed from* https://www.semanticscholar.org/paper/Review-of-trade-agreements-and-issues-Kurzweil-Ledebur/147493dc5d34f05ff16eba5611d9e592886c8906

Leal-Arcas, R., Grasso, C., & Ríos, J. A. (2016). Renewables, preferential trade agreements and EU energy security. In *Energy Security, Trade and the EU* (pp. 244-325). Edward Elgar Publishing. DOI: 10.4337/9781785366741.00012

Leonard, M., Pisani-Ferry, J., Shapiro, J., Tagliapietra, S., & Wolff, G. B. (2021). *The geopolitics of the European green deal* (No. 04/2021). Bruegel policy contribution.

Ludwikowski, R. R. (2020). Overview of the Trade Relations Between the European Community/Union and the United States at the Threshold of Globalization and Post-globalization Era. *Białostockie Studia Prawnicze*, *25*(3), 27–42. DOI: 10.15290/bsp.2020.25.03.02

Maluck, J., Glanemann, N., & Donner, R. V. (2018). Bilateral trade agreements and the interconnectedness of global trade. *Frontiers in Physics (Lausanne)*, *6*, 134. DOI: 10.3389/fphy.2018.00134

Mangala, J. (2010). The European Union and Africa: Old partners in a changing world. In *Africa and the New World Era: From Humanitarianism to a Strategic View* (pp. 167–191). Palgrave Macmillan US. DOI: 10.1057/9780230117303_12

Maskus, K. E., Wilson, J. S., & Otsuki, T. (2000). Quantifying the impact of technical barriers to trade. *World Bank Policy Research Working Paper*, *2512*, 1–51.

Mavroskoti, Z. (2021). The export of EU copyright law: the example of the Free Trade Agreements. In *EU Copyright Law* (pp. 1024–1049). Edward Elgar Publishing. DOI: 10.4337/9781786437808.00036

Meunier, S., & Nicolaidis, K. (2023). The European Union as a Trade Power. *International Relations and the European Union*, *168*, 155–180. DOI: 10.1093/hepl/9780192897343.003.0008

Mossialos, E., & Oliver, A. (2005). An overview of pharmaceutical policy in four countries: France, Germany, the Netherlands and the United Kingdom. *The International Journal of Health Planning and Management*, *20*(4), 291–306. DOI: 10.1002/hpm.816

Neto, P. S. (2024). *Economic Diplomacy in the European Union: Economic Co-operation and Global Influence* (Master's thesis, ISCTE-Instituto Universitario de Lisboa (Portugal)).

Nilsson, M., Zamparutti, T., Petersen, J. E., Nykvist, B., Rudberg, P., & McGuinn, J. (2012). Understanding policy coherence: Analytical framework and examples of sector–environment policy interactions in the EU. *Environmental Policy and Governance*, *22*(6), 395–423. DOI: 10.1002/eet.1589

Öberg, M. L. (2020). Internal market acquis as a tool in EU external relations: from integration to disintegration. *Legal Issues of Economic Integration, 47*(2).

Orefice, G., Piermartini, R., & Rocha, N. (2012). Harmonization and mutual recognition: What are the effects on trade? Accessed from https://ageconsearch.umn.edu/record/332285/files/5808.pdf

Parteka, A. (2012). Trade Diversity and Stages of Development—Evidence on EU Countries. *Ekonomia. Rynek, gospodarka, społeczeństwo*, (30), 23-44.

Pasierbiak, P., & Białowąs, T. (2024). Imbalance in Eu Trade with Selected Asian Economies–A Comparative Analysis Based on Gross Exports and Domestic Value-Added. *Humanities and Social Sciences*, *31*(1), 133–148.

Paukku, M. (2000). *European Union and United States Trade Relations* (No. 723). ETLA Discussion Papers.

Rehman, S. S., & Della Posta, P. (2018). The impact of Brexit on EU27 on trade, investments and financial services. *Global Economy Journal*, *18*(1), 20170097. DOI: 10.1515/gej-2017-0097

Renard, T. (2016). Partnerships for effective multilateralism? Assessing the compatibility between EU bilateralism,(inter-) regionalism and multilateralism. *Cambridge Review of International Affairs*, *29*(1), 18–35. DOI: 10.1080/09557571.2015.1060691

Sassi, M., & Bernini Carri, C. (2009). Scambi commerciali agricoli e accordi di partenariato tra Unione Europea e Africa. *Economia agro-alimentare. Fascicolo, 2*, 1000–1019.

Sharma, T., & Bharti, N. (2025). The Impact of EU Trade Policies on Its Textile and Clothing Imports: A Comparison Between India, Bangladesh, China, and Vietnam. *Economies*, *13*(2), 47. DOI: 10.3390/economies13020047

Smith, M. (2013). The EU, Asia and the Governance of Global Trade. In *The Palgrave Handbook of EU-Asia Relations* (pp. 377–391). Palgrave Macmillan UK. DOI: 10.1057/9780230378704_24

Sotte, F., & Vergamini, D. (2025). The Green Deal and the CAP 2023–2027. In *European Agricultural Policy: History and Analysis* (pp. 219–235). Springer Nature Switzerland. DOI: 10.1007/978-3-031-83313-7_11

Stefanis, C., Stavropoulos, A., Stavropoulou, E., Tsigalou, C., Constantinidis, T. C., & Bezirtzoglou, E. (2024). A spotlight on environmental sustainability in view of the European Green Deal. *Sustainability (Basel)*, *16*(11), 4654. DOI: 10.3390/su16114654

Stojkov, A., & Warin, T. (2025). United Europe: Boundaries and Challenges. In *Western Balkans and the Future of Europe: Between an Enlargement and a Commitment Fatigue* (pp. 1–73). Springer Nature Switzerland. DOI: 10.1007/978-3-031-86465-0_1

Subow, V. (2014). The global governance of trade in agriculture: the role of tariff and non-tariff measures illustrated with an example of agricultural exports from South Africa to the EU.

Togan, S., Nebioğlu, H., & Doğan, S. (2005). *Integration and the manufacturing industry*. Economic Reform and Accession to the European Union.

Trommer, S. (2017). The WTO in an era of preferential trade agreements: Thick and thin institutions in global trade governance. *World Trade Review*, *16*(3), 501–526. DOI: 10.1017/S1474745616000628

Tsakanikas, A., Caloghirou, Y., Dimas, P., & Stamopoulos, D. (2022). Intangibles, innovation, and sector specialization in global value chains: A case study on the EU's and the UK's manufacturing industries. *Technological Forecasting and Social Change*, *177*, 121488. DOI: 10.1016/j.techfore.2022.121488

Van der Vorst, C., Vanoverbeke, D., & Rousseau, S. (2022). Modelling a new economic, environmental and political connectivity: the dynamics of Japan-EU trade.

Van Hove, J. (2010). Variety and quality in intra-European manufacturing trade: The impact of innovation and technological spillovers. *Journal of Economic Policy Reform*, *13*(1), 43–59. DOI: 10.1080/17487870903546275

Varrica, G., & Rusu, E. C. (2023). *Free Movement of Goods Within the Eu Single Market*. EJPAR.

Viju-Miljusevic, C. (2019). European Union adapting to an era of no ruling trade paradigm. *European Foreign Affairs Review*, *24*(3), 387–404. DOI: 10.54648/EERR2019031

Vogel, D. (2010). *Barriers or benefits?: regulation in transatlantic trade*. Brookings Institution Press. DOI: 10.5771/9780815705772

Wallace, H., Pollack, M. A., Roederer-Rynning, C., & Young, A. R. (Eds.). (2020). *Policy-making in the European Union*. Oxford university press. DOI: 10.1093/hepl/9780198807605.001.0001

Westhoek, H., Van Zeijts, H., Witmer, M., Van den Berg, M., Overmars, K., Van der Esch, S., & Van der Bilt, W. (2012). Greening the CAP. An analysis of the effects of the European Commission's proposals for the Common Agricultural Policy 2014-2020.

ADDITIONAL READING

Bacchetta, M., Bekkers, E., Solleder, J. M., & Tresa, E. (2025). The potential impact of environmental goods trade liberalization on trade and emissions. *Energy Economics, 141*, 108051. DOI: 10.1016/j.eneco.2024.108051

Hagemejer, J., Stoll, P. T., Rudloff, B., & Mensah, K. (2025). *An Update on the Economic*. Sustainability and Regulatory Effects of the Trade Part of the EU–Mercosur Partnership Agreement.

Jarosz-Angowska, A., Nowak, A., Kołodziej, E., & Klikocka, H. (2022). Effect of European integration on the competitiveness of the agricultural sector in new member states (EU-13) on the internal EU market. *Sustainability (Basel)*, *14*(20), 13124. DOI: 10.3390/su142013124

Rahman, M. M., & Inkyo, C. (2014). New trade policy of EU: Implications for LDCs. *Journal of International Logistics and Trade*, *12*(1), 43–73. DOI: 10.24006/jilt.2014.12.1.43

Tsiapa, M., Kallioras, D., Manetos, P., & Pérez-Balsalobre, S. (2025). Brexit's ripple effect: Transformations in European interregional trade. *Regional Studies*, *59*(1), 2518279. DOI: 10.1080/00343404.2025.2518279

KEY TERMS AND DEFINITIONS

Common Agricultural Policy (CAP): The Common Agricultural Policy (CAP) is a key policy of the European Union (EU) that supports agriculture, rural development, and food security. It was established in 1962 to ensure a stable supply of affordable food while supporting farmers' livelihoods. CAP has undergone multiple reforms to improve sustainability, environmental protection, and economic efficiency.

EU 15: EU-15 refers to the 15 member states of the European Union before the major enlargement in 2004. These countries were members from 1995 to 2004, consisting mainly of Western European nations. The EU-15 includes Austria, Belgium, Denmark, Finland, France, Germany, Greece, Ireland, Italy, Luxembourg, Netherlands, Portugal, Spain, Sweden, and the United Kingdom. This group is often used in economic comparisons to contrast older, more developed EU economies with newer member states.

EU 27: EU-27 refers to the 27 member states of the European Union after the United Kingdom left on January 31, 2020. It includes all countries that were part of the EU before Brexit, except the UK. The EU-27 is used in economic, trade, and policy discussions to analyze the EU's structure without the UK.

European Economic Area (EEA): The European Economic Area (EEA) is a regional agreement that extends the European Union's (EU) internal market to three non-EU countries: Norway, Iceland, and Liechtenstein. It was established in 1994 to allow these countries to participate in the EU's single market while remaining outside the EU.

European Free Trade Association (EFTA): The European Free Trade Association (EFTA) is an intergovernmental organization established in 1960 as an alternative to the European Economic Community (EEC) (now the European Union, EU). It promotes free trade and economic cooperation among its members.

Chapter 7
Digital Trade and Investment in the 21st Century:
Opportunities, Challenges, and Policy Implications for Sustainable Development

Saizal Pinjaman
http://orcid.org/0000-0002-6790-2688
Universiti Malaysia Sabah, Malaysia

ABSTRACT

This chapter discusses how digital trade and investment have reshaped global economic dynamics in the twenty-first century. It investigates the increasing increase of digital trade and investment, stressing their role in expanding market access, stimulating innovation, and supporting inclusive development. The discussion stresses the revolutionary impact of technologies such as artificial intelligence and cloud computing on trade efficiency and transparency. Regional frameworks are also studied for their role in harmonizing digital legislation. The chapter also addresses important challenges, such as digital inequalities, regulatory fragmentation, protectionism, and cybersecurity risks, while relating digital transformation to Sustainable Development Goals. Policy recommendations stress digital infrastructure investment, FDI facilitation, public-private partnerships, and international cooperation. Ultimately, the chapter demonstrates that digital commerce and investment are vital to attaining sustainable, inclusive, and resilient global economic growth.

DOI: 10.4018/979-8-3373-1782-3.ch007

INTRODUCTION TO DIGITAL TRADE AND INVESTMENT

Digital technologies have transformed the global economy, with digital trade and investment emerging as important drivers of growth and competitiveness. Unlike traditional trade, which is based on the physical exchange of goods, digital trade is the supply of goods and services via electronic channels. It encompasses e-commerce, software, consulting, streaming content, and the data flows that allow for these transactions (González & Ferencz, 2018).

Digital trade is facilitated by a variety of platforms and intermediaries, including online marketplaces such as Amazon, Alibaba, and Etsy; cloud providers such as Microsoft and Salesforce; and service-based platforms like Upwork and Fiverr. Cross-border data transfers are the system's backbone, allowing for payment processing, customer interaction, and logistics. Access to these platforms is not the only requirement for effective participation in digital trade; reliable infrastructure, supportive regulation, and digital literacy are also necessary. As a result, digital trade is multidimensional, encompassing products, technology, and institutional frameworks that influence efficiency and inclusiveness.

For businesses, digital trade lowers international market barriers and reduces reliance on physical presence, which benefits small and medium-sized enterprises (SMEs). However, regulatory inconsistency, inadequate infrastructure, and unequal access to technology continue to be significant constraints, particularly in developing economies.

Digital investment serves as the foundation for the digital economy, while digital trade represents the transactional side. It includes investments in broadband networks, fiber optics, cloud computing, data storage, artificial intelligence tools, and human capital development. These investments increase productivity, lower costs, and promote both domestic and international e-commerce. Attracting digital investment helps developing countries bridge the digital divide, expand internet access, and connect rural areas to larger markets. Countries that invest heavily in digital infrastructure and skills, such as Singapore with its Smart Nation initiative and South Korea with the Digital New Deal, are better positioned to benefit from digital transformation (Ben et al., 2017). Conversely, economies with weak digital systems risk falling behind in the expanding global digital marketplace.

The remainder of the chapter is arranged as follows: The next section, Trends in Digital Trade addresses the rapid expansion of cross-border e-commerce and digital services, concentrating on how technology allows SMEs and developing nations to engage in global markets. Next, the Role of Digital Technologies in Transforming Trade and Investment, studies how artificial intelligence, blockchain, IoT, and cloud computing boost trade efficiency and transparency. Regional Frameworks Supporting Digital Trade looks at activities that create regulatory harmonization while

Opportunities of Digital Trade and Investment in the Global Economy focuses on how digitization fosters growth, resilience, and inclusivity. Challenges and Barriers to Digital Trade discusses subjects such as the digital divide, data governance, and protectionism and Digital Trade and Investment as Enablers of Sustainable Development ties digital transformation to the SDGs. Policy Recommendations for Digital Trade and Investment highlights strategies for FDI, PPPs, and SDG-aligned infrastructure. Finally, the Conclusion outlines how digital trade supports innovation, inclusion, and sustainability, while emphasizing the significance of collaboration and equal access.

TRENDS IN DIGITAL TRADE

Digital trade has rapidly grown from a minor component of the global economy to a significant force influencing international trade, particularly in the aftermath of the COVID-19 epidemic. It encompasses a broad range of activities enabled by digital technologies, including cross-border e-commerce, digital services, data flows, and digital platforms. When used wisely, digital trade opens up unprecedented opportunities for inclusive growth, economic diversification, and structural transformation in developing and least developed countries.

The Cross-Border E-Commerce

One of the most noticeable trends in digital trade is the rapid growth of cross-border e-commerce. Advances in internet penetration, digital payment systems, and shipping technology have enabled businesses, particularly SMEs, to sell their products and services internationally with minimal physical infrastructure.

This trend has significant implications for small and medium-sized enterprises (SMEs) in developing countries. SMEs, which were previously limited by geography, market access, and high transaction costs, can now reach international customers through platforms like Alibaba, Amazon, Shopee, Jumia, and Etsy. These digital marketplaces eliminate many of the barriers to global trade by providing end-to-end services such as shopfront creation, digital marketing, payment processing, and shipping support.

A small clothing manufacturer in Indonesia, for example, or a handcrafted crafts cooperative in Kenya, can now connect directly to global consumers, eliminating the need for costly intermediaries. This not only increases revenue potential, but also promotes product innovation and quality improvement as businesses respond to global competition. In many cases, SMEs that use cross-border e-commerce experience faster growth and higher productivity than their offline counterparts.

Furthermore, the pandemic-induced shift to online shopping increased e-commerce adoption across all regions, including Sub-Saharan Africa, South Asia, and Latin America (Zohra et al., 2025). Governments and development partners have responded by investing in national e-commerce strategies, upgrading digital infrastructure, and encouraging public-private partnerships to improve digital trade readiness.

To fully capitalise on this trend, developing countries must address a number of structural issues, such as customs delays, low digital literacy, inadequate logistics networks, and fragmented regulatory frameworks. Investment in digital infrastructure, e-commerce regulatory harmonisation, and SME capacity building are critical enablers of long-term growth in this sector.

Expansion of Digital Services and Economic Diversification

Another significant trend in digital trade is the growth of cross-border digital services, including financial technology (fintech), software development, cloud computing, online education, digital entertainment, and professional services. These services are typically intangible, delivered in real time, and require few physical resources, making them ideal vehicles for economic diversification in developing countries.

The digital services industry has grown rapidly in response to increased demand for remote work, digital communication, and cloud-based solutions. As businesses around the world look to outsource IT services, customer support, design, and consulting, developing countries with a skilled workforce and reliable internet connectivity are emerging as popular destinations. India and the Philippines, for example, have long enjoyed a comparative advantage in business process outsourcing (BPO), and similar models are emerging in Rwanda, Bangladesh, and Vietnam.

Fintech, in particular, has emerged as a significant driver of financial inclusion and economic growth. Digital payment platforms, mobile money apps, and blockchain-based remittance services are transforming the way people save, borrow, and transact, especially in areas where traditional banking services are limited. M-Pesa in Kenya, for example, has transformed mobile banking in East Africa, enabling millions of unbanked people to participate in the formal economy.

Cloud computing services, which allow businesses to store, analyze, and manage data remotely, are becoming more prevalent. Startups and SMEs can now scale their operations more efficiently by using services such as AWS, Google Cloud, and Microsoft Azure, rather than investing in expensive infrastructure. This has significantly reduced the barriers to innovation and global competitiveness.

The expansion of digital services allows poor countries to diversify their economies, create jobs, and increase resilience (Al-Roubaier et al., 2020). Governments can help new service-based export industries grow by investing in digital skills development, supporting entrepreneurship, and encouraging innovation ecosystems.

THE ROLE OF DIGITAL TECHNOLOGIES IN TRANSFORMING TRADE AND INVESTMENT

The rapid advancement of digital technology in recent decades has altered the global economic environment, reimagining how commerce and investment are conducted, monitored, and optimized. Artificial intelligence (AI), blockchain, the Internet of Things (IoT), and cloud computing are fundamentally altering cross-border business transactions. These technological advancements have not only increased the efficiency and transparency of trade processes, but have also democratized access to global markets, particularly for small and medium-sized businesses (SMEs) and corporations in developing countries.

In the post-pandemic world, where resilience, adaptation, and sustainability are the new imperatives, digital technologies provide essential tools for modern trade. These technologies have become critical to global trade and investment strategies because they lower transaction costs, improve logistical coordination, and enable real-time decision-making. Their role is especially important in achieving the Sustainable Development Goals (SDGs), as it promotes inclusive growth, innovation, and equitable participation in global value chains.

Artificial Intelligence and Big Data: Transforming Market Intelligence

Artificial intelligence (AI) is driving the digital revolution in trade and investment, and it is frequently combined with big data analytics. AI-powered solutions enable companies to process and interpret massive amounts of structured and unstructured data in real time (Ferrari, 2021). This skill has significant implications for international trade.

First, artificial intelligence improves market analysis and demand forecasting. Businesses can use advanced algorithms and machine learning to identify new trends, anticipate consumer needs, and adjust production plans accordingly. For example, AI applications in retail use purchase behavior data to optimize inventory management and personalize marketing efforts, allowing businesses to avoid overproduction and waste. This skill is essential for both sustainability and profitability.

Second, artificial intelligence enables businesses to enter new markets with greater confidence. Predictive analytics can be used by businesses to analyze risks, assess consumer preferences, and tailor products or services to specific local conditions.

This is especially important for businesses entering new or expanding markets, where traditional market research may be insufficient or untrustworthy.

Furthermore, AI simplifies pricing optimization by analyzing competitor strategies, demand elasticity, and customer behavior patterns. Dynamic pricing algorithms can adjust prices in real time based on supply and demand, increasing competition while maintaining margins. Exporters and service providers involved in cross-border e-commerce must be adaptable in extremely volatile international markets.

Finally, AI contributes to fraud detection and cybersecurity. As digital trade grows, so does the likelihood of cyberattacks. AI-powered systems can detect abnormal patterns and unauthorised access, protect the integrity of financial transactions and digital communications, and boost trust in digital ecosystems.

Blockchain: Enhancing Transparency and Trust

Blockchain technology has emerged as a game changer in cross-border trade, enabling decentralized, transparent, and tamper-resistant platforms for recording and confirming transactions. Its fundamental characteristics, such as immutability, transparency, and security, can be applied to a variety of digital trade and investment applications.

Cross-border payments are one of blockchain's most important applications (Sule et al., 2024). Traditional foreign payment methods are frequently slow, costly, and opaque. Blockchain-based platforms enable near-instant and cost-effective transaction settlement, particularly when cryptocurrencies or stablecoins are used. This is especially beneficial for SMEs in emerging economies, which face restrictions on international financial services.

Another blockchain-enabled innovation is smart contracts, which automatically carry out agreements when certain conditions are met. This reduces the need for intermediaries, reduces legal disputes, and improves the efficacy of contractual obligations in international trade. For example, a smart contract can automatically release funds once goods have been confirmed delivered by IoT sensors, eliminating the need for human verification.

Blockchain also increases supply chain transparency. In industries such as agriculture, textiles, and electronics, where ethical sourcing and product traceability are becoming increasingly important, blockchain can provide an indelible record of a product's journey from origin to consumer. This traceability promotes ethical production processes, eliminates fraud, and ensures compliance with environmental and labour regulations. In terms of sustainable development, blockchain technology is an excellent tool for increasing business accountability and consumer trust.

Furthermore, blockchain enables investment ecosystems through tokenization. Blockchain allows for fractional ownership and new investment models by converting physical assets into digital tokens, making capital markets more accessible to a broader range of investors and lowering entry barriers.

Internet of Things (IoT): Optimizing Logistics and Asset Management

The Internet of Things (IoT), which connects physical objects to digital nctworks, is critical to modernizing trade logistics and supply chain management. By embedding sensors and connections into transportation, warehouse, and manufacturing systems, the Internet of Things enables the seamless monitoring and control of commodities throughout the supply chain.

Real-time cargo tracking is one of the most widely used IoT applications in trade (Gnimpieba et al., 2015). GPS-enabled sensors mounted on containers or delivery vehicles provide real-time information on location, temperature, and condition. This data enhances transparency, enables more precise delivery estimates, and reduces losses due to delays, theft, or spoilage, particularly in perishable product trades such as food and pharmaceuticals.

IoT also enables predictive maintenance and increases operational efficiency. Companies that collect data from machinery and infrastructure can anticipate issues, reduce downtime, and reduce operational costs. This competence is critical for multinational manufacturers and exporters to maintain high levels of efficiency and dependability in global supply networks.

Moreover, IoT devices can help with regulatory compliance and customs clearance. Smart packaging, for example, can store complete product information, origin certification, and safety certificates, all of which border authorities can access immediately. This expedites the clearance process and reduces the administrative burden associated with overseas shipments.

In terms of sustainability, IoT enables more efficient resource utilization and environmental monitoring. Smart meters and sensors can track energy and water consumption in real time, allowing businesses to align their operations with environmental goals and contribute to SDGs 13 (Climate Action) and 12 (Responsible Consumption and Production).

Cloud Computing: Empowering Businesses through Scalable Infrastructure

Cloud computing has emerged as the foundation of the digital economy, offering on-demand access to computing power, data storage, and software applications via the internet. This innovation has far-reaching implications for business and investment, especially for small and medium-sized businesses (SMEs) and startups, which frequently lack the resources to design and maintain complex IT systems.

Cloud-based services enable businesses to scale their operations more efficiently and affordably by eliminating the need for large financial investments in physical infrastructure (Kloch et al., 2011). For example, a Kenyan SMEs can use cloud platforms to host an e-commerce website, process online payments, manage inventory, and analyze customer data, allowing them to serve clients across borders without incurring significant overhead costs. This accessibility reduces entry barriers and enables businesses to compete globally.

The scalability of cloud solutions adds to this advantage, allowing businesses to adjust resources in response to seasonal demand or market expansion. This flexibility is especially valuable in international trade, where demand fluctuations and diverse consumer preferences necessitate agility and quick adaptation.

Beyond scalability, cloud computing enhances collaboration and remote work. Companies can use cloud-based communication and project management tools to better coordinate multinational teams, share documents in real time, and manage cross-border operations. This capability is even more important in the post-pandemic era, where remote work and digital connectivity support business resilience and continuity.

At the same time, cloud computing broadens investment opportunities and strengthens innovation ecosystems. Startups and technology companies can quickly develop applications, test prototypes, and deploy services globally without incurring significant infrastructure costs. Recognizing this potential, many governments and international organizations are focusing on cloud infrastructure to promote digital entrepreneurship, innovation, and public-sector efficiency.

Cloud computing also improves data governance by allowing for more localization and compliance with cybersecurity. Leading cloud providers now offer regional data centers and advanced encryption protocols, allowing businesses to meet data sovereignty requirements while protecting user privacy. This ensures that digital transformation is not only efficient but also secure, thereby reinforcing trust in the global digital economy.

REGIONAL FRAMEWORKS SUPPORTING DIGITAL TRADE

Recognizing the potential of digital trade for economic integration and sustainable development, several regional initiatives have emerged to develop unified frameworks for digital transformation. These initiatives play an important role in harmonising regulations, improving cross-border connectivity, and enabling collective capacity building.

ASEAN Digital Economy Framework

The Association of Southeast Asian Nations (ASEAN) has paved the way for digital integration in Southeast Asia with the ASEAN Digital Economy Framework Agreement (DEFA), which is set to be finalized by 2025. The framework aims to improve member nations' digital connections by promoting interoperable standards, harmonizing e-commerce legislation, and facilitating cross-border data flows.

The ASEAN countries collectively represent a thriving digital economy, with over 400 million internet users and a growing number of digital businesses. The DEFA program complements existing regional initiatives such as the ASEAN Agreement on E-Commerce and the ASEAN Digital Masterplan 2025, which outlines policies to promote innovation, improve digital infrastructure, and increase digital inclusion.

These frameworks provide a road map for developing ASEAN countries like Cambodia, Laos, and Myanmar to better integrate into regional and global value chains through digital trade. They also provide channels for exchanging best practices, harmonizing regulatory regimes, and attracting investment in digital infrastructure.

AfCFTA's E-Commerce Protocol

The African Continental Free Trade Area (AfCFTA) is leading efforts to integrate digital trade into its economic agenda. The AfCFTA's Protocol on E-Commerce, which has being negotiated since 2021, aims to establish a consistent legal and regulatory environment for digital commerce across the continent.

This programme is critical for Africa's growth since internet use is rapidly expanding but unevenly distributed. The protocol is expected to cover consumer protection, data privacy, electronic payments, and digital taxation. It will also increase the predictability and security of cross-border e-commerce, attracting additional digital investment.

Jumia, Flutterwave, and Andela already demonstrate Africa's digital economic potential. The AfCFTA protocol, by formalising e-commerce regulations and encouraging interoperability across national networks, has the potential to significantly boost intra-African trade, job creation, and innovation.

OPPORTUNITIES OF DIGITAL TRADE AND INVESTMENT IN THE GLOBAL ECONOMY

In the twenty-first century, digital trade and investment have emerged as major drivers of global economic growth and competition. Digitalization has altered traditional trade, allowing new forms of goods and services, such as software, online education, and virtual consultancy, to be traded internationally. This evolution has increased market access and expedited innovation, particularly during the post-pandemic recovery.

Driving Economic Growth and Job Creation

Digital trade, or the exchange of goods and services enabled by digital technologies, has emerged as a significant driver of worldwide economic growth. It addresses both the selling of digital products including software, cloud computing services, and multimedia material, as well as the facilitation of traditional trade via online platforms. According to the OECD (2020), digital trade now accounts for more than a quarter of global service trade, and this share is increasing as economies speed digital transformation.

Digital platforms enable businesses to reach global markets at a lesser cost by eliminating traditional barriers such as high overhead expenses, geographic limits, and dependency on intermediaries (Abendin & Duan, 2021). This transition is especially beneficial to small and medium-sized businesses (SMEs), who may expand their operations through e-commerce and digital services without requiring significant capital expenditure. As a result, digital trade boosts innovation, productivity, and industrial competitiveness, while directly contributing to long-term economic growth.

Beyond their economic impact, digital trade and investment create a wide range of job opportunities across industries. The digital economy generates new job opportunities in software development, data analytics, digital marketing, finance, and e-commerce, while also indirectly benefiting conventional industries like agriculture, shipping, and manufacturing through more efficient supply chains. Shopify, Lazada, and Amazon have created millions of jobs worldwide in storage, delivery, and customer service. Furthermore, digital labor platforms such as Upwork and Fiverr have created global markets for freelancers, diversifying employment and income opportunities (Saxena & Sirohi, 2025).

Digital transformation also adds flexibility to labour markets. Women, teenagers, and individuals with disabilities can now participate in remote and freelance employment, encouraging inclusivity and aligning with SDG 8 (Decent employment and Economic Growth). Thus, digital commerce and investment not only fuel economic growth, but also foster more diverse, adaptive, and inclusive employment systems that promote long-term development.

Enhancing Global Connectivity and Market Access

Digital trade overcomes geographical and economic gaps, removing conventional barriers to participation in the global economy. Despite numerous infrastructural, financial, and logistical challenges, digital platforms provide unmatched opportunities for developing countries to connect into global value chains and diversify their export offerings.

A compelling example is the rise of internet marketplaces, which enable artists, small farmers, and micro-entrepreneurs in rural areas to interact with international customers. Weavers and craftspeople in rural India, for example, may now sell their products abroad via sites such as Etsy and Amazon, increasing their profits while simultaneously supporting traditional cultural industries. Similarly, African businesses are leveraging fintech and e-commerce to reach out to the diaspora and regional markets, forging new economic links that go beyond traditional trading lines.

This global connectivity is enhanced by investments in digital infrastructure, such as broadband, mobile networks, and digital payment systems, which form the cornerstone of digital commerce. With the correct government and institutional support, digital trade has the potential to be a tremendous economic inclusion engine, allowing even the smallest and remote producers to participate in the global economy.

Fostering Economic Resilience

According to Abidi et al. (2023), the strength of digital trading was most evident during the COVID-19 epidemic. Lockdowns, transit delays, and border restrictions had a significant impact on traditional trade and physical supply chains, although digital trade remained flexible and responsive. E-commerce expanded as businesses and consumers went online, teleworking became prevalent, and digital payments supplanted cash transactions.

This example illustrated the ability of digital trade and investment to provide economic continuity during times of crisis. Companies who had invested in digital platforms before the pandemic were better able to weather disruptions and maintain client relationships. Governments that have developed digital public infrastructure, such as e-government services and mobile payment transfers, are more effective at distributing relief and keeping services operational during lockdowns.

As climate change, pandemics, and geopolitical tensions continue to threaten global supply chains, digital trade boosts economic resilience by reducing reliance on physical infrastructure and allowing for swift reconfiguration of networks. This positions digital investment not only as a development driver, but also as a critical component of national and global risk management strategies.

Attracting Investment and Stimulating Innovation

Investment in digital assets such as data centers, cloud infrastructure, software platforms, and artificial intelligence technologies has emerged as a critical component of modern capital formation. Both public and private investment in digital infrastructure improves trade and fosters innovative hubs. For example, strategic digital investment is directly related to the global expansion of smart cities, fintech centers, and AI research clusters.

Foreign direct investment (FDI) in the digital sector is increasingly being channeled toward emerging markets with undeveloped consumer bases and expanding digital penetration (Götz, 2020). This inflow of capital accelerates technological advancement, creates knowledge spillovers, and increases local capacity. In this strategy, digital investment acts as a conduit for knowledge transfer and capability development, assisting developing countries to strengthen their long-term competitiveness.

Furthermore, digital investment encourages the formation of enabling ecosystems such as digital entrepreneurship, public-private innovation partnerships, and research and development networks. These ecosystems accelerate progress in crucial fields such as health-tech, edtech, agritech, and renewable energy, balancing economic growth with sustainable and equitable development.

Inclusive Growth and Poverty Reduction

Digital trade can help to alleviate poverty and promote inclusive growth by allowing people, microenterprises, and marginalized groups to participate in the global economy. Unlike traditional commerce, which is dominated by huge enterprises, digital platforms provide access to larger markets and new earning opportunities.

Women, kids, and rural communities will benefit the most from this transition. Women entrepreneurs can manage online enterprises from home and reach consumers all over the world, while young people can find freelance work, online education, and remote jobs. Farmers and craftspeople in rural areas communicate directly with buyers via mobile applications. Markets like Farmcrowdy in Nigeria and TaniHub in Indonesia help them get better pricing, minimize waste, and boost transparency.

Digital trade also supports inclusion in fragile and conflict-affected regions. According to Zaballos et al. (2020), digital tools help to sustain education, healthcare, and livelihoods in areas with inadequate infrastructure. For example, Syrian refugee women in Jordan use internet platforms to sell handicrafts and teach languages, therefore restoring income and community stability.

To reap these benefits, governments must bridge the digital gap by expanding cheap internet access, promoting digital literacy, safeguarding data, and supporting local content development. International aid and partnerships should also foster digital inclusion, ensuring that all communities benefit from the digital economy.

CHALLENGES AND BARRIERS TO DIGITAL TRADE

While digital commerce has enormous potential to transform global economic systems and drive long-term development, its growth is impeded by a number of structural, legal, and geopolitical barriers. These limits disproportionately affect poor and least developed countries, resulting in digital inequality and limiting their ability to participate in the global digital economy.

Access to infrastructure and technology alone is insufficient for digital trade; fair and interoperable norms, effective governance structures, and international collaboration are also essential. The disparity in digital preparation across nations has resulted in a fragmented digital commerce sector, undermining the goals of inclusivity and sustainability. This section discusses the primary barriers to digital commerce, with a focus on the digital divide, regulatory fragmentation, digital protectionism, and intellectual property challenges.

The Digital Divide: Connectivity, Skills, and Technology Gaps

The digital divide is the most fundamental hindrance to digital trade, defined as persistent differences in access to digital infrastructure, resources, and literacy between and within countries. According to the International Telecommunication Union (ITU), around 2.6 billion people worldwide remain offline, with the majority living in low-income and rural areas. This lack of connectivity greatly limits the ability of individuals and businesses in developing countries to participate in e-commerce, digital services, and online trading platforms.

Even if basic internet connectivity is available, quality and cost are significant impediments. Many poor countries have uneven internet infrastructure, limited mobile network coverage, and high data charges. This stifles both corporate growth and consumers' ability to participate in digital marketplaces, lowering domestic demand for digital commerce.

Beyond infrastructure, digital skills and literacy are essential to perform digital trade (Chetty et al., 2018). Individuals' capacity to pursue online job or entrepreneurial opportunities is hampered by a lack of training and educational opportunities in coding, digital marketing, data analytics, and cybersecurity, particularly among women and adolescents. Small and medium-sized businesses (SMEs), which are the backbone of most emerging economies, usually lack the skills and resources to integrate digital technology, manage cross-border logistics, or comply with e-commerce regulations.

Closing the digital gap requires investment in affordable infrastructure, the establishment of public–private partnerships to expand digital education, and targeted initiatives that support marginalized communities. Without these reforms, digital trade risks deepening inequality instead of advancing inclusive growth.

Regulatory Challenges: Fragmentation, Compliance, and Cybersecurity

Another key hurdle to digital trade is the growing regulatory complexity and fragmentation across countries. Although digital trade crosses borders, national legislation governing data privacy, cybersecurity, taxation, and digital transactions can vary, creating uncertainty and compliance issues for businesses.

One of the most difficult regulatory considerations is data localisation, which requires data to be housed or processed inside national borders (Mishra, 2015). These regulations, which are sometimes passed in the name of data security or national sovereignty, have the potential to hinder cross-border data flows, raise company operational costs, and discourage international investment. Countries such as India, China, and Russia, for example, have implemented data localization policies that pose challenges for both global cloud service providers and fintech platforms alike.

Data privacy rules, while crucial for consumer protection, can also act as trade barriers when standards differ among countries. The European Union's General Data Protection Regulation (GDPR) has become a global standard, but its extra-territorial reach has created challenges for non-EU businesses that must adhere to severe permission and data processing rules. Many developing countries lack the institutional capacity to comply with such limitations, potentially preventing their businesses from accessing global digital marketplaces.

Concerns regarding cybersecurity complicate the regulatory landscape. The rise in cybercrime, data breaches, and digital espionage has prompted stronger government laws on digital infrastructure and transactions. However, differences in cybersecurity measures risk creating digital silos and undermining trust in digital trading systems. Furthermore, many impoverished countries lack the technological and legislative frameworks necessary to effectively address cybersecurity vulnerabilities.

The strategy aims to enhance regulatory consistency and build capability. International organizations like the World Trade Organization (WTO), the G20, and regional economic communities must work together to create common principles for digital governance, while also aiding poorer states in developing their domestic legal and institutional frameworks.

Digital Protectionism and Geopolitical Tensions

The rise of digital protectionism poses a growing threat to the global digital economy, in which governments impose trade barriers on digital goods and services in order to preserve local industries or achieve strategic goals. These policies include digital product tariffs, restrictions on foreign digital platforms, discriminatory licensing requirements, and bans on cross-border data transfers.

Such protectionist policies have the potential to hinder innovation, limit market competition, and disrupt the global digital ecosystem (Kira et al., 2021). For example, some countries have banned or restricted access to international digital platforms, citing national security concerns, limiting consumer choice, and isolating local businesses from global clients. Trade disputes between major economies, most notably the United States and China, have resulted in reciprocal restrictions on technology companies, chip exports, and telecommunications infrastructure.

These geopolitical considerations also create uncertainty in international digital investment. Companies are increasingly more cautious about where they operate, store data, or collaborate for fear of fines, export prohibitions, or political ramifications. This reduces the predictability needed for cross-border digital transactions and the formation of integrated value chains.

To mitigate the risk of digital fragmentation, global coordination and confidence-building strategies are essential. Trade agreements must include explicit and enforceable digital trade standards, and dispute resolution procedures must be revised to reflect the evolving nature of technology-related concerns. Without such laws, the global digital economy risks fragmenting, impeding its potential to promote equitable and sustainable growth.

Intellectual Property Rights and Digital Market Competition

As digital trade grows, new challenges arise about intellectual property rights (IPRs) and market competitiveness in the digital economy. The rapid proliferation of digital content, which ranges from music and software to e-books and online courses, has raised concerns about copyright infringement, patent protection, and enforcement in the digital realm.

Many countries' inadequate IPR regulations reduce incentives for content creators and technology developers to create and exchange information. Piracy, illegal copying, and digital counterfeiting continue to pose significant risks, particularly in countries with lax or outdated enforcement methods. For developing countries, this offers a delicate balance between promoting access to digital information and innovation while complying to international intellectual property standards.

Furthermore, digital marketplaces are becoming dominated by a small number of prominent technical companies known as "digital giants" or "gatekeepers" (Simone & Laudando, 2025). These businesses control critical platforms, app marketplaces, and data ecosystems, raising concerns about market concentration, anticompetitive behavior, and the abuse of dominant positions.

Platform providers, for example, may utilize their control over user data and algorithms to prioritize their own products or services at the expense of smaller competitors. App developers and e-commerce merchants may face high commission fees or arbitrary changes in platform restrictions, which limit their profitability and independence.

These competitiveness difficulties are particularly critical in developing countries, where local enterprises may lack the resources to compete with global competitors. Stronger antitrust legislation, fair competition standards, and support for open digital ecosystems are crucial for ensuring that digital commerce remains inclusive and vibrant.

DIGITAL TRADE AND INVESTMENT AS ENABLERS OF SUSTAINABLE DEVELOPMENT

In an age of globalization and digitisation, digital trade and investment have emerged as key drivers of long-term growth. As governments attempt to implement the 2030 Agenda for Sustainable Development, it is clear that technological innovation and digital connectivity are vital to achieving the United Nations' Sustainable Development Goals (SDGs). Digital trade, which encompasses e-commerce, cross-border digital services, and data flows, as well as digital investment in infrastructure and human capital, is changing the way economies grow, opportunities are distributed, and resilience and inclusion are achieved.

Digitalisation creates unprecedented prospects for inclusive participation in global trade, allowing previously marginalized people to become economic actors. When effectively integrated into national development frameworks and global economic cooperation, digital trade and investment have the potential to accelerate progress toward many SDGs. This section investigates how digital commerce and investment contribute to sustainable development, with an emphasis on four key SDGs: SDG 8 (Decent Work and Economic Growth), SDG 9 (Industry, Innovation, and Infrastructure), SDG 5 (Gender Equality), and SDG 13 (Climate Action).

SDG 8: Promoting Decent Work and Inclusive Economic Growth

Digital trade promotes economic growth by encouraging entrepreneurship, assisting small and medium-sized businesses (SMEs), and offering a varied range of job prospects (Masongsong et al., 2024). Businesses can reach worldwide consumers at lower prices by using digital platforms and marketplaces, which expands access to international markets and promotes more equitable participation.

Individuals and SMEs can sell directly to worldwide buyers via e-commerce platforms such as Shopify, Etsy, Lazada, and Amazon Marketplace, decreasing the need for physical stores and intermediaries. This transition allows informal enterprises, particularly those in emerging nations, to legitimize and scale operations through online exposure.

Digital trade also promotes the increase of gig and remote labor, allowing people to make money in software development, design, translation, and other digital services via platforms such as Upwork and Fiverr (Wilkins et al., 2022; Charles et al., 2022). While the gig economy presents social protection challenges, good regulation can pave the road for flexible and inclusive work.

Sustained digital investment is essential for long-term employment generation. Programs in digital skills, coding, and entrepreneurship boost worker competitiveness and national output. Digital trade and investment help to achieve SDG 8 by diversifying economies, increasing productivity, and extending access to good and inclusive jobs.

SDG 9: Advancing Industry, Innovation, and Infrastructure

Long-term development requires sustainable industrialization and resilient infrastructure, and SDG 9 is based on digital investment. The modern economy relies on digital infrastructure, which includes broadband networks, mobile connections, data centers, cloud systems, and digital payment platforms. Without these mechanisms, the advantages of digital trade and innovation are out of reach.

Increased digital connectivity, particularly in rural and poor areas, improves access to education, markets, and information. Rural broadband programs in Africa and Southeast Asia have reduced isolation and connected underprivileged populations to the global economy.

Emerging technologies like 5G, AI, and IoT are transforming industries by enabling smart factories, efficient logistics, and connected urban systems (Shafique et al., 2020). Smart infrastructures driven by these technologies increase resource efficiency, reduce emissions, and improve service delivery, hence improving economic and environmental sustainability.

Digital innovation is also altering conventional industries. Industry 4.0 tools in production, such as AI-powered robotics and predictive maintenance, increase productivity and reduce waste, whilst IoT-based precision farming increases yields while lowering environmental impact. Similarly, mobile banking and blockchain technologies increase financial access for small businesses and vulnerable people, boosting economic resilience and inclusive growth.

Integrating digital investment into national infrastructure policies accelerates industrial change, fosters innovation, and promotes equitable, sustainable development in accordance with SDG 9.

SDG 5: Empowering Women Through Digital Trade

Gender equality is critical to long-term development, and digital trade has emerged as an effective tool for economically empowering women. By decreasing traditional obstacles to market entry and financial participation, digital platforms empower women to participate in business, employment, and innovation.

Women in many rural and traditional communities confront movement restrictions, insufficient funding, and societal impediments to formal employment. Digital trade addresses these issues by offering online channels for marketing products, connecting with customers, and accepting digital payments. Platforms like Facebook Marketplace, Instagram Shops, Tokopedia, and Shopee have become indispensable tools for women-owned microbusinesses.

Digital financial services also have a transformational effect. Mobile wallets, peer-to-peer lending, and blockchain-based microfinance increase credit availability for women who were previously excluded from banking systems (Pallavi & Dsa, 2024). These tools promote entrepreneurship, financial independence, and decision-making ability.

Initiatives to enhance capacity help to strengthen inclusiveness even further. SheTrades, a program run by the International Trade Centre, and other public-private partnerships teach women digital skills for cross-border e-commerce and the global workforce.

Nonetheless, women are underrepresented in STEM professions and digital business leadership positions. To achieve SDG 5, gender-responsive policies must be implemented to promote equitable access to infrastructure, education, and capital. Investments in digital literacy, legal reforms, and incentives for women-led businesses can all help break down structural barriers.

Finally, digital trade and investment democratize access to global markets and finance, hastening progress towards gender equality and women's empowerment..

SDG 13: Supporting Climate Action Through Digital Innovation

The impact of digital commerce and investment on SDG 13 (Climate Action) is both direct and systemic. While digital technologies consume energy, when carefully deployed, they can help to improve climate resilience, resource efficiency, and environmental sustainability.

Digital technologies enable the establishment of smart, low-carbon supply chains. IoT-enabled sensors and GPS tracking offer real-time logistics management, lowering fuel usage, shortening delays, and optimising route planning. In manufacturing, AI-powered systems can monitor energy consumption and uncover inefficiencies, allowing businesses to implement energy-saving measures and minimise their carbon impact.

Mouratidis et al. (2021) believe that cloud computing and digital collaboration tools reduce the need for business travel and physical infrastructure, cutting emissions from transportation and real estate. For example, the COVID-19 epidemic has expedited the shift towards virtual meetings and remote work, demonstrating how digital connectivity may promote sector-wide decarbonisation efforts.

Meanwhile, digital trade enables the global exchange of green technologies and services. Businesses that provide solar panels, sustainable energy solutions, energy-efficient appliances, and environmental consulting services can reach international markets more efficiently through digital channels. This interchange is critical for the global spread of climate advances, especially in nations vulnerable to the effects of climate change.

Furthermore, digital investment in climate-resilient infrastructure, such as early warning systems, smart grids, and weather monitoring tools, aids national adaptation plans. These investments improve disaster preparedness, water management, and agricultural planning, reducing the impact of climate disturbances on livelihoods and ecosystems.

POLICY RECOMMENDATIONS FOR DIGITAL TRADE AND INVESTMENT

In the twenty-first century, digital infrastructure has emerged as a critical enabler of economic transformation, social inclusion, and environmental resilience. Broadband networks and data centers, as well as smart grids and digital identity systems, serve as the foundation for the digital economy, promoting cross-border trade, e-governance, and access to financial services. Investment in digital infrastructure is not only a technological requirement for developing and least developed countries; it is also vital for achieving the Sustainable Development Goals.

The Role of FDI in Expanding Digital Infrastructure

Foreign direct investment (FDI) is a powerful driver for developing and expanding digital infrastructure, especially in capital-constrained emerging markets. Multinational technology companies, telecommunications providers, and cloud service providers are increasingly investing in emerging economies to take advantage of fast expanding consumer bases and new economic opportunities.

Broadband infrastructure development has been a key driver of FDI. Access to reliable and reasonably priced high-speed internet is the foundation of digital commerce and services. In Africa, for example, Google's Equiano subsea cable and Facebook's 2Africa cable project are increasing international internet capacity, lowering data rates, and improving access to underserved areas. These investments directly support SDGs 9 (Industry, Innovation, and Infrastructure) and 17 (Partnerships for the Goals) by expanding access to vital digital services and encouraging economic integration.

FDI also contributes to the development of data centres and cloud computing infrastructure, which are essential for digital service delivery, data sovereignty, and company digitisation (Zekos, 2024). Microsoft, Amazon Web Services, and Huawei have made investments in South Africa, Kenya, and Indonesia, enabling local businesses to access scalable digital solutions, foster innovation ecosystems, and support e-government services.

Furthermore, smart city initiatives such as those in Kigali (Rwanda), Pune (India), and Bandar Seri Begawan (Brunei) have drawn foreign direct investment to build integrated urban infrastructure using digital technology. These efforts promote sustainability by establishing intelligent transportation systems, enhancing energy efficiency, and improving public services, so contributing to SDGs 11 (Sustainable Cities and Communities) and 13.

For FDI to be most successful, host countries must create enabling conditions such as clear regulatory frameworks, investor protection measures, and digital governance institutions that ensure fair access and responsible data usage.

Public-Private Partnerships (PPPs) for Financing Digital Transformation

While foreign direct investment (FDI) is an important source of capital, many developing countries rely on public-private partnerships (PPPs) to fund digital infrastructure, especially when economic constraints limit state spending. PPPs combine the public sector's capabilities, such as policy direction, regulatory oversight, and development priorities, with the private sector's knowledge, creativity, and financial resources.

PPPs have been especially effective in last-mile connectivity programs, which seek to deliver internet access to rural and remote areas that are normally too expensive for private operators to operate alone (Tapia, 2019). For example, the World Bank-supported Rural Access Programme in Nepal and Malawi's Broadband for Sustainable Development Project have successfully leveraged PPP models to give internet access to low-income communities.

Colombia's Vive Digital plan, a national strategy to expand ICT access, secured funding from both the public and private sectors to build community access centers, train people in digital skills, and deploy broadband infrastructure. The project resulted in significant increases in internet adoption and digital literacy, with long-term consequences for education, healthcare, and the workplace.

PPPs also fund investments in critical digital infrastructure including e-government platforms, digital ID systems, and smart grids, which are necessary for effective service delivery and inclusive economic participation. Governments can better align digital infrastructure investments with the SDGs by incorporating social goals into PPP contracts, such as targets for gender inclusion, digital literacy, and environmental protection.

However, effective public-private partnerships require strong governance structures, clear contractual frameworks, and open risk-sharing agreements. Governments must ensure that digital infrastructure advancements benefit the public without worsening digital disparities or monopolistic behaviours.

Aligning Digital Infrastructure with the SDGs

To truly support sustainable development, digital infrastructure investments must be designed, implemented, and assessed with an SDG-aligned viewpoint. This requires looking beyond traditional economic metrics to assess social, environmental, and equitable outcomes.

Climate-resilient infrastructure is becoming more critical. As data centres and network towers become more linked into economic and social systems, they must be built to withstand extreme weather, rising temperatures, and power outages. Sustainable digital investments that contribute to SDGs 13 (Climate Action) and 7 (Affordable and Clean Energy) include green data centers powered by renewable energy, smart grids that optimize electricity consumption, and climate-sensitive construction materials.

Digital infrastructure can also help to achieve gender equality (SDG 5). Women and girls commonly face structural barriers to internet access, including cost, a lack of computer expertise, and societal expectations (Mariscal et al., 2019). Infrastructure efforts that incorporate gender-sensitive design and outreach approaches, such as training programs for female entrepreneurs or specialized access points for female users, can assist to close the digital gender gap. For example, the "Girls in ICT" project in Africa and Asia promotes gender equality through infrastructure-based training and mentoring programs.

Furthermore, to promote inclusive growth (SDG 8), digital infrastructure investments must benefit marginalised groups such as rural communities, individuals with disabilities, and ethnic minorities. Universal service funding, subsidized broadband plans, and community-based digital centers are key tools for guaranteeing that no one is left behind during the digital transformation process.

Promoting Digital Trade Cooperation

To improve global digital trade cooperation, especially for sustainable development and inclusiveness, authorities must take strategic and forward-thinking methods. Digital trade agreements should include elements that promote development, such as special and differentiated treatment (SDT), technical assistance, and phased implementation. This ensures that low-capacity countries are not harmed by premature or too stringent commitments. Countries should also collaborate to establish mutual recognition of digital standards for data protection, digital signatures, and cybersecurity. Establishing regional digital regulatory sandboxes allows for experimentation and alignment before making definitive commitments.

Furthermore, trust is critical to digital trade, so governments should establish clear legal frameworks for data governance, consumer protection, and intellectual property. Mechanisms for stakeholder consultation, impact assessment, and restitution must be included in digital policymaking. Equally crucial is the development of infrastructure and capability to support these frameworks. To connect markets, internet access must be expanded, data centers built, and digital logistics investments made, while human capital development projects can increase the skills needed to flourish in digital sectors. To narrow connectivity gaps and promote digital inclusiveness, donor agencies, development banks, and private investors should direct their funds toward these goals.

Finally, open and participatory systems must promote innovation and collaboration in order to ensure long-term digital trade. Governments should support open standards, open-source technologies, and interoperable platforms to avoid proprietary lock-ins and increase opportunities for small and medium-sized businesses, local innovators, and the general public. Open digital ecosystems promote competitiveness while ensuring that the advantages of digitalization are widely distributed. Inclusive policymaking requires active participation from all stakeholders. Multistakeholder platforms like the Internet Governance Forum (IGF) and eTrade for All provide excellent opportunities for public-private conversation and collaborative problem-solving, allowing digital trade policy to be inclusive, innovative, and responsive to global development needs.

CONCLUSION

Digital commerce and investment have emerged as key transformation drivers in the twenty-first century global economy. As technology advances, the way commodities, services, and data are transmitted across borders changes, redefining competition and creating new opportunities for inclusive and sustainable prosperity. This chapter examined how digital trade and investment, such as e-commerce, digital services, cross-border data flows, and infrastructure, can be strategically applied to accomplish the Sustainable Development Goals (SDGs) and promote resilient, equitable development across nations.

The scope of digital trade extends far beyond online transactions. It consists of cloud computing, software exports, digital financial services, and digitally enabled supply chains. Investment in digital infrastructure, such as broadband networks, data centers, and smart city technologies, is vital to enabling these activities. Together, digital commerce and digital investment form a synergistic ecosystem that allows businesses, individuals, and governments to participate in global marketplaces, especially when traditional limits such as distance, time, and scale are eliminated by technological breakthroughs.

This chapter discussed how digital trade can help reach a number of SDGs. It promotes decent work and economic growth (SDG 8) by enabling SMEs and entrepreneurs to enter global markets; it promotes industry and innovation (SDG 9) by expanding ICT infrastructure; it advances gender equality (SDG 5) by empowering women-led businesses; and it contributes to climate action (SDG 13) by digitizing supply chains and implementing resource-efficient operations. Strategic investments, both public and private, have proven successful in Rwanda, India, and across ASEAN, where targeted digital infrastructure initiatives have expanded connectivity, improved service delivery, and raised economic potential.

However, significant hurdles remain to hinder digital trade from reaching its full potential. The continuous digital divide, particularly in developing and least developed nations, limits participation due to unequal access to technology, connectivity, and digital skills. Regulatory fragmentation, such as conflicting data governance legislation, cybersecurity standards, and digital taxation regimes, complicates and impedes cross-border activities. Digital protectionism, growing trade tensions, and concerns about intellectual property and competition have all exacerbated the global digital divide.

To address these challenges, the chapter stressed the importance of clear policy frameworks and international cooperation. Multilateral institutions such as the World Trade Organization, the United Nations Conference on Trade and Development, and the International Telecommunication Union play vital roles in establishing global standards and providing technical assistance and policy debate to poor countries. Regional and plurilateral efforts, such as the CPTPP, RCEP, and USMCA, offer a variety of options for digital trade norms; nevertheless, their implications on poor nations must be carefully managed to avoid further imbalances.

The chapter concludes that achieving sustainable and equitable digital commerce necessitates a multidimensional strategy that involves infrastructure development, legislative alignment, human capital investment, and strategic partnerships. Governments need to prioritize open, secure, and growth-oriented digital ecosystems, while international collaboration should promote interoperability, trust, and equity. Digital commerce has the potential to change the global economy by bridging digital gaps, promoting innovation, and incorporating sustainability into digital investment plans.

REFERENCES

Abendin, S., & Duan, P. (2021). International trade and economic growth in Africa: The role of the digital economy. *Cogent Economics & Finance*, *9*(1), 1911767. DOI: 10.1080/23322039.2021.1911767

Abidi, N., El Herradi, M., & Sakha, S. (2023). Digitalization and resilience during the COVID-19 pandemic. *Telecommunications Policy*, *47*(4), 102522. DOI: 10.1016/j.telpol.2023.102522 PMID: 37051116

Al-Roubaier, A., Hamdan, A., & Sarea, A. M. (2020). Economic diversification in a digital economy. In *Proceedings of the International Conference on Artificial Intelligence and Computer Vision (AICV2020)* (pp. 665-671). Springer International Publishing.

Ben, S., Bosc, R., Jiao, J., Li, W., Simonelli, F., & Zhang, R. (2017). *Digital Infrastructure Overcoming the digital divide in China and the European Union*. Centre for European Policy Studies.

Charles, L., Xia, S., & Coutts, A. P. (2022). *Digitalization and employment: A review*. International Labor Organization.

Chetty, K., Qigui, L., Gcora, N., Josie, J., Wenwei, L., & Fang, C. (2018). Bridging the digital divide: Measuring digital literacy. *Economics*, *12*(1), 20180023. DOI: 10.5018/economics-ejournal.ja.2018-23

Ferrari, A. (2021). Leveraging AI-Driven Techniques for Real-Time Data Integration and Fusion in Modern Enterprise Data Warehousing Systems. *Journal of Computational Innovation*, *1*(1).

Gnimpieba, Z. D. R., Nait-Sidi-Moh, A., Durand, D., & Fortin, J. (2015). Using Internet of Things technologies for a collaborative supply chain: Application to tracking of pallets and containers. *Procedia Computer Science*, *56*, 550–557. DOI: 10.1016/j.procs.2015.07.251

González, J. L., & Ferencz, J. (2018). Digital trade and market openness.

Götz, M. (2020). Attracting foreign direct investment in the era of digitally reshaped international production. The primer on the role of the investment policy and clusters–the case of Poland. *Journal of East-West Business*, *26*(2), 131–160. DOI: 10.1080/10669868.2019.1692985

Kira, B., Sinha, V., & Srinivasan, S. (2021). Regulating digital ecosystems: Bridging the gap between competition policy and data protection. *Industrial and Corporate Change, 30*(5), 1337–1360. DOI: 10.1093/icc/dtab053

Kloch, C., Petersen, E. B., & Madsen, O. B. (2011). Cloud based infrastructure, the new business possibilities and barriers. *Wireless Personal Communications, 58*(1), 17–30. DOI: 10.1007/s11277-011-0286-7

Mariscal, J., Mayne, G., Aneja, U., & Sorgner, A. (2019). Bridging the gender digital gap. *Economics, 13*(1), 20190009. DOI: 10.5018/economics-ejournal.ja.2019-9

Masongsong, A. C., Ulep, S. J., Abante, M. V., Cagang, M. L., & Vigonte, F. (2024, February 27). Digital Transformation of International Trade for SMEs in Developing Countries: Opportunities, Challenges. *Challenges.*

Mishra, N. (2015). Data localization laws in a digital world: Data protection or data protectionism? *The Public Sphere (2016), NUS Centre for International Law Research Paper*, (19/05).

Mouratidis, K., Peters, S., & van Wee, B. (2021). Transportation technologies, sharing economy, and teleactivities: Implications for built environment and travel. *Transportation Research Part D, Transport and Environment, 92*, 102716. DOI: 10.1016/j.trd.2021.102716

OECD. (2020). *Digital Trade and Market Openness.* Retrieved from https://www.oecd.org/trade/topics/digital-trade/

Pallavi, G. P., & Dsa, K. T. (2024). Technological Innovations to Promote Financial Inclusion: A Comprehensive Analysis of Digital Payment Systems and Blockchain Solutions. *The Future of Money Trends in Financial Innovation, 31*, 38.

Saxena, M. P., & Sirohi, N. (2025). Talent Acquisition in the Gig Era: Strategies for Attracting Freelancers. *The Gig Economy Revolution: Rethinking Talent Management*, 86.

Shafique, K., Khawaja, B. A., Sabir, F., Qazi, S., & Mustaqim, M. (2020). Internet of things (IoT) for next-generation smart systems: A review of current challenges, future trends and prospects for emerging 5G-IoT scenarios. *IEEE Access : Practical Innovations, Open Solutions, 8*, 23022–23040. DOI: 10.1109/ACCESS.2020.2970118

Simone, C., & Laudando, A. (2025). Principles and obligations of the Digital Markets Act in regulating the economic power of gatekeepers: Positive, negative or trade-off effects? *Electronic Markets, 35*(1), 1–27. DOI: 10.1007/s12525-025-00788-6

Sule, A. K., Eyo-Udo, N. L., Onukwulu, E. C., Agho, M. O., & Azubuike, C. (2024). Implementing blockchain for secure and efficient cross-border payment systems. *International Journal of Research and Innovation in Applied Science*, *9*(12), 508–535.

Tapia, S. S. (2019). The Global" Last Mile" Solution: High-Altitude Broadband Infrastructure. *Geo. L. Tech. Rev.*, *4*, 47.

Wilkins, D. J., Hulikal Muralidhar, S., Meijer, M., Lascau, L., & Lindley, S. (2022). Gigified knowledge work: understanding knowledge gaps when knowledge work and on-demand work intersect. *Proceedings of the ACM on human-computer interaction*, *6*(CSCW1), 1-27. DOI: 10.1145/3512940

Zaballos, A. G., Rodriguez, E. I., Cave, M., Elbittar, A., Guerrero, R., Mariscal, E., & Webb, W. (2020). The impact of digital infrastructure on the consequences of COVID-19 and on the mitigation of future effects.

Zekos, G. I. (2024). AAI and FDI. In *Artificial Intelligence and Competition: Economic and Legal Perspectives in the Digital Age* (pp. 361–378). Springer Nature Switzerland.

Zohra, B. F., Slimani, I., Douli, S., & Djomana, T. (2025). The impact of the COVID-19 pandemic on digital innovation. *Brazilian Journal of Business*, *7*(1), e78504–e78504. DOI: 10.34140/bjbv7n1-071

ADDITIONAL READING

Baldwin, R. (2019). *The globotics upheaval: Globalization, robotics, and the future of work*. Oxford University Press.

Bukht, R., & Heeks, R. (2017). Defining, conceptualising and measuring the digital economy. *Development Informatics working paper*, (68).

Demirgüç-Kunt, A., Klapper, L., Singer, D., & Ansar, S. (2022). *The Global Findex Database 2021: Financial inclusion, digital payments, and resilience in the age of COVID-19*. World Bank Publications. DOI: 10.1596/978-1-4648-1897-4

Meltzer, J. P. (2019). Governing digital trade. *World Trade Review*, *18*(S1), S23–S48. DOI: 10.1017/S1474745618000502

United Nations Conference on Trade and Development (UNCTAD). (2021). Digital economy report 2021: Cross-border data flows and development – For whom the data flow. United Nations.

Wajda-Lichy, M., Fijorek, K., Denkowska, S., & Kawa, P. (2022). The impact of information and communication technology on services exports: Evidence from developed and developing economies. *International Entrepreneurship Review*, *8*(3), 69–80. DOI: 10.15678/IER.2022.0803.05

KEY TERMS AND DEFINITIONS

Digital Economy: The digital economy is the portion of economic output derived primarily from digital technologies, including digital communication networks, e-commerce, digital services, and data-driven innovation.

Digital Governance: Digital governance encompasses the frameworks, policies, and institutions that regulate digital activities such as data privacy, cybersecurity, competition, and cross-border trade in digital services.

Digital Inclusion: Digital inclusion refers to the equitable access to, and effective use of, digital technologies by all individuals and communities, including those in rural and low-income regions. It involves access to affordable internet, digital literacy, and participation in digital economies.

Digital Investment: Digital investment refers to capital allocation toward digital infrastructure and intangible assets that support the digital economy, such as broadband networks, data centres, cloud computing, artificial intelligence, and human capital development in digital skills.

Digital Trade: Digital trade refers to the production, distribution, marketing, sale, or delivery of goods and services through electronic means, including cross-border data flows that enable such activities.

E-Commerce (Electronic Commerce): E-commerce refers to the buying and selling of goods and services over electronic networks, primarily the internet. It includes business-to-business (B2B), business-to-consumer (B2C), and consumer-to-consumer (C2C) transactions that are digitally ordered and/or digitally delivered.

Chapter 8
Divergence and Convergence in the Bay of Bengal:
India, Bangladesh, and the Pursuit of a Circular Space Economy Through BIMSTEC

Mohammad Rashed Hasan Polas
http://orcid.org/0000-0002-6080-1075
Asia Pacific University of Technology and Innovation, Malaysia

Abdullah Al Fahad
http://orcid.org/0009-0006-2939-9942
United International University, Bangladesh

Mohammad Ekramol Islam
http://orcid.org/0000-0001-6524-6069
Sonargaon University, Bangladesh

Md. Masud Rana
Sonargaon University, Bangladesh

Abu Saleh Md. Sohel-Uz-Zaman
http://orcid.org/0009-0002-0197-3712
United International University, Bangladesh

S. Jobayear Ahmed
http://orcid.org/0000-0001-6356-2666
Bangladesh Foreign Trade Institute, Bangladesh

ABSTRACT

This chapter explores the integration of digital technologies into trade policies for advancing the Blue and Circular Economy (BCE) in emerging economies. It examines how bilateral, multilateral, and regional agreements can enable digital transformation in marine-based sectors such as fisheries, aquaculture, eco-tourism, and green shipping. Based on the theoretical frameworks like the Triple Bottom Line and Technological Innovation Systems, the study highlights the role of AI,

DOI: 10.4018/979-8-3373-1782-3.ch008

blockchain, and IoT in enhancing sustainability, reducing marine pollution, and fostering inclusive economic growth in the industry 4.0 and 5.0. Case studies from Bangladesh, Indonesia, Kenya, and Norway illustrate diverse digital strategies in marine governance and trade. The chapter also emphasizes human capital development, gender inclusion, and the need for ethical safeguards against digital risks. Policy directions and a research roadmap are provided to guide international collaboration and sustainable economic transition through digital BCE models.

1.0 INTRODUCTION

As global climate and economic crises deepen, emerging economies face increasing pressure to balance growth with sustainability in the context of Industry 4.0 and the emerging Industry 5.0 (Upadhyay & Mishra, 2020; Cezarino et al., 2021; Kumar et al., 2023; Tamasiga et al., 2025). Integrating digital technologies into trade policies for the Blue Economy and Circular Economy presents a unique opportunity to align development with environmental and social objectives. Yet, this integration remains underexplored in bilateral, multilateral, and regional trade agreements (Burmaoglu et al., 2023; Tamasiga et al., 2025).

To frame this chapter's analysis, we integrate three complementary perspectives: Technological Innovation Systems (TIS), Diffusion of Innovation (DOI), and the Triple Bottom Line (TBL). TIS explains how institutional structures, networks, and policies shape innovative ecosystems, particularly for digital trade and sustainability. DOI adds a behavioral dimension by clarifying how emerging technologies such as AI, IoT, blockchain, and big data are adopted and diffused across industries and regions. TBL ensures that these technological and policy shifts are assessed holistically through economic, environmental, and social outcomes. Together, these frameworks provide a unified lens to understand how digitalization can transform trade systems while advancing sustainable development goals.

Globally, advanced digital technologies are reshaping how marine resources are monitored, managed, and conserved. In fisheries management, satellite and sensor-based systems track compliance with quotas and biodiversity protection. AI-driven route optimization in maritime logistics reduces fuel use and carbon emissions (Langley et al., 2023). Blockchain enhances transparency and traceability in seafood supply chains, countering illegal and unsustainable fishing. Smart waste management systems, powered by IoT and big data, support circular strategies in coastal cities by identifying pollution hotspots, optimizing waste handling, and converting marine litter into renewable resources (Torgautov et al., 2021). These practices illustrate how trade policies informed by digitalization can align competitiveness with ecological stewardship.

Bangladesh, a deltaic nation with an extensive coastline and rich biodiversity, provides a compelling case for advancing this integration (Kumar et al., 2023). Its economy relies heavily on sectors such as fisheries, shipbreaking, port logistics, and coastal tourism, which are both vulnerable to environmental degradation and ripe for sustainable transformation (Langley et al., 2023). Incorporating circular principles such as recycling ship materials, promoting sustainable aquaculture, and eco-friendly tourism can mitigate risks while enhancing long-term resilience (Torgautov et al., 2021). Digitalization adds further value. AI and geospatial mapping can guide marine spatial planning; mobile platforms can expand access to markets and finance for small-scale fishers; and blockchain can enhance traceability and export competitiveness in seafood (Cezarino et al., 2021).

Despite these opportunities, Bangladesh faces significant barriers to digital adoption, including limited internet access in coastal regions, low digital literacy, and weak institutional frameworks (Geissdoerfer et al., 2017). Overcoming these challenges requires multi-stakeholder collaboration among government agencies, academia, private industry, and international development partners (Sopha et al., 2022). Aligning digital trade policies with the Sustainable Development Goals (SDGs) is equally crucial, for example, real-time marine monitoring advances SDG 14 (Life Below Water), smart logistics supports SDG 9 (Industry, Innovation, and Infrastructure), and digital skill-building contributes to SDG 8 (Decent Work and Economic Growth) (Geissdoerfer et al., 2017; Hagelüken & Goldmann, 2022; Bressanelli et al., 2022). By linking TIS, DOI, and TBL, this chapter shows how digital trade policies can foster innovation, accelerate adoption, and deliver balanced outcomes across economic, environmental, and social dimensions. In doing so, it highlights how global agreements, and regional cooperation can accelerate the transition toward a Blue and Circular Economy in emerging economies, with Bangladesh serving as an illustrative case.

To guide this exploration, the chapter focuses on three key research questions (RQs):

RQ1: *How can digital technologies enhance the integration of Blue and Circular Economy models in emerging economies?*
RQ2: *What role do trade agreements and policy frameworks play in facilitating the digital transformation of sustainable marine-based industries?*
RQ3: *How can inclusive digital strategies empower coastal communities, startups, and marginalized groups within the Blue-Circular Economy?*

Addressing these questions will provide valuable insights into creating resilient, innovative, and equitable pathways for sustainable development in the maritime sector.

This chapter adopts a qualitative synthesis approach, drawing on secondary data from peer-reviewed literature, policy reports, and documented case studies to illustrate the integration of digital technologies within Blue and Circular Economy frameworks. Case examples such as Kenya's "Smart Fish," Indonesia's "Ocean Eye," and Bangladesh's emerging initiatives were selected based on their relevance to marine sustainability and digital innovation in emerging economies. These cases serve as illustrative models rather than primary empirical findings, enabling comparative insights into best practices and contextual challenges. The analysis is guided by the Technological Innovation Systems (TIS), Diffusion of Innovation (DOI), and Triple Bottom Line (TBL) frameworks to ensure theoretical rigor and holistic evaluation.

2.0 TOWARDS SUSTAINABLE TRANSFORMATION: UNITING BLUE, CIRCULAR & DIGITAL ECONOMIES

2.1 Advancing Circular Economy in Emerging Contexts

The Circular Economy (CE) promotes regenerative models that minimize waste and optimize resource use through closed-loop systems such as reuse, recycling, and product-as-a-service (Patwa et al., 2021; Du et al., 2024). In Bangladesh, adoption faces barriers like weak infrastructure, policy gaps, and entrenched linear practices (Malik et al., 2022; Rataj et al., 2024). Yet, CE offers opportunities to convert 3,000 tons of daily plastic waste into economic value through waste-to-wealth strategies, biogas, and e-waste recovery (Teberges Dantas Queiroga et al., 2025). Initiatives like Dhaka's "Waste Concern" and global models from the Netherlands and Sweden illustrate how eco-design and circular fashion can drive sustainability and poverty alleviation (; Murray et al., 2017; Abu-Bakar & Charnley, 2024Ayaz & Tatoglu, 2024).

2.2 Blue Economy: A New Frontier for Trade and Development

The Blue Economy promotes sustainable ocean resource use for economic growth, livelihoods, and ecosystem health, encompassing sectors like fisheries, aquaculture, transport, tourism, and marine biotechnology (Gamage, 2016). It aligns with SDG 14 and global strategies such as the EU's "Blue Growth" and Africa's maritime plan (Onguglo & Eugui, 2018; Zulkifli et al., 2023). For Bangladesh, the Bay of Bengal offers opportunities worth over USD 5 billion annually, supporting 17 million fisheries-dependent people (Liang et al., 2022). Yet, unsustainable practices and weak regulations persist. Regional cooperation through BIMSTEC and blue diplomacy can foster marine trade, biodiversity conservation, and eco-port development (Choudhary et al., 2021; Satizábal et al., 2020; Thoya et al., 2022).

2.3 Smart Sustainability through Industry 4.0

The convergence of Industry 4.0 technologies with Blue and Circular Economy principles enables "smart sustainability," leveraging AI, IoT, blockchain, and big data to optimize marine resource management and waste reduction (Tripathi et al., 2022). Globally, IoT-enabled buoys, GPS tracking, and satellite imaging curb IUU fishing, while blockchain ensures transparency in seafood supply chains, as seen in Norway and Iceland (Xu et al., 2021; Javaid et al., 2022). AI-driven drones monitor coral reefs, and digital twins simulate coastal infrastructure for energy efficiency. In Bangladesh, digital mapping, sensor-based fishery monitoring, and mobile apps for fishers could enhance governance and livelihoods (Fatimah et al., 2020; Beltrami et al., 2021). Smart waste systems using IoT and route optimization can transform urban recycling (Bag et al., 2021). However, progress requires robust infrastructure, skilled human capital, and cybersecurity standards. Aligning initiatives like the Bangladesh Delta Plan 2100 with smart sustainability goals can accelerate adoption (Tripathi et al., 2024).

2.4 Integrated Sustainability for SDG Impact

The intersection of the Blue Economy, Circular Economy, and digitalization aligns closely with several SDGs. For instance, SDG 14 (Life Below Water) benefits from real-time marine ecosystem monitoring. SDG 12 (Responsible Consumption and Production) is advanced through waste reduction and circular manufacturing. SDG 9 (Industry, Innovation, and Infrastructure) is supported by smart port development and digital infrastructure (Rizzato et al., 2024). Importantly, SDG 8 (Decent Work and Economic Growth) is propelled by green job creation in sustainable aquaculture, waste recycling, and digital marine services (Hamad et al., 2023). Realizing the potential of this integrated framework requires collaborative governance involving government bodies, private enterprises, academia, NGOs, and international partners. Policy coherence, cross-sectoral data sharing, and long-term investment in research and innovation are key enablers. Public-private partnerships (PPPs) can drive financing for blue digital startups and circular ventures. Educational institutions must also embed CE, BE, and digitalization in technical and vocational curricula to prepare the future workforce (van Soest et al., 2019; Hamad et al., 2023).

The conceptual framework combining Blue Economy, Circular Economy, and digitalization offers a holistic, future-ready model for sustainable development in Bangladesh and beyond. This integrated approach supports ecological balance, economic resilience, and technological advancement, making it especially suitable for emerging economies seeking inclusive and sustainable transformation. With strategic investments, policy alignment, and stakeholder collaboration, Bangladesh can emerge as a model for digitally enabled blue-circular growth in the Global South (Bilalova et al., 2023).

2.5 Linking Digitalization, Circularity, and Blue Economy

Understanding digitalization in the Blue and Circular Economy (BCE) requires grounding in innovation and sustainability frameworks (Pace et al., 2023). The Technological Innovation System (TIS) lens explains how technologies like AI, IoT, and blockchain emerge and diffuse through systemic functions such as knowledge development and legitimacy building (Nham & Hoa, 2023; Hysa et al., 2024). Diffusion of Innovation (DOI) theory highlights adoption drivers benefits, compatibility, and usability critical for tools like digital waste platforms (Shan et al., 2023). The Triple Bottom Line (TBL) ensures balance across economic, environmental, and social dimensions (Jensen et al., 2021; Vann Yaroson et al., 2024). Complementary perspectives include Systems Theory, emphasizing stakeholder interlinkages, and Institutional Theory, focusing on regulatory and cultural influences (Langley et al., 2023; Seyyedi et al., 2024). Anchored in SDGs 9, 12, and 14, these frameworks collectively guide BCE transitions in emerging economies like Bangladesh.

3.0 DIGITALIZATION AND ECONOMIC COOPERATION IN THE BLUE ECONOMY

The Blue Economy is rapidly evolving in tandem with digitalization, creating new opportunities for economic cooperation, marine conservation, and sustainable development. As nations increasingly integrate digital tools into marine sectors, the importance of bilateral and multilateral trade agreements in facilitating this transition has grown significantly (Liu et al., 2023). Digitalization not only enhances efficiency and transparency in marine industries but also opens up pathways for foreign direct investment (FDI), technology transfer, and regional collaboration especially for emerging economies like Bangladesh that possess vast untapped marine potential (Nham & Hoa, 2023).

3.1 Trade Agreements as Catalysts of Digital Blue Growth

Bilateral and multilateral trade agreements increasingly incorporate digital clauses, which shape the infrastructure and governance needed for digital transformation in the maritime domain. For instance, agreements under the Regional Comprehensive Economic Partnership (RCEP) and the EU–Bangladesh Cooperation Framework lay a foundation for digital technology sharing, e-governance, and capacity building in coastal and marine sectors (Khan et al., 2024). These arrangements encourage harmonized standards for smart port development, marine data sharing, and innovation in logistics and fisheries. Bangladesh, with its strategic access to the Bay of Bengal, can benefit by aligning its national maritime strategies with regional digital trade frameworks that facilitate interoperability and attract FDI in smart port technology and marine digitalization (Midlen, 2024).

3.2 Case Studies on Digital Marine Conservation and Sustainability

Globally, several emerging economies offer compelling case studies on how digitalization supports marine sustainability. In Kenya, the "Smart Fish" initiative uses mobile apps and GPS-enabled tracking systems to empower artisanal fishers with data on legal fishing zones, weather updates, and market prices improving both income and ecological compliance (Picone et al., 2021). Similarly, Indonesia's "Ocean Eye" system uses satellite data and artificial intelligence (AI) to detect illegal fishing vessels and monitor coral reef degradation. These efforts demonstrate how the Internet of Things (IoT), AI, and geospatial technologies can support ecological stewardship while promoting inclusive economic participation (Bruno et al., 2020). Bangladesh can replicate such models by introducing similar digital platforms customized to the needs of local fishers and marine communities. For example, deploying mobile applications in the Sundarbans and Cox's Bazar regions to provide real-time information on tide levels, cyclone alerts, and fish availability could enhance livelihoods and safety. Additionally, AI-powered drones could be used to monitor mangrove health and detect illegal trawling, offering a more efficient alternative to manual patrolling by overburdened authorities (Fang et al., 2024).

3.3 Bangladesh's Maritime Digital Transformation Efforts

The Bangladesh government has initiated several steps toward digitizing its marine economy. The Chattogram Port Authority has begun the transition toward becoming a smart port, aiming to reduce vessel turnaround time and increase throughput via (Amin et al., 2025) automation and digital logistics systems. With technical assistance from development partners like JICA and the World Bank, the integration of blockchain-enabled cargo tracking and AI-assisted logistics planning is under consideration (Fang et al., 2024). These efforts align with the broader vision of "Digital Bangladesh," and contribute directly to the goals set out in the Bangladesh Delta Plan 2100 a national roadmap for integrated and climate-resilient development of coastal and marine resources (Bruno et al., 2020). Moreover, initiatives such as the "Digital Nautical Charting" project under the Department of Hydrography are being used to improve navigational safety and support the Blue Economy's expansion. E-governance tools are gradually being adopted to regulate marine licensing, fishing quotas, and environmental compliance. However, to scale up, Bangladesh must overcome key infrastructural challenges including limited broadband access in coastal areas, a shortage of digitally skilled marine professionals, and weak inter-ministerial coordination (Midlen, 2024).

3.4 The Role of Foreign Direct Investment (FDI) and Public-Private Partnerships

FDI plays a crucial role in accelerating digital maritime infrastructure in developing economies. Countries such as Vietnam and the Philippines have successfully attracted multinational investment in marine technologies, including offshore wind farms, digital shipping platforms, and coastal surveillance systems (Raghutla et al., 2024). Bangladesh, too, is beginning to emerge on investors' radar, particularly due to its geopolitical location, growing blue trade routes, and investor-friendly policies such as the Bangladesh Investment Development Authority (BIDA) incentives for maritime projects. Public-private partnerships (PPPs) can be instrumental in financing smart port infrastructure, digital fisheries management systems, and blue innovation hubs (Carbonara & Pellegrino, 2020). The government may consider establishing a "Blue Digital Innovation Zone" along its coastal belt where tech startups, marine engineers, and sustainability experts collaborate on localized digital solutions. FDI in such zones could focus on AI for marine data analysis, blockchain traceability for seafood exports, and automation tools for port customs clearance. Additionally, leveraging multilateral platforms such as the Indian Ocean Rim Association (IORA) and BIMSTEC can help Bangladesh build regional coalitions to attract investment and share best practices. Joint ventures with technologically advanced nations (e.g., South Korea, Singapore, or Japan) could facilitate knowledge exchange in smart aquaculture, marine robotics, and renewable ocean energy (Ahmad & Raza, 2020).

3.5 Policy Recommendations for Maximizing Digital and Economic Gains

To unlock the full potential of digitalization in the Blue Economy, Bangladesh needs a multi-pronged policy strategy. First, a national "Digital Blue Economy Strategy" should be formulated to align government objectives with private sector capabilities and regional cooperation opportunities (Ahmad & Raza, 2020). This should include investment in fiber optic connectivity along coastal regions, grants for digital marine research, and tax incentives for tech-based blue enterprises. Second, regulatory frameworks must be updated to accommodate data-driven governance models. For example, guidelines for data interoperability, marine cybersecurity, and digital intellectual property rights should be included in maritime legislation. Marine spatial planning and digital twin simulations could be mandated for all large-scale oceanic infrastructure developments to ensure environmental and socio-economic compliance (AlQallaf & Al Mubarak, 2025).

Third, capacity-building initiatives are critical. Universities and vocational institutes should introduce specialized courses in "Digital Marine Economy," covering topics such as GIS mapping, marine data analytics, and IoT deployment (Carbonara & Pellegrino, 2020). Training coastal youth in these digital skills would not only reduce regional inequality but also create a skilled workforce capable of sustaining and expanding the Blue Economy. Finally, data-driven decision-making should become the cornerstone of ocean governance. Establishing a centralized "Blue Digital Dashboard" that aggregates real-time data from sensors, satellites, and field reports would allow policymakers to monitor marine health, predict risks, and optimize economic outputs with greater accuracy ((Carbonara & Pellegrino, 2020; Raghutla et al., 2024). Digitalization offers a transformative pathway for emerging economies like Bangladesh to harness the full potential of the Blue Economy through enhanced economic cooperation, sustainable marine management, and foreign investment. By strategically integrating digital tools into its maritime sectors supported by trade agreements, FDI, and policy coherence Bangladesh can position itself as a regional leader in smart, inclusive, and resilient blue growth. Global examples provide blueprints that can be localized to build a future-ready economy that respects both nature and people (Raghutla et al., 2024).

3.6 Role of Startups and Social Enterprises in the Digital Blue Economy

Digital-native startups and social enterprises are transforming the Blue Economy in Bangladesh by integrating blockchain, IoT, big data, and satellite sensing to improve fisheries, waste management, and biodiversity monitoring (Mirghaderi et al., 2023; Faludi, 2023). Jol Torongo exemplifies grassroots innovation, using mobile platforms to recycle coastal plastic waste and create jobs for women and youth (Kamberidou, 2020). India's FishChain applies blockchain for seafood traceability, addressing IUU fishing (Saebi et al., 2019; Olayele, 2023), while Indonesia's eFishery leverages AI-based feeding systems to boost aquaculture productivity (Yoon & Ho, 2025). Kenya's Blue BioTrade connects small producers to global markets through digital mapping and trade data (Suchek et al., 2022; Tripathi et al., 2024). For Bangladesh, fostering blue innovation hubs, incubation centers, and access to blue finance is critical to scaling sustainable coastal entrepreneurship aligned with SDGs.

4.0 CIRCULAR ECONOMY AND DIGITAL INNOVATION

The integration of digital innovation with circular economy principles presents a promising pathway to address marine pollution, enhance resource efficiency, and promote sustainable growth within ocean-based industries. Across the globe, digital solutions such as Artificial Intelligence (AI), blockchain, and smart waste management systems are transforming how marine ecosystems are monitored and conserved. These technologies not only aid in reducing environmental harm but also enable more efficient use of resources, contributing to economic resilience and ecological sustainability (Del Vecchio et al., 2021).

4.1 Digital Solutions for Marine Pollution Control and Resource Efficiency

Digital technologies are playing a pivotal role in tackling marine pollution and enhancing resource efficiency. Artificial Intelligence (AI) enables real-time detection of oil spills, plastic debris, and illegal dumping through satellite imagery and sensor data (Bruno et al., 2020). Platforms such as Microsoft's AI for Earth and Google Earth Engine provide near real-time monitoring, allowing policymakers to respond swiftly to environmental threats. In Bangladesh, where plastics and industrial waste endanger the Bay of Bengal's ecosystems, AI-driven monitoring could significantly improve early detection and conservation efforts (Bhattacharya & Sachdev, 2024).

Blockchain technology enhances transparency in marine-related supply chains by tracking fishing practices and plastic recycling processes (Bibri & Krogstie, 2020). Initiatives like Plastic Bank show how digital tokens incentivize plastic collection, encouraging proper recycling (Quttainah & Ayadi, 2024). For Bangladesh, blockchain could formalize informal waste sectors and strengthen compliance with environmental regulations. Similarly, IoT-enabled smart waste management systems, tested in cities like Singapore and Amsterdam, optimize collection routes and prevent overflow, reducing plastic leakage into waterways (Fang et al., 2024). Adopting such systems in Bangladesh's coastal cities could curb marine pollution. However, the environmental footprint of digital tools such as energy use and e-waste—must be managed carefully to ensure net ecological benefits (Hu & Li, 2024).

4.2 Investing in Sustainable Blue Economy Sectors

Strategic investment in sustainable ocean industries is vital to balancing economic development with marine ecosystem preservation. Fisheries, aquaculture, and other ocean-based sectors represent significant economic pillars, particularly for countries like Bangladesh, where millions depend on marine resources for their livelihoods (Bennett et al., 2024). In sustainable fisheries, investments focus on implementing ecosystem-based management and technological innovations that reduce environmental impacts. Tools such as vessel tracking systems and bycatch reduction technologies enable responsible harvesting, safeguarding fish populations for future generations (Sarangi, 2023). Bangladesh's fisheries sector, which supports over 17 million people, can greatly benefit from scaling these technologies to improve resource management and compliance.

Aquaculture is the fastest-growing food production sector globally, attracting investment in environmentally sustainable practices. Advanced systems such as Recirculating Aquaculture Systems (RAS), integrated multi-trophic aquaculture (IMTA), and seaweed farming reduce water pollution and reliance on wild stocks (Choudhary et al., 2021). Bangladesh, with its extensive coastal and inland water bodies, has substantial potential to expand sustainable aquaculture using these innovations. Increasingly, investors are funding startups developing sustainable feed alternatives and digital monitoring tools to optimize productivity and animal welfare (Majid & Saimy, 2024). Encouraging such investments can enhance food security while preserving marine biodiversity.

Beyond food production, ocean-based industries like marine biotechnology, renewable ocean energy, and eco-tourism offer promising avenues for innovation-driven growth. Public-private partnerships and blended finance mechanisms are crucial to de-risk investments in these emerging sectors (Pace & Morales-Caselles, 2024). Instruments such as green and blue bonds have gained prominence as effective tools for mobilizing capital dedicated to sustainable ocean development (Lawal, 2024). Incorporating Environmental, Social, and Governance (ESG) criteria alongside international sustainability frameworks like SDG 14 ensures that investments not only yield financial returns but also contribute positively to ocean conservation (Yanlei et al., 2024).

4.3 Trade Policies for Circular Marine Industries

Trade policies are increasingly designed to support circular economy models that link growth with environmental stewardship. In marine biotechnology, policies encourage bio-based innovations from renewable marine resources, promoting waste minimization and reuse (Karakas et al., 2024). Incentives in sustainable trade agreements foster innovations such as bioplastics, pharmaceuticals, and biofuels from marine organisms (Lawal, 2024). For Bangladesh, with its rich coastal biodiversity, these policies could drive research and commercialization of marine biotech products while ensuring ecosystem health. Eco-tourism also benefits from regulations that incentivize low-impact infrastructure and biodiversity protection. In the Sundarbans mangrove forest, a UNESCO World Heritage site, sustainable eco-tourism can provide livelihoods without degrading natural habitats (Pace & Morales-Caselles, 2024).

Green shipping forms another priority. Emission rules, cleaner fuels, and port waste recycling promote energy-efficient vessels and circular waste management (Kyvelou et al., 2023). Subsidies and tariff reductions further accelerate adoption, supported by cross-border standards such as sustainable shipping corridors in the Bay of Bengal (Bhardwaj & Roy, 2025). Finally, integrating digital tools AI, blockchain, and smart waste systems advances monitoring and pollution control (Bhardwaj & Roy, 2025). For Bangladesh and other emerging economies, these integrated trade policies offer a pathway to sustainable ocean development and long-term prosperity (Pace & Morales-Caselles, 2024).

4.4 Education and Skills for a Digital Blue-Circular Economy

The shift to a digitalized Blue and Circular Economy (BCE) requires not only infrastructure and policy but also a workforce equipped with future-ready skills. As marine industries adopt artificial intelligence, blockchain, IoT, and remote sensing, countries like Bangladesh must invest in human capital to remain competitive in the global blue transition (Pranita et al., 2023). Education and training thus form the backbone of this transformation. Universities and Technical and Vocational Education and Training (TVET) centers should update curricula to integrate marine digital technologies, sustainable aquaculture tools, ocean governance, and circular entrepreneurship. Bridging marine sciences with digital competencies is crucial for an innovation-driven coastal economy (Silver et al., 2015; Türkeli et al., 2022).

Practical initiatives could include specialized programs such as a "Blue Economy Digital Bootcamp" developed through partnerships among universities, government, and private tech firms. These would offer short, intensive modules on real-time data analytics, blockchain-enabled traceability, AI-driven pollution monitoring, and marine drone operations (Yeager et al., 2024). Targeting coastal youth and professionals, such programs would enhance employability in fisheries, eco-tourism, conservation, and waste valorization. Regional cooperation also plays a role, with SAARC and ASEAN platforms potentially supporting joint training, exchanges, and certification schemes (Hojnik et al., 2024). Digital learning platforms further expand access. MOOCs and AI-powered systems provide scalable, low-cost education in marine sustainability (Karakas et al., 2024). With growing internet access, Bangladeshi universities can localize global content into blended formats, supported by vernacular resources and workshops (Nunes & Lessa, 2021). AI tutors like ChatGPT and adaptive platforms can personalize learning for students from diverse backgrounds (Ahlström, 2019).

To succeed, these initiatives must be embedded in national development plans, including the Blue Economy Master Plan 2041 and Digital Bangladesh Vision, with emphasis on youth inclusion and gender equity (Cairone et al., 2024). Building ocean-literate, tech-enabled professionals is central to sustainable, inclusive growth in thc digital agc.

4.5 Gender and Social Inclusion in Digital Blue and Circular Economy

A sustainable Blue and Circular Economy (BCE) cannot be achieved without ensuring gender equity and social inclusion. In many coastal regions of developing countries, including Bangladesh, women and marginalized groups face persistent barriers in digital access, financial inclusion, and participation in marine industries (Piao et al., 2023). Bridging these gaps is both a social imperative and a way to unlock innovation and resilience in BCE initiatives. Women in Bangladesh's coastal areas, such as the Sundarbans, are already engaged in small-scale fisheries, crab farming, and eco-tourism (Suarez-Visbal et al., 2022). However, their work often remains informal and undervalued. Digital tools ranging from mobile apps for fish marketing to blockchain-based seafood traceability offer opportunities to formalize and enhance their contributions. Yet, structural barriers such as limited access to smartphones, training, and mobility continue to hinder full participation (Palm et al., 2024).

Global examples highlight how inclusion can be transformative. In the Philippines, women's cooperatives use digital platforms for seaweed farming, weather alerts, and market access, improving both livelihoods and sustainability (Bosone et al., 2023). In Bangladesh, emerging eco-tourism initiatives show how women leverage platforms like Facebook, Google Maps, and TripAdvisor to promote biodiversity hotspots, with some trained in drone operations and digital photography to attract conservation-focused tourism (Pastore & Tommaso, 2024).

Scaling such progress requires gender-sensitive policies. Priority actions include integrating digital literacy for women into BCE training programs (Schröder et al., 2019), improving affordable internet access, and promoting safe online participation (Liu et al., 2021). Institutional reforms should encourage women's leadership in marine governance, cooperatives, and digital blue enterprises (Pastore & Tommaso, 2024). Partnerships with NGOs, private tech firms, and international agencies can accelerate these efforts. Ultimately, gender and social inclusion are not peripheral to BCE they are central. Empowering coastal women and marginalized groups through digital skills, supportive infrastructure, and inclusive governance ensures that the digital BCE transition is equitable, community-driven, and sustainable (Jain & Virk, 2024).

5.0 POLICY IMPLICATIONS AND FUTURE DIRECTIONS

The transition to a Blue and Circular Economy (BCE) depends on coherent policy frameworks, regional cooperation, and strong industry partnerships that foster innovation, efficiency, and environmental stewardship (Pastore & Tommaso, 2024). For Bangladesh, where the Bay of Bengal sustains both livelihoods and fragile ecosystems, strategies must combine climate resilience, sustainable marine industries, and circular economy principles. Existing national policies, including the Bangladesh Delta Plan 2100 and the Blue Economy Development Framework, provide a foundation but require deeper alignment with circular approaches (Pranita et al., 2023). Measures such as Extended Producer Responsibility (EPR) in packaging, fishing, and shipping, along with subsidies for renewable marine energy, seaweed aquaculture, and circular design in shipping, can simultaneously reduce waste and generate green employment.

Regional cooperation is equally crucial, especially for shared challenges such as plastic pollution and overfishing. Platforms like the Bay of Bengal Initiative for Multi-Sectoral Technical and Economic Cooperation (BIMSTEC) can harmonize environmental standards, coordinate research, and deploy digital tools to track marine waste and illegal fishing (Satizábal et al., 2020). Joint investments in AI-based surveillance, blockchain traceability, and drone monitoring could strengthen enforcement across South Asia. A "Blue South Asia Task Force," led by Bangladesh, could promote regional best practices in fisheries, eco-tourism, and circular coastal development. Industry partnerships play a decisive role in scaling BCE solutions. Public-Private Partnerships (PPPs) can mobilize investment for smart ports, sustainable aquaculture, and marine biotech startups (Sopha et al., 2022). Bangladesh's garment sector, for instance, could collaborate with innovators to develop seaweed-based fibers as eco-friendly textile alternatives. Incentives such as green procurement policies and tax benefits can encourage multinational firms to adopt circular supply chains. Institutionalizing collaboration among government, academia, and industry through the triple helix model will also accelerate R&D in blue technologies, environmental monitoring, and circular design (Suarez-Visbal et al., 2022).

Digitalization is a transformative enabler for climate resilience and disaster preparedness. With coastal populations facing cyclones, flooding, and salinity intrusion, technologies such as digital twins of coastal cities can help simulate climate scenarios and guide adaptive planning (Tamasiga et al., 2025). AI-powered early warning systems integrated with community networks could reduce disaster casualties, while blockchain can enhance transparency in emergency relief distribution. IoT sensors in embankments, ports, and aquaculture farms can track sea level rise, salinity, and structural risks, enabling timely interventions. Pilot projects in Satkhira,

Cox's Bazar, and Bhola could serve as scalable models for fisheries forecasting and food security (Thoya et al., 2022).

At the international level, trade policies and multilateral agreements must embed circularity in maritime trade, emissions, and port management (Upadhyay & Mishra, 2020). Bangladesh should leverage the WTO's Aid for Trade initiative to strengthen BCE capacity and engage in global platforms such as the Global Plastics Treaty and the UN Decade of Ocean Science (Yoon & Ho, 2025). Regional trade agreements like SAFTA could extend preferential tariffs to circular products, while the EU's Carbon Border Adjustment Mechanism (CBAM) should incorporate flexibilities for LDCs to ensure a fair transition (Xu et al., 2021). Financing remains a key challenge. Innovative instruments such as blue bonds, debt-for-nature swaps, and climate adaptation funds can bridge gaps (Thoya et al., 2022). Bangladesh Bank can lead by embedding green lending into regulations and incentivizing banks to support coastal circular startups through concessional loans (Yoon & Ho, 2025). Embedding ESG metrics in investment decisions will also ensure long-term environmental and social returns.

Finally, future directions require embedding systems thinking into governance and education. Universities and vocational institutes, especially in coastal regions, should integrate BCE, digital sustainability, and circular entrepreneurship into curricula. Training programs for local officials and fisherfolk cooperatives are essential to democratize technology and finance. The Ministry of Environment, Forest and Climate Change (MoEFCC) could spearhead a National Circular Economy Roadmap for the Blue Economy, co-created with industry, NGOs, and communities. An inclusive, digitally driven, and climate-resilient BCE framework anchored in policy, regional collaboration, and innovation—offers Bangladesh and its neighbors a pathway to prosperity while safeguarding marine ecosystems. By embedding sustainability into trade, finance, and education, Bangladesh can lead a just and future-ready blue transition.

5.1 Ethical and Environmental Risks of Digitalization in the Blue Economy

Digitalization is transforming the Blue and Circular Economy (BCE) through innovations such as AI-driven marine monitoring, blockchain traceability, and IoT-enabled fisheries, offering new efficiency and sustainability pathways (Pace et al., 2023). Yet, these advances also generate ethical and environmental risks, particularly in fragile coastal ecosystems and resource-dependent communities in emerging economies like Bangladesh. One critical issue is the rising volume of electronic waste (e-waste). Devices such as drones, underwater robots, and smart buoys, once obsolete, become hazardous waste that threatens marine biodiversity and coastal livelihoods. In Bangladesh, limited waste management systems often lead to improper disposal, causing water and soil pollution that harms fisheries and public health (Agarwala, 2025).

Another concern involves digital surveillance. While satellite imaging and geolocation tools support fisheries regulation and disaster monitoring, their misuse can infringe on the privacy of coastal and indigenous communities if unregulated (Ekpemuaka et al., 2025). Similarly, the energy intensity of digital infrastructure marine drones, data centers, and sensor networks contributes to carbon emissions. Without renewable energy integration, technologies intended to safeguard ecosystems may paradoxically accelerate climate change. Addressing these risks requires proactive governance. Environmental Impact Assessments (EIAs) should be mandated for large-scale digital deployments in ecologically sensitive zones like the Sundarbans or coral-rich coasts of Indonesia (Fatimah et al., 2020). Ethical AI and data governance frameworks must ensure transparency, fairness, and accountability in marine data use (Hamad et al., 2023). In addition, circular design principles such as modular, repairable, and recyclable ICT devices—can reduce raw material dependence and e-waste.

Ultimately, while digitalization enables sustainability in the Blue Economy, its ethical and environmental risks must be anticipated and mitigated. Responsible innovation is key to ensuring that digital BCE transitions strengthen, rather than undermine, the resilience of marine ecosystems and coastal communities (Jensen et al., 2021).

6.0 COMPARATIVE SPOTLIGHTS ON BLUE-CIRCULAR ECONOMY

To offer practical insights into the integration of digitalization within the Blue and Circular Economy (BCE), this section presents a series of short country spotlights from both emerging and developed economies. These case studies drawn from Bangladesh, Indonesia, Kenya, and Norway highlight diverse pathways in digital marine policy, community engagement, and sustainable trade. They illustrate how contextual realities shape digital BCE adoption and underscore the contrast between resource-constrained innovations and high-tech models.

a. Bangladesh: Grassroots Digital Inclusion in Coastal Communities

As a low-lying coastal nation highly vulnerable to climate change, Bangladesh is taking strategic steps to harness digitalization for sustainable marine resource management. The government, through the Blue Economy Cell, has started integrating GIS mapping, marine drones, and satellite monitoring into national fisheries oversight. Notably, digital eco-tourism initiatives in the Sundarbans, led by community youth groups, are creating income while preserving biodiversity. Pilot initiatives such as the proposed "Blue Economy Digital Bootcamp" are designed to equip rural youth and fisherfolk with skills in marine data analytics, digital marketing of coastal products, and innovations in aquaculture. Despite limited resources, Bangladesh's community-driven and low-cost digitalization efforts stand as a model for inclusive development (Zafarullah & Ferdous, 2021).

b. Indonesia: Digital Marine Governance and Aquaculture Startups

Indonesia, the world's largest archipelagic nation, has made impressive progress in digitizing marine governance. Through its One Map Policy and e-ocean zoning system, the government ensures transparent marine spatial planning to prevent resource conflicts and overfishing. Startups like eFishery use IoT-based feeding systems and AI to optimize aquaculture operations, increasing yields and reducing environmental impacts. Additionally, platforms like JALA Tech collect real-time water quality data from shrimp farms, empowering small-scale farmers with predictive analytics. These digital interventions are backed by government investment and international development partnerships, positioning Indonesia as a regional leader in marine tech (Teniwut et al., 2022).

c. Kenya: Blue BioTrade and Blockchain for Coastal Livelihoods

On the east coast of Africa, Kenya is innovating through its Blue Economy Implementation Framework, focused on biodiversity conservation, youth employment, and digital trade facilitation. The Blue BioTrade platform leverages blockchain to ensure traceability and sustainability certification for marine products such as sea cucumbers and mangrove honey. This enhances Kenya's access to premium markets while promoting sustainable harvesting. Additionally, digital learning hubs in Mombasa and Lamu provide coastal youth with training in marine spatial planning, GPS navigation, and drone piloting for coastal surveillance. Kenya's approach emphasizes digital empowerment and ethical trade as tools for climate resilience (Phang et al., 2023).

d. Norway: High-Tech Marine Sustainability in a Developed Context

As a developed nation with strong maritime traditions, Norway leads globally in digital marine technologies and circular aquaculture systems. The Norwegian government supports AI-powered marine robotics, autonomous ships, and blockchain-based supply chains for cod and salmon. Institutions like SINTEF and NTNU collaborate with industry to develop real-time environmental sensors that monitor fish health, ocean acidity, and marine waste. Norway's Fisheries Directorate utilizes big data analytics to enforce fishing quotas and marine conservation zones efficiently. Furthermore, circularity principles are applied in the reuse of aquaculture waste for biogas and fertilizer, exemplifying closed-loop innovation at scale (Luthman et al., 2022).

6.0 CONCLUSION

The integration of digital transformation within the Blue and Circular Economy (BCE) presents a paradigm shift in how coastal and marine resources are managed, conserved, and commercialized, particularly for developing countries like Bangladesh. This chapter has outlined the pivotal role of digital technologies such as artificial intelligence, blockchain, big data analytics, and IoT in enhancing resource efficiency, transparency, and resilience across marine industries including fisheries, aquaculture, tourism, and port logistics. Key insights reveal that digital tools not only support circularity in production and consumption but also strengthen climate resilience, disaster preparedness, and ecological sustainability in vulnerable coastal zones (Majid & Saimy, 2024).

Policy recommendations emerging from this discourse emphasize the need for an enabling environment that fosters inclusive, sustainable, and technology-driven growth. For countries like Bangladesh, strategic investment in digital infrastructure, the upskilling of coastal communities and strong public-private-academic partnerships are essential to localize BCE innovation (Milhem et al., 2024). Governments must enact forward-thinking policies such as digital marine zoning, climate-smart port modernization, and incentives for green marine entrepreneurship. At the same time, regional cooperation through platforms like BIMSTEC and SAFTA must be deepened to harmonize environmental regulations, share data, and co-develop digital solutions for marine governance. International trade bodies should revise existing protocols to accommodate and promote circular goods and services, particularly from the Global South, ensuring a fair and green transition (Midlen, 2024).

Furthermore, a global roadmap for future research and collaboration is essential. Priority research areas should include measuring the digital readiness of coastal communities, assessing the circular potential of blue industries, and developing inclusive indicators to track digital BCE progress (Nunes & Lessa, 2021). Interdisciplinary collaborations involving ocean scientists, digital innovators, economists, and policymakers are crucial to generate scalable, evidence-based solutions. Bangladesh can serve as a model for other developing nations by launching pilot projects that combine indigenous knowledge with frontier technologies in sustainable marine resource use. Multilateral institutions and donor agencies should channel more funding into South-South cooperation, innovation hubs, and technology transfer programs that empower local actors and bridge the digital divide. The convergence of digital transformation and the Blue and Circular Economy offers a compelling pathway toward sustainable, inclusive, and climate-resilient growth. For countries like Bangladesh, this intersection provides not only a development opportunity but a strategic imperative for ensuring a thriving future for both people and the planet (Olayele, 2023).

REFERENCES

Abu-Bakar, H., & Charnley, F. (2024). Developing a strategic methodology for circular economy roadmapping: A theoretical framework. *Sustainability (Basel), 16*(15), 6682. DOI: 10.3390/su16156682

Agarwala, N. (2025). Smart Governance for a Sustainable Blue Economy. In *Handbook of Sustainable Blue Economy* (pp. 1–35). Springer Nature Switzerland. DOI: 10.1007/978-3-031-32671-4_37-1

Ahlström, H. (2019). Policy hotspots for sustainability: Changes in the EU regulation of sustainable business and finance. *Sustainability (Basel), 11*(2), 499. DOI: 10.3390/su11020499

Ahmad, M., & Raza, M. Y. (2020). Role of public-private partnerships investment in energy and technological innovations in driving climate change: Evidence from Brazil. *Environmental Science and Pollution Research International, 27*(24), 30638–30648. DOI: 10.1007/s11356-020-09307-w

AlQallaf, S. J. S., & Al Mubarak, M. (2025). Maximization of Business Strategies Through Digital Technology: Opportunities and Challenges. *Innovative and Intelligent Digital Technologies. Towards an Increased Efficiency, 2*, 957–975.

Amin, R., Muppani, V. R., Sairam, P. S., Arora, R., Haque, M., & Islam, S. (2025). Digitalizing the Shipping Containers of Bangladesh Sustainable Solutions Amidst Challenges. In *Developing Dynamic and Sustainable Supply Chains to Achieve Sustainable Development Goals* (pp. 283–310). IGI Global Scientific Publishing. DOI: 10.4018/979-8-3693-6284-6.ch010

Ayaz, O., & Tatoglu, E. (2024). Unveiling the power of social value: Catalyzing circular economy in emerging market SMEs. *Journal of Cleaner Production, 453*, 142245. DOI: 10.1016/j.jclepro.2024.142245

Bag, S., Telukdarie, A., Pretorius, J. C., & Gupta, S. (2021). Industry 4.0 and supply chain sustainability: Framework and future research directions. *Benchmarking, 28*(5), 1410–1450.

Beltrami, M., Orzes, G., Sarkis, J., & Sartor, M. (2021). Industry 4.0 and sustainability: Towards conceptualization and theory. *Journal of Cleaner Production, 312*, 127733. DOI: 10.1016/j.jclepro.2021.127733

Bennett, M., March, A., & Failler, P. (2024). Blue economy financing solutions for the fisheries and aquaculture sectors of Caribbean Island states. *Fishes, 9*(8), 305. DOI: 10.3390/fishes9080305

Bhardwaj, A., & Roy, M. (2025). Blue Economy vs. Green Economy: A Case Study for Sustainable Economy in India. In *Securing Sustainable Futures Through Blue and Green Economies* (pp. 195-218). IGI Global Scientific Publishing. DOI: 10.4018/979-8-3693-7893-9.ch008

Bhattacharya, S., & Sachdev, B. K. (2024). Impact of Scientific Innovation in Coastal Resource Management: Fostering Blue Economic Development, Environmental Mitigation, and Pollution Control. In *Scientific Innovations for Coastal Resource Management* (pp. 1–32). IGI Global. DOI: 10.4018/979-8-3693-2436-3.ch001

Bibri, S. E., & Krogstie, J. (2020). Environmentally data-driven smart sustainable cities: Applied innovative solutions for energy efficiency, pollution reduction, and urban metabolism. *Energy Informatics*, *3*(1), 29. DOI: 10.1186/s42162-020-00130-8

Bilalova, S., Newig, J., Tremblay-Lévesque, L. C., Roux, J., Herron, C., & Crane, S. (2023). Pathways to water sustainability? A global study assessing the benefits of integrated water resources management. *Journal of Environmental Management*, *343*, 118179. DOI: 10.1016/j.jenvman.2023.118179

Bosone, M., Casola, M., Daldanise, G., & Vito, D. (2023). Stimulating Circular Urban Regeneration through Cultural and Sustainable Communities: The Proposal for a Green Blue Youth Vision 2030. *Sustainability (Basel)*, *15*(14), 11294. DOI: 10.3390/su151411294

Bressanelli, G., Adrodegari, F., Pigosso, D. C., & Parida, V. (2022). Towards the smart circular economy paradigm: A definition, conceptualization, and research agenda. *Sustainability (Basel)*, *14*(9), 4960. DOI: 10.3390/su14094960

Bruno, F., Ricca, M., Lagudi, A., Kalamara, P., Manglis, A., Fourkiotou, A., Papadopoulou, D., & Veneti, A. (2020). Digital technologies for the sustainable development of the accessible underwater cultural heritage sites. *Journal of Marine Science and Engineering*, *8*(11), 955. DOI: 10.3390/jmse8110955

Burmaoglu, S., Ozdemir Gungor, D., Kirbac, A., & Saritas, O. (2023). Future research avenues at the nexus of circular economy and digitalization. *International Journal of Productivity and Performance Management*, *72*(8), 2247–2269. DOI: 10.1108/IJPPM-01-2021-0026

Cairone, S., Hasan, S. W., Choo, K. H., Li, C. W., Zarra, T., Belgiorno, V., & Naddeo, V. (2024). Integrating artificial intelligence modeling and membrane technologies for advanced wastewater treatment: Research progress and future perspectives. *The Science of the Total Environment*, *944*, 173999. DOI: 10.1016/j.scitotenv.2024.173999

Carbonara, N., & Pellegrino, R. (2020). The role of public private partnerships in fostering innovation. *Construction Management and Economics*, *38*(2), 140–156. DOI: 10.1080/01446193.2019.1610184

Cezarino, L. O., Liboni, L. B., Oliveira Stefanelli, N., Oliveira, B. G., & Stocco, L. C. (2021). Diving into emerging economies bottleneck: Industry 4.0 and implications for circular economy. *Management Decision*, *59*(8), 1841–1862. DOI: 10.1108/MD-10-2018-1084

Choudhary, P., Khade, M., Savant, S., Musale, A., Chelliah, M. S., & Dasgupta, S. (2021). Empowering blue economy: From underrated ecosystem to sustainable industry. *Journal of Environmental Management*, *291*, 112697. DOI: 10.1016/j.jenvman.2021.112697

Del Vecchio, P., Passiante, G., Barberio, G., & Innella, C. (2021). Digital innovation ecosystems for circular economy: The case of ICESP, the Italian circular economy stakeholder platform. *International Journal on Management of Innovation & Technology*, *18*(01), 2050053. DOI: 10.1142/S0219877020500534

Du, Y., Xu, J., & Yuan, X. (2024). The development relationship between circular economy and advanced digital technology: Based on an innovative literature review method. *Environmental Technology Reviews*, *13*(1), 614–638. DOI: 10.1080/21622515.2024.2406988

Ekpemuaka, E., Odunlade, O. R., & Maiyaki, S. F. (2025). Resilience in Africa's Transition to a Sustainable Digital and Blue Economy: Policy and Regulatory Framework in Nigeria. In *Securing Sustainable Futures Through Blue and Green Economies* (pp. 149–172). IGI Global Scientific Publishing. DOI: 10.4018/979-8-3693-7893-9.ch006

Faludi, J. (2023). How to create social value through digital social innovation? Unlocking the potential of the social value creation of digital start-ups. *Journal of Social Entrepreneurship*, *14*(1), 73–90. DOI: 10.1080/19420676.2020.1823871

Fang, X., Zhang, Y., Yang, J., & Zhan, G. (2024). An evaluation of marine economy sustainable development and the ramifications of digital technologies in China coastal regions. *Economic Analysis and Policy*, *82*, 554–570. DOI: 10.1016/j.eap.2024.03.022

Fatimah, Y. A., Govindan, K., Murniningsih, R., & Setiawan, A. (2020). Industry 4.0 based sustainable circular economy approach for smart waste management system to achieve sustainable development goals: A case study of Indonesia. *Journal of Cleaner Production*, *269*, 122263. DOI: 10.1016/j.jclepro.2020.122263

Gamage, R. N. (2016). Blue economy in Southeast Asia: Oceans as the new frontier of economic development. *Maritime Affairs*, *12*(2), 1–15. DOI: 10.1080/09733159.2016.1244361

Geissdoerfer, M., Savaget, P., Bocken, N. M., & Hultink, E. J. (2017). The Circular Economy–A new sustainability paradigm? *Journal of Cleaner Production*, *143*, 757–768. DOI: 10.1016/j.jclepro.2016.12.048

Hagelüken, C., & Goldmann, D. (2022). Recycling and circular economy—Towards a closed loop for metals in emerging clean technologies. *Mineral Economics*, *35*(3), 539–562. DOI: 10.1007/s13563-022-00319-1

Hamad, S., Lai, F. W., Shad, M. K., Khatib, S. F., & Ali, S. E. A. (2023). Assessing the implementation of sustainable development goals: Does integrated reporting matter? *Sustainability Accounting. Management and Policy Journal*, *14*(1), 49–74.

Hojnik, J., Ruzzier, M., Ruzzier, M. K., Sučić, B., Soltwisch, B., & Rus, M. (2024). Review of EU projects with a focus on environmental quality: Innovation, eco-innovation, and circular-economy elements. *International Journal of Innovation Studies*, *8*(1), 1–12. DOI: 10.1016/j.ijis.2023.10.001

Hu, J., & Li, Q. (2024). From bits to green: Unraveling the digital economy's influence on natural resource efficiency. *Journal of Environmental Management*, *365*, 121203. DOI: 10.1016/j.jenvman.2024.121203

Hysa, E., Manta, O., Ailincă, A. G., Piciu, G. C., & Yue, X. G. (2024). Digitalization as an instrument in support of covering the circularity gap in the European Union economy. *Environment, Development and Sustainability*, *27*(11), 1–21. DOI: 10.1007/s10668-024-04772-6

Jain, N., & Virk, S. (2024). Circular Economy in Agriculture. In *Impact of Women in Food and Agricultural Development* (pp. 79–88). IGI Global. DOI: 10.4018/979-8-3693-3037-1.ch005

Javaid, M., Haleem, A., Singh, R. P., Suman, R., & Gonzalez, E. S. (2022). Understanding the adoption of Industry 4.0 technologies in improving environmental sustainability. *Sustainable operations and computers, 3*, 203-217.

Jensen, H. H., Andersen, M. M., Dao, A., Lind, M., Pandey, V., Bapuji, G., & Turos, A. (2021). Digitalisation in a maritime circular economy. In *Maritime Informatics: Additional Perspectives and Applications* (pp. 17–37). Springer International Publishing. DOI: 10.1007/978-3-030-72785-7_2

Kamberidou, I. (2020). "Distinguished" women entrepreneurs in the digital economy and the multitasking whirlpool. *Journal of Innovation and Entrepreneurship*, *9*(1), 3. DOI: 10.1186/s13731-020-0114-y

Karakas, S., Acar, A. Z., & Kirmizi, M. (2024). Maritime Sustainability: Navigating Complex Challenges and Ecological Footprints. In *Sustainable Development Seen Through the Lenses of Ethnoeconomics and the Circular Economy* (pp. 19–47). Springer Nature Switzerland. DOI: 10.1007/978-3-031-72676-7_2

Khan, M., Chang, Y. C., & Bibi, A. (2024). Navigating Pakistan's Maritime Industry potential in context of blue economy: An analysis of the necessity for ratification of maritime labour convention 2006. *Marine Policy*, *165*, 106150. DOI: 10.1016/j.marpol.2024.106150

Kumar, S., Darshna, A., & Ranjan, D. (2023). A review of literature on the integration of green energy and circular economy. *Heliyon*, *9*(11), e21091. DOI: 10.1016/j.heliyon.2023.e21091

Kyvelou, S. S., Ierapetritis, D. G., & Chiotinis, M. (2023). The future of fisheries co-management in the context of the sustainable blue economy and the green deal: There is no green without blue. *Sustainability (Basel)*, *15*(10), 7784. DOI: 10.3390/su15107784

Langley, D. J., Rosca, E., Angelopoulos, M., Kamminga, O., & Hooijer, C. (2023). Orchestrating a smart circular economy: Guiding principles for digital product passports. *Journal of Business Research*, *169*, 114259. DOI: 10.1016/j.jbusres.2023.114259

Lawal, O. T. (2024). Blue Bioeconomy and Industrial Innovation. In *Marine Bioprospecting for Sustainable Blue-bioeconomy* (pp. 119–141). Springer Nature Switzerland. DOI: 10.1007/978-3-031-68911-6_7

Liang, J., Yin, Z., Yang, J., Li, Y., Xu, M., Li, J., Yang, M., & Niu, L. (2022). Bibliometrics and visualization analysis of research in the field of sustainable development of the blue economy (2006–2021). *Frontiers in Marine Science*, *9*, 936612. DOI: 10.3389/fmars.2022.936612

Liu, Y., Jiang, Y., Pei, Z., Xia, N., & Wang, A. (2023). Evolution of the coupling coordination between the marine economy and digital economy. *Sustainability (Basel)*, *15*(6), 5600. DOI: 10.3390/su15065600

Liu, Z., Liu, J., & Osmani, M. (2021). Integration of digital economy and circular economy: Current status and future directions. *Sustainability (Basel)*, *13*(13), 7217. DOI: 10.3390/su13137217

Luthman, O., Jonell, M., Rönnbäck, P., & Troell, M. (2022). Strong and weak sustainability in Nordic aquaculture policies. *Aquaculture (Amsterdam, Netherlands)*, *550*, 737841. DOI: 10.1016/j.aquaculture.2021.737841

Majid, M. A., & Saimy, I. S. (2024, April). Strategic Marketing of Blue Financing for Advancing Blue Economy Activities: A Comprehensive Review. In *International Conference on Business and Technology* (pp. 219-229). Cham: Springer Nature Switzerland. DOI: 10.1007/978-3-031-67431-0_21

Malik, A., Sharma, P., Vinu, A., Karakoti, A., Kaur, K., Gujral, H. S., & Laker, B. (2022). Circular economy adoption by SMEs in emerging markets: Towards a multilevel conceptual framework. *Journal of Business Research*, *142*, 605–619. DOI: 10.1016/j.jbusres.2021.12.076

Midlen, A. (2024). Enacting the blue economy in the Western Indian Ocean: A 'collaborative blue economy governmentality'. *Environment and Planning. E, Nature and Space*, *7*(2), 627–653. DOI: 10.1177/25148486231198010

Milhem, M., Ateeq, A., Al Astal, A., Alzoraiki, M., Ateeq, R. A., Shafie, D. I., & Santhanamery, T. (2024). Advancing Sustainability: Embracing the Circular Economy for Environmental and Economic Resilience. In *Business Sustainability with Artificial Intelligence (AI): Challenges and Opportunities* (Vol. 2, pp. 57–68). Springer Nature Switzerland.

Mirghaderi, S. A., Aboumasoudi, A. S., & Amindoust, A. (2023). Developing an open innovation model in the startup ecosystem industries based on the attitude of organizational resilience and blue ocean strategy. *Computers & Industrial Engineering*, *181*, 109301. DOI: 10.1016/j.cie.2023.109301

Murray, A., Skene, K., & Haynes, K. (2017). The circular economy: An interdisciplinary exploration of the concept and application in a global context. *Journal of Business Ethics*, *140*(3), 369–380. DOI: 10.1007/s10551-015-2693-2

Nham, N. T. H., & Hoa, T. T. M. (2023). Influences of digitalization on sustaining marine minerals: A path toward sustainable blue economy. *Ocean and Coastal Management*, *239*, 106589. DOI: 10.1016/j.ocecoaman.2023.106589

Nunes, D., & Lessa, J. (2021). Design as a Driver for Behavioural Change: Oceans and Plastics, Approaches for a Shift Towards Sustainability. In *Advances in Design and Digital Communication: Proceedings of the 4th International Conference on Design and Digital Communication, Digicom 2020, November 5–7, 2020, Barcelos, Portugal* (pp. 456-469). Springer International Publishing.

Olayele, F. (2023). Innovation and value creation in Canadas ocean sector: A blue economy imperative. In *Regional Economic Systems after* [Edward Elgar Publishing.]. *COVID*, *19*, 225–240.

Onguglo, B. F., & Eugui, D. V. (2018). Small island developing states and the ocean economy: widening the development frontier. In *Handbook of Small States* (pp. 530–549). Routledge. DOI: 10.4324/9781351181846-28

Pace, L. A., & Morales-Caselles, C. (2024). Sustainability-Oriented Innovation in Blue Economy Sectors: Pathways Toward Specialization in Island Territories of the Western Mediterranean Basin. In *Handbook of Sustainable Blue Economy* (pp. 1–25). Springer Nature Switzerland. DOI: 10.1007/978-3-031-32671-4_29-1

Pace, L. A., Saritas, O., & Deidun, A. (2023). Exploring future research and innovation directions for a sustainable blue economy. *Marine Policy*, *148*, 105433. DOI: 10.1016/j.marpol.2022.105433

Palm, J., Lazoroska, D., Valencia, M., Bocken, N., & Södergren, K. (2024). A gender perspective on the circular economy: A literature review and research agenda. *Journal of Industrial Ecology*, *28*(6), 1670–1683. DOI: 10.1111/jiec.13554

Pastore, P., & Tommaso, S. (2024). Women in Firms and Circular Economy Actions: A Systematic Literature Review with a Bibliometric Analysis. *Gender Issues in the Sustainable Development Era*, 189-220.

Patwa, N., Sivarajah, U., Seetharaman, A., Sarkar, S., Maiti, K., & Hingorani, K. (2021). Towards a circular economy: An emerging economies context. *Journal of Business Research*, *122*, 725–735. DOI: 10.1016/j.jbusres.2020.05.015

Phang, S., March, A., Touron-Gardic, G., Deane, K., & Failler, P. (2023). A review of the blue economy, potential, and opportunities in seven Caribbean nations pre-COVID-19. *ICES Journal of Marine Science*, *80*(8), 2233–2243. DOI: 10.1093/icesjms/fsac230

Piao, R. S., de Vincenzi, T. B., da Silva, A. L. F., de Oliveira, M. C. C., Vazquez-Brust, D., & Carvalho, M. M. (2023). How is the circular economy embracing social inclusion? *Journal of Cleaner Production*, *411*, 137340. DOI: 10.1016/j.jclepro.2023.137340

Picone, F., Buonocore, E., Chemello, R., Russo, G. F., & Franzese, P. P. (2021). Exploring the development of scientific research on Marine Protected Areas: From conservation to global ocean sustainability. *Ecological Informatics*, *61*, 101200. DOI: 10.1016/j.ecoinf.2020.101200

Pranita, D., Sarjana, S., Musthofa, B. M., Kusumastuti, H., & Rasul, M. S. (2023). Blockchain technology to enhance integrated blue economy: A case study in strengthening sustainable tourism on smart islands. *Sustainability (Basel), 15*(6), 5342. DOI: 10.3390/su15065342

Quttainah, M. A., & Ayadi, I. (2024). The impact of digital integration on corporate sustainability: Emissions reduction, environmental innovation, and resource efficiency in the European. *Journal of Innovation & Knowledge, 9*(3), 100525. DOI: 10.1016/j.jik.2024.100525

Raghutla, C., Malik, M. N., Hameed, A., & Chittedi, K. R. (2024). Impact of public-private partnerships investment and FDI on CO2 emissions: A study of six global investment countries. *Journal of Environmental Management, 360*, 121213. DOI: 10.1016/j.jenvman.2024.121213

Rataj, O., Kemp, R., & Mordaszewska, K. (2024). Mainstreaming innovative circular economy solutions—A comparative study between entrepreneurs in developed versus emerging markets and developing economies. *Business Strategy and the Environment, 33*(8), 8946–8964. DOI: 10.1002/bse.3957

Rizzato, F., Tonelli, A., Fiandrino, S., & Devalle, A. (2024). Analysing SDG disclosure and its impact on integrated thinking and reporting. *Meditari Accountancy Research, 32*(3), 803–831. DOI: 10.1108/MEDAR-07-2022-1751

Saebi, T., Foss, N. J., & Linder, S. (2019). Social entrepreneurship research: Past achievements and future promises. *Journal of Management, 45*(1), 70–95. DOI: 10.1177/0149206318793196

Sarangi, U. (2023, February). Blue economy, blue finance and ocean governance for achieving sustainable development goals. [). Oxford, UK: Blackwell Publishing Ltd.]. *Natural Resources Forum, 47*(1), 3–21. DOI: 10.1111/1477-8947.12267

Satizábal, P., Dressler, W. H., Fabinyi, M., & Pido, M. D. (2020). Blue economy discourses and practices: Reconfiguring ocean spaces in the Philippines. *Maritime Studies, 19*(2), 207–221. DOI: 10.1007/s40152-020-00168-0

Schröder, P., Anantharaman, M., Anggraeni, K., & Foxon, T. J. (2019). The circular economy and the Global South. *The Circular Economy and the Global South. Routledge.* Https://Doi. Org/10.4324, *978042*(9434), 006.

Seyyedi, S. R., Kowsari, E., Gheibi, M., Chinnappan, A., & Ramakrishna, S. (2024). A comprehensive review integration of digitalization and circular economy in waste management by adopting artificial intelligence approaches: Towards a simulation model. *Journal of Cleaner Production*, *460*, 142584. DOI: 10.1016/j.jclepro.2024.142584

Shan, S., Mirza, N., Umar, M., & Hasnaoui, A. (2023). The nexus of sustainable development, blue financing, digitalization, and financial intermediation. *Technological Forecasting and Social Change*, *195*, 122772. DOI: 10.1016/j.techfore.2023.122772

Silver, J. J., Gray, N. J., Campbell, L. M., Fairbanks, L. W., & Gruby, R. L. (2015). Blue economy and competing discourses in international oceans governance. *Journal of Environment & Development*, *24*(2), 135–160. DOI: 10.1177/1070496515580797

Sopha, B. M., Purnamasari, D. M., & Ma'mun, S. (2022). Barriers and enablers of circular economy implementation for electric-vehicle batteries: From systematic literature review to conceptual framework. *Sustainability (Basel)*, *14*(10), 6359. DOI: 10.3390/su14106359

Suarez-Visbal, L., Stuckrath, C., & Carreón, J. R. (2022). Assessing through a gender-inclusion lens the social impact of circular strategies in the apparel value chain: the dutch case. In *Social and Cultural Aspects of the Circular Economy* (pp. 136–159). Routledge. DOI: 10.4324/9781003255246-9

Suchek, N., Ferreira, J. J., & Fernandes, P. O. (2022). A review of entrepreneurship and circular economy research: State of the art and future directions. *Business Strategy and the Environment*, *31*(5), 2256–2283. DOI: 10.1002/bse.3020

Tamasiga, P., Mfuni, H., Onyeaka, H., & Ouassou, E. H. (2025). Green industrial policy as an enabler of the transition to sustainability: Challenges, opportunities and policy implications for developing countries. *Environment, Development and Sustainability*, *27*(1), 355–376. DOI: 10.1007/s10668-023-03952-0

Teberges Dantas Queiroga, A., Elf, P., & Macário de Oliveira, V. (2025). Circular economy business models as context-forging opportunities: The role of circular managers in driving sustainable innovation in emerging markets. *Journal of Tropical Futures*, 27538931251342187.

Teniwut, W. A., Hasyim, C. L., & Pentury, F. (2022). Towards smart government for sustainable fisheries and marine development: An intelligent web-based support system approach in small islands. *Marine Policy*, *143*, 105158. DOI: 10.1016/j.marpol.2022.105158

Thoya, P., Horigue, V., Möllmann, C., Maina, J., & Schiele, K. S. (2022). Policy gaps in the East African Blue economy: Perspectives of small-scale fishers on port development in Kenya and Tanzania. *Frontiers in Marine Science*, *9*, 933111. DOI: 10.3389/fmars.2022.933111

Torgautov, B., Zhanabayev, A., Tleuken, A., Turkyilmaz, A., Mustafa, M., & Karaca, F. (2021). Circular economy: Challenges and opportunities in the construction sector of Kazakhstan. *Buildings (Basel, Switzerland)*, *11*(11), 501. DOI: 10.3390/buildings11110501

Tripathi, V., Chattopadhyaya, S., Mukhopadhyay, A. K., Saraswat, S., Sharma, S., Li, C., Rajkumar, S., & Georgise, F. B. (2022). A novel smart production management system for the enhancement of industrial sustainability in Industry 4.0. *Mathematical Problems in Engineering*, *2022*(1), 6424869. DOI: 10.1155/2022/6424869

Tripathi, V., Chattopadhyaya, S., Mukhopadhyay, A. K., Sharma, S., Kumar, V., Li, C., & Singh, S. (2024). Lean, green, and smart manufacturing: An ingenious framework for enhancing the sustainability of operations management on the shop floor in industry 4.0. *Proceedings of the Institution of Mechanical Engineers. Part E, Journal of Process Mechanical Engineering*, *238*(4), 1976–1990. DOI: 10.1177/09544089231159834

Türkeli, S., Bleisteiner, I., Cenci, L., Dominicis, R. D., Demanet, E., Ramirez, G. L., & Müller, D. (2022). X economies: towards comprehensive policy intelligence among Economy visions and practices in Europe and Latin America. In *Towards a circular economy: transdisciplinary approach for business* (pp. 297–332). Springer International Publishing. DOI: 10.1007/978-3-030-94293-9_17

Upadhyay, D. K., & Mishra, M. (2020). Blue economy: Emerging global trends and India's multilateral cooperation. *Maritime affairs: journal of the national maritime foundation of india, 16*(1), 30-45.

van Soest, H. L., van Vuuren, D. P., Hilaire, J., Minx, J. C., Harmsen, M. J., Krey, V., Popp, A., Riahi, K., & Luderer, G. (2019). Analysing interactions among sustainable development goals with integrated assessment models. *Global Transitions*, *1*, 210–225. DOI: 10.1016/j.glt.2019.10.004

Vann Yaroson, E., Chowdhury, S., Mangla, S. K., Dey, P., Chan, F. T., & Roux, M. (2024). A systematic literature review exploring and linking circular economy and sustainable development goals in the past three decades (1991–2022). *International Journal of Production Research*, *62*(4), 1399–1433. DOI: 10.1080/00207543.2023.2270586

Xu, X., Lu, Y., Vogel-Heuser, B., & Wang, L. (2021). Industry 4.0 and Industry 5.0—Inception, conception and perception. *Journal of Manufacturing Systems*, *61*, 530–535. DOI: 10.1016/j.jmsy.2021.10.006

Yeager, E., Bee, B., Hou, A., Cash, T., Dew, K., Dickerson, D., & Jones, S. (2024). A Process for Asset Mapping to Develop a Blue Economy Corridor. *Journal of Higher Education Outreach & Engagement*, *28*(1), 125–143.

Yoon, S., & Ho, J. Y. (2025). Delivering sustainable development via social innovation: Cases of social entrepreneurship in South Korea and Singapore. *Sustainable Development (Bradford)*, *33*(1), 416–430. DOI: 10.1002/sd.3127

Zafarullah, H., & Ferdous, J. (2021). Cyberspace at the grassroots: E-governance and citizen/stakeholder perceptions at the local level in Bangladesh. *Journal of Development Policy and Practice*, *6*(2), 168–187. DOI: 10.1177/24551333211034082

Zulkifli, R., Ozora, E., Ramadhan, M. A., Kacaribu, J. P., & Mahendra, R. (2023). Indonesia's blue economy initiative: Oceans as the new frontier of economic development. *Jurnal Perdagangan Internasional*, *1*(1), 10–16. DOI: 10.33197/jpi.v1i1.1083

Chapter 9
The Role of Bilateral, Regional, and Multilateral Trade Agreements:
Facilitating Sustainable Economic Development Through Agriculture, Manufacturing, and Services

Mallika Roy
http://orcid.org/0000-0002-5854-5084
Central Queensland University, Australia & University of Chittagong, Bangladesh

Runa Saha
http://orcid.org/0009-0002-6975-4137
University of Chittagong, Bangladesh

Mohammad Mamun Morshed Bhuyan
http://orcid.org/0009-0007-9689-7359
University of Chittagong, Bangladesh

ABSTRACT

In today's interconnected global economy, trade agreements are vital instruments shaping development in agriculture, manufacturing, and services. While bilateral, regional, and multilateral agreements aim to enhance growth, their role in promoting sustainable development remains uneven and underexplored. Although trade liberalization has been widely studied, there is limited understanding of how different

DOI: 10.4018/979-8-3373-1782-3.ch009

trade frameworks impact sustainability across sectors and countries. This study fills that gap through a comprehensive review of literature from diverse economies, examining how trade agreements influence environmental, social, and economic outcomes. The findings reveal that trade can foster technology transfer, resource efficiency, and inclusive growth, but these benefits depend on strong governance, enforcement, and the inclusion of sustainability provisions. By synthesizing global evidence, this research offers actionable insights for policymakers to craft trade policies that align economic progress with long-term sustainability.

INTRODUCTION

Trade agreements—whether bilateral, regional, or multilateral—are central to shaping modern global economic relations. By reducing trade barriers, improving market access, and fostering cooperation, these agreements play a significant role in driving economic growth and integration (Eyo-Udo et al., 2025; Freund & Ornelas, 2010). For developing and emerging economies, trade agreements have become strategic tools for stimulating sustainable economic development, especially in critical sectors such as agriculture, manufacturing, and services (Meijerink & Roza, 2007; Okolo et al., 2025). On the whole, the negative impact of digital mobility, geographic mobility, and bilateral trade in technology-related goods and services was overshadowed by the positive effect of bilateral trade in computers and communication technology on sustainable trade-adjusted development. To facilitate the power between technical bilateral trade and geographical mobility in benefiting sustainable trade, high levels of digital mobility are requisite (Shahzad et al., 2025).

As a result, the welfare gains from trade liberalization under multilateral terms are more or less the same for all countries, and substantially larger than those from preferential agreements (Brown, Deardorff & Stern; 2003). The impact of comprehensive trade agreements on services trade is greatly positive in the case of trade between high-income countries, low-income countries, as well as between high- and low-income countries, but there is no significant effect on trade from low- to high-income countries. In addition, rather extensive trade agreements are believed to be more favorable to the developing area like China. The method of matched pairs shows that deep trade agreements are more effective than GTAs in reducing service trade costs and improving the business environment (Chen & Shen, 2024).

These agreements influence key developmental drivers such as technology transfer, inclusive economic growth, environmental sustainability, and social equity (Ncube & De Beer, 2024). Since 1990, the number of RTAs in force has increased sixfold—from fewer than 50 to nearly 300 by 2024. All 164 WTO member countries now participate in at least one RTA, with the average member having about 11 such partnerships. For example, the United States began negotiating Free Trade Agreements (FTAs) in the 1980s and by 2018 was engaged in 14 FTAs with 20 countries.

However, the multilateral system has made limited progress in launching broad new liberalization efforts since the Uruguay Round of the 1990s. Despite some successes, such as the Trade Facilitation Agreement, multilateral negotiations have slowed, prompting a shift toward RTAs as a complementary or alternative mechanism. These developments highlight the intersection between WTO frameworks and regional arrangements, particularly in contexts like the Atlantic Space, where alignment varies based on the economic maturity of member states (Goswami, 2025; Khorana et al., 2014).

In light of increasing global challenges such as climate change and the COVID-19 pandemic—both of which have disrupted food systems and heightened food security concerns—trade liberalization has become even more critical. Many developing countries have used expanded trade opportunities to boost exports and drive recovery (Wang et al., 2023; Thompson, 2019). The Comprehensive and Progressive Agreement for Trans-Pacific Partnership (CPTPP) has come out after the COVID-19 pandemic as the main regional trade agreement for digital trade with a market-oriented approach (Ni, 2024).

This paper examines the role of trade agreements in advancing sustainable economic development, particularly across agriculture, manufacturing, and services. Through a thematic review of global literature, it identifies implementation challenges, highlights sustainability gaps, and offers policy recommendations for more inclusive and environmentally aligned trade governance with literary works.

THEORETICAL PERSPECTIVES OF TRADE AGREEMENTS AND ECONOMIC DEVELOPMENT

Trade agreements play a crucial role in economic development, particularly for developing countries. The terms of trade theory suggests that unilateral tariff policies lead to a prisoner's dilemma, necessitating reciprocal tariff reductions through agreements (Beshkar & Bond, 2019). These agreements can significantly contribute to economic growth by increasing exports, GDP, and attracting foreign direct investment (Geller, 2023). However, their impact varies across countries, influenced by factors such as institutional arrangements and targeted industries (Geller, 2023). The design of trade agreements incorporates flexibility mechanisms and dispute settlement processes to address challenges in implementation (Beshkar & Bond, 2019). Regional Trade Agreements (RTAs) in the Asia-Pacific region have been found to significantly impact material progress, with varying benefits and costs for different countries (Siddique, 2007). The structural modifications in China and its lifting to the status of an economic power, particularly after the WTO membership in 2001, have significantly altered the global trade balance (Erten & Leight, 2021), which was indicated by the annual rate of export growth being around 8% and the import growth being at 16% (Glauber, 2021).

3. TRADE AGREEMENTS IN THE AGRICULTURAL SECTOR

3.1 The Impact of WTO's Agreement on Agriculture (AoA) on Global Food Security

The World Trade Organization (WTO) is still the most preferred platform for the international trade rule negotiations but it has to deal with major problems in agriculture discussions. The non-success of Doha round of negotiations has left many significant issues in agriculture unresolved (Mensah, 2024). The global trade system is desperate for a multisectoral approach that is collaborative and encompasses the whole food chain—from production to consumption—that will ensure sustainability and fairness along with food security (McMahon, 2024).

The AoA systematically favours agricultural producers in industrialized nations at the expense of farmers in developing countries (Gonzalez, 2002). This imbalance allows developed countries to continue subsidizing their agricultural sector while requiring market openness in developing nations, negatively impacting food security (Gonzalez, 2002; Birovljev & Ćetković, 2013). To address these inequities and enhance food security, reforms are necessary to level the playing field between industrialized and developing countries (Birovljev & Ćetković, 2013). However, trade rule reforms alone are insufficient; proper implementation of existing human rights commitments is also crucial (Häberli, 2012).

3.1.1 Trade Liberalization and Food Security

Trade liberalization's impact on food security in developing countries, particularly in Africa, remains contentious. While promoted by international institutions as a means to improve food security (Eba Nguema & Assoumou Ella, 2014). The increasing free trade could benefit low-income countries and those that suffer from acute food shortages, however, the positive impact depends on the trade freedom level being neither too low nor too high. Moreover, famine conditions spread in countries that are poor or have been hit hard by a recession, in landlocked nations, in rural places with high exchange rates, in areas with rapid population rise and little agricultural output, in conflict-affected regions, in places prone to natural disasters, and in hot, dry climates (Ferreira et al., 2025).

To address food security challenges in Africa, reforms in agricultural policies, fair multilateral trade, improved access to international markets, and maintaining a balance between multilateralism and regionalism have been proposed as necessary conditions (Eba Nguema & Assoumou Ella, 2014). National perspectives are usually the basis of empirical studies on the relationship between trade liberalization and food consumption inequality, and they produce inconsistent outcomes (Zhang & Li; 2024). It is possible that the trade liberalization which may follow between China and Africa, will play a major role in the prosperity of the African countries by augmenting real incomes and increasing access to food for households (Ma et al.; 2025).

3.1.2 Agricultural Subsidies and Market Distortions

The World Trade Organization (WTO) agreements have significantly impacted agricultural policies and trade. While the WTO did not substantially reduce total agricultural support, it prompted a shift from distortionary to less distortionary instruments (Swinnen et al., 2012). The existing multilateral trade rules monitored by the Agreement on Agriculture (AoA) and the Agreement on Subsidies and Countervailing Measures (ASM) regarding agricultural subsidies, are not designed to ensure or promote the enormously important policy goal of food security (Makore & Osode, 2025).

High tariffs remain the primary factor restricting world trade (Diao et al., 2001; Burfisher, 2001). The WTO negotiations continue to address these issues, focusing on liberalizing tariffs, tariff-rate quotas, domestic support, and export subsidies (Diao et al., 2001; Burfisher, 2001).

3.1.3 WTO Agreement Impacts on Developing Countries

Developing countries play an increasingly important role in the WTO, viewing trade as vital for development (Rena, 2012). In order to turn the WTO Agreement into a worldwide trade system that is advantageous for both developed and developing countries, especially regarding the protection of human rights, a change of WTO principles is warranted, thereby making the WTO a fair-trade agreement rather than simply a free trade agreement (Liyew, 2025). Despite the fact that many developing countries have made great strides in their trade liberalization efforts, the resulting progress and development have often been uneven and, especially in the poorest countries, very small (Rodrik, 2022).

However, developing countries have much to gain from trade liberalization, particularly in agriculture, which is crucial for their economies (Mccalla, 2001). To enhance food security, reforms are needed to level the playing field between industrialized and developing countries (Birovljev & Ćetković, 2013). Overall, a fair, open, and rules-based international trading environment is critical for reducing poverty in developing countries (Mccalla, 2001).

These findings highlight the complex interplay between food security, subsidy agricultural trade, and efficiency in different regional contexts.

3.2 Regional Trade Agreements and Intra-Regional Agricultural Trade (e.g., AfCFTA, ASEAN)

Regional trade agreements (RTAs) have shown positive impacts on agricultural trade and efficiency in various regions. The ASEAN Free Trade Agreement, COMESA, and MERCOSUR have increased intra-regional agricultural trade without significant trade diversion (Korinek & Melatos, 2009). The African Continental Free Trade Area (AfCFTA) is expected to significantly impact agricultural value chains, with varying effects on backward and forward integration across countries (Fusacchia et al., 2022). RTAs have been found to improve agricultural technical efficiency through technology transfer, although the effects differ by product and membership (Sunge & Ngepah, 2020). Institutional factors also play a role, with regulatory quality reducing inefficiency while control of corruption surprisingly increases it (Sunge & Ngepah, 2020).

These findings highlight the complex interplay between RTAs, agricultural trade, and efficiency in different regional contexts.

3.2.1 Trade Facilitation and Market Integration

Trade facilitation and regional integration play crucial roles in enhancing agricultural trade and economic development in various regions. Studies show that economic integration significantly facilitates trade within ECOWAS, positively impacting agricultural exports (Olayiwola et al., 2011). In the Middle East and North Africa, regional trade agreements and trade facilitation improvements lead to substantial welfare gains, with EU integration offering greater benefits than intra-regional integration (Dennis, 2006). For South Asia, enhancing trade facilitation capacity to East Asian levels could potentially increase intraregional trade by 60% (Wilson & Otsuki, 2007). In Africa, trade-related costs hinder both global and regional integration, highlighting the importance of implementing the Trade Facilitation Agreement (TFA) alongside ongoing regional integration efforts (Valensisi et al., 2016). The AfCFTA has led to better policy alignment and increased regional discussions, yet the related difficulties of infrastructure, institutional capability, and political differences will still be a major stop for collaborating progress (Khan, 2025).

These findings underscore the significance of trade facilitation measures in promoting market integration and agricultural trade performance across different regions, emphasizing the need for targeted policies and capacity-building initiatives.

3.2.2 Food Security and Agricultural Value Chains

Regional integration and agricultural value chains play a crucial role in enhancing food security and economic growth, particularly in developing regions. The African Continental Free Trade Area (AfCFTA) agreement is expected to significantly impact trade patterns and value-added structures in agriculture and food sectors (Fusacchia et al., 2022). Value chain-based perspectives can offer valuable guidance to policymakers in addressing food security challenges and implementing effective solutions (Dixit, 2014). In the context of ECOWAS, regional trade linked to the creation of value chains among member countries has been identified as a potential engine for growth and food security, while international trade alone may not be sufficient to boost economic growth (Tinta et al., 2018). These studies emphasize the importance of strengthening regional integration and promoting intra-regional trade to stimulate sustained growth and improve food security outcomes in developing regions.

3.2.3 Policy Harmonization and Sustainable Agriculture

Regional cooperation in agricultural research, policy harmonization, and trade liberalization can significantly enhance sustainable agriculture and economic growth in Africa. Permitting greater cross-border technology transfers could yield spillover benefits up to four times the direct gains within innovating countries (Abdulai et al., 2005). The land management recognizes and supports actions and infrastructures that come together through probable good regulatory practices to increase productivity, operational efficiency and agricultural sustainability (Babazov & Li, 2025). Reducing trade barriers and improving cross-border transport could increase agricultural incomes by up to 10% (Abdulai et al., 2006). However, current free trade and industrialized agriculture practices may hinder sustainability, necessitating alternatives like organic farming and fair trade (Rehber & Grega, 2008). Trade policies should aim to safeguard food security, address economic-environmental trade-offs, and strengthen agrifood system resilience.

Several studies have illustrated the influence of WTO trade agreements on food security subsidies as well as the role of international trade agreements in facilitating market integration through policy harmonization for sustainable economic development. However, we limit our inquiry to examining the simultaneous impact on agriculture.

3.3 Case Studies

Developing Countries

Agricultural trade liberalization presents complex challenges and opportunities for developing countries. While some nations benefit from expanded market access and diversification, others face significant difficulties. (Kumar & Wu, 2025) recommend that developing countries should go for two-prong adoption of sustainable trade policies comprising one that integrates environmental considerations into their national legislation and one that involves signing trade agreements that allow for such considerations. One of these initiatives is strengthening of environmentally friendly product labels, support for sustainable supply chains, and waiving of trade barriers for eco-friendly goods.

However, net trade positions in many developing countries have deteriorated due to economic policies and population pressures (Díaz-Bonilla et al., 2002). The Doha Round emphasizes tariff reductions but risks eroding preferential market access for some countries, while non-tariff barriers such as sanitary and phytosanitary standards remain major unresolved hurdles (Bureau et al., 2006). Developing countries often face constraints in financial and human resources rather than legal barriers under the Agreement on Agriculture. (Díaz-Bonilla et al., 2002).

In Bangladesh, agricultural trade liberalization has yielded mixed results. Talukder (2014) finds that it generally improves rural household welfare and the broader economy, but success depends heavily on complementary reforms in non-trade sectors. Domestic liberalization may reduce output and employment in import-competing sectors but stimulates growth in export-oriented ones (Raihan, 2011). Tariff reforms aimed at protecting agriculture could foster sector expansion, improve welfare, ensure food security, and alleviate poverty (Ahmed, 2022). Consequently, Bangladesh's agricultural trade policies require careful consideration of domestic, regional, and global frameworks (Raihan, 2011). Rashid (2025) reported that the positive impact of Bangladesh's GDP on exports and the impact of trade agreements on GDP have been significantly intertwined in the case of Bangladesh.

India's agricultural trade policies have evolved considerably since independence, with major reforms in the 1980s and 1990s (Loganathan, 2023). WTO agreements have reduced trade barriers and subsidies but introduced challenges like plant variety patenting (Hans & Prasanna, 2023). WTO and free trade agreements have liberalized the sector, influencing GDP growth, employment, and economic development (Ratna et al., 2021). Key issues include market price support, import surges, food security, and special treatment clauses (Ratna et al., 2021). Favorable agricultural trade terms can shift income away from industry, affecting savings and capital formation (Hans, 2024). Despite progress in tariff reductions, non-tariff measures have become new barriers, complicating India's balancing act between liberalization and domestic concerns (Loganathan, 2023).

African Countries

Trade agreements play a significant role in agricultural trade and food security in African countries. Studies show that free trade agreements positively impact agricultural trade flows, particularly among ECOWAS members (Manu, 2021). However, the WTO Agreement on Agriculture has been criticized for favouring developed countries' producers over those in developing nations, including Africa (Hailu, 2010). South Africa plays a dominant role in intra-African agricultural trade, primarily as an exporter of diverse value-added products, while imports remain concentrated in commodities (Daya et al., 2006).Despite comparative advantages in agriculture, many Sub-Saharan African countries face food insecurity challenges (Hailu, 2010). The Africa Agriculture Trade Monitor highlights the importance of addressing non-tariff measures and improving competitiveness in key value chains to enhance intra-African trade (Bouët et al., 2020). West African countries have taken positions on various WTO issues, which sometimes differ from those of major trade partners (Nouve et al., 2002). Ongoing negotiations and reforms in agricultural trade policies are crucial for promoting food security in the region (Hailu, 2010).

Trade agreements have shown positive impacts on agricultural trade flows in various African regions. Studies on North African countries (Algeria, Egypt, Morocco, Tunisia) and West Africa (focusing on Ghana) found that free trade agreements (FTAs) generally increase agricultural trade volume, with potential for trade creation (Hndi et al., 2016; Manu, 2021). It has been shown that financial inclusion is the main driving force behind the relationship between trade liberalization and sustainable economic growth in a positive way, whereas trade liberalization to a greater extent connects financial inclusion to sustainable economic growth (Logan et al., 2025).However, the effects can vary for specific agricultural subsectors, with some experiencing negative impacts (Hndi et al., 2016).

European Countries

Trade agreements play a significant role in shaping agricultural trade between the European Union (EU) and other countries. Regional trade agreements (RTAs) generally support agricultural exports from developing countries to the EU market, offering an attractive alternative to multilateral free trade (Pishbahar & Huchet, 2008). However, the Comprehensive Economic and Trade Agreement (CETA) between the EU and Canada achieved little agricultural trade liberalization, maintaining protectionist interests (Hobbs, 2015).

Bojnec and Hartmann (2004) analyze Slovenia's agricultural trade, finding low intra-industry trade and high protection despite free trade agreements. Hodo (2014) reports positive effects of Albania's trade agreements on agricultural imports and exports, while noting the need for structural changes. Pishbahar and Huchet (2008) assess EU preferential trade agreements, concluding that most support developing countries' agricultural exports to the EU, though some have negative effects. The studies suggest that while trade agreements can benefit agricultural sectors, they may also have unintended consequences on trade patterns, competitiveness, and the environment, necessitating targeted policies to address these issues (Bojnec & Hartmann, 2004; Hodo, 2014; Pishbahar & Huchet, 2008; Runge, 1992). According to Nam et al. 2025, too much openness can slow financial development in Eastern Europe, pointing out the necessity of a balanced approach to financial globalization in emerging markets.

Australia

Australia's free trade agreements (FTAs) have significantly impacted agricultural trade. Studies show that FTAs with China, Korea, USA, and Japan have created substantial trade in the agricultural sector, particularly in sugar and wine (Timsina & Culas, 2020). The trade creation effects of FTAs on agriculture appear higher than in non-agricultural sectors (Timsina & Culas, 2020). Despite potential threats to Japan's protected agricultural sector, foreign policy goals, including regional leadership and resource security, have influenced Japan's decision to negotiate an FTA with Australia (Mulgan, 2008). ChAFTA was mainly responsible for the steep rise in forest and fishery product imports, followed by textiles and farm goods from 2000 to 2020 (Cai et al., 2025).

. For instance, Victoria benefits from dairy exports, Queensland from beef, and New South Wales from summer crops and wool (Culas & Timsina, 2019). Although wheat is excluded from ChAFTA, Australia shows a high Revealed Comparative Advantage in wheat trade with China, suggesting potential for future negotiations (Culas & Timsina, 2019). The potential for products from sectors where trade between the two countries could be profitable, which is one case of the free trade agreement (FTA) being advantageous for both India and Australia (Aman et al., 2025).

Generally, regional trade agreements in agriculture tend to increase trade between member countries without significant trade diversion (Korinek & Melatos, 2009). Trade openness, in particular, has been seen as a cornerstone of modern economic policy. It refers to the ease of crossborder capital movement, which makes it possible to acquire international finance and make investments in other markets. According to conventional economic theories, financial openness promotes sustainability, improved access to external resourcs, and efficient capital allocation.

4. TRADE AGREEMENTS AND INDUSTRIAL GROWTH IN THE MANUFACTURING SECTOR

4.1 Role of Bilateral and Regional Trade Agreements in Facilitating Industrialization (e.g., NAFTA/USMCA, EU Trade Policies)

As the structure of international trade continues to evolve, Regional Trade Agreements (RTAs) are gaining growing importance and influence. Since the mid-20th century, global trade has been liberalized through multilateral agreements, a process accelerated by the Bretton Woods institutions. Alongside these multilateral efforts, countries have increasingly pursued trade liberalization through bilateral, regional, and interregional arrangements (Dilek, 2024). Over the past two decades, bilateral investment treaties (BITs) have become the leading international legal mechanism for fostering and regulating foreign direct investment (Colen, Persyn & Guariso, 2016).

4.2 Technology Transfer and Foreign Direct Investment (FDI) in Manufacturing

FDI has no discernible impact in the Central and Western regions, but it has a detrimental impact on industrialization in the developed East and a beneficial impact in the less developed Northeast.Policymakers should use spatially diversified approaches to attain balanced industrialization (Yang et al., 2025). Moreover, technology transfer through FDI can generate positive spillover effects, benefiting downstream firms across various sectors (Blalock & Gertler, 2008). As a mechanism for international technology transfer (ITT), FDI is gaining increasing importance. ITT through FDI can occur either horizontally—where the full set of technologies for producing a good is transferred—or vertically along the supply chain. Empirical evidence consistently shows that foreign-owned firms in developing countries tend to exhibit higher productivity levels than their locally owned counterparts (Glass et al., 2008).

In industry, FDI, especially green field investments, significantly boosts production capability through new technologies, and innovation ecosystems enhance industrial progress by enabling technical improvements and new market possibilities.

4.2.1 Trade Liberalization and Technology Transfer

World trade has been greatly liberalized since 1950 in a number of ways, such as the establishment of customs unions, free trade zones, unilateral tariff reductions, and reductions in non-tariff trade obstacles (Thirlwall, 2000). Reducing import tariffs can restrict the diffusion of foreign ideas by reducing technology transfers (de Souza et al., 2025). Through imported inputs and foreign investment, foreign technology transfer has also been connected to the industrial sector's success (Goldar, Chawla, & Behera, 2020). The Research and development of foreign firms is positively impacted by trade liberalization, which improves local and global welfare by transferring better technology to domestic firms (Hwang, Marjit, & Peng, 2016). In summary, even though the network of informal and personal interactions serves as the primary conduit for knowledge spill overs, in the case of formal Technology transfer (TT), transfer to the firm is aided by entrepreneurial motivation and a propensity to connect with universities that are interested in commercializing academic research ((Cardamone, Pupo & Ricotta, 2015).

4.2.2 NAFTA/USMCA, EU Trade Policies on Developing Countries

Trade policies are a crucial component of industrial policy, and when trade policies are moved from the state level to the regional level, industrial policies should follow suit. If not, coordination issues will occur, and industrial policies will be less effective (Odijie, 2019). NAFTA was one of the first bilateral trade agreements to connect a developing nation with a major industrialized economy, therefore its implications could help clarify other bilateral trade deals that are being negotiated (Baylis, Garduño-Rivera & Piras, 2012). The European Union's trade policy has become more neoliberal, which has had significant effects on its economic diplomacy with the developing economies of the African, Caribbean, and Pacific region (Siles-Brügge, 2014). Tiwari (2025) observed that WTO is no longer the central authority in global trade governance, having been operationally, tactically, and legally supplanted by a system increasingly valuing regional blocs, national sovereignty, and geopolitical alignment.

4.2.3 The Role of Labour and Environmental Regulations

Capital-labour endowments and/or environmental restrictions are the cause of compositional changes in pollution brought on by trade liberalization (Cole & Elliott, 2003). Even in developing nations, market-based environmental rules have the potential to simultaneously preserve the environment and create jobs (Ren et al., 2020). The production process became more mechanized as a result of the industrial revolution. Many countries have heavily relied on primary energy from fossil fuels for industrial goods that emit greenhouse gases (GHGs) and significantly lead to global warming (Ojekemi et al., 2023).

Different studies have explained the effects of WTO trade agreements facts, on industrial exploration with trade libarization and trade agreements on manufacturing for laour enrolment to establish market integration with sustainable environment quality. However, our concern is estimating the simultaneous impact on manufactures.

4.3 Case Studies

Developing Countries

Developing nations often rely heavily on agriculture, face high unemployment, and engage in labour-intensive farming, making them vulnerable to discriminatory trade policies of wealthier countries (Devadoss, 2006). Globalization, while affecting environmental quality and resource use, has opened trade opportunities, especially under WTO frameworks (Coxhead & Jayasuriya, 2003; Fukui, 2019). Manufacturing and exports have become vital for economic growth and job creation in these regions (Collier & Venables, 2007). Despite environmental concerns, trade positively influences sustainable development (Kindo, Adams & Mohammed, 2024). In Bangladesh, both bilateral and regional FTAs enhance employment, real wages, exports, and consumer benefits (Raihan, 2011). Bangladesh and China can adopt several efforts to minimize enormous trade deficits such as 98% duty-free goods export, trade liberalization based on comparative advantages, labor-intensive infrastructure, bilateral negotiation, and so on. While Bangladesh is a labor-intensive country China favors technology (Alam, 2025).

African Countries

Over the past ten to fifteen years, Africa's manufacturing sector has generally been quite poor (Mauritius is a notable exception). Given the competitive dominance of China and Southeast Asia in the global markets for manufactured goods, Africa confronts significant obstacles in expanding its manufacturing sector (Kaplinsky & Morris, 2019).Despite this, many people still think that manufacturing can be a driver of growth on the continent by modernizing the economy, creating skilled jobs, and having positive spillover effects (Bigsten & Söderbom, 2006). African nations find it challenging to realize the potential advantages of regional trade agreements (RTAs) due to their small markets, inadequate transportation infrastructure, and high trading expenses (Yang & Gupta, 2007).In Botswana Many attempts have been made by governmental and non-governmental organizations to support the growth of small and medium-sized businesses (SMEs) in order to diversify the economy away from mining, create jobs, produce revenue, and reduce poverty (Temtime & Pansiri, 2004). Industrialization greatly moderates the favorable benefits of trade liberalization and labor force participation on productive capacity in Africa (Ogbuabor et al.; 2025).

European Countries

To help poorer countries benefit from trade, the European Union has committed to enhancing capacity-building, improving market access, offering special and differential treatment, and reforming the Common Agricultural Policy (CAP) to reduce its trade-distorting effects. These initiatives, part of the European Consensus, highlight the important role of trade and regional integration in development (Rodríguez, 2009). The EU-Korea bilateral trade relationship has seen significant positive impacts due to these measures. Additionally, the link between environmental policies and international trade is crucial as Europe expands trade flows while enforcing effective environmental regulations. Eco-innovations and environmental policies in European countries promote economic growth, job creation, and competitiveness (Stojanović & Radukić, 2006), with Romania's exports benefiting from compliance with environmental standards (Arouri et al., 2012). The challenges of decoupling international agri-food trade and land conversion for EU imports of Brazilian commodities, based on current estimates and projections of the potential impact that the EU-Mercosur Trade Agreement (EMTA) could have on land-use change in Brazil (de Oliveira et al., 2024).

Australia

For a long time, the manufacturing sector has been a vital component of the Australian economy. Instead of limiting production, Australian producers have concentrated on reducing labour costs. The enactment of the Workplace Relations Act has made this goal possible and has resulted in previously unheard-of productivity increases for the industry (Bowden, 2000). Western Australia will benefit more from China-Australia Free Trade Agreement (ChAFTA) than other States and Territories, as evidenced by its dominance in the overall goods export market and its low share of import merchandise trade with China (Culas, & Timsina, 2019). In spite of the industry's success, there are some structural flaws in Australia's supply chains, and the interactions between the participants are complicated (Singh, Smith & Sohal, 2005). The Korea-Australia Free Trade Agreement (KAFTA) eliminates or reduces barriers to investments and trade between Korea and Australia. This benefits Australian businesses that seek to export Australian goods to Korea or want to import

Korean goods for sale in Australia (Quansah, & Ahn, 2017). Liu (2024) observed that due to the increased pursuit of bilateral and regional economic cooperation between Australia and China, industrial total factor productivity improvement and specialized commodity trade shifts.

5. SERVICES TRADE AND THE DIGITAL ECONOMY

5.1 The Rise of Services Trade Under GATS and CPTPP

Recent research highlights a positive correlation between broadband internet, information and communication technology (ICT), and economic growth (Bertschek et al., 2015; Niebel, 2018). Beyond economic growth, the internet significantly improves education (Derksen et al., 2022), employment (Hjort and Poulsen, 2019), productivity and innovation through knowledge diffusion (Paunov and Rollo, 2016), and reduces government corruption via e-government (Elbahnasawy, 2014). Burri and Polanco (2020) emphasize the complex regulations in preferential trade agreements (PTAs) regarding digital trade governance, using the TAPED dataset. Duval and Mengjing (2017) classify paperless trade measures and analyze their coverage in regional trade agreements (RTAs). Burri (2021) examines digital challenges from evolving technologies, noting that PTAs have yet to fully adapt the GATS framework for services. Neeraj (2019) discusses the difficulty of fitting digital trade into the WTO's goods vs. services classification. Burri (2021) compares e-commerce clauses in PTAs and WTO proposals. Wang and Zhao (2022) show that symmetric free trade agreements benefit members, encouraging less digitally advanced nations to pursue such agreements. The CPTPP, covering about 13% of global GDP, offers modern, flexible provisions on digital trade, intellectual property, labour, and the environment, fostering innovation among members despite the absence of the US (Petri & Plummer, 2019).

5.2 Digital Trade Agreements: Data Flows, E-commerce

Digital platforms trade and share data to enter new markets and boost profits, driving economies of scale amid imperfect competition (Nuccio & Guerzoni, 2019). Governments pursue strategic trade policies to support domestic digital industries, with the US, EU, China, and India adopting different approaches focused on digital platforms and data governance (Chen & Gao, 2022; Fefer et al., 2017; Gereffi et al., 2021). Adding digital trade elements to agreements benefits both high- and low-income countries, with internet usage having a stronger impact on trade in low- and middle-income nations (Herman & Oliver, 2023; Clarke and Wallsten, 2006; Meijers,

2014 Contractor and Lorange (2002) emphasize the knowledge-driven economy's reliance on IT, regulatory, economic, and competitive factors in alliance formation.

5.3 Challenges: Data privacy, Digital Divide and Regulatory Gaps

Bridging the digital divide in the EU requires efficient regional and national strategies targeting connectivity, human resources, internet usage, digital business integration, and public services. Promoting local economic development, higher education, R&D investment, and reducing early school dropouts are crucial steps (Răileanu Szeles, 2018). Although the EU shows a limited regional digital divide, it reflects income disparities, with cultural and institutional factors playing a larger role than the rural-urban gap in ICT adoption (Vincente & Lopez, 2011). In Africa, the ICT divide hinders financial system development and bilateral trade, with financial development indices confirming the negative impact of digital disparities (Mignamissi, 2021). Freund and Weinhold (2004) documented the Internet's positive effect on global trade, while Sridhar (2016) found trans-border data flows strongly boost economic growth, especially in low- and middle-income countries. Chander and Le (2014) warn that government actions fragmenting the web over surveillance concerns do not improve privacy or security. Taylor (2020) argues that Internet localization diminishes its benefits, supported by Bauer et al. (2014), who estimated GDP losses due to data localization in India, Indonesia, and Vietnam. Meltzer and Lovelock (2018) provide further analysis of data flow restrictions in Asia.

5.3 Case Studies

African Countries

Karakara and Osabuohien (2020) emphasize policies enhancing firms' access to ICTs to boost innovation in West Africa. Agyapong (2021) highlights Ghana's digital economy transformation, noting financial institutions' adoption of technologies for improved, cost-effective services. Digitalization in Africa has accelerated, acting as a catalyst for economic growth and innovation amid trade infrastructure challenges. Adams et al. (2024) examine AfCFTA's impact on ICT and Digital Technologies sectors across 43 African countries (2014–2021), finding trade liberalization and improved productive capacities promote sectoral trade and spillover benefits. Luke (2019) notes AfCFTA's potential to strengthen trust, predictability, and rule of law in African trade. Studies by Adeleye and Eboagu (2019) and Myovella et al. (2020) reveal positive digital technology impacts on economic development and financial inclusion. Sawadogo and Wandaogo (2021) find mobile money services boost intra-African trade, while Banga et al. (2021) explore ICT's influence on regional commerce. Regulatory challenges remain critical for digital trade within AfCFTA (Banga et al., 2021).

European Countries

Chen and Gao (2022) highlight that the United States, European Union, China, and India adopt diverse digital trade policies and data governance approaches, reflecting their digital industries' strengths. Governments strategically shape trade policies to influence digital trade benefits and expand their digital sectors by regulating cross-border data flows. Evangelista et al. (2014) argue that access to ICT alone is insufficient for digital transformation; the quality and extent of technology use, along with enabling conditions, are crucial. Within the EU, bridging the digital divide requires coordinated regional and national strategies focusing on connectivity, human capital, internet usage, business digital integration, and public digital services. Key measures include fostering local economic growth, improving higher education outcomes, increasing R&D investments, and reducing early school dropouts (Răileanu Szeles, 2018). Though the EU's regional digital divide is relatively limited, it correlates with income disparities (Vincente & Lopez, 2011). Cultural and institutional factors influence ICT adoption more significantly than rural-urban divides, while regional policies have positively affected technology uptake.

Developing Countries

Anukoonwattaka et al. (2018) highlight that despite growing internet access in Asia-Pacific economies, women's participation in the digital economy remains low, especially in low-income countries, with cybersecurity improvements needed. Promoting inclusive digital transformation can enhance network effects and accelerate a sustainable regional digital economy.). Inclusive E-commerce policies must strengthen formal institutions, promote less-developed countries' participation, and support SMEs (Ahi et al., 2023). Gao (2018) contrasts the US and China's digital trade strategies, noting the US focuses on the "digital" aspect, while China emphasizes traditional "trade." Salisu et al. (2025) emphasize the importance of national, regional, and global regulations for e-commerce growth, highlighting ASEAN's initiatives like the e-ASEAN Task Force and ICT Master Plan, supported by harmonized electronic signature standards. Li et al. (2023) show that the digital economy boosts service export competitiveness, particularly in low- and middle-income countries and low ICT-intensity sectors. Albiman and Sulong (2017) find lower-middle-income countries gain more first-mover ICT advantages than others. Asian economies displaying stronger performance than many in Africa and Latin

America. As the results show, trade openness can generate growth if supported by sound institutions and policies tailored to country needs. Trade facilitation can be a powerful driver of the economic growth and development process in transition economies by way of sector-specific policy reform, enhanced trade management capacity, application of digital trade solutions, and promotion of multi-stakeholder collaboration.

6. POLICY RECOMMENDATIONS FOR SUSTAINABLE TRADE AGREEMENTS

Examining digital trade regulations across leading economies reveals critical insights for shaping collaborative and interoperable data governance frameworks. Strengthening dialogue among governments and stakeholders in the public, private, and social sectors is essential to manage digital trade effectively and maximize economic and social benefits. Coordinated efforts can reduce conflicts in digital trade strategies and promote sustainable global growth. Halting environmental degradation and anthropogenic climate change causes, in addition to responding and adapting to inevitable changes, requires determination by policymakers and substantial financial investments. Strong environmental policy is called for with responsible implementation, and the reduction of green trade obstacles is urged.

The following table summarizes the practical implications of digital trade governance, ICT impacts, and environmental considerations linked to trade agreements.

Table 1.

Theme	Key Points	References
Collaborative Digital Trade Governance	Emphasizes the need for interoperability in data governance and enhanced government-stakeholder dialogue to reduce conflicts and promote sustainable growth.	-
ICT Impact on Sectors	ICT adoption lowers product and labour costs in manufacturing, improves productivity in agriculture, and boosts overall business sustainability.	Rafikov & Ansary (2020); Andreoni et al. (2021); Chauhan et al. (2021)
Trade and Environmental Outcomes	Trade can have mixed environmental effects; RTAs promote equitable regional development and improve export product quality in China.	Antweiler, Copeland & Taylor (2001); Yao et al. (2019); Wang & Zhang (2024)
Environmental Provisions in Trade Agreements	Environmental clauses in PTAs reduce environmental impact shifting; international pacts are less effective; green economy policies are crucial for sustainability globally.	Presberger & Bernauer (2020)

6. CHALLENGES IN IMPLEMENTING SUSTAINABLE TRADE AGREEMENTS

Implementing sustainable trade agreements presents complex challenges due to the need to balance economic growth with environmental protection and social equity. Differences in national priorities, regulatory standards, and enforcement capacities often hinder uniform implementation across countries. Additionally, developing nations may face resource constraints and institutional weaknesses that limit their ability to fully comply with sustainability provisions.

6.1 Trade Imbalances and Unequal Benefits for Developing Countries

In emerging nations, the issue of inequality poses a considerable hurdle, as it deepens gaps in different elements such as distribution of income, educational accessibility, healthcare provisions, and opportunities for growth (Tabash et al., 2024). Through imports and exports, trading with high-income nations exacerbates the income disparity in developing countries (Meschi & Vivarelli, 2009). Finally, the trade balance is improved by greater domestic absorption and increased manufacturing sector productivity (Tran & Dinh, 2014).

6.2 Fair Trade and Labour Rights in Developing Countries

Fair trade influences local and regional employment, bargaining conditions, and strengthens farmers' organizations, with significant benefits in capitalizing farmers despite modest direct income effects (Ruben, Fort & Zúñiga-Arias, 2009). After the failure of WTO negotiations, we observed a rapid development of preferential trade agreements, including different types of labour clauses. labour provisions are connected with a lower level of labour standards infractions, but also with the number of conventions (Bazillier & Rana, 2025). The 2008 EU-Cariforum Economic Partnership Agreement incorporated sustainable development chapters, including commitments to labor and environmental standards (Bartels, 2013). Yet, the International Labour Organization notes limited empirical evidence on the effects of labor rights clauses in trade agreements (Marx, Lein & Brando, 2016). Trade theory suggests globalization may reduce the wage premium for education in developing countries (Rama, 2003).

6.3 Deforestation, Carbon Emission Risk in Sustainable Trade Agreements

The main reasons for deforestation include changes in land use, such as large-scale agriculture, lack of stable tenure, soil quality, market accessibility, and population densities and changes (Fry, 2008). The agricultural sector's production is negatively impacted by both forest area and natural resource variables, but it is positively impacted by the usage of renewable energy sources (Chopra, et al.,2022). Developing nations in the tropics are the main drivers of deforestation and the expansion of agricultural land, indicating that trade liberalization may cause deforestation to occur in ecologically vulnerable areas in addition to increasing net deforestation (Abman & Lundberg, 2020). A Free Trade Agreement (FTA) has been signed by several nations, although free trade agreements (FTAs) have economic benefits, they also raise the possibility of carbon leakage, which raises greenhouse gas emissions (Kinoshita et al.,2023).

6.4 Institutional and Regulatory Challenges in Trade Governance

Today's institutionally fragmented governance architecture, which mixes a network of bilateral and regional superstructures with a uniform bedrock of multilateral standards, is ingrained in global economic interactions (Trommer, 2017). The majority of WTO analyses consider the organization as though it exists on a different level from nation states, one that deals with interstate relations and global governance

(Shaffer, 2015).Since the WTO and other trade agreements are now unable to adequately handle these issues, the EU and the USA are prepared to look outside the conventional process of drafting international treaties in order to investigate new opportunities for international regulatory cooperation (Alemanno, 2015). In addition to providing reciprocal benefits (such as for export-oriented industries), the reciprocal liberalization commitments and non-discrimination requirements would assist governments in overcoming domestic protectionist pressures and removing discriminatory, welfare-reducing border barriers (Petersmann, 2005).

CONCLUSION

Trade agreements have become essential instruments in shaping global economic relations, influencing patterns of growth, investment, and sustainability across various sectors. This study has explored the critical role that bilateral, regional, and multilateral trade agreements play in promoting sustainable economic development across the agriculture, manufacturing, and services sectors. These agreements not only enhance market access and investment flows but also foster the transfer of technology, skills, and environmentally responsible practices. By aligning trade liberalization with social and environmental objectives, such agreements can serve as powerful instruments for inclusive and long-term growth. However, realizing their full potential requires coordinated efforts to ensure policy coherence, equitable participation of developing economies, and effective implementation of sustainability provisions. It advocates for responsible implementation of sound environmental policies and the reduction of obstacles to green trade. Risk management and compliance have become integral in helping organizations maintain operational integrity and competitive advantage in a globally expanding market. The intricacies of international trade, coupled with legal complications and rapid technological changes, pose problems that call for strategic changes. While being enlightening, this research also has some limitations. Longer-term studies may further probe into how sustainability and technological adoption related to trade deals impact organizational resilience. Future studies, based on these findings, will afford us a better understanding. Strengthening institutional capacities and promoting fair trade practices will be essential to harness the benefits of these trade agreements in a way that supports resilient and sustainable development pathways.

REFERENCES

Abdulai, A., Diao, X., & Johnson, M. (2005). Achieving regional growth dynamics in African agriculture. *Accessed from* https://ageconsearch.umn.edu/record/58371/files/dsgdp17.pdf

Abdulai, A., Johnson, M., & Diao, X. (2006). Leveraging regional growth dynamics in African agriculture. *African Journal of Agricultural and Resource Economics, 1*(1), 49–66.

Abman, R., & Lundberg, C. (2020). Does free trade increase deforestation? The effects of regional trade agreements. *Journal of the Association of Environmental and Resource Economists, 7*(1), 35–72. DOI: 10.1086/705787

Adams, K., Attah-Boakye, R., Yu, H., Chu, I., & Mali, D. (2024). African continental free trade area and regional trade in ICT and digital technologies. *Journal of International Management, 30*(4), 101156. DOI: 10.1016/j.intman.2024.101156

Adeleye, N., & Eboagu, C. (2019). Evaluation of ICT development and economic growth in Africa. *NETNOMICS: Economic Research and Electronic Networking, 20*(1), 31–53. DOI: 10.1007/s11066-019-09131-6

Agyapong, D. (2021). Implications of digital economy for financial institutions in Ghana: An exploratory inquiry. *Transnational Corporations Review, 13*(1), 51–61. DOI: 10.1080/19186444.2020.1787304

Ahi, A. A., Sinkovics, N., & Sinkovics, R. R. (2023). E-commerce policy and the global economy: A path to more inclusive development? *MIR. Management International Review, 63*(1), 27–56. DOI: 10.1007/s11575-022-00490-1

Ahmed, S. M. U. (2022). A General Equilibrium Analysis on the Impact of Tariff Reforms to Protect Agricultural Sector in Bangladesh. *Center for Development Economic Studies, 9*(11), 20–28. DOI: 10.53422/JDMS.2022.91103

Alam, M. J. (2025). Trade Between Bangladesh and China: Challenges and Opportunities. *Bangladesh–China Connectivity: History, Trade and Diplomacy, and Society*, 113-124.

Albiman, M. M., & Sulong, Z. (2017). The linear and non-linear impacts of ICT on economic growth, of disaggregate income groups within SSA region. *Telecommunications Policy, 41*(7-8), 555–572. DOI: 10.1016/j.telpol.2017.07.007

Alemanno, A. (2015). The regulatory cooperation chapter of the transatlantic trade and investment partnership: Institutional structures and democratic consequences. *Journal of International Economic Law*, *18*(3), 625–640. DOI: 10.1093/jiel/jgv026

Aman, A., Alam, I., Singh, G. J., Ghali, Z., Fatma, R., & Khan, K. (2025). Bridging Markets, Building Alliances: Assessing the India-Australia Economic Cooperation through the Lens of Trade Liberalization and Geoeconomic Strategy. *International Journal of Economics and Financial Issues*, *15*(4), 187–195. DOI: 10.32479/ijefi.19025

Arouri, M. E. H., Caporale, G. M., Rault, C., Sova, R., & Sova, A. (2012). Environmental regulation and competitiveness: Evidence from Romania. *Ecological Economics*, *81*, 130–139. DOI: 10.1016/j.ecolecon.2012.07.001

Babazov, Z., & Li, C. (2025). Exploring the Relationship Between Cultivated Land Regulations, Agricultural Productivity, and Trade Efficiency: A Comparative Analysis Among China, Russia, and Kyrgyzstan Under the Belt and Road Initiative. *Sustainability (Basel)*, *17*(10), 4723. DOI: 10.3390/su17104723

Banga, K., Gharib, M., Mendez-Parra, M., & Macleod, J. (2021). E-commerce in preferential trade agreements: Implications for African firms and the AfCFTA. *ODI Report*.

Bartels, L. (2013). Human rights and sustainable development obligations in EU free trade agreements. *Legal Issues of Economic Integration, 40*(4).

Bauer, M., Lee-Makiyama, H., Van der Marel, E., & Verschelde, B. (2014). *The costs of data localisation: Friendly fire on economic recovery* (No. 3/2014). ECIPE occasional paper.

Baylis, K., Garduño-Rivera, R., & Piras, G. (2012). The distributional effects of NAFTA in Mexico: Evidence from a panel of municipalities. *Regional Science and Urban Economics*, *42*(1-2), 286–302. DOI: 10.1016/j.regsciurbeco.2011.09.006

Bazillier, R., & Rana, A. T. (2025). Social Clauses in Free Trade Agreements: An Efficient Tool to Improve Labour Standards? *World Economy*, *48*(6), 1251–1281. DOI: 10.1111/twec.13675

Bertschek, I., Briglauer, W., Hüschelrath, K., Kauf, B., & Niebel, T. (2015). The economic impacts of broadband internet: A survey. *Review of Network Economics*, *14*(4), 201–227. DOI: 10.1515/rne-2016-0032

Beshkar, M., & Bond, E. (2019). Trade agreements: Theoretical foundations. In *Oxford Research Encyclopedia of Economics and Finance*.

Bigsten, A., & Söderbom, M. (2006). What have we learned from a decade of manufacturing enterprise surveys in Africa? *The World Bank Research Observer*, *21*(2), 241–265. DOI: 10.1093/wbro/lkl003

Birovljev, J., & Ćetković, B. (2013). The impact of the WTO agreement on agriculture on food security in developing countries.

Blalock, G., & Gertler, P. J. (2008). Welfare gains from foreign direct investment through technology transfer to local suppliers. *Journal of International Economics*, *74*(2), 402–421. DOI: 10.1016/j.jinteco.2007.05.011

Bojnec, S., & Hartmann, M. (2004). Agricultural and food trade in Central and Eastern Europe: The case of Slovenian intra-industry trade. *Access from* https://ageconsearch.umn.edu/record/92027/files/dp65.pdf https://ageconsearch.umn.edu/record/51136/files/Liberalization%20and%20Food%20Security%20Paper%20for%20IAAE-%20China%202009%20Final.pdf

Bouët, A., Odjo, S. P., & Zaki, C. (2020). *Africa agriculture trade monitor 2020*. Intl Food Policy Res Inst. https://books.google.com/books?hl=en&lr=&id=7gYBEAAAQBAJ&oi=fnd&pg=PR8&dq=Africa+agriculture+trade+monitor+2020&ots=jrxjpPfTtY&sig=a1rPX-ByzOI09qvcMn9H4W6txFc

Bowden, B. (2000). Competing to Survive? Productivity, Workplace Reform and International Competitiveness in the Australian Coal Industry. In *paper presented*.

Brown, D. K., Deardorff, A. V., & Stern, R. M. (2003). Multilateral, Regional and Bilateral Trade-Policy Options for the United States and Japan. *World Economy*, *26*(6), 803–828. DOI: 10.1111/1467-9701.00549

Bureau, J. C., Jean, S., & Matthews, A. (2006). The consequences of agricultural trade liberalization for developing countries: Distinguishing between genuine benefits and false hopes. *World Trade Review*, *5*(2), 225–249. DOI: 10.1017/S147474560600276X

Burfisher, M. E. (2001). Agricultural Policy Reform in the WTO: Challenges for Analysts.

Burri, M. (2021). Towards a new treaty on digital trade. *Journal of World Trade*, *55*(1), 77–100. DOI: 10.54648/TRAD2021003

Burri, M., & Polanco, R. (2020). Digital trade provisions in preferential trade agreements: Introducing a new dataset. *Journal of International Economic Law*, *23*(1), 187–220. DOI: 10.1093/jiel/jgz044

Cai, Y., Chen, W., & Zeng, X. (2025). The impact of the China-Australia free trade agreement on China's agricultural imports. *Frontiers in Sustainable Food Systems*, *9*, 1553373. DOI: 10.3389/fsufs.2025.1553373

Cardamone, P., Pupo, V., & Ricotta, F. (2015). University Technology Transfer and Manufacturing Innovation: The Case of I taly. *The Review of Policy Research*, *32*(3), 297–322. DOI: 10.1111/ropr.12125

Chander, A., & Lê, U. P. (2014). Data nationalism. *Emory Law Journal*, *64*, 677.

Chen, Q., & Shen, Y. (2024). Deep trade agreements and services trade: An analysis based on service trade provisions. *World Economy*, *47*(7), 2909–2946. DOI: 10.1111/twec.13563

Chen, Y., & Gao, Y. (2022). Comparative analysis of digital trade development strategies and governance approaches. *Journal of Digital Economy*, *1*(3), 227–238. DOI: 10.1016/j.jdec.2023.02.001

Chopra, R., Magazzino, C., Shah, M. I., Sharma, G. D., Rao, A., & Shahzad, U. (2022). The role of renewable energy and natural resources for sustainable agriculture in ASEAN countries: Do carbon emissions and deforestation affect agriculture productivity? *Resources Policy*, *76*, 102578. DOI: 10.1016/j.resourpol.2022.102578

Clarke, G. R., & Wallsten, S. J. (2006). Has the internet increased trade? Developed and developing country evidence. *Economic Inquiry*, *44*(3), 465–484. DOI: 10.1093/ei/cbj026

Cole, M. A., & Elliott, R. J. (2003). Determining the trade–environment composition effect: The role of capital, labor and environmental regulations. *Journal of Environmental Economics and Management*, *46*(3), 363–383. DOI: 10.1016/S0095-0696(03)00021-4

Colen, L., Persyn, D., & Guariso, A. (2016). Bilateral investment treaties and FDI: Does the sector matter? *World Development*, *83*, 193–206. DOI: 10.1016/j.worlddev.2016.01.020

Collier, P., & Venables, A. J. (2007). Rethinking trade preferences: How Africa can diversify its exports. *World Economy*, *30*(8), 1326–1345. DOI: 10.1111/j.1467-9701.2007.01042.x

Contractor, F. J., & Lorange, P. (2002). The growth of alliances in the knowledge-based economy. *International Business Review*, *11*(4), 485–502. DOI: 10.1016/S0969-5931(02)00021-5

Coxhead, I., & Jayasuriya, S. (2003). The open economy and the environment: development, trade and resources in Asia. In *The Open Economy and the Environment*. Edward Elgar Publishing. DOI: 10.4337/9781781952856.00009

Culas, R. J., & Timsina, K. P. (2019). Impacts of China-Australia free trade agreement on Australian agriproducts trade. *Australasian Agribusiness Review, 24*(6), 128–148.

Daya, Y., Ranoto, T., & Letsoalo, M. A. (2006). Intra-Africa agricultural trade: A South African perspective. *Acta Commercii, 6*(1), 99–113. DOI: 10.4102/ac.v6i1.99

de Oliveira, S. E. C., Visentin, J. C., Pavani, B. F., Branco, P. D., de Maria, M., & Loyola, R. (2024). The European Union-Mercosur Free Trade Agreement as a tool for environmentally sustainable land use governance. *Environmental Science & Policy, 161*, 103875. DOI: 10.1016/j.envsci.2024.103875

de Souza, G., Gaetani, R., & Mestieri, M. (2025). More Trade, Less Diffusion: Technology Transfers and the Dynamic Effects of Import Liberalization.

Dennis, A. (2006). The impact of regional trade agreements and trade facilitation in the Middle East and North Africa region. *World Bank Policy Research Working Paper*, (3837). *Accessed from* https://papers.ssrn.com/sol3/Delivery.cfm?abstractid=922963

Derksen, L., Michaud-Leclerc, C., & Souza, P. C. (2022). Restricted access: How the internet can be used to promote reading and learning. *Journal of Development Economics, 155*, 102810. DOI: 10.1016/j.jdeveco.2021.102810

Devadoss, S. (2006). Why do developing countries resist global trade agreements? *The Journal of International Trade & Economic Development, 15*(2), 191–208. DOI: 10.1080/09638190600690895

Diao, X., Somwaru, A., & Roe, T. (2001). A global analysis of agricultural reform in WTO member countries.

Díaz-Bonilla, E., Robinson, S., Thomas, M., & Yanoma, Y. (2002). WTO, agriculture, and developing countries: a survey of issues. *Accessed from* https://cgspace.cgiar.org/bitstreams/e98499e4-3d3b-4013-8ca9-eb8748c8170a/download

Dilek, Ş. (2024). Rising Regionalization: An Assessment of Regional Trade Agreements. *Avrasya Etüdleri*, (63), 131–158.

Dixit, D. (2014). Agricultural value chains and food security. *Journal of World Trade, 48*(5).

Duval, Y., & Mengjing, K. (2017). *Digital trade facilitation: Paperless trade in regional trade agreements* (No. 747). ADBI Working Paper.

Eba Nguema, I., & Assoumou Ella, G. (2014). Trade liberalization and food security: For a new green revolution in Africa. *Accessed from* https://ageconsearch.umn.edu/record/332519/files/7160.pdf

Erten, B., & Leight, J. (2021). Exporting out of agriculture: The impact of WTO accession on structural transformation in China. *The Review of Economics and Statistics*, *103*(2), 364–380. DOI: 10.1162/rest_a_00852

Evangelista, R., Guerrieri, P., & Meliciani, V. (2014). The economic impact of digital technologies in Europe. *Economics of Innovation and New Technology*, *23*(8), 802–824. DOI: 10.1080/10438599.2014.918438

Eyo-Udo, N. L., Apeh, C. E., Bristol-Alagbariya, B., Udeh, C. A., & Ewim, C. P. M. (2025). International trade law in the modern world: A review of evolving practices and agreements. *International Journal of Multidisciplinary Research and Growth Evaluation*.

Fefer, R. F., Akhtar, S. I., & Morrison, W. M. (2017). Digital trade and US trade policy. *Current Politics and Economics of the United States, Canada and Mexico*, *19*(1), 1–52.

Ferreira, C. R. C., Gomide, M. R., & Firme, V. D. A. C. (2025). The impacts of trade freedom on food insecurity from countries with different profiles: An empirical analysis. *Revista de Economia Política*, *45*(4), e253664. DOI: 10.1590/0101-31572025-3664

Freund, C., & Ornelas, E. (2010). Regional trade agreements. *Annual Review of Economics*, *2*(1), 139–166. DOI: 10.1146/annurev.economics.102308.124455

Fry, I. (2008). Reducing emissions from deforestation and forest degradation: Opportunities and pitfalls in developing a new legal regime. *Review of European Community & International Environmental Law*, *17*(2), 166–182. DOI: 10.1111/j.1467-9388.2008.00597.x

Fukui, S. (2019). Economic development in developing countries and the future of trade agreements. *Japanese Journal of Agricultural Economics*, *21*(0), 50–55. DOI: 10.18480/jjae.21.0_50

Fusacchia, I., Balié, J., & Salvatici, L. (2022). The AfCFTA impact on agricultural and food trade: A value added perspective. *European Review of Agriculture Economics*, *49*(1), 237–284. DOI: 10.1093/erae/jbab046

Gao, H. (2018). Digital or trade? The contrasting approaches of China and US to digital trade. *Journal of International Economic Law*, *21*(2), 297–321. DOI: 10.1093/jiel/jgy015

Gereffi, G., Lim, H. C., & Lee, J. (2021). Trade policies, firm strategies, and adaptive reconfigurations of global value chains. *Journal of International Business Policy, 4*(4), 506–522. DOI: 10.1057/s42214-021-00102-z

Glass, A., Saggi, K., Dutt, A., & Ros, J. (2008). The role of foreign direct investment in international technology transfer. *International handbook of development economics, 2*, 137-149.

Goldar, B., Chawla, I., & Behera, S. R. (2020). Trade liberalization and productivity of Indian manufacturing firms. *Indian Growth and Development Review, 13*(1), 73–98. DOI: 10.1108/IGDR-10-2018-0108

Gonzalez, C. G. (2002). Institutionalizing inequality: The WTO Agreement on Agriculture, food security, and developing countries. *Colum. J. Envtl. L., 27*, 433.

Häberli, C. (2012). Do WTO rules improve or impair the right to food? In *Research Handbook on the WTO Agriculture Agreement*. Edward Elgar Publishing. DOI: 10.4337/9781781001233.00009

Hailu, M. B. (2010, July). Food Security and Agricultural Trade Liberalization. In *Society of International Economic Law (SIEL), Second Biennial Global Conference, University of Barcelona.*

Hans, V., & Prasanna, G. (2023). International Trade in Agriculture, Terms of Trade and WTO With Reference to India. *International Trade in Agriculture, Terms of Trade and WTO With Reference to India (July 11, 2023).*

Hans, V. B. (2024). International Trade in Agriculture, Terms of Trade, and the World Trade Organization with Reference to India. *Acta Scientific Agriculture, 8*(2), 3–15. https://actascientific.com/ASAG/pdf/ASAG-08-1339.pdf. DOI: 10.31080/ASAG.2024.08.1339

Herman, P. R., & Oliver, S. (2023). Trade, policy, and economic development in the digital economy. *Journal of Development Economics, 164*, 103135. DOI: 10.1016/j.jdeveco.2023.103135

Hjort, J., & Poulsen, J. (2019). The arrival of fast internet and employment in Africa. *The American Economic Review, 109*(3), 1032–1079. DOI: 10.1257/aer.20161385

Hndi, B. M., Maitah, M., & Mustofa, J. (2016). Trade impacts of selected free trade agreements on agriculture: The case of selected North African countries. *AGRIS On-Line Papers in Economics and Informatics, 8*(3), 39–50. DOI: 10.7160/aol.2016.080304

Hobbs, J. E. (2015). A protectionist bargain?: Agriculture in the European Union—Canada Trade Agreement. *Journal of World Trade*, *49*(3), 437–456. DOI: 10.54648/TRAD2015018

Hodo, M. (2014). The impact of trade agreements on agriculture sector, import and export: Albanian case. *Journal of Educational and Social Research*, *4*(4), 421–425. DOI: 10.5901/jesr.2014.v4n4p421

Hwang, H., Marjit, S., & Peng, C. H. (2016). Trade liberalization, technology transfer, and endogenous R&D. *Oxford Economic Papers*, *68*(4), 1107–1119. DOI: 10.1093/oep/gpw034

Kaplinsky, R., & Morris, M. (2019). Trade and industrialisation in Africa: SMEs, manufacturing and cluster dynamics. *Journal of African Trade*, *6*(1), 47–59. DOI: 10.2991/jat.k.190812.001

Karakara, A. A. W., & Osabuohien, E. (2020). ICT adoption, competition and innovation of informal firms in West Africa: A comparative study of Ghana and Nigeria. *Journal of Enterprising Communities: People and Places in the Global Economy*, *14*(3), 397–414. DOI: 10.1108/JEC-03-2020-0022

Khan, A. M. (2025). Regional integration in Africa: The political economy of the African Continental Free Trade Area (Afcfta). *Policy Journal of Social Science Review*, *3*(4), 320–330.

Khorana, S., McGuire, S., & Perdikis, N. (2014). *Multilateral Agreements and Global Governance of International Trade Regimes. Scientific Paper FP-7*. ATLANTIC FUTURE Project.

Kindo, M. D., Adams, A. A., & Mohammed, J. (2024). The impact of trade on environmental quality and sustainable development in Ghana. *World Development Sustainability*, *4*, 100134. DOI: 10.1016/j.wds.2024.100134

Kinoshita, Y., Nagao, T., Ijuin, H., Nagasawa, K., Yamada, T., & Gupta, S. M. (2023). Utilization of free trade agreements to minimize costs and carbon emissions in the global supply chain for sustainable logistics. *Logistics (Basel)*, *7*(2), 32. DOI: 10.3390/logistics7020032

Korinek, J., & Melatos, M. (2009). Trade impacts of selected regional trade agreements in agriculture. *OECD Trade Policy Papers, 2009*.

Kumar, P., & Wu, H. (2025). Evaluating the dual impact of economic drivers on environmental degradation in developing countries: A study of technology innovation, foreign direct investment, and trade openness. *Journal of Energy and Environmental Policy Options*, *8*(1), 24–36.

Li, H., Han, J., & Xu, Y. (2023). The effect of the digital economy on services exports competitiveness and ternary margins. *Telecommunications Policy*, *47*(7), 102596. DOI: 10.1016/j.telpol.2023.102596

Liu, T. (2024). *Empirical analysis of the impact of regional trade agreements for Australia and China* (Doctoral dissertation, RMIT University).

Liyew, E. B. (2025). World Trade Organization Agreement Acceding Impacts on the Developing Countries' Human Rights System. [DSSR]. *Dialogue Social Science Review*, *3*(3), 232–241.

Logan, C. S., Manasseh, C. O., & Ede, K. K. (2025). Trade Liberalization, Foreign Investment and Economic Growth: Experience from Non-Oil Producing Countries in Africa. *International Journal of Economics and Financial Issues*, *15*(1), 101–112. DOI: 10.32479/ijefi.16912

Loganathan, V. (2023). Seventy-Five Years of India's Trade Policies With Special Reference to Agricultural Sector: An Overview. *Shanlax International Journal of Economics*, *11*(4), 46–51. DOI: 10.34293/economics.v11i4.6666

Luke, D. (2019). Making the case for the African continental free trade area. In *Inclusive trade in Africa* (pp. 5–12). Routledge. DOI: 10.4324/9780429401121-2

MA, Z., WANG, R., LIN, F., ZHANG, Q., & OTUMAWU-APREKU, K. (2025). Impact of China–Africa agricultural trade on food security: Facts and quantitative analysis. *Frontiers of Agricultural Science and Engineering*, *12*(4).

Makore, S. T. M., & Osode, P. C. (2025). Shifting the Paradigms of International Agricultural Subsidies Regulation to Advance the Human Right to Food. *African Journal of International and Comparative Law*, *33*(1), 53–81. DOI: 10.3366/ajicl.2025.0512

Manu, C. (2021). The Impact of Trade Agreement on Agricultural Trade Flow in West Africa. *International Journal of Economics and Finance*, *13*(1), 1–89.

Marx, A., Lein, B., & Brando, N. (2016). The protection of labour rights in trade agreements: The case of the EU-Colombia agreement. *Journal of World Trade*, *50*(4), 587–610. DOI: 10.54648/TRAD2016025

McCalla, A. F. (2001). What the developing countries want from the WTO. *Estey Journal of International Law and Trade Policy*, *2*(1), 165–177.

McMahon, J. A. (2024). Negotiations on food security at the WTO: A never-ending story? *Journal of International Trade Law & Policy*, *23*(2/3), 101–116. DOI: 10.1108/JITLP-03-2024-0018

Meijerink, G., & Roza, P. (2007). *The role of agriculture in economic development* (Vol. 4). Wageningen UR.

Meijers, H. (2014). Does the internet generate economic growth, international trade, or both? *International Economics and Economic Policy*, *11*(1-2), 137–163. DOI: 10.1007/s10368-013-0251-x

Meltzer, J. P., & Lovelock, P. (2018). Regulating for a Digital Economy-Understanding the Importance of Cross-Border Data Flows in Asia. *Available at SSRN* 3164401.

Mensah, K. (2024). *The World Trade Organization at a crossroad: Agricultural negotiations and what it means for developing countries* (No. 237). ZEF Working Paper Series.

Meschi, E., & Vivarelli, M. (2009). Trade and income inequality in developing countries. *World Development*, *37*(2), 287–302. DOI: 10.1016/j.worlddev.2008.06.002

Mignamissi, D., & Djijo T, A. J. (2021). Digital divide and financial development in Africa. *Telecommunications Policy*, *45*(9), 102199. DOI: 10.1016/j.telpol.2021.102199

Mulgan, A. G. (2008). Japan's FTA politics and the problem of agricultural trade liberalisation. *Australian Journal of International Affairs*, *62*(2), 164–178. DOI: 10.1080/10357710802060535

Myovella, G., Karacuka, M., & Haucap, J. (2020). Digitalization and economic growth: A comparative analysis of Sub-Saharan Africa and OECD economies. *Telecommunications Policy*, *44*(2), 101856. DOI: 10.1016/j.telpol.2019.101856

Nam, H. J., Batten, J. A., & Ryu, D. (2025). Do institutional quality and trade openness enhance the role of financial openness in Eastern European financial development? *Global Finance Journal*, *64*, 101071. DOI: 10.1016/j.gfj.2024.101071

Ncube, C. B., & De Beer, J. (2024, April). *Trade Rules as Regulatory Tools for Inclusive Innovation: Connecting Digital Trade and Clean Technology to Achieve Sustainable Development Goals.*

Neeraj, R. S. (2019). Trade rules for the digital economy: Charting new waters at the WTO. *World Trade Review*, *18*(S1), S121–S141. DOI: 10.1017/S1474745618000423

Ni, K. J. (2024). Can the CPTPP's Digital Format on Data Flows Serve a Role Model for the WTO? *Journal of World Trade*, *58*(6), 989–1006. DOI: 10.54648/TRAD2024048

Niebel, T. (2018). ICT and economic growth–Comparing developing, emerging and developed countries. *World Development*, *104*, 197–211. DOI: 10.1016/j.worlddev.2017.11.024

Nouve, K., Staatz, J. M., Schweikhardt, D. B., & Yade, M. (2002). Trading out of Poverty: WTO Agreements and the West African Agriculture. A Report of the Food Security II Cooperative Agreement.

Nuccio, M., & Guerzoni, M. (2019). Big data: Hell or heaven? Digital platforms and market power in the data-driven economy. *Competition & Change*, *23*(3), 312–328. DOI: 10.1177/1024529418816525

Odijie, M. E. (2019). The need for industrial policy coordination in the African Continental Free Trade Area. *African Affairs*, *118*(470), 182–193. DOI: 10.1093/afraf/ady054

Ogbuabor, J. E., Emeka, E. T., & Iheonu, C. O. (2025). Do industrialization, trade openness, and labor force participation enhance Africa's productive capacity? *Innovation and Development*, *15*(1), 207–232. DOI: 10.1080/2157930X.2023.2286718

Ojekemi, O. S., Ağa, M., & Magazzino, C. (2023). Towards achieving sustainability in the BRICS economies: The role of renewable energy consumption and economic risk. *Energies*, *16*(14), 528728. DOI: 10.3390/en16145287

Olayiwola, W. K., Osabuohien, E., & Okodua, H. (2011). *Economic Integration, Trade Facilitation, and Agricultural Exports Performance in ECOWAS Countries*. Economic Policy Analysis Unit, Department of Macroeconomic Policy, ECOWAS Commision. Accessed from https://citeseerx.ist.psu.edu/document?repid=rep1&type=pdf&doi=5e19c498d850c8b999d9fe3e0c1cca8a82752774

Pasadilla, G. O. (2006). *Preferential trading agreements and agricultural liberalization in East and Southeast Asia* (No. 11). ARTNeT Working Paper Series. Accessed from https://www.econstor.eu/bitstream/10419/178369/1/awp-11.pdf

Paunov, C., & Rollo, V. (2016). Has the internet fostered inclusive innovation in the developing world? *World Development*, *78*, 587–609. DOI: 10.1016/j.worlddev.2015.10.029

Petersmann, E. U. (2005). Addressing Institutional Challenges to the WTO in the New Millennium: A longer-term perspective. *Journal of International Economic Law*, *8*(3), 647–665. DOI: 10.1093/jiel/jgi040

Petri, P. A., & Plummer, M. (2019). *China should join the new trans-pacific partnership* (No. PB19-1).

Pishbahar, E., & Huchet, M. (2008). *European Union's preferential trade agreements in agricultural sector: a gravity approach* (Doctoral dissertation, auto-saisine).

Presberger, D., & Bernauer, T. (2023). Economic and political drivers of environmental impact shifting between countries. *Global Environmental Change*, *79*, 10263727. DOI: 10.1016/j.gloenvcha.2023.102637

Quansah, K. A., & Ahn, W. C. (2017). The effect of the Korea-Australia free trade agreement (KAFTA) on the Korea-Australia trade structure. *The Asian Journal of Shipping and Logistics*, *33*(4), 229–235. DOI: 10.1016/j.ajsl.2017.12.006

Raihan, S. (2011). Economic Reforms and Agriculture in Bangladesh: Assessment of Impacts using Economy-wide Simulation Models. *Accessed from* https://mpra.ub.uni-muenchen.de/37886/1/MPRA_paper_37886.pdf

Raihan, S. (2011). Employment Effects of FTA Agreements: The Perspectives from Bangladesh. *Accessed from* https://mpra.ub.uni-muenchen.de/id/eprint/37885

Rama, M. (2003). Globalization and workers in developing countries. *World Bank Policy Research Working Paper*, •••, 2958.

Rashid, H. (2025). Trade Agreements and Export Performance of Bangladesh: A Gravity Model Analysis. *Available at SSRN* 5379852.

Ratna, R. S., Sharma, S. K., & Dobhal, A. (2021). Indian agriculture under WTO and FTAs: An assessment. In *Indian Agriculture Under the Shadows of WTO and FTAs: Issues and Concerns* (pp. 3–25). Springer Singapore. DOI: 10.1007/978-981-33-6854-5_1

Rehber, E., & Grega, L. (2008). Agriculture, trade and sustainability. *The European Legacy, Toward New Paradigms*, *13*(4), 463–479. DOI: 10.1080/10848770802180755

Ren, S., Liu, D., Li, B., Wang, Y., & Chen, X. (2020). Does emissions trading affect labor demand? Evidence from the mining and manufacturing industries in China. *Journal of Environmental Management*, *254*, 109789. DOI: 10.1016/j.jenvman.2019.109789

Rena, R. (2012). Impact of WTO policies on developing countries: Issues and perspectives. *Transnational Corporations Review*, *4*(3), 77–88. DOI: 10.1080/19186444.2012.11658336

Rodríguez, E. V. (2009). The European Union Free Trade Agreements: Implications for Rodrik, D. (2022). An industrial policy for good jobs. *Hamilton Project—Policy proposal. Washington, DC: Brookings Institution*. Developing Countries. *Real Instituto Elcano. Working Paper*, *8*, 5–6.

Ruben, R., Fort, R., & Zúñiga-Arias, G. (2009). Measuring the impact of fair trade on development. *Development in Practice, 19*(6), 777–788. DOI: 10.1080/09614520903027049

Runge, C. F. (1992). Environmental effects of trade in the agricultural sector: a case study. Accessed from https://ageconsearch.umn.edu/record/14449/files/wp92-01.pdf

Salisu, M. A., Marafa, L., Bamiro, N. B., Shokunbi, M. O., & Raimi, B. O. (2025). Systematic review of post-COVID policies and strategies for strengthening e-commerce cooperation among ASEAN countries. *Journal of Economic and Administrative Sciences.*

Sawadogo, F., & Wandaogo, A. A. (2021). Does mobile money services adoption foster intra-African goods trade? *Economics Letters, 199*, 109681. DOI: 10.1016/j.econlet.2020.109681

Shaffer, G. (2015). How the World Trade Organization shapes regulatory governance. *Regulation & Governance, 9*(1), 1–15. DOI: 10.1111/rego.12057

Shahzad, U., Miao, C., & Muhammad, S. (2025). Digital and geographical mobility: Correlating technological bilateral trade impact on sustainable trade development between China and East Asia. *Environment, Development and Sustainability*, •••, 1–28. DOI: 10.1007/s10668-025-06128-0

Siles-Brügge, G. (2014). *Constructing European Union trade policy: A global idea of Europe*. Palgrave Macmillan. DOI: 10.1057/9781137331663

Singh, P. J., Smith, A., & Sohal, A. S. (2005). Strategic supply chain management issues in the automotive industry: An Australian perspective. *International Journal of Production Research, 43*(16), 3375–3399. DOI: 10.1080/00207540500095738

Stanford, J. (2019). North American free trade: history, structure and prospects. In *The Handbook of Globalisation* (3rd ed., pp. 272–303). Edward Elgar Publishing. DOI: 10.4337/9781788118606.00026

Stojanović, B., & Radukić, S. (2006). EU environmental policy and competitiveness. *Panoeconomicus, 53*(4), 471–485. DOI: 10.2298/PAN0604471S

Sunge, R., & Ngepah, N. (2020). Agricultural trade liberalization, regional trade agreements and agricultural technical efficiency in Africa. *Outlook on Agriculture, 49*(1), 66–76. DOI: 10.1177/0030727019870551

Swinnen, J., Olper, A., & Vandemoortele, T. (2012). Impact of the WTO on Agricultural and Food Policies. *World Economy, 35*(9), 1089–1101. DOI: 10.1111/j.1467-9701.2012.01472.x

Szeles, M. R. (2018). New insights from a multilevel approach to the regional digital divide in the European Union. *Telecommunications Policy*, *42*(6), 452–463. DOI: 10.1016/j.telpol.2018.03.007

Tabash, M. I., Elsantil, Y., Hamadi, A., & Drachal, K. (2024). Globalization and income inequality in developing economies: A comprehensive analysis. *Economies*, *12*(1), 23. DOI: 10.3390/economies12010023

Talukder, D. (2014). Agricultural trade liberalisation and welfare of rural households in Bangladesh: A complementary policy framework. *Journal of Economic and Social Policy*, *16*(2), 89–128.

Taylor, R. D. (2020). "Data localization": The internet in the balance. *Telecommunications Policy*, *44*(8), 102003. DOI: 10.1016/j.telpol.2020.102003

Temtime, Z. T., & Pansiri, J. (2004). Small business critical success/failure factors in developing countries: some evidence from Botswana.

Thirlwall, A. P. (2000). Trade agreements, trade liberalization and economic growth: A selective survey. *African Development Review*, *12*(2), 129–160. DOI: 10.1111/1467-8268.00020

Timsina, K. P., & Culas, R. J. (2020). Impacts of Australia's free trade agreements on trade in agricultural products: An aggregative and disaggregative analysis. *The Australian Journal of Agricultural and Resource Economics*, *64*(3), 889–919. DOI: 10.1111/1467-8489.12377

Tinta, A. A., Sarpong, D. B., Ouedraogo, I. M., Al Hassan, R., Mensah-Bonsu, A., & Onumah, E. E. (2018). Assessing the impact of integration on economic growth and food security in ECOWAS. *Theoretical and Practical Research in Economic Fields*, *9*(1 (17)), 32–44. DOI: 10.14505/tpref.v9.1(17).04

Tiwari, M. (2025). The Rise of Geo-Economic Fragmentation: Is the WTO Obsolete? *Available at SSRN* 5501579. *SSRN*: https://ssrn.com/abstract=5501579 or http://dx.doi.org/DOI: 10.2139/ssrn.5501579

Tran, T. A. D., & Dinh, T. T. B. (2014). FDI inflows and trade imbalances: Evidence from developing Asia. *The European Journal of Comparative Economics*, *11*(1), 147.

Trommer, S. (2017). The WTO in an era of preferential trade agreements: Thick and thin institutions in global trade governance. *World Trade Review*, *16*(3), 501–526. DOI: 10.1017/S1474745616000628

Valensisi, G., Lisinge, R., & Karingi, S. (2016). The trade facilitation agreement and Africa's regional integration. Canadian Journal of Development Studies. *Canadian Journal of Development Studies*, *37*(2), 239–259. DOI: 10.1080/02255189.2016.1131672

Vicente, M. R., & López, A. J. (2011). Assessing the regional digital divide across the European Union-27. *Telecommunications Policy*, *35*(3), 220–237. DOI: 10.1016/j.telpol.2010.12.013

Wang, X. H., & Zhao, J. (2022). Bilateral free trade agreements in a four-country model with a digital technology perspective. *Journal of Digital Economy*, *1*(3), 192–208. DOI: 10.1016/j.jdec.2023.01.001

Weber, R. H. (2015). Digital trade and E-commerce: Challenges and opportunities of the Asia-Pacific regionalism. *Asian J. WTO & Int'l Health L & Pol'y*, *10*, 321.

Wilson, J. S., & Otsuki, T. (2007). Regional integration in South Asia: What role for trade facilitation? *World Bank Policy Research Working Paper*, (4423).

Yang, Y., & Gupta, S. (2007). Regional trade arrangements in Africa: Past performance and the way forward. *African Development Review*, *19*(3), 399–431. DOI: 10.1111/j.1467-8268.2007.00169.x

Yang, Z., Anwar, S., & Yang, Y. (2025). The Impact of Foreign Direct Investment on Industrialization in China: A Spatial Panel Analysis. *Economies*, *13*(2), 42. DOI: 10.3390/economies13020042

Yao, X., Yasmeen, R., Li, Y., Hafeez, M., & Padda, I. U. H. (2019). Free trade agreements and environment for sustainable development: A gravity model analysis. *Sustainability (Basel)*, *11*(3), 597. DOI: 10.3390/su11030597

Yu, H., Wang, R., & Zhang, A. (2024). Unraveling the impact of environmental provisions in preferential trade agreements on green total factor energy efficiency. *Journal of Environmental Management*, *362*, 121205. DOI: 10.1016/j.jenvman.2024.121205

Yusuf, M. (2009, July). The evils of agriculture subsidy. In *Competition Forum* (Vol. 7, No. 2, p. 427). American Society for Competitiveness.

Zhang, Y., & Li, S. (2024). The effects of trade liberalization on inequality in nutrition intake: Empirical evidence from Indian districts. *BMC Public Health*, *24*(1), 1317. DOI: 10.1186/s12889-024-18749-7

ADDITIONAL READINGS

Baker, P. R. (2021). Handbook on negotiating sustainable development provisions in preferential trade agreements: update.

Chauffour, J. P., & Maur, J. C. (Eds.). (2011). *Preferential trade agreement policies for development: A handbook*. World Bank Publications.

Hoekman, B. M., & Evenett, S. J. (Eds.). (2005). *Economic development and multilateral trade cooperation*. World Bank Publications.

Looney, R. E. (Ed.). (2018). *Handbook of International Trade Agreements: Country, regional and global approaches*. Routledge. DOI: 10.4324/9781351046954

KEY TERMS AND DEFINITIONS

Bilateral Trade Agreement: A bilateral trade agreement is a pact between two countries that reduces or removes trade barriers such as tariffs and quotas. Its goal is to increase trade and economic cooperation between the two nations. These agreements are usually easier to negotiate because only two parties are involved.

Multilateral Trade Agreement: A multilateral trade agreement involves three or more countries working together to establish common trade rules. These agreements aim to reduce global trade barriers and promote economic cooperation on a broader scale. The World Trade Organization (WTO) negotiations are a common platform for such agreements.

Regional Trade Agreement: A regional trade agreement (RTA) is a treaty among several countries within the same geographic region to promote free or preferential trade. RTAs often focus on reducing tariffs and improving market access among member states. Examples include the European Union (EU) and the ASEAN Free Trade Area.

Sustainable Trade Agreement: A sustainable trade agreement is a trade pact that incorporates environmental protection, social welfare, and economic development objectives into trade rules. It ensures that increased trade does not harm ecosystems, labour rights, or long-term resource security. These agreements promote responsible production, clean technologies, and fair labour practices alongside economic gains.

Trade Facilitation: Trade facilitation refers to simplifying and harmonising international trade processes to make the movement of goods across borders faster, cheaper, and more efficient. It includes improving customs procedures, documentation, logistics, and infrastructure. The goal is to reduce delays, decrease cost of doing business, and enhance global competitiveness of firms.

Compilation of References

Abdi, H. A., Zaidi, M. A. S., & Karim, Z. A. (2023). Economic complexity and trade flows in selected COMESA and Asia countries. *Technological and Economic Development of Economy*, *29*(3), 188–205. DOI: 10.3846/tede.2023.18682

Abdulai, A., Diao, X., & Johnson, M. (2005). Achieving regional growth dynamics in African agriculture. *Accessed from* https://ageconsearch.umn.edu/record/58371/files/dsgdp17.pdf

Abdulai, A., Johnson, M., & Diao, X. (2006). Leveraging regional growth dynamics in African agriculture. *African Journal of Agricultural and Resource Economics*, *1*(1), 49–66.

Abendin, S., & Duan, P. (2021). International trade and economic growth in Africa: The role of the digital economy. *Cogent Economics & Finance*, *9*(1), 1911767. DOI: 10.1080/23322039.2021.1911767

Abidi, N., El Herradi, M., & Sakha, S. (2023). Digitalization and resilience during the COVID-19 pandemic. *Telecommunications Policy*, *47*(4), 102522. DOI: 10.1016/j.telpol.2023.102522 PMID: 37051116

Abman, R., & Lundberg, C. (2020). Does free trade increase deforestation? The effects of regional trade agreements. *Journal of the Association of Environmental and Resource Economists*, *7*(1), 35–72. DOI: 10.1086/705787

Abu-Bakar, H., & Charnley, F. (2024). Developing a strategic methodology for circular economy roadmapping: A theoretical framework. *Sustainability (Basel)*, *16*(15), 6682. DOI: 10.3390/su16156682

Acar, S., Aşıcı, A. A., & Yeldan, A. E. (2022). Potential effects of the EU's carbon border adjustment mechanism on the Turkish economy. Environment, Development and Sustainability, 24(6), 8162-8194. springer.comDOI: 10.1007/s10668-021-01779-1

Adams, K., Attah-Boakye, R., Yu, H., Chu, I., & Mali, D. (2024). African continental free trade area and regional trade in ICT and digital technologies. *Journal of International Management*, *30*(4), 101156. DOI: 10.1016/j.intman.2024.101156

Adedokun, A. S. (2024). Improving Intra-African trade for AfCFTA and non-AfCFTA Trade flows through trade policy regime: Lessons from European Union. In *Africa-EU Relations and the African Continental Free Trade Area: Redefining the Dynamics of Power and Economic Partnership in a Complex Global Order* (pp. 53–77). Springer Nature Switzerland. DOI: 10.1007/978-3-031-57992-9_4

Adeleye, N., & Eboagu, C. (2019). Evaluation of ICT development and economic growth in Africa. *NETNOMICS: Economic Research and Electronic Networking*, *20*(1), 31–53. DOI: 10.1007/s11066-019-09131-6

Adetula, V., & Osegbue, C. (2020). Trade and the Economic Partnership Agreements in EU-Africa relations. In *The Routledge Handbook of EU-Africa Relations* (pp. 211–223). Routledge. DOI: 10.4324/9781315170916-20

Afzal, S. (2025). Unlocking economic potential: The TAPI pipeline's role in regional integration. *The Diplomatic Herald Journal*. https://tdhj.org/blog/post/tapi-pipeline-role-integration/

Agarwala, N. (2025). Smart Governance for a Sustainable Blue Economy. In *Handbook of Sustainable Blue Economy* (pp. 1–35). Springer Nature Switzerland. DOI: 10.1007/978-3-031-32671-4_37-1

Aggarwal, V. K., & Urata, S. (2006). *Bilateral Tade Agreements in the Asia-Pacific: Origins Evolutions, and Implications* (1st ed.). Routledge., DOI: 10.4324/9781315020976

Agyapong, D. (2021). Implications of digital economy for financial institutions in Ghana: An exploratory inquiry. *Transnational Corporations Review*, *13*(1), 51–61. DOI: 10.1080/19186444.2020.1787304

Ahi, A. A., Sinkovics, N., & Sinkovics, R. R. (2023). E-commerce policy and the global economy: A path to more inclusive development? *MIR. Management International Review*, *63*(1), 27–56. DOI: 10.1007/s11575-022-00490-1

Ahlström, H. (2019). Policy hotspots for sustainability: Changes in the EU regulation of sustainable business and finance. *Sustainability (Basel)*, *11*(2), 499. DOI: 10.3390/su11020499

Ahmad, M., & Raza, M. Y. (2020). Role of public-private partnerships investment in energy and technological innovations in driving climate change: Evidence from Brazil. *Environmental Science and Pollution Research International, 27*(24), 30638–30648. DOI: 10.1007/s11356-020-09307-w

Ahmadov, N. (2021). Azerbaijan, Afghanistan, and Turkmenistan sign trilateral roadmap for cooperation on Eurasian connectivity. *Eurasia Daily Monitor, 18*(23). The Jamestown Foundation. https://jamestown.org/program/azerbaijan-afghanistan-and-turkmenistan-sign-trilateral-roadmap-for-cooperation-on-eurasian-connectivity/

Ahmad, S. S., & Wani, N. U. H. (2018). Trade potential of Afghanistan against SAARC: An application of Gravity Model Approach. *Kardan Journal of Economics and Management Sciences, 1*(4), 1–19. DOI: 10.31841/KJEMS.2021.66

Ahmed, S. M. U. (2022). A General Equilibrium Analysis on the Impact of Tariff Reforms to Protect Agricultural Sector in Bangladesh. *Center for Development Economic Studies, 9*(11), 20–28. DOI: 10.53422/JDMS.2022.91103

Aiyar, S., Chen, J., Ebeke, C. H., Garcia-Saltos, R., Gudmundsson, T., Ilyina, A., . . . Trevino, J. P. (2023). Geo-economic fragmentation and the future of multilateralism. *International Monetary Fund.* https://www.imf.org/en/Publications/WP/Issues/2023/01/13/Geo-Economic-Fragmentation-and-the-Future-of-Multilateralism-528208

Akram, H. W., Ciddikie, M. D., & Khan, M. A. (2014). India's trade relationship with SAFTA countries: A review. *Journal of Indian Research, 2*(1), 46–58.

Alam, M. J. (2025). Trade Between Bangladesh and China: Challenges and Opportunities. *Bangladesh–China Connectivity: History, Trade and Diplomacy, and Society*, 113-124.

Alam, M. S., & Zubayer, M. (2010). Intra regional foreign direct investment (FDI) prospect in South Asian Association of Regional Cooperation (SAARC) region. *International Journal of Economics and Finance, 2*(3), 114–121. DOI: 10.5539/ijef.v2n3p114

Alamoush, A. S., Ballini, F., & Ölçer, A. I. (2021). Revisiting port sustainability as a foundation for the implementation of the United Nations Sustainable Development Goals (UN SDGs). Journal of Shipping and Trade. springer.comDOI: 10.1186/s41072-021-00101-6

Albiman, M. M., & Sulong, Z. (2017). The linear and non-linear impacts of ICT on economic growth, of disaggregate income groups within SSA region. *Telecommunications Policy, 41*(7-8), 555–572. DOI: 10.1016/j.telpol.2017.07.007

Alekberli-Museyibova, N. (2023). Revitalization of the Lapis Lazuli Corridor: From Afghanistan to Europe. *Eurasia Daily Monitor, 20*(110). The Jamestown Foundation. https://jamestown.org/program/revitalization-of-the-lapis-lazuli-corridor-from-afghanistan-to-europe/

Alemanno, A. (2015). The regulatory cooperation chapter of the transatlantic trade and investment partnership: Institutional structures and democratic consequences. *Journal of International Economic Law, 18*(3), 625–640. DOI: 10.1093/jiel/jgv026

Ali, I., & Mufti, A. (2020). Saarc and Safta: Dynamic of Trade Facilitation in South Asia. Available at *SSRN* 3753321. DOI: 10.2139/ssrn.3753321

Ali, M. M., & Medhekar, A. (2016). Bilateral Trade through official channel between India and Bangladesh: An analysis with the use of Time Series forecasting models. *Journal of Economic Cooperation and Development, 37*(3), 135–170.

Alimov, R. (2017). The role of the Shanghai Cooperation Organization in counteracting threats to peace and security. *UN Chronicle.* https://www.un.org/en/chronicle/article/role-shanghai-cooperation-organization-counteracting-threats-peace-and-security

Ali-Yrkkö, J., Foster-McGregor, N., Hanzl-Weiss, D., Rouvinen, P., Seppälä, T., Stehrer, R., Stöllinger, R., & Ylä-Anttila, P. (2011). Trade in Intermediate Products and EU Manufacturing Supply Chains. *WIIW Research Reports.* Accessed from https://www.econstor.eu/bitstream/10419/204141/1/wiiw-research-rep-369.pdf

Almeida, T. F. (2025). Environmental Protection or Domestic Protectionism? The EU Deforestation-Free Regulation and its Shift from Exporter to Importer of Foreign Capital. In *EU External Relations Law and Sustainability: The EU, Third States and International Organizations* (pp. 167–201). TMC Asser Press. [HTML], DOI: 10.1007/978-94-6265-655-0_8

AlQallaf, S. J. S., & Al Mubarak, M. (2025). Maximization of Business Strategies Through Digital Technology: Opportunities and Challenges. *Innovative and Intelligent Digital Technologies. Towards an Increased Efficiency, 2*, 957–975.

Al-Roubaier, A., Hamdan, A., & Sarea, A. M. (2020). Economic diversification in a digital economy. In *Proceedings of the International Conference on Artificial Intelligence and Computer Vision (AICV2020)* (pp. 665-671). Springer International Publishing.

Aman, A., Alam, I., Singh, G. J., Ghali, Z., Fatma, R., & Khan, K. (2025). Bridging Markets, Building Alliances: Assessing the India-Australia Economic Cooperation through the Lens of Trade Liberalization and Geoeconomic Strategy. *International Journal of Economics and Financial Issues*, *15*(4), 187–195. DOI: 10.32479/ijefi.19025

Amin, R., Muppani, V. R., Sairam, P. S., Arora, R., Haque, M., & Islam, S. (2025). Digitalizing the Shipping Containers of Bangladesh Sustainable Solutions Amidst Challenges. In *Developing Dynamic and Sustainable Supply Chains to Achieve Sustainable Development Goals* (pp. 283–310). IGI Global Scientific Publishing. DOI: 10.4018/979-8-3693-6284-6.ch010

Anderson, J. E., & van Wincoop, E. (2003). Gravity with Gravitas: A Solution to the Border Puzzle. *The American Economic Review*, *93*(1), 170–192. DOI: 10.1257/000282803321455214

Andreescu, C. V., & Sfetea, R. C. (2013). EU-US Trade Relationship. *Knowledge Horizons. Economics*, *5*(4), 62.

Antimiani, A., & Salvatici, L. (2015). Regionalism versus multilateralism: The case of the European Union trade policy. *Journal of World Trade*, *49*(2).

Arouri, M. E. H., Caporale, G. M., Rault, C., Sova, R., & Sova, A. (2012). Environmental regulation and competitiveness: Evidence from Romania. *Ecological Economics*, *81*, 130–139. DOI: 10.1016/j.ecolecon.2012.07.001

Arvis, J.-F., Raballand, G., & Marteau, J.-F. (2010) The cost of being landlocked. The World Bank. Pages, Washington DC. DOI: 10.1596/978-0-8213-8408-4

Aryal, S. K. (2022). *State of regional integration in South Asia: Does post-Sri Lanka crisis have positive impact?* The Geopolitics. https://thegeopolitics.com/state-of-regional-integration-in-south-asia-does-post-sri-lanka-crisis-have-positive-impact/

Asian Development Bank. (2005). *Opening transport corridors between Central Asia and South Asia* (Regional Business Roundtable, Bishkek, Kyrgyz Republic, 3—4 November 2005). Central Asia Regional Economic Cooperation (CAREC) Program. https://www.carecprogram.org/uploads/Paper-Opening-Transport-Corridors-Central-and-South-Asia.pdf

Asian Development Bank. (2009). *Study on intraregional trade and investment in South Asia*. https://www.adb.org/sites/default/files/publication/28658/intraregional-trade-investment.pdf

Aune, F. R., Dalen, H. M., & Hagem, C. (2012). Implementing the EU renewable target through green certificate markets. *Energy Economics*, *34*(4), 992–1000. DOI: 10.1016/j.eneco.2011.07.006

Austarlian Border Force. (2020). RECEP -Free Trade Agreements. https://www.abf.gov.au/importing-exporting-and-manufacturing/fta/free-trade-agreements/regional-comprehensive-economic-partnership-agreement

Austarlian Government DFAT. (2025). Comprehensive and Progressive Agreement for Trans-Pacific Partnership (CPTPP). https://www.dfat.gov.au/trade/agreements/in-force/cptpp/comprehensive-and-progressive-agreement-for-trans-pacific-partnership

Australian Government. (2025). Free Trade Agreements https://business.gov.au/products-and-services/exporting/free-trade-agreements

Ayaz, O., & Tatoglu, E. (2024). Unveiling the power of social value: Catalyzing circular economy in emerging market SMEs. *Journal of Cleaner Production*, *453*, 142245. DOI: 10.1016/j.jclepro.2024.142245

Aziz, M. (2016). Afghanistan: The geopolitics of regional economic integration. The emergence of China as the new facilitator. CIDOB. https://www.cidob.org/sites/default/files/2024-11/313-342_afghanistan_the_geopolitics_of_regional_economic_integration_the_emergence_of_china_as_the_new_facilitator.pdf

Babazov, Z., & Li, C. (2025). Exploring the Relationship Between Cultivated Land Regulations, Agricultural Productivity, and Trade Efficiency: A Comparative Analysis Among China, Russia, and Kyrgyzstan Under the Belt and Road Initiative. *Sustainability (Basel)*, *17*(10), 4723. DOI: 10.3390/su17104723

Baena-Rojas, J. J., & Herrero-Olarte, S. (2020). From Preferential Trade Arrangements to Free Trade Agreements: One of the Downturns of Cooperation in International Relations? *Social Sciences (Basel, Switzerland)*, *9*(8), 139. DOI: 10.3390/socsci9080139

Bag, S., Telukdarie, A., Pretorius, J. C., & Gupta, S. (2021). Industry 4.0 and supply chain sustainability: Framework and future research directions. *Benchmarking*, *28*(5), 1410–1450.

Balassa, B. (1965). Trade Liberalization and Revealed Comparative Advantage. *Manchester School*, *33*(2), 99–123. DOI: 10.1111/j.1467-9957.1965.tb00050.x

Balassa, B. (1966). Tariff Reductions and Trade in Manufactures Among Industrial Countries. *The American Economic Review*, *56*, 466–473.

Balogh, J. M., & Aguiar, M. B. (2022). Determinants of Latin American and the Caribbean Agricultural Trade: A Gravity Model Approach. *Zemedelská Ekonomika*, *68*(4), 127–136. DOI: 10.17221/405/2021-AGRICECON

Balogh, J. M., & Leitão, N. C. (2019). A Gravity Approach of Agricultural Trade: The Nexus of the EU and African, Caribbean and Pacific Countries. *Zemedelská Ekonomika*, *65*(11), 509–519. DOI: 10.17221/131/2019-AGRICECON

Banga, K., Gharib, M., Mendez-Parra, M., & Macleod, J. (2021). E-commerce in preferential trade agreements: Implications for African firms and the AfCFTA. *ODI Report*.

Bangladesh Bank. (2024). Trading in Local Currencies: Problems and Prospects for the SAARC Countries. Bangladesh Bank. *Accessed from* https://www.bb.org.bd/pub/special/aug282024_bb_special_publication.pdf

Barsha, S., & Munshi, S. A. (2023). Implementing artificial intelligence in library services: A review of current prospects and challenges of developing countries. [HTML]. *Library Hi Tech News*. Advance online publication. DOI: 10.1108/LHTN-07-2023-0126

Bartels, L. (2013). Human rights and sustainable development obligations in EU free trade agreements. *Legal Issues of Economic Integration, 40*(4).

Bauer, M., Lee-Makiyama, H., Van der Marel, E., & Verschelde, B. (2014). *The costs of data localisation: Friendly fire on economic recovery* (No. 3/2014). ECIPE occasional paper.

Baylis, K., Garduño-Rivera, R., & Piras, G. (2012). The distributional effects of NAFTA in Mexico: Evidence from a panel of municipalities. *Regional Science and Urban Economics*, *42*(1-2), 286–302. DOI: 10.1016/j.regsciurbeco.2011.09.006

Baysan, T., Panagariya, A., & Pitigala, N. (2006). Preferential Trading in South Asia. *World Bank Policy Research Working Paper*, (3813).

Bazillier, R., & Rana, A. T. (2025). Social Clauses in Free Trade Agreements: An Efficient Tool to Improve Labour Standards? *World Economy*, *48*(6), 1251–1281. DOI: 10.1111/twec.13675

Beghin, J., & Bureau, J. C. (2001). Quantification of Sanitary, Phytosanitary, and Technical Barriers To Trade for Trade Policy Analysis. Iowa State University, Center for Agricultural and Rural Development *Working Paper 01-WP-291*.

Bellmann, C., & Bulatnikova, A. (2022). *Incorporating environmental provisions in regional trade agreements in chapters and articles dealing with trade in services.* OECD Trade and Environment. [HTML], DOI: 10.1787/6e976798-

Beltrami, M., Orzes, G., Sarkis, J., & Sartor, M. (2021). Industry 4.0 and sustainability: Towards conceptualization and theory. *Journal of Cleaner Production, 312*, 127733. DOI: 10.1016/j.jclepro.2021.127733

Bennett, M., March, A., & Failler, P. (2024). Blue economy financing solutions for the fisheries and aquaculture sectors of Caribbean Island states. *Fishes, 9*(8), 305. DOI: 10.3390/fishes9080305

Ben, S., Bosc, R., Jiao, J., Li, W., Simonelli, F., & Zhang, R. (2017). *Digital Infrastructure Overcoming the digital divide in China and the European Union.* Centre for European Policy Studies.

Bergstrand, J. H., & Clance, M. W. (2023). and Matthew W. Clance, Quantile Gravity: Economic Integration Agreements, Least Traded Goods, and Least Developed Economies, September 2023, *Working Papers.*

Berlingher, R. D. (2018). Regulating free movement of goods within the european union. *Journal of Legal Studies. Vasile Goldiş, 21*(35), 61–77.

Bertelsmann Stiftung. (2024). *BTI 2024 Country Report — Afghanistan.* https://bti-project.org/en/reports/country-report/AFG

Bertschek, I., Briglauer, W., Hüschelrath, K., Kauf, B., & Niebel, T. (2015). The economic impacts of broadband internet: A survey. *Review of Network Economics, 14*(4), 201–227. DOI: 10.1515/rne-2016-0032

Beshkar, M., & Bond, E. (2019). Trade agreements: Theoretical foundations. In *Oxford Research Encyclopedia of Economics and Finance.*

Bhardwaj, A., & Roy, M. (2025). Blue Economy vs. Green Economy: A Case Study for Sustainable Economy in India. In *Securing Sustainable Futures Through Blue and Green Economies* (pp. 195-218). IGI Global Scientific Publishing. DOI: 10.4018/979-8-3693-7893-9.ch008

Bhattacharya, S. K., & Das, G. G. (2011). Do South-South Trade Agreements Enhance Member Countries' Trade? Evaluating Implications for Development Potentials in the Context of SAARC. *Evaluating Implications for Development Potentials in the Context of SAARC (November 1, 2011). UNU-CRIS Working Papers W-20011/2.*

Bhattacharya, S. K., & Das, G. G. (2014). Can South–South trade agreements reduce development deficits? An exploration of SAARC during 1995–2008. *Journal of South Asian Development, 9*(3), 253–285. DOI: 10.1177/0973174114549129

Bhattacharya, S., & Sachdev, B. K. (2024). Impact of Scientific Innovation in Coastal Resource Management: Fostering Blue Economic Development, Environmental Mitigation, and Pollution Control. In *Scientific Innovations for Coastal Resource Management* (pp. 1–32). IGI Global. DOI: 10.4018/979-8-3693-2436-3.ch001

Bibri, S. E., & Krogstie, J. (2020). Environmentally data-driven smart sustainable cities: Applied innovative solutions for energy efficiency, pollution reduction, and urban metabolism. *Energy Informatics, 3*(1), 29. DOI: 10.1186/s42162-020-00130-8

Bigsten, A., & Söderbom, M. (2006). What have we learned from a decade of manufacturing enterprise surveys in Africa? *The World Bank Research Observer, 21*(2), 241–265. DOI: 10.1093/wbro/lkl003

Bilalova, S., Newig, J., Tremblay-Lévesque, L. C., Roux, J., Herron, C., & Crane, S. (2023). Pathways to water sustainability? A global study assessing the benefits of integrated water resources management. *Journal of Environmental Management, 343*, 118179. DOI: 10.1016/j.jenvman.2023.118179

Birovljev, J., & Ćetković, B. (2013). The impact of the WTO agreement on agriculture on food security in developing countries.

Blalock, G., & Gertler, P. J. (2008). Welfare gains from foreign direct investment through technology transfer to local suppliers. *Journal of International Economics, 74*(2), 402–421. DOI: 10.1016/j.jinteco.2007.05.011

Bojnec, S., & Hartmann, M. (2004). Agricultural and food trade in Central and Eastern Europe: The case of Slovenian intra-industry trade. *Access from* https://ageconsearch.umn.edu/record/92027/files/dp65.pdf https://ageconsearch.umn.edu/record/51136/files/Liberalization%20and%20Food%20Security%20Paper%20for%20IAAE-%20China%202009%20Final.pdf

Bojnec, Š., & Fertő, I. (2015). Does enlargement has caused intra and extra European Union agri-food trade? *Bulgarian Journal of Agricultural Science, 21*(1), 1–15.

Bollyky, T. J., & Mavroidis, P. C. (2017). Trade, Social Preferences and Regulatory Cooperation The New WTO-Think. *Journal of International Economic Law, 20*(1), 1–30. DOI: 10.1093/jiel/jgw076

Borangaziev, A. (2024). *Is Afghanistan ready for dialogue with Central Asia on water issues?* Times of Central Asia. https://timesca.com/is-afghanistan-ready-for-dialogue-with-central-asia-on-water-issues/

Bosone, M., Casola, M., Daldanise, G., & Vito, D. (2023). Stimulating Circular Urban Regeneration through Cultural and Sustainable Communities: The Proposal for a Green Blue Youth Vision 2030. *Sustainability (Basel), 15*(14), 11294. DOI: 10.3390/su151411294

Bouët, A., Odjo, S. P., & Zaki, C. (2020). *Africa agriculture trade monitor 2020.* Intl Food Policy Res Inst. https://books.google.com/books?hl=en&lr=&id=7gYBEAAAQBAJ&oi=fnd&pg=PR8&dq=Africa+agriculture+trade+monitor+2020&ots=jrxjpPfTtY&sig=a1rPX-ByzOI09qvcMn9H4W6txFc

Bourdet, Y., & Persson, M. (2012). Completing the European Union Customs Union: The effects of trade procedure harmonization. *Journal of Common Market Studies, 50*(2), 300–314. DOI: 10.1111/j.1468-5965.2011.02203.x

Bowden, B. (2000). Competing to Survive? Productivity, Workplace Reform and International Competitiveness in the Australian Coal Industry. In *paper presented.*

Bradford, A. (2015). Exporting standards: The externalization of the EU's regulatory power via markets. *International Review of Law and Economics, 42*, 158–173. DOI: 10.1016/j.irle.2014.09.004

Bradford, A. (2020). *The Brussels effect: How the European Union rules the world.* Oxford University Press. DOI: 10.1093/oso/9780190088583.001.0001

Brenton, P., Sheehy, J., & Vancauteren, M. (2001). Technical barriers to trade in the European Union: Importance for accession countries. *Journal of Common Market Studies, 39*(2), 265–284. DOI: 10.1111/1468-5965.00288

Bressanelli, G., Adrodegari, F., Pigosso, D. C., & Parida, V. (2022). Towards the smart circular economy paradigm: A definition, conceptualization, and research agenda. *Sustainability (Basel), 14*(9), 4960. DOI: 10.3390/su14094960

Breton, A. (1999). *Exploring the Economics of Language.* New Canadian Perspectives, Canadian Heritage.

BRICS. (2026). Launch of BRICS India 2026 Logo, Theme and Website by the External Affairs Minister. https://www.mea.gov.in/press-releases.htm?dtl/40585/Launch_of_BRICS_India_2026_Logo_Theme_and_Website_by_the_External_Affairs_Minister

Brkić, B. (2025). Central Asian countries push for regional development at Termez Dialogue. *Euronews.* https://www.euronews.com/2025/05/21/central-asian-countries-push-for-regional-development-at-termez-dialogue

Brown, D. K., Deardorff, A. V., & Stern, R. M. (2003). Multilateral, Regional and Bilateral Trade-Policy Options for the United States and Japan. *World Economy*, *26*(6), 803–828. DOI: 10.1111/1467-9701.00549

Bruno, F., Ricca, M., Lagudi, A., Kalamara, P., Manglis, A., Fourkiotou, A., Papadopoulou, D., & Veneti, A. (2020). Digital technologies for the sustainable development of the accessible underwater cultural heritage sites. *Journal of Marine Science and Engineering*, *8*(11), 955. DOI: 10.3390/jmse8110955

Bureau, J. C., Jean, S., & Matthews, A. (2006). The consequences of agricultural trade liberalization for developing countries: Distinguishing between genuine benefits and false hopes. *World Trade Review*, *5*(2), 225–249. DOI: 10.1017/S147474560600276X

Burfisher, M. E. (2001). Agricultural Policy Reform in the WTO: Challenges for Analysts.

Burmaoglu, S., Ozdemir Gungor, D., Kirbac, A., & Saritas, O. (2023). Future research avenues at the nexus of circular economy and digitalization. *International Journal of Productivity and Performance Management*, *72*(8), 2247–2269. DOI: 10.1108/IJPPM-01-2021-0026

Burri, M. (2021). Towards a new treaty on digital trade. *Journal of World Trade*, *55*(1), 77–100. DOI: 10.54648/TRAD2021003

Burri, M., & Polanco, R. (2020). Digital trade provisions in preferential trade agreements: Introducing a new dataset. *Journal of International Economic Law*, *23*(1), 187–220. DOI: 10.1093/jiel/jgz044

Burstall, M. L., Reuben, B. G., & Reuben, A. J. (1999). Pricing and reimbursement regulation in Europe: An update on the industry perspective. *Drug Information Journal*, *33*(3), 669–688. DOI: 10.1177/009286159903300304

Bywalec, G. (2020). Dynamics and determinants of trade exchange between the European Union and India. *Optimum. Economic Studies*, *101*(3), 123–139.

Cairone, S., Hasan, S. W., Choo, K. H., Li, C. W., Zarra, T., Belgiorno, V., & Naddeo, V. (2024). Integrating artificial intelligence modeling and membrane technologies for advanced wastewater treatment: Research progress and future perspectives. *The Science of the Total Environment*, *944*, 173999. DOI: 10.1016/j.scitotenv.2024.173999

Cai, Y., Chen, W., & Zeng, X. (2025). The impact of the China-Australia free trade agreement on China's agricultural imports. *Frontiers in Sustainable Food Systems*, *9*, 1553373. DOI: 10.3389/fsufs.2025.1553373

Capoani, L. (2023). Review of the Gravity Model: Origins and Critical Analysis of its Theoretical Development. *SN Business & Economics*, *3*(5), 95. DOI: 10.1007/s43546-023-00461-0

Capoani, L. (2024). The Gravity Equation in International Trade: An Overview of the Introduction of Gravity to the Study of Economics and Its Systematic Barriers. *European Journal of the History of Economic Thought*, *31*(3), 487–520. DOI: 10.1080/09672567.2024.2329064

Carbonara, N., & Pellegrino, R. (2020). The role of public private partnerships in fostering innovation. *Construction Management and Economics*, *38*(2), 140–156. DOI: 10.1080/01446193.2019.1610184

Carbone, M. (2008). Mission impossible: The European Union and policy coherence for development. *European integration, 30*(3), 323-342.

Cardamone, P., Pupo, V., & Ricotta, F. (2015). University Technology Transfer and Manufacturing Innovation: The Case of I taly. *The Review of Policy Research*, *32*(3), 297–322. DOI: 10.1111/ropr.12125

Carll, E. (2021). An Afghanistan at peace could connect South and Central Asia. *Atlantic Council — New Atlanticist.* https://www.atlanticcouncil.org/blogs/new-atlanticist/an-afghanistan-at-peace-could-connect-south-and-central-asia/

Carnegie Endowment for International Peace. (2025). *BRICS expansion and the future of world order: Perspectives from member states, partners, and aspirants.* https://carnegieendowment.org/research/2025/03/brics-expansion-and-the-future-of-world-order-perspectives-from-member-states-partners-and-aspirants

Caspian Policy Center. (2023). China, Russia, and great power politics in Afghanistan and Central Asia. https://www.caspianpolicy.org/research/guest-contributions/china-russia-and-great-power-politics-in-afghanistan-and-central-asia

Caspian Policy Center. (2024). China, Russia, and great power politics in Afghanistan and Central Asia. https://www.caspianpolicy.org/research/central-asia/china-russia-and-great-power-politics-in-afghanistan-and-central-asia

Center for Preventive Action. (2025). Instability in Afghanistan. Council on Foreign Relations. https://www.cfr.org/global-conflict-tracker/conflict/war-afghanistan

Center for Strategic and International Studies [CSIS]. (2024). How sanctions have reshaped Russia's future. https://www.csis.org/analysis/how-sanctions-have-reshaped-russias-future

CEPII. (*Centre d'Informations Internationales) GeoDist* Database. Notes on CEPII's distances measures: The GeoDist database Thierry Mayer & Soledad Zignago (2011). No 2011- 25 December DOCUMENT DE TRAVAIL. Available at: https://www.cepii.fr/cepii/en/bdd_modele/bdd_modele_item.asp?id=6

Cezarino, L. O., Liboni, L. B., Oliveira Stefanelli, N., Oliveira, B. G., & Stocco, L. C. (2021). Diving into emerging economies bottleneck: Industry 4.0 and implications for circular economy. *Management Decision*, *59*(8), 1841–1862. DOI: 10.1108/MD-10-2018-1084

Chakraborty, D., & Dey, O. (2024). Non-tariff Barriers and Trade Flows. In *Influence of WTO and Global Dynamics on Trade Flows: A Machine-Generated Literature Overview* (pp. 245–287). Springer Nature Singapore. DOI: 10.1007/978-981-99-7375-0_3

Chanda, R. (2015). Challenges to regional services integration in South Asia. *South Asia Economic Journal*, *16*(2, suppl), 19S–38S. DOI: 10.1177/1391561415594730

Chander, A., & Lê, U. P. (2014). Data nationalism. *Emory Law Journal*, *64*, 677.

Charles, L., Xia, S., & Coutts, A. P. (2022). *Digitalization and employment: A review*. International Labor Organization.

Chaturvedi, P., Hussain, Z., & Nag, B. (2015). SAARC geopolitics and trade: Missing intra-regional connectivity a hindrance to further economic integration. *South Asian Survey*, *22*(1), 78–106. DOI: 10.1177/0971523117708963

Chatzilazarou, L. A., & Dadakas, D. (2024). Trade potential in European Union manufacturing. *Journal of Economic Studies (Glasgow, Scotland)*, *51*(5), 1144–1163. DOI: 10.1108/JES-06-2023-0292

Chen, M. X., & Mattoo, A. (2008). Regionalism in standards: Good or bad for trade? *The Canadian Journal of Economics. Revue Canadienne d'Economique*, *41*(3), 838–863. DOI: 10.1111/j.1540-5982.2008.00488.x

Chen, Q., & Shen, Y. (2024). Deep trade agreements and services trade: An analysis based on service trade provisions. *World Economy*, *47*(7), 2909–2946. DOI: 10.1111/twec.13563

Chen, Y., & Gao, Y. (2022). Comparative analysis of digital trade development strategies and governance approaches. *Journal of Digital Economy*, *1*(3), 227–238. DOI: 10.1016/j.jdec.2023.02.001

Chen, Y., Ma, Q., & Tao, R. (2024). Addressing the fixed effects in gravity model based on higher-order origin destination pairs. *International Journal of Geographical Information Science*. Advance online publication. DOI: 10.1080/13658816.2024.2343763

Chen, Y., Yao, Z., & Zhong, K. (2022). Do environmental regulations of carbon emissions and air pollution foster green technology innovation: Evidence from China's prefecture-level cities. [HTML]. *Journal of Cleaner Production*, *350*, 131537. Advance online publication. DOI: 10.1016/j.jclepro.2022.131537

Chernozhukov, V., Fernández-Val, I., & Weidner, M. (2024). Network and Panel Quantile Effects via Distribution Regression. *Journal of Econometrics*, *240*(2), 105009. DOI: 10.1016/j.jeconom.2020.08.009

Chetty, K., Qigui, L., Gcora, N., Josie, J., Wenwei, L., & Fang, C. (2018). Bridging the digital divide: Measuring digital literacy. *Economics*, *12*(1), 20180023. DOI: 10.5018/economics-ejournal.ja.2018-23

Chopra, R., Magazzino, C., Shah, M. I., Sharma, G. D., Rao, A., & Shahzad, U. (2022). The role of renewable energy and natural resources for sustainable agriculture in ASEAN countries: Do carbon emissions and deforestation affect agriculture productivity? *Resources Policy*, *76*, 102578. DOI: 10.1016/j.resourpol.2022.102578

Choudhary, P., Khade, M., Savant, S., Musale, A., Chelliah, M. S., & Dasgupta, S. (2021). Empowering blue economy: From underrated ecosystem to sustainable industry. *Journal of Environmental Management*, *291*, 112697. DOI: 10.1016/j.jenvman.2021.112697

Choudhury, R., & Nayak, D. (2019). Relationship between Trade and Investment in the SAARC Region. *World Scientific Book Chapters*, 99-135.

Christen, E., Meyer, B., Oberhofer, H., Hinz, J., Kamin, K., & Wanner, J. (2022). *The Brussels effect 2.0: How the EU sets global standards with its trade policy* (No. 2022-07). FIW-Research Reports.

Clarke, G. R., & Wallsten, S. J. (2006). Has the internet increased trade? Developed and developing country evidence. *Economic Inquiry*, *44*(3), 465–484. DOI: 10.1093/ei/cbj026

Coenen, J., Bager, S., Meyfroidt, P., Newig, J., & Challies, E. (2021). Environmental governance of China's belt and road initiative. Environmental Policy and Governance, 31(1), 3-17. wiley.comDOI: 10.1002/eet.1901

Cole, M. A., & Elliott, R. J. (2003). Determining the trade–environment composition effect: The role of capital, labor and environmental regulations. *Journal of Environmental Economics and Management, 46*(3), 363–383. DOI: 10.1016/S0095-0696(03)00021-4

Colen, L., Persyn, D., & Guariso, A. (2016). Bilateral investment treaties and FDI: Does the sector matter? *World Development, 83*, 193–206. DOI: 10.1016/j.worlddev.2016.01.020

Collier, P., & Venables, A. J. (2007). Rethinking trade preferences: How Africa can diversify its exports. *World Economy, 30*(8), 1326–1345. DOI: 10.1111/j.1467-9701.2007.01042.x

Collier, S. J. (2009). Topologies of power: Foucault's analysis of political government beyond "governmentality.". *Theory, Culture & Society, 26*(6), 78–108. DOI: 10.1177/0263276409347694

Congressional Research Service. (2018). *China-India great power competition in the Indian Ocean region: Issues for Congress* (CRS Report R45194). https://www.crs.gov/

Contractor, F. J. (2017a). What is globalization? How to measure it and why many oppose it (part 1). GlobalBusiness.blog, May 8. Accessed from: https://globalbusiness.blog/2017/05/08/what-is-globalization-part-1-how-to-measure-it-and-why-many-oppose-it/.

Contractor, F. J. (2017b). What is Globalization Part 2: Global Leadership in an Era of Growing Nationalism, Protectionism, and Anti-Globalization (Part 1 & Part 2), accessed from: https://globalbusiness.blog/2017/06/02/global-leadership-in-an-era-of-growing-nationalism-protectionism-and-anti-globalization-part-2

Contractor, F. J., & Lorange, P. (2002). The growth of alliances in the knowledge-based economy. *International Business Review, 11*(4), 485–502. DOI: 10.1016/S0969-5931(02)00021-5

Council of the European Union. (2024). Sanctions against Russia explained. https://www.consilium.europa.eu/en/policies/sanctions-against-russia-explained

Coxhead, I., & Jayasuriya, S. (2003). The open economy and the environment: development, trade and resources in Asia. In *The Open Economy and the Environment*. Edward Elgar Publishing. DOI: 10.4337/9781781952856.00009

Crespo, N., & Fontoura, M. (2004). Intra-industry Trade by Types: What Can We Learn from Portuguese data? *Review of World Economics, 140*(1), 53–79. DOI: 10.1007/BF02659710

Cross-border Paperless Trade in Asia and the Pacific [UNESCAP]. (2014). *ECO: Rail-based intermodal transport corridors.* https://www.unescap.org/sites/default/files/ECO.pdf

Culas, R. J., & Timsina, K. P. (2019). Impacts of China-Australia free trade agreement on Australian agriproducts trade. *Australasian Agribusiness Review*, *24*(6), 128–148.

CUTS International. CPR, AF. (2016). Non-Tariff Measures to Food Trade in India: A Case Study of Selected Ports. CUTS International, Centre for Policy Research, Asia Foundation. *Accessed from* https://cprindia.org/wp-content/uploads/2021/12/NTB-report.pdf

Dağdemir, E. U. (2014). From Economic Protectorate to the Transatlantic Trade and Investment Partnership: A New-Age Relationship between the European Union and the United States? *Marmara Üniversitesi Avrupa Araştırmaları Enstitüsü Avrupa Araştırmaları Dergisi*, *22*(1), 31–63.

Dasgupta, A., & Maskay, N. M. (2003). Financial Policy Cooperation in SAARC: A First Step Towards Greater Monetary Integration in South Asia. *South Asia Economic Journal*, *4*(1), 133–143. DOI: 10.1177/139156140300400109

Daya, Y., Ranoto, T., & Letsoalo, M. A. (2006). Intra-Africa agricultural trade: A South African perspective. *Acta Commercii*, *6*(1), 99–113. DOI: 10.4102/ac.v6i1.99

de Oliveira, S. E. C., Visentin, J. C., Pavani, B. F., Branco, P. D., de Maria, M., & Loyola, R. (2024). The European Union-Mercosur Free Trade Agreement as a tool for environmentally sustainable land use governance. *Environmental Science & Policy*, *161*, 103875. DOI: 10.1016/j.envsci.2024.103875

de Souza, G., Gaetani, R., & Mestieri, M. (2025). More Trade, Less Diffusion: Technology Transfers and the Dynamic Effects of Import Liberalization.

Debrah, Y. A., Olabode, O. E., Olan, E., & Nyuur, R. B. (2024). The African continental free trade area (AfCFTA): Taking stock and looking ahead for international business research. *Journal of International Management*, *30*(2), 101120. Advance online publication. DOI: 10.1016/j.intman.2024.101120

Del Vecchio, P., Passiante, G., Barberio, G., & Innella, C. (2021). Digital innovation ecosystems for circular economy: The case of ICESP, the Italian circular economy stakeholder platform. *International Journal on Management of Innovation & Technology*, *18*(01), 2050053. DOI: 10.1142/S0219877020500534

Dembatapitiya, P., & Weerahewa, J. (2015). Effects of regional trading agreements on South Asian trade: A gravity model analysis. *Tropical Agricultural Research, 26*(3).

Dennis, A. (2006). The impact of regional trade agreements and trade facilitation in the Middle East and North Africa region. *World Bank Policy Research Working Paper*, (3837). *Accessed from* https://papers.ssrn.com/sol3/Delivery.cfm?abstractid =922963

De, P. (2011). Why is trade at borders a costly affair in South Asia? An empirical investigation. *Contemporary South Asia*, *19*(4), 441–464. DOI: 10.1080/09584935.2011.602666

De, P., & Iyengar, K. (2014). *Developing economic corridors in South Asia. Mandaluyong City, Philippines*. Asian Development Bank.

Derksen, L., Michaud-Leclerc, C., & Souza, P. C. (2022). Restricted access: How the internet can be used to promote reading and learning. *Journal of Development Economics*, *155*, 102810. DOI: 10.1016/j.jdeveco.2021.102810

Devadoss, S. (2006). Why do developing countries resist global trade agreements? *The Journal of International Trade & Economic Development*, *15*(2), 191–208. DOI: 10.1080/09638190600690895

Dhingra, S., Freeman, R., & Huang, H. (2023). The impact of non-tariff barriers on trade and welfare. Economica. wiley.comDOI: 10.1111/ecca.12450

Diao, X., Somwaru, A., & Roe, T. (2001). A global analysis of agricultural reform in WTO member countries.

Díaz-Bonilla, E., Robinson, S., Thomas, M., & Yanoma, Y. (2002). WTO, agriculture, and developing countries: a survey of issues. *Accessed from* https://cgspace .cgiar.org/bitstreams/e98499e4-3d3b-4013-8ca9-eb8748c8170a/download

Dihel, N., & Walkenhorst, P. (2002). European Union trade and non-tariff measures.

Dilek, Ş. (2024). Rising Regionalization: An Assessment of Regional Trade Agreements. *Avrasya Etüdleri*, (63), 131–158.

Dimnwobi, S. K., Okere, K. I., Onuoha, F. C., Uzoechina, B. I., Ekesiobi, C., & Nwokoye, E. S. (2023). Energizing environmental sustainability in Sub-Saharan Africa: the role of governance quality in mitigating the environmental impact of energy poverty. Environmental Science and Pollution Research, 30(45), 101761-101781. https://hdl.handle.net/10419/298246 econstor.eu

Disdier, A. C., Fontagné, L., & Mimouni, M. (2015). Tariff Liberalization and Trade Integration of Emerging Countries. *Review of International Economics*, *23*(5), 946–971. DOI: 10.1111/roie.12198

Dixit, D. (2014). Agricultural value chains and food security. *Journal of World Trade, 48*(5).

Doanh, N. K., & Heo, Y. (2018). Horizontal Intra-industry Trade in Korea: A Dynamic Panel Data Analysis. *Journal of International Logistics and Trade, 16*(1), 1–10. DOI: 10.24006/jilt.2018.16.1.1

Dür, A. (2025). EU trade agreements and external differentiation: A large language model approach. *West European Politics, 48*(5), 1059–1085. DOI: 10.1080/01402382.2024.2425549

Duval, Y., & Mengjing, K. (2017). *Digital trade facilitation: Paperless trade in regional trade agreements* (No. 747). ADBI Working Paper.

Du, Y., Xu, J., & Yuan, X. (2024). The development relationship between circular economy and advanced digital technology: Based on an innovative literature review method. *Environmental Technology Reviews, 13*(1), 614–638. DOI: 10.1080/21622515.2024.2406988

Earl-Slater, A. (1997). Recent legal and policy developments affecting the EU pharmaceutical business environment. *European Business Review, 97*(6), 267–278. DOI: 10.1108/09555349710189978

Eba Nguema, I., & Assoumou Ella, G. (2014). Trade liberalization and food security: For a new green revolution in Africa. *Accessed from* https://ageconsearch.umn.edu/record/332519/files/7160.pdf

Economic and Social Commission for Asia and the Pacific [ESCAP]. (2018). Unlocking the Potential of Regional Economic Cooperation and Integration in South Asia Potential, Challenges and the Way Forward. ESCAP, Bangkok, Thailand.

Economic Cooperation Organization [ECO]. (2020). ECO—KTAI Road Corridor Test Run Kicks Off from Iran. https://eco.int/eco-ktai-road-corridor-test-run-kicks-off-from-iran

Egan, M. (2014). *Single markets: Economic integration in Europe and the United States*. OUP Oxford.

Egger, P. H., Li, J., & Ouyang, J. (2024). Taking Grubel and Lloyd to Dance in the City: Domestic Intra-Industry Trade in China. *Economics Letters, 244*, 111925. DOI: 10.1016/j.econlet.2024.111925

Egger, P. H., & Staub, K. E. (2016). GLM Estimation of Trade Gravity Models with Fixed Effects. *Empirical Economics, 50*(1), 137–175. DOI: 10.1007/s00181-015-0935-x

Ekanayake, R., & Perera, N. (2015). Stimulating Intra-Regional Investment in SAARC: Is a Regional Investment Agreement the Way Forward? *South Asia Economic Journal*, *16*(2, suppl), 75S–101S. DOI: 10.1177/1391561415594731

Ekpemuaka, E., Odunlade, O. R., & Maiyaki, S. F. (2025). Resilience in Africa's Transition to a Sustainable Digital and Blue Economy: Policy and Regulatory Framework in Nigeria. In *Securing Sustainable Futures Through Blue and Green Economies* (pp. 149–172). IGI Global Scientific Publishing. DOI: 10.4018/979-8-3693-7893-9.ch006

Elliot, K. A. (2018). *The WTO and Regional/Bilateral Trade Agreements. The Handbook of International Trade Agreements. Edn. (1)*. Routledge.

Elliott, K. A. (2018). The WTO and regional/bilateral trade agreements. In *Handbook of International Trade Agreements* (pp. 17–28). Routledge. DOI: 10.4324/9781351046954-3

Emon, M. M. H., Khan, T., Rahman, M. A., Hamid, A. B. A., & Yaakub, N. I. (2025). GreenTech revolution: Navigating challenges and seizing opportunities. In *AI and green technology applications in society* (pp. 63–90). IGI Global Scientific Publishing. [HTML], DOI: 10.4018/979-8-3693-9879-1.ch003

Enchelmaier, S. (2019). The Foundations of the Internal Market: Free Trade Area and Customs Union under Articles 28-31 TFEU. *Erasmus L. Rev.*, *12*(3), 219–228. DOI: 10.5553/ELR.000138

Erten, B., & Leight, J. (2021). Exporting out of agriculture: The impact of WTO accession on structural transformation in China. *The Review of Economics and Statistics*, *103*(2), 364–380. DOI: 10.1162/rest_a_00852

Erum, N., Hussain, S., & Yousaf, A. (2016). Foreign direct investment and economic growth in SAARC countries. *The Journal of Asian Finance, Economics and Business*, *3*(4), 57–66. DOI: 10.13106/jafeb.2016.vol3.no4.57

European External Action Service. (2021). South Asian Association for Regional Cooperation (SAARC). https://www.eeas.europa.eu/eeas/south-asian-association-regional-cooperation-saarc_en

European Union Institute for Security Studies [EUISS]. (2023). *Annual report 2023* (EUISS-DIR-CA(2024)1). https://www.iss.europa.eu/sites/default/files/Annual_report_2023.pdf

European Union. (2025). Trade and Economic Security. https://policy.trade.ec.europa.eu/eu-trade-relationships-country-and-region/negotiations-and-agreements_en

Eurostat (2022). A growing population until 2020. Accessed from https://ec.europa.eu/eurostat/cache/digpub/demography_2022/bloc-1a.html?lang=en

Eurostat (2023). International trade in goods by partner. https://ec.europa.eu/eurostat/statistics-explained/index.php?title=International_trade_in_goods_by_partner

Eurostat. (2024). Russia-EU — international trade of main product groups. European Commission. https://ec.europa.eu/eurostat/statistics-explained/index.php?title=Russia-EU_-_international_trade_of_main_product_groups&oldid=558089

Evangelista, R., Guerrieri, P., & Meliciani, V. (2014). The economic impact of digital technologies in Europe. *Economics of Innovation and New Technology*, *23*(8), 802–824. DOI: 10.1080/10438599.2014.918438

Eyo-Udo, N. L., Apeh, C. E., Bristol-Alagbariya, B., Udeh, C. A., & Ewim, C. P. M. (2025). International trade law in the modern world: A review of evolving practices and agreements. *International Journal of Multidisciplinary Research and Growth Evaluation.*

Faludi, J. (2023). How to create social value through digital social innovation? Unlocking the potential of the social value creation of digital start-ups. *Journal of Social Entrepreneurship*, *14*(1), 73–90. DOI: 10.1080/19420676.2020.1823871

Fang, M. M. & Zhou, W. (2022). Greening the road: China's low-carbon energy transition and international trade regulation. Leiden Journal of International Law. cambridge.orgDOI: 10.1017/S0922156521000704

Fang, X., Zhang, Y., Yang, J., & Zhan, G. (2024). An evaluation of marine economy sustainable development and the ramifications of digital technologies in China coastal regions. *Economic Analysis and Policy*, *82*, 554–570. DOI: 10.1016/j.eap.2024.03.022

Farasoo [EFSAS]. (2019). *The Chabahar Port: A potential game changer for Afghanistan.* https://www.efsas.org/commentaries/the-chabahar-port-a-potential-game-changer-for-afghanistan/

Farasoo, A. (2016). Afghanistan's quest for regional cooperation. *Fair Observer — Central & South Asia.* https://www.fairobserver.com/region/central_south_asia/afghanistan-pakistan-south-asia-economy-terrorism-news-67132/

Fatimah, Y. A., Govindan, K., Murniningsih, R., & Setiawan, A. (2020). Industry 4.0 based sustainable circular economy approach for smart waste management system to achieve sustainable development goals: A case study of Indonesia. *Journal of Cleaner Production*, *269*, 122263. DOI: 10.1016/j.jclepro.2020.122263

Faustino, H. C., & Leitão, N. C. (2007). Intra-Industry-Trade: A Static and Dynamic Panel Data Analysis. *International Advances in Economic Research, 13*(3), 313–333. DOI: 10.1007/s11294-007-9097-8

Faustino, H. C., & Leitão, N. C. (2011). Fragmentation in the Automobile Manufacturing Industry: Evidence from Portugal. *Journal of Economic Studies (Glasgow, Scotland), 38*(3), 287–300. DOI: 10.1108/01443581111152409

Faye, M. L., Mcarthur, J., Sachs, J. D., & Snow, T. (2004). The Challenges Facing Landlocked Developing Countries. *Journal of Human Development, 5*(1), 31–68. DOI: 10.1080/14649880310001660201

Fazl-e-Haider, S. (2023). *Revival of TAPI pipeline project brings serious geopolitical implications for Russia. Eurasia Daily Monitor, 20(91)*. The Jamestown Foundation.

Fefer, R. F., Akhtar, S. I., & Morrison, W. M. (2017). Digital trade and US trade policy. *Current Politics and Economics of the United States, Canada and Mexico, 19*(1), 1–52.

Fernandes, A., & Forte, R. (2022). The Impact of Economic Diplomacy on Exports: The Portuguese Case. *International Journal (Toronto, Ont.), 77*(2), 216–247. DOI: 10.1177/00207020221135382

Ferrari, A. (2021). Leveraging AI-Driven Techniques for Real-Time Data Integration and Fusion in Modern Enterprise Data Warehousing Systems. *Journal of Computational Innovation, 1*(1).

Ferreira, C. R. C., Gomide, M. R., & Firme, V. D. A. C. (2025). The impacts of trade freedom on food insecurity from countries with different profiles: An empirical analysis. *Revista de Economia Política, 45*(4), e253664. DOI: 10.1590/0101-31572025-3664

Fertő, I., Kheyirkhabarli, M., & Sass, M. (2022). Gravity Models with TiVA Data: Do They Bring New Results? *Applied Economics Letters, 31*(8), 702–705. DOI: 10.1080/13504851.2022.2145010

Feruni, N., & Hysa, E. (2020). Free Trade and Gravity Model: Albania as Part of Central European Free Trade Agreement (CEFTA). In Christiansen, B., & Shuwaikh, F. (Eds.), *Theoretical and Applied Mathematics in International Business* (pp. 60–90). IGI Global Scientific Publishing., DOI: 10.4018/978-1-5225-8458-2.ch004

Fidrmuc, J. (2005). Trade Structure during Accession to the EU. *Post-Communist Economies, 17*(2), 225–234. DOI: 10.1080/14631370500104943

Foletti, L., & Shingal, A. (2014). *Trade effects of MRL harmonization in the EU* (No. 720).

France24. (2024). World Bank approves $300 mn in new funding for Afghanistan. https://www.france24.com/en/live-news/20240215-world-bank-approves-300-mn-in-new-funding-for-afghanistan

Freund, C., & Ornelas, E. (2010). Regional trade agreements. *Annual Review of Economics*, *2*(1), 139–166. DOI: 10.1146/annurev.economics.102308.124455

Fry, I. (2008). Reducing emissions from deforestation and forest degradation: Opportunities and pitfalls in developing a new legal regime. *Review of European Community & International Environmental Law*, *17*(2), 166–182. DOI: 10.1111/j.1467-9388.2008.00597.x

Fukui, S. (2019). Economic development in developing countries and the future of trade agreements. *Japanese Journal of Agricultural Economics*, *21*(0), 50–55. DOI: 10.18480/jjae.21.0_50

Fusacchia, I., Balié, J., & Salvatici, L. (2022). The AfCFTA impact on agricultural and food trade: A value added perspective. *European Review of Agriculture Economics*, *49*(1), 237–284. DOI: 10.1093/erae/jbab046

Gamage, R. N. (2016). Blue economy in Southeast Asia: Oceans as the new frontier of economic development. *Maritime Affairs*, *12*(2), 1–15. DOI: 10.1080/09733159.2016.1244361

Gandou, A., K., S. & Sönmez, A. (2023). The Role of Industrialization in Trade: A Panel Data Gravity Model Analysis on ECOWAS Countries (1995-2020*). Jass Studies-The Journal of Academic Social Science Studies*, 16(98), 395 414. DOI: 10.29228/JASSS.72786

Ganslandt, M., & Maskus, K. E. (2004). Parallel imports and the pricing of pharmaceutical products: Evidence from the European Union. *Journal of Health Economics*, *23*(5), 1035–1057. DOI: 10.1016/j.jhealeco.2004.03.005

Gao, H. (2018). Digital or trade? The contrasting approaches of China and US to digital trade. *Journal of International Economic Law*, *21*(2), 297–321. DOI: 10.1093/jiel/jgy015

Garattini, S., Natsis, Y., & Banzi, R. (2021). Pharmaceutical strategy for Europe: Reflections on public health-driven drug development, regulation, and policies. *Frontiers in Pharmacology*, *12*, 685604. DOI: 10.3389/fphar.2021.685604

Garlick, J. (2025). Beyond Central Asia: The ever-expanding influence of the Shanghai Cooperation Organization. *European Hub for Security Studies*. https://eh4s.eu/publication/beyond-central-asia-the-ever-expanding-influence-of-the-shanghai-cooperation-organization

Garnizova, E. (2018). *The new political economy of trade: understanding the treatment of non-tariff measures in European Union trade policy* (Doctoral dissertation, London School of Economics and Political Science).

Gastinger, M. (2023). EU Trade Agreements and European Integration. Routledge. *Accessed from* https://www.taylorfrancis.com/books/mono/10.4324/9781003342427/eu-trade-agreements-european-integration-markus-gastinger

Gaurav, K., & Bharti, N. (2019). Has trade improved from SAPTA to SAFTA? Evidence from the gravity model. *International Journal of Business and Globalisation, 23*(4), 532–548. DOI: 10.1504/IJBG.2019.104832

Geissdoerfer, M., Savaget, P., Bocken, N. M., & Hultink, E. J. (2017). The Circular Economy–A new sustainability paradigm? *Journal of Cleaner Production, 143*, 757–768. DOI: 10.1016/j.jclepro.2016.12.048

Geldner, T. (2024). Exchange Rates and Trade Balance Dynamics: A Quantile Regression Analysis. *Applied Economics*. Advance online publication. DOI: 10.1080/00036846.2024.2311067

Gereffi, G., Lim, H. C., & Lee, J. (2021). Trade policies, firm strategies, and adaptive reconfigurations of global value chains. *Journal of International Business Policy, 4*(4), 506–522. DOI: 10.1057/s42214-021-00102-z

Ghemawat, P., & Altman, S. A. (2016). *DHL Global Connectedness Index 2016: The State of Globalization in an Age of Ambiguity*. Deutsche Post DHL Group.

Gill, D. M. (2020). Challenges to Regional Cooperation in South Asia: An Overview. *Journal of International Affairs, 3*(1), 42–51. DOI: 10.3126/joia.v3i1.29081

Giri, P., Karinje, P., & Verma, R., JSSATE, N., & Noida, I. J. (2015). A study and analysis of challenges, achievements and hurdles faced by SAARC nations in trade integration and growth. *International Journal of Engineering Technology. Management and Applied Sciences, 3*(1), 204–215.

Glass, A., Saggi, K., Dutt, A., & Ros, J. (2008). The role of foreign direct investment in international technology transfer. *International handbook of development economics, 2*, 137-149.

Global Business Outlook. (2025, June 27). Why BRICS+ backs local currency trade? https://globalbusinessoutlook.com/magazine/banking-and-finance-magazine/why-brics-backs-local-currency-trade/

Gnimpieba, Z. D. R., Nait-Sidi-Moh, A., Durand, D., & Fortin, J. (2015). Using Internet of Things technologies for a collaborative supply chain: Application to tracking of pallets and containers. *Procedia Computer Science*, *56*, 550–557. DOI: 10.1016/j.procs.2015.07.251

Gohel, S. M. (2010). Iran's ambiguous role in Afghanistan. *CTC Sentinel, 3*(3). https://ctc.westpoint.edu/irans-ambiguous-role-in-afghanistan/

Goldar, B., Chawla, I., & Behera, S. R. (2020). Trade liberalization and productivity of Indian manufacturing firms. *Indian Growth and Development Review*, *13*(1), 73–98. DOI: 10.1108/IGDR-10-2018-0108

González, J. L., & Ferencz, J. (2018). Digital trade and market openness.

Gonzalez, C. G. (2002). Institutionalizing inequality: The WTO Agreement on Agriculture, food security, and developing countries. *Colum. J. Envtl. L.*, *27*, 433.

Gormley, D. (2009). Getting more from international partnerships. Naval Postgraduate School Center for Contemporary Conflict. https://www.academia.edu/12734832/Getting_More_from_International_Partnerships

Gormley, L. W. (2009). *EU law of free movement of goods and customs union*. Oxford university press. DOI: 10.1093/oso/9780199229000.001.0001

Götz, M. (2020). Attracting foreign direct investment in the era of digitally reshaped international production. The primer on the role of the investment policy and clusters–the case of Poland. *Journal of East-West Business*, *26*(2), 131–160. DOI: 10.1080/10669868.2019.1692985

Gould, D. (1994). Immigrant Links to The Home Country: Empirical Implications for U.S. Bilateral Trade Flows. *The Review of Economics and Statistics*, *76*(2), 302–316. DOI: 10.2307/2109884

Gouveia, S., Rebelo, J., & Lourenço-Gomes, L. (2018). Port Wine Exports: A Gravity Model Approach. *International Journal of Wine Business Research*, *30*(2), 218–242. DOI: 10.1108/IJWBR-02-2017-0008

Greaney, T. M., & Kiyota, K. (2020). The Gravity Model and Trade in Intermediate Inputs. *World Economy*, *43*(8), 2034–2049. DOI: 10.1111/twec.12947

Greenaway, D., Hine, R., & Milner, C. (1995). Vertical and horizontal intra-industry trade: A Cross Industry Analysis for the United Kingdom. *Economic Journal (London), 105*(433), 1505–1518. DOI: 10.2307/2235113

Grossman, G. M. (2016). The Purpose of Trade Agreements. Chapter 7. *Handbook of Commercial Policy*, 1(Part-A), 379-434. DOI: 10.3386/w22070

Grubel, H. G., & Lloyd, P. J. (1975). *Intra-Industry Trade: The Theory and Measurement of International Trade in Differentiated Products*. Macmillan Press.

Gu, R., Guo, J., Huang, Y., & Wu, X. (2023). Impact of the EU carbon border adjustment mechanism on economic growth and resources supply in the BASIC countries. [HTML]. *Resources Policy, 85*, 104034. Advance online publication. DOI: 10.1016/j.resourpol.2023.104034

Haastrup, T., Mah, L., & Duggan, N. (Eds.). (2020). *The Routledge handbook of EU-Africa relations*. Routledge. DOI: 10.4324/9781315170916

Häberli, C. (2012). Do WTO rules improve or impair the right to food? In *Research Handbook on the WTO Agriculture Agreement*. Edward Elgar Publishing. DOI: 10.4337/9781781001233.00009

Hagelüken, C., & Goldmann, D. (2022). Recycling and circular economy—Towards a closed loop for metals in emerging clean technologies. *Mineral Economics, 35*(3), 539–562. DOI: 10.1007/s13563-022-00319-1

Hailu, M. B. (2010, July). Food Security and Agricultural Trade Liberalization. In *Society of International Economic Law (SIEL), Second Biennial Global Conference, University of Barcelona*.

Hamad, S., Lai, F. W., Shad, M. K., Khatib, S. F., & Ali, S. E. A. (2023). Assessing the implementation of sustainable development goals: Does integrated reporting matter? *Sustainability Accounting. Management and Policy Journal, 14*(1), 49–74.

Hans, V., & Prasanna, G. (2023). International Trade in Agriculture, Terms of Trade and WTO With Reference to India. *International Trade in Agriculture, Terms of Trade and WTO With Reference to India (July 11, 2023)*.

Hans, V. B. (2024). International Trade in Agriculture, Terms of Trade, and the World Trade Organization with Reference to India. *Acta Scientific Agriculture, 8*(2), 3–15. https://actascientific.com/ASAG/pdf/ASAG-08-1339.pdf. DOI: 10.31080/ASAG.2024.08.1339

Haq, M., Ahmad, I., & Jabeen, A. (2021). Financial sector development, trade openness and economic growth nexus: evidence from SAARC countries. *Forman Journal of Economic Studies, 17*(1).

Hart, J., Miljkovic, D., & Shaik, S. (2015). The impact of trade openness on technical efficiency in the agricultural sector of the European Union. *Applied Economics, 47*(12), 1230–1247. DOI: 10.1080/00036846.2014.993134

Harvard Kennedy School. (2025). *Development diplomacy in action: The CASA-1000 electricity grid* (HKS Case Program). https://case.hks.harvard.edu/development-diplomacy-in-action-the-casa-1000-electricity-grid/

Hasan, M. D. (2021). The relationship between trade openness and economic growth in Bangladesh: An empirical analysis. *Journal of Economic Studies (Glasgow, Scotland), 48*(3), 456–472.

Hasibul, I. R., & John, K. (2017). Impact of foreign direct investment on economic growth of the SAARC countries. *Journal of Economics and Sustainable Development, 8*, 58–66.

Hassan, M. U., Rana, A. T., Khan, M., & Gillani, S. (2024). Trade agreements and CO2 emissions in Asian countries: Accounting for institutional heterogeneity. [HTML]. *Environmental Science and Pollution Research International, 31*(6), 9197–9217. DOI: 10.1007/s11356-023-31684-1 PMID: 38191733

Hayakawa, K., & Yoshimi, T. (2023). Tariff Rates in Gravity. *The Journal of International Trade & Economic Development, 33*(8), 1477–1494. DOI: 10.1080/09638199.2023.2277779

Hayes, C. (2025). India-Afghanistan thaw: A geopolitical pivot to regional trade dominance. *A Invest.* https://www.ainvest.com/news/india-afghanistan-thaw-geopolitical-pivot-regional-trade-dominance-2505/

Hecker, P. (2019). EU TRADE LAW AND PHARMACEUTICALS. In *EU Law of Competition and Trade in the Pharmaceutical Sector* (pp. 377–404). Edward Elgar Publishing. DOI: 10.4337/9781785362613.00018

Heckscher, E., & Ohlin, B. (1933). *International and Inter-Regional Trade*. Harvard University Press.

Hegedüs, Z., & Kiss, J. (2014). The impact of ten years of European Union membership on Hungarian agricultural trade. *Studies in Agricultural Economics (Budapest), 116*(2), 87–94. DOI: 10.7896/j.1407

Herman, P. R., & Oliver, S. (2023). Trade, policy, and economic development in the digital economy. *Journal of Development Economics, 164*, 103135. DOI: 10.1016/j.jdeveco.2023.103135

Hertel, T. W., & Mirza, T. (2009). The role of trade facilitation in South Asian economic integration. *Study on intraregional trade and investment in South Asia*, 12-39.

Heyl, K., Ekardt, F., Roos, P., Stubenrauch, J., & Garske, B. (2021). Free trade, environment, agriculture, and plurilateral treaties: the ambivalent example of Mercosur, CETA, and the EU–Vietnam free trade agreement. Sustainability. mdpi.comDOI: 10.3390/su13063153

Hirantha, S. W. (2004). *From SAPTA to SAFTA: Gravity analysis of South Asian free trade. European Trade Study Group*. ETSG.

Hjort, J., & Poulsen, J. (2019). The arrival of fast internet and employment in Africa. *The American Economic Review, 109*(3), 1032–1079. DOI: 10.1257/aer.20161385

Hladnik, A. (2022). *Comparative Analysis of Legal and Economic Aspects of the EU's Free Trade Agreements with Selected Asian Economies* (Master's thesis, ISCTE-Instituto Universitario de Lisboa (Portugal)).

Hndi, B. M., Maitah, M., & Mustofa, J. (2016). Trade impacts of selected free trade agreements on agriculture: The case of selected North African countries. *AGRIS On-Line Papers in Economics and Informatics, 8*(3), 39–50. DOI: 10.7160/aol.2016.080304

Hobbs, J. E. (2015). A protectionist bargain?: Agriculture in the European Union—Canada Trade Agreement. *Journal of World Trade, 49*(3), 437–456. DOI: 10.54648/TRAD2015018

Hodo, M. (2014). The impact of trade agreements on agriculture sector, import and export: Albanian case. *Journal of Educational and Social Research, 4*(4), 421–425. DOI: 10.5901/jesr.2014.v4n4p421

Hoffmeister, F. (2015). The European Union as an international trade negotiator. In *The European Union as a diplomatic actor* (pp. 138–154). Palgrave Macmillan UK. DOI: 10.1057/9781137356857_9

Hojnik, J., Ruzzier, M., Ruzzier, M. K., Sučić, B., Soltwisch, B., & Rus, M. (2024). Review of EU projects with a focus on environmental quality: Innovation, eco-innovation, and circular-economy elements. *International Journal of Innovation Studies, 8*(1), 1–12. DOI: 10.1016/j.ijis.2023.10.001

Homewood, M. J., Homewood, M., & Smith, C. (2022). *EU Law Concentrate: Law Revision and Study Guide*. Oxford University Press. DOI: 10.1093/he/9780192865663.001.0001

Huang, Y., Haseeb, M., Usman, M., & Ozturk, I. (2022). … between ICT, renewable energy, economic complexity and ecological footprint: Is there any difference between E-7 (developing) and G-7 (developed) countries? [HTML]. *Technology in Society*, *68*, 101853. Advance online publication. DOI: 10.1016/j.techsoc.2021.101853

Huchet-Bourdon, M., Le Mouël, C., & Vijil, M. (2018). The relationship between trade openness and economic growth: Some new insights on the openness measurement issue. *World Economy*, *41*(1), 59–76. DOI: 10.1111/twec.12586

Hu, J., & Li, Q. (2024). From bits to green: Unraveling the digital economy's influence on natural resource efficiency. *Journal of Environmental Management*, *365*, 121203. DOI: 10.1016/j.jenvman.2024.121203

Hunter, M., & Ginn, P. (2025). Treasure hunt: Why is Afghanistan part of the great extractives race? *Global Initiative Against Transnational Organized Crime*. https://globalinitiative.net/analysis/why-is-afghanistan-part-of-the-great-extractives-race/

Hussain, F., & Nawaz, S. (2021). Geostrategic imperatives for Pakistan of Gwadar Port. *Asian Journal of Peacebuilding*, *9*(2), 427–441. DOI: 10.18588/202111.00a205

Hwang, H., Marjit, S., & Peng, C. H. (2016). Trade liberalization, technology transfer, and endogenous R&D. *Oxford Economic Papers*, *68*(4), 1107–1119. DOI: 10.1093/oep/gpw034

Hysa, E., Manta, O., Ailincă, A. G., Piciu, G. C., & Yue, X. G. (2024). Digitalization as an instrument in support of covering the circularity gap in the European Union economy. *Environment, Development and Sustainability*, *27*(11), 1–21. DOI: 10.1007/s10668-024-04772-6

Ibrahimi, S. Y. (2007). Afghans divided on regional integration. *Institute for War & Peace Reporting*. https://iwpr.net/global-voices/afghans-divided-regional-integrationiwpr.net

Iftekhar, A. & Cui, X. (2021). Blockchain-based traceability system that ensures food safety measures to protect consumer safety and COVID-19 free supply chains. Foods. mdpi.comDOI: 10.3390/foods10061289

Ijirshar, V. U. (2022). Trade facilitation and economic growth among middle-income countries. *arXiv*. https://arxiv.org/pdf/2204.11088

Indeo, F. (2025). TAPI gas pipeline: A paradigm of the Central Asian pragmatic approach toward Taliban. *Trends Research and Advisory.* https://trendsresearch.org/insight/tapi-gas-pipeline-a-paradigm-of-the-central-asian-pragmatic-approach-toward-taliban/

Institute for the Study of Ancient Cultures, University of Chicago. (n.d.). Afghanistan. https://isac.uchicago.edu/explore-oi/afghanistan

Intellinews. (2024). Pakistan-Afghanistan transit trade drops 59% in FY2023/24. https://www.intellinews.com/pakistan-afghanistan-transit-trade-drops-59-in-fy2023-24-340687/

International Crisis Group. (2022). Afghanistan's security challenges under the Taliban. https://www.crisisgroup.org/asia/south-asia/afghanistan/afghanistans-security-challenges-under-taliban

International Crisis Group. (2022). *The Taliban's neighborhood: Regional diplomacy in Afghanistan* (Report No. 337). https://www.crisisgroup.org/asia/south-asia/afghanistan/337-talibans-neighbourhood-regional-diplomacy-afghanistan

International Road Transport Union [IRU]. (2020). *Final report: Project for development of Kyrgyz-Tajikistan-Afghanistan-Iran (KTAI) road transport corridor.* https://www.iru.org/system/files/Final%20report%20-%20Project%20for%20development%20of%20Kyrgyz-Tajikistan-%20Afghanistan-Iran%20%28KTAI%29%20road%20transport%20corridor.pdf

International Road Transport Union [IRU]. (2020). *TIR helps open India—Iran—Afghanistan intermodal trade*. IRU. https://www.iru.org/news-resources/newsroom/tir-helps-open-india-iran-afghanistan-intermodal-trade

International Secretariat for CASA-1000. (n.d.). *About CASA-1000*. Retrieved June 12, 2025, from https://www.casa-1000.org/about-casa-1000/

Isard, W. (1969). Some Notes on the Linkage of the Ecologic and Economic Systems. *Papers in Regional Science*, *22*(1), 85–96. DOI: 10.1111/j.1435-5597.1969.tb01455.x

Ishikawa, K. (2021). The ASEAN Economic Community and ASEAN economic integration. Journal of Contemporary East Asia Studies. tandfonline.comDOI: 10.1080/24761028.2021.1891702

Islam, A.M. (2021b). Is Economic Globalization Under Strain? *Management and Economics Research Journal*, 7(1),1-4, Article ID 9900039. DOI: DOI: 10.18639/MERJ.2021.9900039

Islam, A. M. (2021a). Impact of Covid-19 Pandemic on Global Output, Employment and Prices-An Assessment. *Transnational Corporations Review, 13*(2), 189–201. DOI: 10.1080/19186444.2021.1936852

Jadhav, S., & Ghosh, I. (2024). Future Prospects of the Gravity Model of Trade: A Bibliometric Review (1993–2021). *Foreign Trade Review, 59*(1), 26–61. DOI: 10.1177/00157325221140154

Jadoon, A. (2025). Decoding Pakistan's 2024 airstrikes in Afghanistan. *War on the Rocks.* https://warontherocks.com/2025/03/decoding-pakistans-2024-airstrikes-in-afghanistan/

Jain, N., & Virk, S. (2024). Circular Economy in Agriculture. In *Impact of Women in Food and Agricultural Development* (pp. 79–88). IGI Global. DOI: 10.4018/979-8-3693-3037-1.ch005

Jámbor, A., Balogh, J., & Kucsera, P. (2016). Country and Industry Specific Determinants of Intra-Industry Agri-Food Trade in the Baltic Countries. *Agricultural Economic Czech*, 62, 2016 (6): 280–291. DOI: 10.17221/153/2015-AGRICECON

Jameel, A., Imran, M., Adam, N. A., Mirzaliev, S., Khidirov, M., & Yingying, G. (2025). Safeguarding tourism economies: Managing the financial and ecological challenges of oil spills on coastal destinations. [HTML]. *Marine Pollution Bulletin, 213*, 117668. DOI: 10.1016/j.marpolbul.2025.117668 PMID: 39970791

Jančiūtė, L. (2018). *EU politics and the making of the General Data Protection Regulation: Consociationalism, policy networks and institutionalism in the process of balancing actor interests* (Doctoral dissertation, University of Westminster).

Javaid, M., Haleem, A., Singh, R. P., Suman, R., & Gonzalez, E. S. (2022). Understanding the adoption of Industry 4.0 technologies in improving environmental sustainability. *Sustainable operations and computers, 3*, 203-217.

Javaid, F. (2024). Challenges and opportunities for regional connectivity: Afghanistan's role between Pakistan and the Central Asian region. In Pietrzak, P. (Ed.), *Analyzing global responses to contemporary regional conflicts* (pp. 275–297). IGI Global., DOI: 10.4018/979-8-3693-2837-8.ch013

Jensen, H. H., Andersen, M. M., Dao, A., Lind, M., Pandey, V., Bapuji, G., & Turos, A. (2021). Digitalisation in a maritime circular economy. In *Maritime Informatics: Additional Perspectives and Applications* (pp. 17–37). Springer International Publishing. DOI: 10.1007/978-3-030-72785-7_2

Jones, R., & Kierzkowski, H. (1990). The role of services in production and international trade: A theoretical framework. In Jones, R., & Krueger, A. (Eds.), *The political economy of international trade: Festschrift in Honor of Robert Baldwin*. Basil Blackwell.

Josephs, J. (2026- Jan). How tariff disruption will continue reshaping the global economy in 2026. https://www.bbc.com/news/articles/czejp3gep63o

Joshi, S. & Sharma, M. (2024). Intelligent algorithms and methodologies for low-carbon smart manufacturing: Review on past research, recent developments and future research directions. IET Collaborative Intelligent .... wiley.comDOI: 10.1049/cim2.12094

Jovanović, M. N. (2015). The economics of international integration. In *The Economics of International Integration* (2nd ed.). Edward Elgar Publishing.

Kaitila, V. (2010). *Quality-adjusted similarity of EU-countries' export structure* (No. 1227). ETLA Discussion Papers.

Kaleji, V. (2025). *The first phase of the TAPI gas pipeline: From Serhetabat, Turkmenistan to Herat*. Central Asia-Caucasus Analyst.

Kamberidou, I. (2020). "Distinguished" women entrepreneurs in the digital economy and the multitasking whirlpool. *Journal of Innovation and Entrepreneurship*, *9*(1), 3. DOI: 10.1186/s13731-020-0114-y

Kamidza, R. (2017). *From Antagonism to Re-engagement: Zimbabwes Trade Negotiations with the European Union, 2000-2016*. African Books Collective.

Kandel, D. I. (2021). Political and Economic Challenge of SAARC. *IOSR Journal of Humanities and Social Science*, *26*(1), 1–5.

Kandel, I. P. (2023). Political and Economic Relation in The SAARC Countries. *Researcher CAB. Journal of Research and Development (Srinagar)*, *2*(1), 129–143.

Kaplinsky, R., & Morris, M. (2019). Trade and industrialisation in Africa: SMEs, manufacturing and cluster dynamics. *Journal of African Trade*, *6*(1), 47–59. DOI: 10.2991/jat.k.190812.001

Karakara, A. A. W., & Osabuohien, E. (2020). ICT adoption, competition and innovation of informal firms in West Africa: A comparative study of Ghana and Nigeria. *Journal of Enterprising Communities: People and Places in the Global Economy*, *14*(3), 397–414. DOI: 10.1108/JEC-03-2020-0022

Karakas, S., Acar, A. Z., & Kirmizi, M. (2024). Maritime Sustainability: Navigating Complex Challenges and Ecological Footprints. In *Sustainable Development Seen Through the Lenses of Ethnoeconomics and the Circular Economy* (pp. 19–47). Springer Nature Switzerland. DOI: 10.1007/978-3-031-72676-7_2

Karakosta, O., & Petropoulou, D. (2022). The EU electricity market: Renewables targets, Tradable Green Certificates and electricity trade. *Energy Economics*, *111*, 106034. DOI: 10.1016/j.eneco.2022.106034

Kathuria, S. (2018). *A glass half full: The promise of regional trade in South Asia*. World Bank Publications. DOI: 10.1596/978-1-4648-1294-1

Kazancoglu, I., Sagnak, M., Kumar Mangla, S., & Kazancoglu, Y. (2021). Circular economy and the policy: A framework for improving the corporate environmental management in supply chains. Business Strategy and the Environment, 30(1), wiley.comDOI: 10.1002/bse.2641

Khan, H. (2024). Afghanistan's lithium: Sovereignty vs. foreign exploitation. *The Diplomat*. https://thediplomat.com/2024/08/afghanistans-lithium-sovereignty-vs-foreign-exploitation/

Khan, H. (2024). Charting Afghanistan's economic future: Recommendations for reform. *Stimson Center*. https://www.stimson.org/2024/charting-afghanistans-economic-future-recommendations-for-reform/

Khan, H., & Sayed, N. (2025). *How Afghanistan can benefit from China's investments*. The Diplomat. https://thediplomat.com/2025/02/how-afghanistan-can-benefit-from-chinas-investments/

Khan, A. M. (2025). Regional integration in Africa: The political economy of the African Continental Free Trade Area (Afcfta). *Policy Journal of Social Science Review*, *3*(4), 320–330.

Khandekar, G. (2012). The Changing Landscape of EU-Asia Relations. *Jindal Journal of International Affairs*, *2*(1), 72–89. DOI: 10.54945/jjia.v2i1.31

Khan, M., Chang, Y. C., & Bibi, A. (2024). Navigating Pakistan's Maritime Industry potential in context of blue economy: An analysis of the necessity for ratification of maritime labour convention 2006. *Marine Policy*, *165*, 106150. DOI: 10.1016/j.marpol.2024.106150

Khati, P., & Kim, C. (2022). Impact of India's free trade agreement with ASEAN on its goods exports: A gravity model analysis. *Economies*, *11*(1), 1–19. DOI: 10.3390/economies11010008

Khorana, S., & Soo, K. T. (2016). Barriers to Exporting to the EU: Evidence from Textiles and Leather. *A Project Funded by the British High Commission*, 2-21.

Khorana, S., McGuire, S., & Perdikis, N. (2014). *Multilateral Agreements and Global Governance of International Trade Regimes. Scientific Paper FP-7.* ATLANTIC FUTURE Project.

Khorana, S., & Narayanan, B. G. (2017). Modelling effects of tariff liberalisation on India's key export sectors: Analysis of the EU–India free trade agreement. *Margin*, *11*(1), 1–22. DOI: 10.1177/0973801016676016

Khushboo, D. (2025). The challenges of SAARC as a regional organization: A special reference to the Indo-Pak conflict. *International Journal for Research Trends and Innovation*, *10*(4). https://www.ijrti.org

Kim, P. M., Aydıntaşbaş, A., Stent, A., & Varma, T. (2024). The China-Russia relationship and threats to vital US interests. *Brookings Institution.* https://www.brookings.edu/articles/the-china-russia-relationship-and-threats-to-vital-us-interests/

Kindo, M. D., Adams, A. A., & Mohammed, J. (2024). The impact of trade on environmental quality and sustainable development in Ghana. *World Development Sustainability*, *4*, 100134. DOI: 10.1016/j.wds.2024.100134

Kinoshita, Y., Nagao, T., Ijuin, H., Nagasawa, K., Yamada, T., & Gupta, S. M. (2023). Utilization of free trade agreements to minimize costs and carbon emissions in the global supply chain for sustainable logistics. *Logistics (Basel)*, *7*(2), 32. DOI: 10.3390/logistics7020032

Kira, B., Sinha, V., & Srinivasan, S. (2021). Regulating digital ecosystems: Bridging the gap between competition policy and data protection. *Industrial and Corporate Change*, *30*(5), 1337–1360. DOI: 10.1093/icc/dtab053

Kiryluk-Dryjska, E., & Baer-Nawrocka, A. (2021). Regional differences in benefits from the EU Common Agricultural Policy in Poland and their policy implications. *Agriculture*, *11*(4), 288. DOI: 10.3390/agriculture11040288

Kloch, C., Petersen, E. B., & Madsen, O. B. (2011). Cloud based infrastructure, the new business possibilities and barriers. *Wireless Personal Communications*, *58*(1), 17–30. DOI: 10.1007/s11277-011-0286-7

Komkova, A. & Habert, G. (2023). Environmental impact assessment of alkali-activated materials: Examining impacts of variability in constituent production processes and transportation. Construction and Building Materials. sciencedirect.comDOI: 10.1016/j.conbuildmat.2022.129032

Konwer, , SHazarika, , O.B. (2025). India and the BIMSTEC- regionalism, multilateral frameworks and a changing global order. Australian *Journal of International Affairs, 79*(6), 969-987. https://doi.org/10.1080/10357718.2025.2548934

Korinek, J., & Melatos, M. (2009). Trade impacts of selected regional trade agreements in agriculture. *OECD Trade Policy Papers, 2009.*

Krugman, P. (1979). Increasing Returns, Monopolistic Competition, and International Trade. *Journal of International Economics*, *9*(4), 469–479. DOI: 10.1016/0022-1996(79)90017-5

Krugman, P. (1991). Increasing Returns and Economic Geography. *Journal of Political Economy*, *99*(3), 483–499. DOI: 10.1086/261763

Krugman, P. R., Obstfeld, M., & Melitz, M. (2018). *International Economics* (11th ed.). Pearson.

Kübek, G. (2022). Sustainable development chapters in EU FTAs and dispute settlement: lessons learned from Ukraine-Wood Products and Korea-Labour Rights. Understanding the EU as a Good Global Actor. rug.nlDOI: 10.4337/9781802202984.00026

Kubo, H. (2013). EU-Asia Trade Relations. In *The Palgrave Handbook of EU-Asia Relations* (pp. 247–262). Palgrave Macmillan UK. DOI: 10.1057/9780230378704_16

Kumar, P., Kumar, A., Patil, M., Hussain, S., Sharma, S., Singh, S., . . . Singh, A. N. (2022). Biodiversity Resources and Ecosystem Services in the Context of the Industrialized World. In Biodiversity (pp. 23-39). CRC Press. [HTML]DOI: 10.1201/9781003220398-3

Kumar, R. (n.d.). SAARC: Changing realities, opportunities, and challenges. Paper presented at the DIE Conference on Regional Economic Integration Beyond Europe, Bonn. https://www.idos-research.de/fileadmin/_migrated/content_uploads/SAARC_changingrealities.pdf

Kumar, J., Xi, C., Kumari, J., & Huang, J. (2025). Macroeconomic and Institutional Determinants of Foreign Direct Investment in SAARC Countries. *Problemy Ekorozwoju*, *20*(1), 271–287. DOI: 10.35784/preko.6747

Kumar, P., & Wu, H. (2025). Evaluating the dual impact of economic drivers on environmental degradation in developing countries: A study of technology innovation, foreign direct investment, and trade openness. *Journal of Energy and Environmental Policy Options*, *8*(1), 24–36.

Kumar, R. (2021). South Asia: Multilateral trade agreements and untapped regional trade integration. *International Journal of Finance & Economics*, *26*(2), 2891–2903. DOI: 10.1002/ijfe.1941

Kumar, S., Darshna, A., & Ranjan, D. (2023). A review of literature on the integration of green energy and circular economy. *Heliyon*, *9*(11), e21091. DOI: 10.1016/j.heliyon.2023.e21091

Kunroo, M. A., & Ahmad, I. (2023). Heckscher-Ohlin Theory or the Modern Trade Theory: How the Overall Trade Characterizes at the Global Level? *Journal of Quantitative Economics*, *21*(1), 151–174. DOI: 10.1007/s40953-022-00330-x

Kurin, R. (2002). The Silk Road: Connecting people and cultures. In *The Silk Road: Connecting peoples and cultures* [Program Book]. Smithsonian Center for Folklife & Cultural Heritage. https://festival.si.edu/2002/the-silk-road/the-silk-road-connecting-peoples-and-cultures/smithsonian

Kurzweil, M., Ledebur, O. V., & Salamon, P. (2003). Review of trade agreements and issues. *Accessed from* https://www.semanticscholar.org/paper/Review-of-trade-agreements-and-issues-Kurzweil-Ledebur/147493dc5d34f05ff16eba5611d9e592886c8906

Kyvelou, S. S., Ierapetritis, D. G., & Chiotinis, M. (2023). The future of fisheries co-management in the context of the sustainable blue economy and the green deal: There is no green without blue. *Sustainability (Basel)*, *15*(10), 7784. DOI: 10.3390/su15107784

Lancaster, K. (1980). Intra-Industry Trade under Perfect Monopolistic Competition. *Journal of International Economics*, *10*(2), 151–175. DOI: 10.1016/0022-1996(80)90052-5

Langley, D. J., Rosca, E., Angelopoulos, M., Kamminga, O., & Hooijer, C. (2023). Orchestrating a smart circular economy: Guiding principles for digital product passports. *Journal of Business Research*, *169*, 114259. DOI: 10.1016/j.jbusres.2023.114259

Laurens, N., Dove, Z., Morin, J. F., & Jinnah, S. (2022). NAFTA and the Environment: Decades of Measured Progress. NAFTA 2.0: From the first NAFTA to the United States-Mexico-Canada Agreement, 157-180. ulaval.caDOI: 10.1007/978-3-030-81694-0_11

Lawal, O. T. (2024). Blue Bioeconomy and Industrial Innovation. In *Marine Bioprospecting for Sustainable Blue-bioeconomy* (pp. 119–141). Springer Nature Switzerland. DOI: 10.1007/978-3-031-68911-6_7

Leal-Arcas, R., Grasso, C., & Ríos, J. A. (2016). Renewables, preferential trade agreements and EU energy security. In *Energy Security, Trade and the EU* (pp. 244-325). Edward Elgar Publishing. DOI: 10.4337/9781785366741.00012

Lehmen, A. & Vidigal, G. (2025). Trade and Environment in EU-Mercosur Relations: Negotiating in the Shadow of Unilateralism. European Foreign Affairs Review. httpss:// [HTML]DOI: 10.54648/EERR2025004

Leitão, N. C. (2023). The Impact of Geopolitical Risk on Portuguese Exports. *Economies*, *11*(12), 291. DOI: 10.3390/economies11120291

Leitão, N. C. (2024). Gravity Model and International Trade: A Survey of Literature. *Administrative Sciences*, *14*(9), 219. DOI: 10.3390/admsci14090219

Leitão, N. C., Faustino, H., & Yoshida, Y. (2010). Fragmentation, Vertical Intra-industry Trade, and Automobile Components. *Economic Bulletin*, *30*, 1006–1015.

Lemon, E., & Norov, R. (2025). *How China is adapting to Tajikistan's demand for security cooperation.* Carnegie Endowment for International Peace. https://carnegieendowment.org/posts/2025/03/how-china-is-adapting-to-tajikistans-demand-for-security-cooperation?lang=en

Leonard, M., Pisani-Ferry, J., Shapiro, J., Tagliapietra, S., & Wolff, G. B. (2021). *The geopolitics of the European green deal* (No. 04/2021). Bruegel policy contribution.

Liang, J., Yin, Z., Yang, J., Li, Y., Xu, M., Li, J., Yang, M., & Niu, L. (2022). Bibliometrics and visualization analysis of research in the field of sustainable development of the blue economy (2006–2021). *Frontiers in Marine Science*, *9*, 936612. DOI: 10.3389/fmars.2022.936612

Li, H., Han, J., & Xu, Y. (2023). The effect of the digital economy on services exports competitiveness and ternary margins. *Telecommunications Policy*, *47*(7), 102596. DOI: 10.1016/j.telpol.2023.102596

Li, J., & Wang, F. (2024). A Study on the Competitiveness and Influencing Factors of the Digital Service Trade. *Sustainability (Basel)*, *16*(8), 3116. DOI: 10.3390/su16083116

Liu, T. (2024). *Empirical analysis of the impact of regional trade agreements for Australia and China* (Doctoral dissertation, RMIT University).

Liu, W., & Heugens, P. P. (2024). Cross-sector collaborations in global supply chains as an opportunity structure: How NGOs promote corporate sustainability in China. [HTML]. *Journal of International Business Studies*, *55*(4), 429–449. Advance online publication. DOI: 10.1057/s41267-023-00644-9

Liu, Y., Jiang, Y., Pei, Z., Xia, N., & Wang, A. (2023). Evolution of the coupling coordination between the marine economy and digital economy. *Sustainability (Basel), 15*(6), 5600. DOI: 10.3390/su15065600

Liu, Z., Liu, J., & Osmani, M. (2021). Integration of digital economy and circular economy: Current status and future directions. *Sustainability (Basel), 13*(13), 7217. DOI: 10.3390/su13137217

Liyew, E. B. (2025). World Trade Organization Agreement Acceding Impacts on the Developing Countries' Human Rights System. [DSSR]. *Dialogue Social Science Review, 3*(3), 232–241.

Loganathan, V. (2023). Seventy-Five Years of India's Trade Policies With Special Reference to Agricultural Sector: An Overview. *Shanlax International Journal of Economics, 11*(4), 46–51. DOI: 10.34293/economics.v11i4.6666

Logan, C. S., Manasseh, C. O., & Ede, K. K. (2025). Trade Liberalization, Foreign Investment and Economic Growth: Experience from Non-Oil Producing Countries in Africa. *International Journal of Economics and Financial Issues, 15*(1), 101–112. DOI: 10.32479/ijefi.16912

Luck, P. (2025). How sanctions have reshaped Russia's future. *Center for Strategic and International Studies.* https://www.csis.org/analysis/how-sanctions-have-reshaped-russias-future

Ludwikowski, R. R. (2020). Overview of the Trade Relations Between the European Community/Union and the United States at the Threshold of Globalization and Post-globalization Era. *Białostockie Studia Prawnicze, 25*(3), 27–42. DOI: 10.15290/bsp.2020.25.03.02

Luke, D. (2019). Making the case for the African continental free trade area. In *Inclusive trade in Africa* (pp. 5–12). Routledge. DOI: 10.4324/9780429401121-2

Lupan, R. (2018). Non-tariff barriers and deepening economic integration within the European Union. In *Simpozion Ştiinţific Internaţional al Tinerilor Cercetători* (pp. 18-21).

Lü, Q. Q., Henderson, J., Wang, Y., & Wang, B. (2021). Natron glass beads reveal the proto-Silk Road between the Mediterranean and China in the 1st millennium BCE. *Scientific Reports, 11*(1), 3537. DOI: 10.1038/s41598-021-82245-w PMID: 33574376

Luthman, O., Jonell, M., Rönnbäck, P., & Troell, M. (2022). Strong and weak sustainability in Nordic aquaculture policies. *Aquaculture (Amsterdam, Netherlands), 550*, 737841. DOI: 10.1016/j.aquaculture.2021.737841

MA, Z., WANG, R., LIN, F., ZHANG, Q., & OTUMAWU-APREKU, K. (2025). Impact of China–Africa agricultural trade on food security: Facts and quantitative analysis. *Frontiers of Agricultural Science and Engineering*, *12*(4).

Macrotrends (2025). Portugal Tariff Rates 1988-2025. Available at: https://www.macrotrends.net/global-metrics/countries/PRT/portugal/tariff-rates

Mahalik, M. K., Mallick, H., & Padhan, H. (2021). Do educational levels influence the environmental quality? The role of renewable and non-renewable energy demand in selected BRICS countries with a new policy…. [HTML]. *Renewable Energy*, *164*, 419–432. Advance online publication. DOI: 10.1016/j.renene.2020.09.090

Majid, M. A., & Saimy, I. S. (2024, April). Strategic Marketing of Blue Financing for Advancing Blue Economy Activities: A Comprehensive Review. In *International Conference on Business and Technology* (pp. 219-229). Cham: Springer Nature Switzerland. DOI: 10.1007/978-3-031-67431-0_21

Makore, S. T. M., & Osode, P. C. (2025). Shifting the Paradigms of International Agricultural Subsidies Regulation to Advance the Human Right to Food. *African Journal of International and Comparative Law*, *33*(1), 53–81. DOI: 10.3366/ajicl.2025.0512

Malik, A., Sharma, P., Vinu, A., Karakoti, A., Kaur, K., Gujral, H. S., & Laker, B. (2022). Circular economy adoption by SMEs in emerging markets: Towards a multilevel conceptual framework. *Journal of Business Research*, *142*, 605–619. DOI: 10.1016/j.jbusres.2021.12.076

Malingrey, L., & Duval, Y. (2023). Identifying a Sustainable Path for RCEP: Global Overview and Comparative Analysis of Sustainable Development Provisions in Three Mega Regional Trade Agreements. [HTML]. *Journal of Asian Economic Integration*, *5*(2), 109–128. DOI: 10.1177/26316846231184936

Maluck, J., Glanemann, N., & Donner, R. V. (2018). Bilateral trade agreements and the interconnectedness of global trade. *Frontiers in Physics (Lausanne)*, *6*, 134. DOI: 10.3389/fphy.2018.00134

Mangala, J. (2010). The European Union and Africa: Old partners in a changing world. In *Africa and the New World Era: From Humanitarianism to a Strategic View* (pp. 167–191). Palgrave Macmillan US. DOI: 10.1057/9780230117303_12

Manu, C. (2021). The Impact of Trade Agreement on Agricultural Trade Flow in West Africa. *International Journal of Economics and Finance*, *13*(1), 1–89.

Mariscal, J., Mayne, G., Aneja, U., & Sorgner, A. (2019). Bridging the gender digital gap. *Economics*, *13*(1), 20190009. DOI: 10.5018/economics-ejournal.ja.2019-9

Maritime Gateway. (2025). Taliban looks to develop Chabahar Port to cut Pakistani port dependency. https://www.maritimegateway.com/taliban-looks-to-develop-chabahar-port-to-cut-pakistani-port-dependency/

Martin-Mayoral, F., Carofilis, G. M., & Guijarro, J. C. (2016). The Effects of Integration Agreements in Western Hemisphere trade, 1970–2014. *The Journal of International Trade & Economic Development*, *25*(5), 724–756. DOI: 10.1080/09638199.2015.1125519

Martin, P., Mayer, T., & Thoenig, M. (2012). The Geography of Conflicts and Regional Trade Agreements. *American Economic Journal. Macroeconomics*, *4*(4), 1–35. https://www.aeaweb.org/articles?id=10.1257/mac.4.4.1. DOI: 10.1257/mac.4.4.1

Marx, A., Lein, B., & Brando, N. (2016). The protection of labour rights in trade agreements: The case of the EU-Colombia agreement. *Journal of World Trade*, *50*(4), 587–610. DOI: 10.54648/TRAD2016025

Maskus, K. E., Wilson, J. S., & Otsuki, T. (2000). Quantifying the impact of technical barriers to trade. *World Bank Policy Research Working Paper*, *2512*, 1–51.

Masomy, M. J. (2021). Afghanistan as a land bridge between Central Asia and South Asia. *Electronic Journal of Social and Strategic Studies*, *2*(1), 77–91. DOI: 10.47362/EJSSS.2021.2113

Masongsong, A. C., Ulep, S. J., Abante, M. V., Cagang, M. L., & Vigonte, F. (2024, February 27). Digital Transformation of International Trade for SMEs in Developing Countries: Opportunities, Challenges. *Challenges*.

Masood, S., Khurshid, N., Haider, M., Khurshid, J., & Khokhar, A. M. (2023). Trade Potential of Pakistan with the South Asian Countries: A Gravity Model Approach. *Asia Pacific Management Review*, *28*(1), 45–51. DOI: 10.1016/j.apmrv.2022.02.001

Mavroskoti, Z. (2021). The export of EU copyright law: the example of the Free Trade Agreements. In *EU Copyright Law* (pp. 1024–1049). Edward Elgar Publishing. DOI: 10.4337/9781786437808.00036

McCalla, A. F. (2001). What the developing countries want from the WTO. *Estey Journal of International Law and Trade Policy*, *2*(1), 165–177.

McMahon, J. A. (2024). Negotiations on food security at the WTO: A never-ending story? *Journal of International Trade Law & Policy*, *23*(2/3), 101–116. DOI: 10.1108/JITLP-03-2024-0018

Medhekar, A., & Kaur, H. (2022). Look-East Act-East Policy: India and Southeast Asian Economic Cooperation. In Medhekar, A., & Kaur, H. (Eds.), "*Evaluating Trade and Economic Relations Between India and Southeast Asia*," (Ch1, pp.1-22). USA: IGI Global Publishing. DOI: DOI: 10.4018/978-1-7998-5774-7.ch001

Medhekar, A. (2019). Trade in healthcare services and Economic Development: case of Kenya & South Africa. In Evelyn, F. W., & Peter, J. N. (Eds.), *The Service Sector and Economic Development in Africa. Studies in Development Economics* (pp. 181–195). Routledge.

Medhekar, A. (2021). Australia- India: Bilateral Trade Opportunities and Challenges. In Hooke, (Eds.), *Emerging Business and Trade Opportunities Between Oceania and Asia* (pp. 57–86). IGI Global., DOI: 10.4018/978-1-7998-4126-5.ch004

Medhekar, A. (2022). Australia's Bilateral and Multilateral Health Sector Partnership with South Asian Nations: Opportunities and Challenges. In Medhekar, (Eds.), *Strategic Cooperation and Partnerships Between Australia and South Asia: Economic Development, Trade, and Investment Opportunities Post-COVID-19* (pp. 1–21). IGI Global., DOI: 10.4018/978-1-7998-8657-0.ch001

Medhekar, A., & Ali, M. M. (2012). A Cross-Border Trade in Healthcare services: Bangladesh to India. *The Business and Management Review*, *2*(1), 1–13.

Medhekar, A., & Haq, F. (2020). Cross-Border Cooperation for Bilateral Trade, Travel and Tourism: A Challenge for India and Pakistan. In Castanho, R. A. (Ed.), *Cross-Border Cooperation (CBC) Strategies for Sustainable Development* (pp. 168–191). IGI Global., DOI: 10.4018/978-1-7998-2513-5.ch010

Mehrzai, M. E. (2019). Economic benefits and importance of TAPI Project. *IJRDO —. Journal of Historical Geography*, *1*(1). https://ijrdo.org/index.php/history/article/view/3095

Meijerink, G., & Roza, P. (2007). *The role of agriculture in economic development* (Vol. 4). Wageningen UR.

Meijers, H. (2014). Does the internet generate economic growth, international trade, or both? *International Economics and Economic Policy*, *11*(1-2), 137–163. DOI: 10.1007/s10368-013-0251-x

Meltzer, J. P., & Lovelock, P. (2018). Regulating for a Digital Economy-Understanding the Importance of Cross-Border Data Flows in Asia. *Available at SSRN* 3164401.

Mensah, K. (2024). *The World Trade Organization at a crossroad: Agricultural negotiations and what it means for developing countries* (No. 237). ZEF Working Paper Series.

Meschi, E., & Vivarelli, M. (2009). Trade and income inequality in developing countries. *World Development, 37*(2), 287–302. DOI: 10.1016/j.worlddev.2008.06.002

Meunier, S., & Nicolaidis, K. (2023). The European Union as a Trade Power. *International Relations and the European Union, 168*, 155–180. DOI: 10.1093/hepl/9780192897343.003.0008

Midlen, A. (2024). Enacting the blue economy in the Western Indian Ocean: A 'collaborative blue economy governmentality'. *Environment and Planning. E, Nature and Space, 7*(2), 627–653. DOI: 10.1177/25148486231198010

Mignamissi, D., & Djijo T, A. J. (2021). Digital divide and financial development in Africa. *Telecommunications Policy, 45*(9), 102199. DOI: 10.1016/j.telpol.2021.102199

Milhem, M., Ateeq, A., Al Astal, A., Alzoraiki, M., Ateeq, R. A., Shafie, D. I., & Santhanamery, T. (2024). Advancing Sustainability: Embracing the Circular Economy for Environmental and Economic Resilience. In *Business Sustainability with Artificial Intelligence (AI): Challenges and Opportunities* (Vol. 2, pp. 57–68). Springer Nature Switzerland.

Ministry of External Affairs. Government of India [MEA]. (2024). Rajya Sabha: Question No. 44 — Chabahar Port Project. https://www.mea.gov.in/rajya-sabha.htm?dtl/38631/QUESTION+NO+44+CHABAHAR+PORT+PROJECT

Ministry of Foreign Affairs of Afghanistan. (2022). *RECCA Brief Policy Series — Issue 1: How can regional economic cooperation be accelerated within the RECCA region?* https://recca.mfa.gov.af/wp-content/uploads/2022/11/RECCA-BPS-ISSUE-1.pdf

Ministry of Mines and Petroleum [MoMP]. (2025). TAPI Project. Government of the Islamic Emirate of Afghanistan. Retrieved August 10, 2025, from https://momp.gov.af/tapi-project

Mir, A. (2023). No good choices: The counterterrorism dilemmas in Afghanistan and Pakistan. *CTC Sentinel, 16*(10). https://ctc.westpoint.edu/commentary-no-good-choices-the-counterterrorism-dilemmas-in-afghanistan-and-pakistan/

Mirghaderi, S. A., Aboumasoudi, A. S., & Amindoust, A. (2023). Developing an open innovation model in the startup ecosystem industries based on the attitude of organizational resilience and blue ocean strategy. *Computers & Industrial Engineering, 181*, 109301. DOI: 10.1016/j.cie.2023.109301

Mirzaye, S., & Mohiuddin, M. (2025). Digital Transformation in International Trade: Opportunities, Challenges, and Policy Implications. *Journal of Risk and Financial Management, 18*(8), 421. DOI: 10.3390/jrfm18080421

Mishra, N. (2015). Data localization laws in a digital world: Data protection or data protectionism? *The Public Sphere (2016), NUS Centre for International Law Research Paper*, (19/05).

Mohy-ud-Din, K., Shahbaz, M., & Du, A. M. (2025). Corporate social responsibility and climate change mitigation: Discovering the interaction role of green audit and sustainability committee. [HTML]. *Corporate Social Responsibility and Environmental Management, 32*(1), 1198–1212. DOI: 10.1002/csr.3011

Molua, E. L., Sonwa, D., Bele, Y., Foahom, B., Mate Mweru, J. P., Wa Bassa, S. M., ... & Masumbuko, E. M. (2023). Climate-smart conservation agriculture, farm values and tenure security: implications for climate change adaptation and mitigation in the Congo Basin. Tropical Conservation Science, 16, 19400829231169980. sagepub.comDOI: 10.1177/19400829231169980

Morozkina., & Skryabina, V. (2021). BRICS and Partnerships for Sustainable Development: Prospects for Trade with Least Developed Countries. *International Organisations Research Journal, 16*(1). https://doi.org/DOI: 10.17323/1996-7845-2021-01-04

Moshenski-Dubov, G. (2022). The Protection of Environmental Law under NAFTA and CUSMA: A Canadian Perspective. Can.-USLJ. https://scholarlycommons.law.case.edu/cuslj/vol46/iss1/15 case.edu

Moshood, T. D., Nawanir, G., Mahmud, F., Mohamad, F., Ahmad, M. H., & AbdulGhani, A. (2022). Biodegradable plastic applications towards sustainability: A recent innovations in the green product. Cleaner Engineering and Technology, 6, 100404. sciencedirect.comDOI: 10.1016/j.clet.2022.100404

Mossialos, E., & Oliver, A. (2005). An overview of pharmaceutical policy in four countries: France, Germany, the Netherlands and the United Kingdom. *The International Journal of Health Planning and Management, 20*(4), 291–306. DOI: 10.1002/hpm.816

Mouratidis, K., Peters, S., & van Wee, B. (2021). Transportation technologies, sharing economy, and teleactivities: Implications for built environment and travel. *Transportation Research Part D, Transport and Environment, 92*, 102716. DOI: 10.1016/j.trd.2021.102716

Msigwa, G., Ighalo, J. O., & Yap, P. S. (2022). Considerations on environmental, economic, and energy impacts of wind energy generation: Projections towards sustainability initiatives. [HTML]. *The Science of the Total Environment, 849*, 157755. Advance online publication. DOI: 10.1016/j.scitotenv.2022.157755 PMID: 35921924

Mulgan, A. G. (2008). Japan's FTA politics and the problem of agricultural trade liberalisation. *Australian Journal of International Affairs*, *62*(2), 164–178. DOI: 10.1080/10357710802060535

Murray, A., Skene, K., & Haynes, K. (2017). The circular economy: An interdisciplinary exploration of the concept and application in a global context. *Journal of Business Ethics*, *140*(3), 369–380. DOI: 10.1007/s10551-015-2693-2

Mushtaq, M., Ahmad, K., Ahmed, S., & Nadeem, M. (2014). Impact of FDI on income distribution in selected SAARC countries. *Journal of Applied Environmental and Biological Sciences*, *4*, 1–10.

Myovella, G., Karacuka, M., & Haucap, J. (2020). Digitalization and economic growth: A comparative analysis of Sub-Saharan Africa and OECD economies. *Telecommunications Policy*, *44*(2), 101856. DOI: 10.1016/j.telpol.2019.101856

Nadal, J. R., & Gallego, M. S. (2022). Gravity Models for Tourism Demand Modeling: Empirical Review and Outlook. *Journal of Economic Surveys*, *36*(5), 1358–1409. https://wileyonlinelibrary.com/journal/joes. DOI: 10.1111/joes.12502

Nam, H. J., Batten, J. A., & Ryu, D. (2025). Do institutional quality and trade openness enhance the role of financial openness in Eastern European financial development? *Global Finance Journal*, *64*, 101071. DOI: 10.1016/j.gfj.2024.101071

National Geographic Education. (n.d.). The Silk Road. https://education.nationalgeographic.org/resource/silk-road/

National Intelligence Council. (2002). *Afghanistan and regional geopolitical dynamics after 11 September: Conference proceedings, 18—19 April 2002* (CR 2002-02). Office of the Director of Central Intelligence. https://www.dni.gov/files/documents/afghanistan_2002.pdf

Nawaz, S. (2020). Institutions, Regional Integration and Bilateral Trade in South Asia: PPML-based evidence. *Pakistan Development Review*, *59*(2), 221–241. https://www.jstor.org/stable/27184732. DOI: 10.30541/v59i2pp.221-242

Ncube, C. B., & De Beer, J. (2024, April). *Trade Rules as Regulatory Tools for Inclusive Innovation: Connecting Digital Trade and Clean Technology to Achieve Sustainable Development Goals.*

NDTV. (2024). Chabahar Port would benefit landlocked Afghanistan, Central Asia: India. https://www.ndtv.com/india-news/chabahar-port-would-benefit-landlocked-afghanistan-central-asia-india-5688770

Neeraj, R. S. (2019). Trade rules for the digital economy: Charting new waters at the WTO. *World Trade Review*, *18*(S1), S121–S141. DOI: 10.1017/S1474745618000423

Neto, P. S. (2024). *Economic Diplomacy in the European Union: Economic Co-operation and Global Influence* (Master's thesis, ISCTE-Instituto Universitario de Lisboa (Portugal)).

Ngaibiakching, N., & Pande, A. (2020). India's Act East Policy and ASEAN: Building a Regional Order Through Partnership in the Indo-Pacific. *International Studies*, *57*(1), 67–78. DOI: 10.1177/0020881719885526

Nguy n, H. V., & Phan, T. T. (2025). Impact of economic growth, international trade, and FDI on sustainable development in developing countries. [HTML]. *Environment*. Advance online publication. DOI: 10.1007/s10668-023-04060-9

Nham, N. T. H., & Hoa, T. T. M. (2023). Influences of digitalization on sustaining marine minerals: A path toward sustainable blue economy. *Ocean and Coastal Management*, *239*, 106589. DOI: 10.1016/j.ocecoaman.2023.106589

Niebel, T. (2018). ICT and economic growth–Comparing developing, emerging and developed countries. *World Development*, *104*, 197–211. DOI: 10.1016/j.worlddev.2017.11.024

Ni, K. J. (2024). Can the CPTPP's Digital Format on Data Flows Serve a Role Model for the WTO? *Journal of World Trade*, *58*(6), 989–1006. DOI: 10.54648/TRAD2024048

Nilsson, M., Zamparutti, T., Petersen, J. E., Nykvist, B., Rudberg, P., & McGuinn, J. (2012). Understanding policy coherence: Analytical framework and examples of sector–environment policy interactions in the EU. *Environmental Policy and Governance*, *22*(6), 395–423. DOI: 10.1002/eet.1589

Noorzi, M. Y. (2021). Afghanistan: Regional connectivity hub. *Eastern Studies*, *15*, 287–300. DOI: 10.4467/20827695WSC.21.014.14721

North Atlantic Treaty Organization. (n.d.). NATO and Afghanistan. https://www.nato.int/cps/en/natohq/topics_8189.htm

Nouve, K., Staatz, J. M., Schweikhardt, D. B., & Yade, M. (2002). Trading out of Poverty: WTO Agreements and the West African Agriculture. A Report of the Food Security II Cooperative Agreement.

Nuccio, M., & Guerzoni, M. (2019). Big data: Hell or heaven? Digital platforms and market power in the data-driven economy. *Competition & Change*, *23*(3), 312–328. DOI: 10.1177/1024529418816525

Nunes, D., & Lessa, J. (2021). Design as a Driver for Behavioural Change: Oceans and Plastics, Approaches for a Shift Towards Sustainability. In *Advances in Design and Digital Communication: Proceedings of the 4th International Conference on Design and Digital Communication, Digicom 2020, November 5–7, 2020, Barcelos, Portugal* (pp. 456-469). Springer International Publishing.

Öberg, M. L. (2020). Internal market acquis as a tool in EU external relations: from integration to disintegration. *Legal Issues of Economic Integration, 47*(2).

Odijie, M. E. (2019). The need for industrial policy coordination in the African Continental Free Trade Area. *African Affairs, 118*(470), 182–193. DOI: 10.1093/afraf/ady054

OECD. (2020). *Digital Trade and Market Openness*. Retrieved from https://www.oecd.org/trade/topics/digital-trade/

Ogbuabor, J. E., Emeka, E. T., & Iheonu, C. O. (2025). Do industrialization, trade openness, and labor force participation enhance Africa's productive capacity? *Innovation and Development, 15*(1), 207–232. DOI: 10.1080/2157930X.2023.2286718

OilPrice.com. (2024). Why Russia and China are vying for influence in Afghanistan. https://oilprice.com/Geopolitics/International/Why-Russia-and-China-are-Vying-For-Influence-in-Afghanistan.html

Ojekemi, O. S., Ağa, M., & Magazzino, C. (2023). Towards achieving sustainability in the BRICS economies: The role of renewable energy consumption and economic risk. *Energies, 16*(14), 528728. DOI: 10.3390/en16145287

Olayele, F. (2023). Innovation and value creation in Canadas ocean sector: A blue economy imperative. In *Regional Economic Systems after* [Edward Elgar Publishing.]. *COVID, 19*, 225–240.

Olayiwola, W. K., Osabuohien, E., & Okodua, H. (2011). *Economic Integration, Trade Facilitation, and Agricultural Exports Performance in ECOWAS Countries*. Economic Policy Analysis Unit, Department of Macroeconomic Policy, ECOWAS Commision. Accessed from https://citeseerx.ist.psu.edu/document?repid=rep1&type=pdf&doi=5e19c498d850c8b999d9fe3e0c1cca8a82752774

Omarkhail, I., & Zahid, A. (2025). Afghanistan's perspectives on the Belt and Road Initiative: Strengths, weaknesses, opportunities, and threats. *Asian Journal of Political Science, 33*(3), 481–505. Advance online publication. DOI: 10.1080/02185377.2025.2473887

Onguglo, B. F., & Eugui, D. V. (2018). Small island developing states and the ocean economy: widening the development frontier. In *Handbook of Small States* (pp. 530–549). Routledge. DOI: 10.4324/9781351181846-28

Oppong-Baah, T., Bo, Y., Twi-Brempong, C., Amoah, E. O., Prempeh, N. A., & Addai, M. (2022). The Impact of trade openness on economic growth: The case of Ghana and Nigeria. *Journal of Human Resource and Sustainability Studies*, *10*(1), 142–160. DOI: 10.4236/jhrss.2022.101010

Orefice, G., Piermartini, R., & Rocha, N. (2012). Harmonization and mutual recognition: What are the effects on trade? Accessed from https://ageconsearch.umn.edu/record/332285/files/5808.pdf

Pace, L. A., Saritas, O., & Deidun, A. (2023). Exploring future research and innovation directions for a sustainable blue economy. *Marine Policy*, *148*, 105433. DOI: 10.1016/j.marpol.2022.105433

Pacheco, L. M., & Matos, A. P. (2022). Foreign Presence and Export Performance: The Role of Portuguese Commercial Diplomacy. *The International Trade Journal*, *36*(2), 147–169. DOI: 10.1080/08853908.2021.1907262

Pachori, S. (2019). Conflicts in South Asia–challenges to SAARC regionalism. *Int J Res Geogr*, *5*, 34–41.

Pallavi, G. P., & Dsa, K. T. (2024). Technological Innovations to Promote Financial Inclusion: A Comprehensive Analysis of Digital Payment Systems and Blockchain Solutions. *The Future of Money Trends in Financial Innovation*, *31*, 38.

Palmer, M. (2024). Beyond Tariff Reduction: A Libertarian Approach to Reducing Non-Tariff Barriers. [HTML]. *Liberty and Security in an Anarchical World*, *I*, 281–313. Advance online publication. DOI: 10.1007/978-3-031-70525-0_10

Palm, J., Lazoroska, D., Valencia, M., Bocken, N., & Södergren, K. (2024). A gender perspective on the circular economy: A literature review and research agenda. *Journal of Industrial Ecology*, *28*(6), 1670–1683. DOI: 10.1111/jiec.13554

Pandey, N., de Coninck, H., & Sagar, A. D. (2022). Beyond technology transfer: Innovation cooperation to advance sustainable development in developing countries. Wiley Interdisciplinary Reviews: Energy and Environment, 11(2), e422. wiley.comDOI: 10.1002/wene.422

Parihar, M. (2022). A study of South Asian Association for Regional Cooperation (SAARC) along with its role, challenges and prospects. *International Journal of Humanities and Social Science Invention*, *11*(1), 68–81.

Parliament, U. K. (2024). Russia: Overseas Trade. Written question and answer — UIN 15290. https://questions-statements.parliament.uk/written-questions/detail/2024-02-22/15290

Parteka, A. (2012). Trade Diversity and Stages of Development—Evidence on EU Countries. *Ekonomia. Rynek, gospodarka, społeczeństwo*, (30), 23-44.

Pasadilla, G. O. (2006). *Preferential trading agreements and agricultural liberalization in East and Southeast Asia* (No. 11). ARTNeT Working Paper Series. Accessed from https://www.econstor.eu/bitstream/10419/178369/1/awp-11.pdf

Pasierbiak, P., & Białowąs, T. (2024). Imbalance in Eu Trade with Selected Asian Economies–A Comparative Analysis Based on Gross Exports and Domestic Value-Added. *Humanities and Social Sciences, 31*(1), 133–148.

Pastore, P., & Tommaso, S. (2024). Women in Firms and Circular Economy Actions: A Systematic Literature Review with a Bibliometric Analysis. *Gender Issues in the Sustainable Development Era*, 189-220.

Patro, B. (2024). India should take a proactive interest in the TAPI pipeline. *Stimson Center.* https://www.stimson.org/2024/india-should-take-a-proactive-interest-in-the-tapi-pipeline/

Pattanaik, S. S. (2006). Making sense of regional cooperation: SAARC at twenty. *Strategic Analysis, 30*(1), 139–160. DOI: 10.1080/17540054.2006.12288822

Patwa, N., Sivarajah, U., Seetharaman, A., Sarkar, S., Maiti, K., & Hingorani, K. (2021). Towards a circular economy: An emerging economies context. *Journal of Business Research, 122*, 725–735. DOI: 10.1016/j.jbusres.2020.05.015

Paukku, M. (2000). *European Union and United States Trade Relations* (No. 723). ETLA Discussion Papers.

Paunov, C., & Rollo, V. (2016). Has the internet fostered inclusive innovation in the developing world? *World Development, 78*, 587–609. DOI: 10.1016/j.worlddev.2015.10.029

Pauwelyn, J. & Pelc, K. (2022). WTO Rulings and the Veil of Anonymity. European Journal of International Law. ejil.orgDOI: 10.1093/ejil/chac027

Petersmann, E. U. (2005). Addressing Institutional Challenges to the WTO in the New Millennium: A longer-term perspective. *Journal of International Economic Law, 8*(3), 647–665. DOI: 10.1093/jiel/jgi040

Petri, P. A., & Plummer, M. (2019). *China should join the new trans-pacific partnership* (No. PB19-1).

Phang, S., March, A., Touron-Gardic, G., Deane, K., & Failler, P. (2023). A review of the blue economy, potential, and opportunities in seven Caribbean nations pre-COVID-19. *ICES Journal of Marine Science*, *80*(8), 2233–2243. DOI: 10.1093/icesjms/fsac230

Piao, R. S., de Vincenzi, T. B., da Silva, A. L. F., de Oliveira, M. C. C., Vazquez-Brust, D., & Carvalho, M. M. (2023). How is the circular economy embracing social inclusion? *Journal of Cleaner Production*, *411*, 137340. DOI: 10.1016/j.jclepro.2023.137340

Picone, F., Buonocore, E., Chemello, R., Russo, G. F., & Franzese, P. P. (2021). Exploring the development of scientific research on Marine Protected Areas: From conservation to global ocean sustainability. *Ecological Informatics*, *61*, 101200. DOI: 10.1016/j.ecoinf.2020.101200

Pishbahar, E., & Huchet, M. (2008). *European Union's preferential trade agreements in agricultural sector: a gravity approach* (Doctoral dissertation, auto-saisine).

Pleis, L. J., Lliteras, R., Wood, D. A., Bain, M. D., & Hendrickson, S. J. (2015). The Afghanistan National Railway: A plan of opportunity. *Joint Force Quarterly*. https://ndupress.ndu.edu/Media/News/News-Article-View/Article/577556/the-afghanistan-national-railway-a-plan-of-opportunity/

Poletti, A., Sicurelli, D., & Yildirim, A. B. (2021). Promoting sustainable development through trade? EU trade agreements and global value chains. Italian political science review/rivista italiana di scienza politica, 51(3), 339-354. cambridge.orgDOI: 10.1017/ipo.2020.33

Pomfret, R. (2020). *Regionalism" and The Global Trade System. Discussion Paper Jean Monnet Chair in the Economics of European Integration*. University of Adelaide., https://iit.adelaide.edu.au/ua/media/2066/2020-05-regionalism-rp-final.pdf

Pöyhönen, P. (1963). A Tentative Model for the Volume of Trade between Countries. *Weltwirtschaftliches Archiv*, *90*, 93–100. https://www.jstor.org/stable/40436776

Pranita, D., Sarjana, S., Musthofa, B. M., Kusumastuti, H., & Rasul, M. S. (2023). Blockchain technology to enhance integrated blue economy: A case study in strengthening sustainable tourism on smart islands. *Sustainability (Basel)*, *15*(6), 5342. DOI: 10.3390/su15065342

Presberger, D., & Bernauer, T. (2023). Economic and political drivers of environmental impact shifting between countries. *Global Environmental Change*, *79*, 10263727. DOI: 10.1016/j.gloenvcha.2023.102637

Qiang, O., Tian-Tian, W., Ying, D., Zhu-Ping, L., & Jahanger, A. (2021). The impact of environmental regulations on export trade at provincial level in China: evidence from panel quantile regression. Environmental Science and Pollution Research, 1-14. springer.comDOI: 10.1007/s11356-021-17676-z

Qiang, X., & Jia, L. (2025). Russia's new Eurasian security architecture: Implications for the Eurasian region. *Horizons, 29.* https://www.cirsd.org/en/horizons/horizons-winter-2025-issue-no-29/russias-new-eurasian-security-architecture

Quansah, K. A., & Ahn, W. C. (2017). The effect of the Korea-Australia free trade agreement (KAFTA) on the Korea-Australia trade structure. *The Asian Journal of Shipping and Logistics*, *33*(4), 229–235. DOI: 10.1016/j.ajsl.2017.12.006

Quttainah, M. A., & Ayadi, I. (2024). The impact of digital integration on corporate sustainability: Emissions reduction, environmental innovation, and resource efficiency in the European. *Journal of Innovation & Knowledge*, *9*(3), 100525. DOI: 10.1016/j.jik.2024.100525

Raghutla, C., Malik, M. N., Hameed, A., & Chittedi, K. R. (2024). Impact of public-private partnerships investment and FDI on CO2 emissions: A study of six global investment countries. *Journal of Environmental Management*, *360*, 121213. DOI: 10.1016/j.jenvman.2024.121213

Rahim, S. A. (2018). Afghanistan's dependence on Pakistan: Transit trade and the cost of being landlocked. *Kardan Journal of Economics & Management Sciences, 1*(4), 68—79. https://kardan.edu.af/data/public/files/KJEMS-4th-3.pdf

Rahim, S. A. (2019). Lapis Lazuli Corridor: Meeting the economic aspirations of Afghanistan and member countries. *Kardan Journal of Economics and Management Sciences, 2*(3), 67-78. https://kardan.edu.af/Research/CurrentIssue.aspx?j=KJEMS

Rahman, S. H., Khatri, S., & Brunner, H. P. (2012). *Regional Integration and Economic Development in South Asia.* The Asian Development Bank and Edward Elgar Publishing., Accessed from https://www.adb.org/sites/default/files/publication/29871/regional-integration-economic-development-south-asia.pdf DOI: 10.4337/9781781005248

Rahman, S. Z., & Bristy, J. F. (2015). Macroeconomic impact of foreign direct investment: A study on SAARC countries. *European Journal of Business and Management*, *7*(34), 59–70.

Raihan, S. (2011). Economic Reforms and Agriculture in Bangladesh: Assessment of Impacts using Economy-wide Simulation Models. *Accessed from* https://mpra.ub.uni-muenchen.de/37886/1/MPRA_paper_37886.pdf

Raihan, S. (2011). Employment Effects of FTA Agreements: The Perspectives from Bangladesh. *Accessed from* https://mpra.ub.uni-muenchen.de/id/eprint/37885

Rai, K. S., & Sharma, K. A. (2020). Causal nexus between FDI inflows and its determinants in SAARC countries. *South Asia Economic Journal, 21*(2), 193–215. DOI: 10.1177/1391561420940838

Rama, M. (2003). Globalization and workers in developing countries. *World Bank Policy Research Working Paper*, •••, 2958.

Rashid, H. (2025). Trade Agreements and Export Performance of Bangladesh: A Gravity Model Analysis. *Available at SSRN* 5379852.

Rataj, O., Kemp, R., & Mordaszewska, K. (2024). Mainstreaming innovative circular economy solutions—A comparative study between entrepreneurs in developed versus emerging markets and developing economies. *Business Strategy and the Environment, 33*(8), 8946–8964. DOI: 10.1002/bse.3957

Ratna, R. S. (2020). South Asian integration: Dream or reality. In *Regional and Multilateral Trade in Developing Countries* (pp. 95–105). Routledge India. DOI: 10.4324/9780367817985-7

Ratna, R. S., Sharma, S. K., & Dobhal, A. (2021). Indian agriculture under WTO and FTAs: An assessment. In *Indian Agriculture Under the Shadows of WTO and FTAs: Issues and Concerns* (pp. 3–25). Springer Singapore. DOI: 10.1007/978-981-33-6854-5_1

Reddy, G. J. (2019). Regional imbalances and implications for South Asian economic integration. In *New Futures for South Asia* (pp. 161–173). Routledge India. DOI: 10.4324/9780367816827-13

Rehber, E., & Grega, L. (2008). Agriculture, trade and sustainability. *The European Legacy, Toward New Paradigms, 13*(4), 463–479. DOI: 10.1080/10848770802180755

Rehman, S. S., & Della Posta, P. (2018). The impact of Brexit on EU27 on trade, investments and financial services. *Global Economy Journal, 18*(1), 20170097. DOI: 10.1515/gej-2017-0097

Reina, J. C., Cuaresma, J. C., Fenz, K., Zellmann, J., Yankov, T., & Taha, A. (2024). Gravity Models for Global Migration Flows: A Predictive Evaluation. *Population Research and Policy Review, 43*(2), 29. DOI: 10.1007/s11113-024-09867-6

Reiners, K. & Versluis, E. (2023). NGOs as new Guardians of the Treaties? Analysing the effectiveness of NGOs as decentralised enforcers of EU law. Journal of European Public Policy. tandfonline.comDOI: 10.1080/13501763.2022.2084146

Rena, R. (2012). Impact of WTO policies on developing countries: Issues and perspectives. *Transnational Corporations Review*, *4*(3), 77–88. DOI: 10.1080/19186444.2012.11658336

Renard, T. (2016). Partnerships for effective multilateralism? Assessing the compatibility between EU bilateralism,(inter-) regionalism and multilateralism. *Cambridge Review of International Affairs*, *29*(1), 18–35. DOI: 10.1080/09557571.2015.1060691

Ren, S., Liu, D., Li, B., Wang, Y., & Chen, X. (2020). Does emissions trading affect labor demand? Evidence from the mining and manufacturing industries in China. *Journal of Environmental Management*, *254*, 109789. DOI: 10.1016/j.jenvman.2019.109789

Reuters. (2024). India signs 10-year deal with Iran to operate Chabahar port. https://www.reuters.com/world/india/india-sign-10-year-pact-with-iran-chabahar-port-management-et-reports-2024-05-13/

Ricardo, D. (1817) *The Theory of Comparative Advantage*. In: Ricardo, D., Vol. 1 Ed. By Pierro Sraffa with Collaboration of M.H. Dobb, Principles of Political Economy and Taxation, Cambridge University Press, Cambridge, London.

Ricardo, D. (2004). *(1817/1821). On the Principles of Political Economy and Taxation, Collated Text of all Three Editions*. Liberty Fund Press.

Richard, B. E. (2014). Multilateralising 21st Century Regionalism, OECD *Report (46 pages)*, International Economic Department. OECD: Paris. https://repository.graduateinstitute.ch/record/286980/references?v=pdf

Rismawati, R., Darsono, T., Pujotomo, D., Tunjungsari, H., Numberi, A., Korniawan, R., & Agustiyanto, A. (2024). Exploring the relationship between sustainable supply chain and sustainable development goals on the financial performance of SMEs. *Uncertain Supply Chain Management*, *12*(3), 1911–1922. DOI: 10.5267/j.uscm.2024.2.012

Rizzato, F., Tonelli, A., Fiandrino, S., & Devalle, A. (2024). Analysing SDG disclosure and its impact on integrated thinking and reporting. *Meditari Accountancy Research*, *32*(3), 803–831. DOI: 10.1108/MEDAR-07-2022-1751

Rlung, A. S. (2024). Effect of Afghanistan—Pakistan Transit Trade Agreement on trade cost parity. *MPRA Paper*. https://mpra.ub.uni-muenchen.de/123183/

Rodríguez-Delgado, J. D. (2007). SAFTA: Living in a world of regional trade agreements. *Accessed from* https://papers.ssrn.com/sol3/Delivery.cfm?abstractid=961753

Rodríguez, E. V. (2009). The European Union Free Trade Agreements: Implications for Rodrik, D. (2022). An industrial policy for good jobs. *Hamilton Project—Policy proposal. Washington, DC: Brookings Institution*. Developing Countries. *Real Instituto Elcano. Working Paper*, *8*, 5–6.

Romer, P. (2021). Growth Theory. *Endogenous Growth in Historical Perspective: From Adam Smith to Paul Romer*, 251.

Roos, D. (2021). *The Silk Road: 8 goods traded along the ancient network.* History. A&E Television Networks. (Last updated May 28, 2025.) https://www.history.com/articles/silk-road-trade-goods

Roy, J., & Banerjee, P. (2010). Connecting South Asia: The centrality of trade facilitation for regional economic integration. In *Promoting Economic Cooperation in South Asia: Beyond SAFTA* (pp. 110-138). SAGE Publications India Pvt Ltd.

Ruben, R., Fort, R., & Zúñiga-Arias, G. (2009). Measuring the impact of fair trade on development. *Development in Practice*, *19*(6), 777–788. DOI: 10.1080/09614520903027049

Runde, D. F., Pforzheimer, A., Bryja, T., & Smutny, C. (2024). *The future of assistance to Afghanistan: A dilemma.* Center for Strategic and International Studies. https://www.csis.org/analysis/future-assistance-afghanistan-dilemma

Runge, C. F. (1992). Environmental effects of trade in the agricultural sector: a case study. Accessed from https://ageconsearch.umn.edu/record/14449/files/wp92-01.pdf

Saboor, A., Ahmed, S., & Shabbir, T. (2021). Post-withdrawal situation of US troops from Afghanistan: Role of Shanghai Cooperation Organization (SCO). *Global International Relations Review*, *4*(4), 43–54. Advance online publication. DOI: 10.31703/girr.2021(IV-IV).05

Sadat, S. M. (2015). *TAPI and CASA-1000: Win-win trade between Central Asia and South Asia* (Policy Brief No. 25). OSCE Academy in Bishkek. https://osce-academy.net/upload/file/Policy_Brief_25.pdf

Sadiqi, M. K., & Wani, N. U. H. (2018). Latency of Afghanistan-SAARC merchandise trade relation: An economic evaluation. *Kardan Journal of Economics and Management Sciences*, *1*(2), 101–120. DOI: 10.31841/KJEMS.2021.82

Saebi, T., Foss, N. J., & Linder, S. (2019). Social entrepreneurship research: Past achievements and future promises. *Journal of Management*, *45*(1), 70–95. DOI: 10.1177/0149206318793196

Safi, M., & Alizada, B. (2018). *Integrating Afghanistan into the Belt and Road Initiative: Review, analysis, and prospects.* Friedrich Ebert Stiftung. https://library.fes.de/pdf-files/bueros/kabul/15587.pdf

Sahoo, P., Nataraj, G., & Dash, R. K. (2014). *Foreign direct investment in South Asia. Policy, Impact, Determinants and Challenges.* Springer. DOI: 10.1007/978-81-322-1536-3

SAIS Review of International Affairs. (2024). From Balochistan to beyond: How Iran emerged as a senior partner to Pakistan. https://saisreview.sais.jhu.edu/from-balochistan-to-beyond-how-iran-emerged-as-a-senior-partner-to-pakistan/

Salahi, Z. (2022). Afghanistan: A Junction of Asia's Connectivity. *The National Bureau of Asian Research.* https://www.nbr.org/publication/afghanistan-a-junction-of-asias-connectivity/

Salem, H. S., Pudza, M. Y., & Yihdego, Y. (2023). … in the Arabian Gulf region, considering population, climate change impacts, ecological and carbon footprints, and United Nations' Sustainable Development Goals. Sustainable Earth Reviews. springer.comDOI: 10.1186/s42055-023-00057-4

Salimova-Tekay, J. (2022). Infrastructure financing in Kyrgyzstan (PER Series Working Paper). Macroeconomic Policy & Financing for Development Division.

Salisu, M. A., Marafa, L., Bamiro, N. B., Shokunbi, M. O., & Raimi, B. O. (2025). Systematic review of post-COVID policies and strategies for strengthening e-commerce cooperation among ASEAN countries. *Journal of Economic and Administrative Sciences.*

Sanchez Cacicedo, A. (2022). Unlocking Afghanistan's connectivity potential: Opportunities for the EU. *EUISS Brief No. 15.* https://www.iss.europa.eu/publications/briefs/unlocking-afghanistans-connectivity-potential-opportunities-eu

Sands, P. (2023). Environmental protection in the twenty-first century: Sustainable development and international law. [HTML]. *Global Environment.* Advance online publication. DOI: 10.4324/9781003421368

Sangar, K. (2017). *Russia and China in the age of grand Eurasian projects: Prospects for integration between the Silk Road Economic Belt and the Eurasian Economic Union.* Cambridge Journal of Eurasian Studies., DOI: 10.22261/YDG5KF

Santeramo, F. G., & Lamonaca, E. (2022). Standards and regulatory cooperation in regional trade agreements: What the effects on trade?. Applied Economic Perspectives and Policy, 44(4), 1682-1701. wiley.comDOI: 10.1002/aepp.13276

Santos Silva, J. M. C., & Tenreyro, S. (2011). Further Simulation Evidence on the Performance of the Poisson Pseudo-Maximum Likelihood Estimator. *Economics Letters*, *112*(2), 220–222. DOI: 10.1016/j.econlet.2011.05.008

Santos-Silva, J. M. C., & Tenreyro, S. (2006). The Log of Gravity. *The Review of Economics and Statistics*, *88*(4), 641–658. DOI: 10.1162/rest.88.4.641

Sarangi, U. (2023, February). Blue economy, blue finance and ocean governance for achieving sustainable development goals. []). Oxford, UK: Blackwell Publishing Ltd.]. *Natural Resources Forum*, *47*(1), 3–21. DOI: 10.1111/1477-8947.12267

Sassi, M., & Bernini Carri, C. (2009). Scambi commerciali agricoli e accordi di partenariato tra Unione Europea e Africa. *Economia agro-alimentare. Fascicolo*, *2*, 1000–1019.

Satizábal, P., Dressler, W. H., Fabinyi, M., & Pido, M. D. (2020). Blue economy discourses and practices: Reconfiguring ocean spaces in the Philippines. *Maritime Studies*, *19*(2), 207–221. DOI: 10.1007/s40152-020-00168-0

Savic, B. (2025). Sanctions and the geopolitics of trade. *Geopolitical Intelligence Services*. https://www.gisreportsonline.com/r/sanctions-trade-routes

Sawadogo, F., & Wandaogo, A. A. (2021). Does mobile money services adoption foster intra-African goods trade? *Economics Letters*, *199*, 109681. DOI: 10.1016/j.econlet.2020.109681

Saxena, M. P., & Sirohi, N. (2025). Talent Acquisition in the Gig Era: Strategies for Attracting Freelancers. *The Gig Economy Revolution: Rethinking Talent Management*, 86.

Schröder, P., Anantharaman, M., Anggraeni, K., & Foxon, T. J. (2019). The circular economy and the Global South. *The Circular Economy and the Global South. Routledge*. Https://Doi. Org/10.4324, *978042*(9434), 006.

Sedra, M. (2014). An uncertain future for Afghanistan's security sector. *Stability*, *3*(1), 35. Advance online publication. DOI: 10.5334/sta.ei

Sehgal, S., Pandey, P., Deisting, F., & McMillan, D. (2018). Time varying integration amongst the South Asian equity markets: An empirical study. *Cogent Economics & Finance*, *6*(1), 1452328. DOI: 10.1080/23322039.2018.1452328

Sehgal, S., Saini, S., & Pandey, P. (2020). Economic and financial integration in the South Asian region: A survey. In *Economic and Financial Integration in South Asia* (pp. 16–32). Routledge India. DOI: 10.4324/9781003097563-3

Seyyedi, S. R., Kowsari, E., Gheibi, M., Chinnappan, A., & Ramakrishna, S. (2024). A comprehensive review integration of digitalization and circular economy in waste management by adopting artificial intelligence approaches: Towards a simulation model. *Journal of Cleaner Production*, *460*, 142584. DOI: 10.1016/j.jclepro.2024.142584

Shaffer, G. (2015). How the World Trade Organization shapes regulatory governance. *Regulation & Governance*, *9*(1), 1–15. DOI: 10.1111/rego.12057

Shafique, K., Khawaja, B. A., Sabir, F., Qazi, S., & Mustaqim, M. (2020). Internet of things (IoT) for next-generation smart systems: A review of current challenges, future trends and prospects for emerging 5G-IoT scenarios. *IEEE Access : Practical Innovations, Open Solutions*, *8*, 23022–23040. DOI: 10.1109/ACCESS.2020.2970118

Shah, Z., Ahmad, B., & Alam, A. (2023). Understanding Convergence and Divergence in Pak-Iran Relations. *Journal of Development and Social Sciences*, *4*(3), 1265–1276. DOI: 10.47205/jdss.2023(4-III)117

Shahzad, U., Miao, C., & Muhammad, S. (2025). Digital and geographical mobility: Correlating technological bilateral trade impact on sustainable trade development between China and East Asia. *Environment, Development and Sustainability*, •••, 1–28. DOI: 10.1007/s10668-025-06128-0

Shan, S., Mirza, N., Umar, M., & Hasnaoui, A. (2023). The nexus of sustainable development, blue financing, digitalization, and financial intermediation. *Technological Forecasting and Social Change*, *195*, 122772. DOI: 10.1016/j.techfore.2023.122772

Sharma, P., Rohatgi, S., & Jasuja, D. (2022). Scientific Mapping of Gravity Model of International Trade Literature: A Bibliometric Analysis. *Journal of Scientometric Research*, *11*(3), 447–457. DOI: 10.5530/jscires.11.3.48

Sharma, T., & Bharti, N. (2025). The Impact of EU Trade Policies on Its Textile and Clothing Imports: A Comparison Between India, Bangladesh, China, and Vietnam. *Economies*, *13*(2), 47. DOI: 10.3390/economies13020047

Shukla, A. (2024). The Chabahar Port and India-Iran Agreement. *International Council for Policy Studies*. https://www.icpsnet.org/issuebrief/The-Chabahar-Port-and-India-Iran-Agreement

Sidaway, J. D., Rowedder, S. C., Woon, C. Y., Lin, S., & Pholsena, V. (2020). *Introduction: Research agendas raised by the Belt and Road Initiative*. Environment and Planning C. *Politics and Space*, *38*(5), 795–802. DOI: 10.1177/2399654420911410

Siles-Brügge, G. (2014). *Constructing European Union trade policy: A global idea of Europe*. Palgrave Macmillan. DOI: 10.1057/9781137331663

Silver, J. J., Gray, N. J., Campbell, L. M., Fairbanks, L. W., & Gruby, R. L. (2015). Blue economy and competing discourses in international oceans governance. *Journal of Environment & Development*, *24*(2), 135–160. DOI: 10.1177/1070496515580797

Simone, C., & Laudando, A. (2025). Principles and obligations of the Digital Markets Act in regulating the economic power of gatekeepers: Positive, negative or trade-off effects? *Electronic Markets*, *35*(1), 1–27. DOI: 10.1007/s12525-025-00788-6

Singapore Ministry of Trade & International Economic Relations. {SMTIER} (2025). Regional Comprehensive Economic Partnership. https://www.mti.gov.sg/trade-international-economic-relations/agreements/free-trade-agreements-fta/rcep/

Singh, N. (2024). Promoting Multi-stakeholder Collaboration for Nature-Based Sustainable Development. In Nature-Based Solutions in Achieving Sustainable Development Goals: Harmonizing Nature and Progress (pp. 289-316). Cham: Springer Nature Switzerland. [HTML]DOI: 10.1007/978-3-031-76128-7_10

Singh, P. J., Smith, A., & Sohal, A. S. (2005). Strategic supply chain management issues in the automotive industry: An Australian perspective. *International Journal of Production Research*, *43*(16), 3375–3399. DOI: 10.1080/00207540500095738

Skylence. (n.d.). The Silk Road of China. https://www.skylence.com/blogs/journal/the-silk-road-of-china

Small, A. (2015). *The China—Pakistan Axis: Asia's New Geopolitics*. London: Hurst; New York: Oxford University Press.

Smith, A. (1776). *The Wealth of Nations*. W. strahan and T. Cadell, London.

Smith, A. (1776/1784). *An Inquiry into the Nature and Causes of the Wealth of Nations*. Liberty Fund Press.

Songwe, V., MacLeod, J. M., & Karingi, S. (2021). The African Continental Free Trade Area: A Historical Moment for Development in Africa. *Journal of African Trade*, *8*(2), 9. Advance online publication. DOI: 10.2991/jat.k.211208.001

Sopha, B. M., Purnamasari, D. M., & Ma'mun, S. (2022). Barriers and enablers of circular economy implementation for electric-vehicle batteries: From systematic literature review to conceptual framework. *Sustainability (Basel)*, *14*(10), 6359. DOI: 10.3390/su14106359

Sotirov, M., Azevedo-Ramos, C., Rattis, L., & Berning, L. (2022). Policy options to regulate timber and agricultural supply-chains for legality and sustainability: The case of the EU and Brazil. [HTML]. *Forest Policy and Economics*, *144*, 102818. DOI: 10.1016/j.forpol.2022.102818

Sotte, F., & Vergamini, D. (2025). The Green Deal and the CAP 2023–2027. In *European Agricultural Policy: History and Analysis* (pp. 219–235). Springer Nature Switzerland. DOI: 10.1007/978-3-031-83313-7_11

Southgate, L. (2025). Explaining ASEAN institutional balancing success and failure. *Asian Security, 21*(2), 149–167. DOI: 10.1080/14799855.2025.2527885

Stanford, J. (2019). North American free trade: history, structure and prospects. In *The Handbook of Globalisation* (3rd ed., pp. 272–303). Edward Elgar Publishing. DOI: 10.4337/9781788118606.00026

Statistical Portugal (2024). Instituto Nacional de Estatística (INE), and PORDATA-International Trade in Goods Statistics.

Stavytskyy, A., Kharlamova, G., Giedraitis, V., & Sengul, E. C. (2019). Gravity model analysis of globalization process in transition economies. *Journal of International Students, 12*(2), 322–341. DOI: 10.14254/2071-8330.2019/12-2/21

Stefanis, C., Stavropoulos, A., Stavropoulou, E., Tsigalou, C., Constantinidis, T. C., & Bezirtzoglou, E. (2024). A spotlight on environmental sustainability in view of the European Green Deal. *Sustainability (Basel), 16*(11), 4654. DOI: 10.3390/su16114654

Stojanović, B., & Radukić, S. (2006). EU environmental policy and competitiveness. *Panoeconomicus, 53*(4), 471–485. DOI: 10.2298/PAN0604471S

Stojkov, A., & Warin, T. (2025). United Europe: Boundaries and Challenges. In *Western Balkans and the Future of Europe: Between an Enlargement and a Commitment Fatigue* (pp. 1–73). Springer Nature Switzerland. DOI: 10.1007/978-3-031-86465-0_1

Suarez-Visbal, L., Stuckrath, C., & Carreón, J. R. (2022). Assessing through a gender-inclusion lens the social impact of circular strategies in the apparel value chain: the dutch case. In *Social and Cultural Aspects of the Circular Economy* (pp. 136–159). Routledge. DOI: 10.4324/9781003255246-9

Subow, V. (2014). The global governance of trade in agriculture: the role of tariff and non-tariff measures illustrated with an example of agricultural exports from South Africa to the EU.

Suchek, N., Ferreira, J. J., & Fernandes, P. O. (2022). A review of entrepreneurship and circular economy research: State of the art and future directions. *Business Strategy and the Environment, 31*(5), 2256–2283. DOI: 10.1002/bse.3020

Suhail, P., & Sreejesh, S. (2011). The bilateral trade agreements and export performance of South Asian nations with special reference to India Sri Lanka Free Trade Agreement. *Romanian Economic Journal, 14*(42).

Sule, A. K., Eyo-Udo, N. L., Onukwulu, E. C., Agho, M. O., & Azubuike, C. (2024). Implementing blockchain for secure and efficient cross-border payment systems. *International Journal of Research and Innovation in Applied Science, 9*(12), 508–535.

Sultana, S., & Asrat, J. (2014). South Asian Countries in Regional Integration Perspective: A Critical Review. *Journal of Business and Technology (Dhaka), 9*(2), 43–59. DOI: 10.3329/jbt.v9i2.26195

Summers, T. (2016). China's 'new silk roads': Sub-national regions and networks of global political economy. *Third World Quarterly, 37*(9), 1628–1643. DOI: 10.1080/01436597.2016.1153415

Sunge, R., & Ngepah, N. (2020). Agricultural trade liberalization, regional trade agreements and agricultural technical efficiency in Africa. *Outlook on Agriculture, 49*(1), 66–76. DOI: 10.1177/0030727019870551

Swinnen, J., Olper, A., & Vandemoortele, T. (2012). Impact of the WTO on Agricultural and Food Policies. *World Economy, 35*(9), 1089–1101. DOI: 10.1111/j.1467-9701.2012.01472.x

Szeles, M. R. (2018). New insights from a multilevel approach to the regional digital divide in the European Union. *Telecommunications Policy, 42*(6), 452–463. DOI: 10.1016/j.telpol.2018.03.007

Tabash, M. I., Elsantil, Y., Hamadi, A., & Drachal, K. (2024). Globalization and income inequality in developing economies: A comprehensive analysis. *Economies, 12*(1), 23. DOI: 10.3390/economies12010023

Talukder, D. (2014). Agricultural trade liberalisation and welfare of rural households in Bangladesh: A complementary policy framework. *Journal of Economic and Social Policy, 16*(2), 89–128.

Tamasiga, P., Mfuni, H., Onyeaka, H., & Ouassou, E. H. (2025). Green industrial policy as an enabler of the transition to sustainability: Challenges, opportunities and policy implications for developing countries. *Environment, Development and Sustainability, 27*(1), 355–376. DOI: 10.1007/s10668-023-03952-0

Taneja, N., Prakash, S., & Kalita, P. (2013). India's Role in Facilitating Trade under SAFTA. Working Paper 263. Indian Council for Research on International Economic Relations.

Tan, R., Hou, K., & Wu, H. (2025). The cost of biodiversity protection: National key ecological functional zone and labor demand in China. [HTML]. *Journal of Asian Economics*, *97*, 101895. Advance online publication. DOI: 10.1016/j.asieco.2025.101895

Tapia, S. S. (2019). The Global" Last Mile" Solution: High-Altitude Broadband Infrastructure. *Geo. L. Tech. Rev.*, *4*, 47.

Tariq, M. T. (2023). The Importance of Lapis Lazuli Corridor for Afghanistan. *International Journal of Research in Academic Humanities*, *3*(5), 276–280. Advance online publication. DOI: 10.55544/ijrah.3.5.28

Taylor, R. D. (2020). "Data localization": The internet in the balance. *Telecommunications Policy*, *44*(8), 102003. DOI: 10.1016/j.telpol.2020.102003

Teberges Dantas Queiroga, A., Elf, P., & Macário de Oliveira, V. (2025). Circular economy business models as context-forging opportunities: The role of circular managers in driving sustainable innovation in emerging markets. *Journal of Tropical Futures*, 27538931251342187.

Temtime, Z. T., & Pansiri, J. (2004). Small business critical success/failure factors in developing countries: some evidence from Botswana.

Teniwut, W. A., Hasyim, C. L., & Pentury, F. (2022). Towards smart government for sustainable fisheries and marine development: An intelligent web-based support system approach in small islands. *Marine Policy*, *143*, 105158. DOI: 10.1016/j.marpol.2022.105158

Tewari, M. (2008). *Deepening intraregional trade and investment in South Asia: The case of the textiles and clothing industry* (No. 213). Working Paper.

The Fund for Peace. (2024). *Fragile States Index 2024: Global data.* https://fragilestatesindex.org/global-data/

Thirlwall, A. P. (2000). Trade agreements, trade liberalization and economic growth: A selective survey. *African Development Review*, *12*(2), 129–160. DOI: 10.1111/1467-8268.00020

Thoya, P., Horigue, V., Möllmann, C., Maina, J., & Schiele, K. S. (2022). Policy gaps in the East African Blue economy: Perspectives of small-scale fishers on port development in Kenya and Tanzania. *Frontiers in Marine Science*, *9*, 933111. DOI: 10.3389/fmars.2022.933111

Thrasher, R.D., & Gallagher, K.P. (2008). 21st century trade agreements: implications for long-run development policy. The Frederick S. Pardee Centre for the Study of Longer-Range Future. Boston University. Paper No-2

Thu, L. A., Fang, S., & Kessani, S. S. (2019). Factors influencing Vietnam's handicraft export with the gravity model. *Journal of Economic Development, 21*(2), 156–171. DOI: 10.1108/JED-08-2019-0021

Thuy Van, L. T. (2011). *Study on Intraregional Trade and Investment in South Asia–By Thomas W.* Hertel. DOI: 10.1111/j.1943-0787.2011.01285.x

Tian, G., Zaki, Z., & Haihua, Y. (2024). Strategic Alliance: The Contribution of the "Belt and Road Initiative "to Easing Trade Restrictions for Afghanistan. *Research in Business & Social Science, 13*(7), 326–342. DOI: 10.20525/ijrbs.v13i7.3658

Timsina, K. P., & Culas, R. J. (2020). Impacts of Australia's free trade agreements on trade in agricultural products: An aggregative and disaggregative analysis. *The Australian Journal of Agricultural and Resource Economics, 64*(3), 889–919. DOI: 10.1111/1467-8489.12377

Tinbergen, J. (1962). *Shaping the world economy: suggestions for an International Economic Policy*. The Twentieth Century Fund.

Tinbergen, J. (1962). *Shaping the world economy; Suggestions for an international economic policy*. Twentieth Century Fund.

Tinta, A. A., Sarpong, D. B., Ouedraogo, I. M., Al Hassan, R., Mensah-Bonsu, A., & Onumah, E. E. (2018). Assessing the impact of integration on economic growth and food security in ECOWAS. *Theoretical and Practical Research in Economic Fields, 9*(1 (17)), 32–44. DOI: 10.14505/tpref.v9.1(17).04

Tiwari, M. (2025). The Rise of Geo-Economic Fragmentation: Is the WTO Obsolete? *Available at SSRN* 5501579. *SSRN*: https://ssrn.com/abstract=5501579 or http://dx.doi.org/DOI: 10.2139/ssrn.5501579

Todaro, M. P., & Smith, S. C. (2020). *Economic Development*. Pearson.

Togan, S., Nebioğlu, H., & Doğan, S. (2005). *Integration and the manufacturing industry*. Economic Reform and Accession to the European Union.

Torgautov, B., Zhanabayev, A., Tleuken, A., Turkyilmaz, A., Mustafa, M., & Karaca, F. (2021). Circular economy: Challenges and opportunities in the construction sector of Kazakhstan. *Buildings (Basel, Switzerland), 11*(11), 501. DOI: 10.3390/buildings11110501

TRACECA. (n.d.). *Lapis Lazuli Corridor*. Retrieved November 10, 2025, from https://traceca.ge/en/route/silk-road/lapislazulicorridor

Transparency International. (2024). *Corruption Perceptions Index 2024: Afghanistan*. https://www.transparency.org/en/cpi/2024/index/afg

Tran, T. A. D., & Dinh, T. T. B. (2014). FDI inflows and trade imbalances: Evidence from developing Asia. *The European Journal of Comparative Economics*, *11*(1), 147.

Tripathi, V., Chattopadhyaya, S., Mukhopadhyay, A. K., Saraswat, S., Sharma, S., Li, C., Rajkumar, S., & Georgise, F. B. (2022). A novel smart production management system for the enhancement of industrial sustainability in Industry 4.0. *Mathematical Problems in Engineering*, *2022*(1), 6424869. DOI: 10.1155/2022/6424869

Tripathi, V., Chattopadhyaya, S., Mukhopadhyay, A. K., Sharma, S., Kumar, V., Li, C., & Singh, S. (2024). Lean, green, and smart manufacturing: An ingenious framework for enhancing the sustainability of operations management on the shop floor in industry 4.0. *Proceedings of the Institution of Mechanical Engineers. Part E, Journal of Process Mechanical Engineering*, *238*(4), 1976–1990. DOI: 10.1177/09544089231159834

Trommer, S. (2017). The WTO in an era of preferential trade agreements: Thick and thin institutions in global trade governance. *World Trade Review*, *16*(3), 501–526. DOI: 10.1017/S1474745616000628

Tsakanikas, A., Caloghirou, Y., Dimas, P., & Stamopoulos, D. (2022). Intangibles, innovation, and sector specialization in global value chains: A case study on the EU's and the UK's manufacturing industries. *Technological Forecasting and Social Change*, *177*, 121488. DOI: 10.1016/j.techfore.2022.121488

Türkeli, S., Bleisteiner, I., Cenci, L., Dominicis, R. D., Demanet, E., Ramirez, G. L., & Müller, D. (2022). X economies: towards comprehensive policy intelligence among Economy visions and practices in Europe and Latin America. In *Towards a circular economy: transdisciplinary approach for business* (pp. 297–332). Springer International Publishing. DOI: 10.1007/978-3-030-94293-9_17

Turkson, E., Oduro, A. D., Baffour, P. T., & Quartey, P. (2023). Regional integration and non-tariff barriers to Intra-Sub-Saharan Africa trade. [HTML]. *World Economy*, *46*(2), 396–414. DOI: 10.1111/twec.13365

Uddin, M. R., Sadik, N., & Rahman, M. M. (2025). Globalization, physical capital, and human capital nexus with economic growth: Evidence from BIMSTEC. *Research in Globalisation*, *10*, 100284. DOI: 10.1016/j.resglo.2025.100284

UNCTAD. (2019). *Islamic Republic of Afghanistan: Rapid eTrade readiness assessment* (UNCTAD/DTL/STICT/2019/5). *United Nations Conference on Trade and Development.*

United Nations Economic and Social Commission for Asia and the Pacific [UN-ESCAP]. (n.d.). *Framework Agreement on Facilitation of Cross-border Paperless Trade in Asia and the Pacific (CPTA).* https://www.unescap.org/projects/cpta

United Nations Office for South-South Cooperation [UNOSSC]. (2022). *Digital trade integration: Role of South-South and triangular cooperation* (South-South Ideas Paper). https://southsouth-galaxy.org/wp-content/uploads/2023/08/South-South-Ideas-Digital-Trade-Integration-Role-of-South-South-and-Triangular-Cooperation.pdf

United Nations Office on Drugs and Crime [UNODC]. (2011). *The global Afghan opium trade: A threat assessment.* https://www.unodc.org/documents/data-and-analysis/Studies/Global_Afghan_Opium_Trade_2011-web.pdf

United Nations Trade and Development (UNCTAD). (2024). The reshaping of global trade: How developing countries can strategize. https://unctad.org/news/reshaping-global-trade-how-developing-countries-can-strategize#:~:text

Upadhyay, D. K., & Mishra, M. (2020). Blue economy: Emerging global trends and India's multilateral cooperation. *Maritime affairs: journal of the national maritime foundation of india, 16*(1), 30-45.

Usanas Foundation. (2024). Why South Asia is needed in Afghanistan. https://usanasfoundation.com/why-south-asia-is-needed-in%20Afghanistan

Valensisi, G., Lisinge, R., & Karingi, S. (2016). The trade facilitation agreement and Africa's regional integration. Canadian Journal of Development Studies. *Canadian Journal of Development Studies, 37*(2), 239–259. DOI: 10.1080/02255189.2016.1131672

Van der Vorst, C., Vanoverbeke, D., & Rousseau, S. (2022). Modelling a new economic, environmental and political connectivity: the dynamics of Japan-EU trade.

Van Hove, J. (2010). Variety and quality in intra-European manufacturing trade: The impact of innovation and technological spillovers. *Journal of Economic Policy Reform, 13*(1), 43–59. DOI: 10.1080/17487870903546275

van Soest, H. L., van Vuuren, D. P., Hilaire, J., Minx, J. C., Harmsen, M. J., Krey, V., Popp, A., Riahi, K., & Luderer, G. (2019). Analysing interactions among sustainable development goals with integrated assessment models. *Global Transitions, 1*, 210–225. DOI: 10.1016/j.glt.2019.10.004

Vann Yaroson, E., Chowdhury, S., Mangla, S. K., Dey, P., Chan, F. T., & Roux, M. (2024). A systematic literature review exploring and linking circular economy and sustainable development goals in the past three decades (1991–2022). *International Journal of Production Research*, *62*(4), 1399–1433. DOI: 10.1080/00207543.2023.2270586

Varghese, P. (2018). Indian Economic Strategy 2035. Department of Foreign Affairs and Trade. Retrieved from https://dfat.gov.au/geo/india/ies/index.html

Varrica, G., & Rusu, E. C. (2023). *Free Movement of Goods Within the Eu Single Market*. EJPAR.

Venables, A. J. (2006). Shifts in Economic Geography and their Causes. CEP Discussion Paper No 767. 1-21.

Vicente, M. R., & López, A. J. (2011). Assessing the regional digital divide across the European Union-27. *Telecommunications Policy*, *35*(3), 220–237. DOI: 10.1016/j.telpol.2010.12.013

Viju-Miljusevic, C. (2019). European Union adapting to an era of no ruling trade paradigm. *European Foreign Affairs Review*, *24*(3), 387–404. DOI: 10.54648/EERR2019031

Vogel, D. (2010). *Barriers or benefits?: regulation in transatlantic trade*. Brookings Institution Press. DOI: 10.5771/9780815705772

Voumik, L. C., Rahman, M. H., Rahman, M. M., Ridwan, M., Akter, S., & Raihan, A. (2023). Toward a sustainable future: Examining the interconnectedness among Foreign Direct Investment (FDI), urbanization, trade openness, economic growth, and energy usage in Australia. Regional Sustainability, 4(4), 405-415. sciencedirect.comDOI: 10.1016/j.regsus.2023.11.003

Wafa, N., & Mazloum Yar, F. G. (2023). Geopolitical influence of Afghanistan's neighbors on the country's domestic and foreign policies. *Devotion: Journal of Research and Community Service.*

Wallace, H., Pollack, M. A., Roederer-Rynning, C., & Young, A. R. (Eds.). (2020). *Policy-making in the European Union*. Oxford university press. DOI: 10.1093/hepl/9780198807605.001.0001

Wang, X. H., & Zhao, J. (2022). Bilateral free trade agreements in a four-country model with a digital technology perspective. *Journal of Digital Economy*, *1*(3), 192–208. DOI: 10.1016/j.jdec.2023.01.001

Wani, A. (2024). The Chabahar gambit: India's play for influence in Central Asia. https://www.orfonline.org/research/the-chabahar-gambit-india-s-play-for-influence-in-central-asia

Watson, M. (2017). Historicising Ricardo's comparative advantage theory, challenging the normative foundations of liberal International Political Economy. *New Political Economy*, *22*(3), 257–272. DOI: 10.1080/13563467.2016.1216535

Weber, R. H. (2015). Digital trade and E-commerce: Challenges and opportunities of the Asia-Pacific regionalism. *Asian J. WTO & Int'l Health L & Pol'y*, *10*, 321.

Weinbaum, M. G., & Ali, N. (2025). US disengagement and new regional security dynamics in Afghanistan's neighborhood. *Middle East Institute.* https://www.mei.edu/publications/us-disengagement-and-new-regional-security-dynamics-afghanistans-neighborhood

Westhoek, H., Van Zeijts, H., Witmer, M., Van den Berg, M., Overmars, K., Van der Esch, S., & Van der Bilt, W. (2012). Greening the CAP. An analysis of the effects of the European Commission's proposals for the Common Agricultural Policy 2014-2020.

Wilkins, D. J., Hulikal Muralidhar, S., Meijer, M., Lascau, L., & Lindley, S. (2022). Gigified knowledge work: understanding knowledge gaps when knowledge work and on-demand work intersect. *Proceedings of the ACM on human-computer interaction, 6*(CSCW1), 1-27. DOI: 10.1145/3512940

Wilson, J. S., & Otsuki, T. (2007). Regional integration in South Asia: What role for trade facilitation? *World Bank Policy Research Working Paper*, (4423).

Wishnick, E. (2021). Prospects for Sino-Russian coordination in Afghanistan. *War on the Rocks.* https://warontherocks.com/2021/11/prospects-for-sino-russian-coordination-in-afghanistan/

World Bank. (2018). *Project appraisal document on a proposed loan…* (P145010). https://documents1.worldbank.org/curated/en/283351468170975849/pdf/832500PAD0P145010Box382156B00OUO090.pdf

World Bank. (2023). https://blogs.worldbank.org/en/trade/africa-pursues-free-trade-amid-global-fragmentation

World Bank. (2024). Afghanistan overview. https://www.worldbank.org/en/country/afghanistan/overview

World Bank. (2024). Q&A: CASA-1000 Resumption in Afghanistan. https://www.worldbank.org/en/news/statement/2024/02/23/casa1000resumptionafghanistan

World Bank. (2024). *The World Bank in Afghanistan: Overview.* https://www.worldbank.org/en/country/afghanistan/overview

World Bank. (2024). World Bank Group announces next phase of support for people of Afghanistan. https://www.worldbank.org/en/news/press-release/2024/02/15/world-bank-group-announces-next-phase-of-support-for-people-of-afghanistan

World Bank. (2024). World Development Indicators (WDI). Available at: https://data.worldbank.org/indicator

World Bank. (2025). *Afghanistan development update: Unlocking youth potential for resilience and economic recovery.* https://thedocs.worldbank.org/en/doc/71dd45bbb425564ee41e22e1dc2c2f57-0310012025/original/Afghanistan-Development-Update-April-2025-Final.pdf

World Economic Forum. [WEF]. (2025). Global trade is changing — and these cities are seizing the opportunity. https://www.weforum.org/stories/2025/03/cities-global-trade-changing-seize-moment/

World Tade Organisation. (2025). Regional Trade Agreements and the WTO. https://www.wto.org/english/tratop_e/region_e/scope_rta_e.htm

World Trade Organization [WTO]. (2015). *World Trade Report 2015: Speeding up trade — Benefits and challenges of implementing the WTO Trade Facilitation Agreement.* https://www.wto.org/english/res_e/booksp_e/world_trade_report15_e.pdf

WTO. (2020). Seventh Trade Policy Review: India, Report by India & Report by the WTO Secretariat, World Trade Organization, Geneva.

WTO. (2022). Fifth Trade Policy Review: Pakistan, Report by the WTO Secretariat, World Trade Organization, Geneva.

WTO. (2025). Fourth Trade Policy Review: Maldives, Report by the WTO Secretariat, World Trade Organization, Geneva.

Xu, X., Lu, Y., Vogel-Heuser, B., & Wang, L. (2021). Industry 4.0 and Industry 5.0—Inception, conception and perception. *Journal of Manufacturing Systems, 61*, 530–535. DOI: 10.1016/j.jmsy.2021.10.006

Yadav, B. K. (2023). Impact of regulation and conformity assessment procedures on global trade. In Handbook of Quality System, Accreditation and Conformity Assessment (pp. 1-21). Singapore: Springer Nature Singapore. [HTML]DOI: 10.1007/978-981-99-4637-2_14-1

Yang, Y., & Gupta, S. (2007). Regional trade arrangements in Africa: Past performance and the way forward. *African Development Review*, *19*(3), 399–431. DOI: 10.1111/j.1467-8268.2007.00169.x

Yang, Z., Anwar, S., & Yang, Y. (2025). The Impact of Foreign Direct Investment on Industrialization in China: A Spatial Panel Analysis. *Economies*, *13*(2), 42. DOI: 10.3390/economies13020042

Yao, X., Yasmeen, R., Li, Y., Hafeez, M., & Padda, I. U. H. (2019). Free trade agreements and environment for sustainable development: A gravity model analysis. *Sustainability (Basel)*, *11*(3), 597. DOI: 10.3390/su11030597

Yar, F. G. M., Zahid, S., & Miakhil, J. M. (2023). Afghanistan's geopolitical and geo-economic significance in regional connectivity and development. *Journal of Political and Legal Sovereignty*, *1*(2), 78–86. DOI: 10.38142/jpls.v1i2.86

Yawar, M. E., & Rasooli, M. (2024). *Examining the position of Afghanistan in the new plan of China's Belt and Road Initiative (with emphasis on media strategies).* Law and Humanities Quarterly Reviews, 3(1). Available at *SSRN*: https://ssrn.com/abstract=4687249

Yeager, E., Bee, B., Hou, A., Cash, T., Dew, K., Dickerson, D., & Jones, S. (2024). A Process for Asset Mapping to Develop a Blue Economy Corridor. *Journal of Higher Education Outreach & Engagement*, *28*(1), 125–143.

Yoon, S., & Ho, J. Y. (2025). Delivering sustainable development via social innovation: Cases of social entrepreneurship in South Korea and Singapore. *Sustainable Development (Bradford)*, *33*(1), 416–430. DOI: 10.1002/sd.3127

Yu, H., Wang, R., & Zhang, A. (2024). Unraveling the impact of environmental provisions in preferential trade agreements on green total factor energy efficiency. [HTML]. *Journal of Environmental Management*, *362*, 121205. Advance online publication. DOI: 10.1016/j.jenvman.2024.121205 PMID: 38823299

Yussuf, A. (2026-Jan-7). Why does Trump want Greenland and why it is so important? https://www.abc.net.au/news/2026-01-07/why-does-trump-want-greenland-and-why-is-it-so-important/106203650

Yusuf, M. (2009, July). The evils of agriculture subsidy. In *Competition Forum* (Vol. 7, No. 2, p. 427). American Society for Competitiveness.

Zaballos, A. G., Rodriguez, E. I., Cave, M., Elbittar, A., Guerrero, R., Mariscal, E., & Webb, W. (2020). The impact of digital infrastructure on the consequences of COVID-19 and on the mitigation of future effects.

Zafarullah, H., & Ferdous, J. (2021). Cyberspace at the grassroots: E-governance and citizen/stakeholder perceptions at the local level in Bangladesh. *Journal of Development Policy and Practice*, *6*(2), 168–187. DOI: 10.1177/24551333211034082

Zapata, A. N., Vacas, M. A., & Payá, J. H. (2023). Drivers of Technological Export Performance in Spain: A Regional Approach, 2000–2016. *Regional Statistics*, *13*(6), 997–1025. DOI: 10.15196/RS130601

Zekos, G. I. (2024). AAI and FDI. In *Artificial Intelligence and Competition: Economic and Legal Perspectives in the Digital Age* (pp. 361–378). Springer Nature Switzerland.

Zhang, Y. (2024). RETRACTED ARTICLE: Promoting sustainable growth through eco-innovation, energy transition, and human capital: a comparative analysis of G-7 economies. [HTML]. *Economic Change and Restructuring*, *57*(6), 186. Advance online publication. DOI: 10.1007/s10644-024-09770-2

Zhang, Y., & Li, S. (2024). The effects of trade liberalization on inequality in nutrition intake: Empirical evidence from Indian districts. *BMC Public Health*, *24*(1), 1317. DOI: 10.1186/s12889-024-18749-7

Zhong, J. & Pei, J. (2024). Carbon border adjustment mechanism: a systematic literature review of the latest developments. Climate Policy. iqcyg.comDOI: 10.1080/14693062.2023.2190074

Zohra, B. F., Slimani, I., Douli, S., & Djomana, T. (2025). The impact of the COVID-19 pandemic on digital innovation. *Brazilian Journal of Business*, *7*(1), e78504–e78504. DOI: 10.34140/bjbv7n1-071

Zulkifli, R., Ozora, E., Ramadhan, M. A., Kacaribu, J. P., & Mahendra, R. (2023). Indonesia's blue economy initiative: Oceans as the new frontier of economic development. *Jurnal Perdagangan Internasional*, *1*(1), 10–16. DOI: 10.33197/jpi.v1i1.1083

About the Contributors

Anita Medhekar is a senior lecturer in economics and holds a PhD from Deakin University, Australia. She has completed her double master's in education and pure Economics from Pune University and University of New England, Australia. She has taught at undergraduate and post graduate levels in India, Indonesia, and Australia and has more than 30 years of teaching and research experience. Currently, she is teaching at Central Queensland University, Australia. Her research interests are in applied International Trade, Tourism Economics, Health Economics, Gender and Development Economics, Asia-Pacific Economies, Public Finance, South-Asia, Australian Economy, Bilateral Trade and Development for Peace, Supply Chains, Public Policy, and Public-Private Partnerships. She has presented papers at numerous international conferences and received best research paper awards. Anita has numerous refereed publications in journals, conference proceedings, with edited books, and book chapters to her credit

Anisul M. Islam is currently serving in the rank of Professor of Economics and Chairman at the FISER (Finance, Info Systems, Economics and Risk Management) Department at University of Houston-Downtown, U.S.A. He has earned his Ph.D. degree in Economics from the University of Alberta (1985). Currently he is the Course Coordinator for Economics He is the past President of the Southwestern Society of Economists and Chapter Chair of the Academy of International Business-US Southwest Chapter. Dr. Islam has co-authored several books, many book chapters, and published numerous articles in peer-reviewed academic journals in international economics, international finance and economic development. He is currently the Editor-in-Chief of the Journal of Global Economy, Trade and International Business and serves in editorial boards of several other professional and peer reviewed academic journals.

S.Jobayear Ahmed is a motivated Research Associate with the Bangladesh Foreign Trade Institute, Ministry of Commerce. He has four master's degrees in applied Statistics and Data Science(MSc), Entrepreneurship Economics(MSS), Marketing(MBA), and Political Economy(MSS). Currently he is involved in international trade related research (associated with EPA/FTA GVC, RVC, and WTO dispute settlement), trade related training need assessment and capacity building of the government officials, chambers and business associations and WTO related policy advocacy including the smooth transitioning strategy after LDC graduation of Bangladesh in 2026. Jobayear brings in first-hand experience of international trade policy formulation, export, import, branding, testing, certification and standardization of the products and services project management through complex field operations conducting field work for 8 years (2016-2025) in Bangladesh Foreign Trade Institute (BFTI), International Rice Research Institute (IRRI), BRAC International and Light Castle Partners. In 2022, he won a Stanford University Fellowship in Frontiers of Social Innovation, and in 2021, he was awarded IOM Scholarship for Certificate Course in Migration. He was also selected as a Young Talent for 2021, to work on United Nations Sustainable Development Goal- 4 on Inclusive and Equitable Quality Education for All; Besides achieved a Japan Foundation Scholarship in 2017.

***

Bablo Biswas has been working as a Research Assistant since 2013, specializing in data collection, report writing, and data curation. Over the past decade, he has contributed to multiple research projects by systematically gathering, organizing, and analyzing data to ensure accuracy and reliability. His responsibilities have included designing and implementing data collection strategies, preparing research reports, and managing datasets to support evidence-based findings. With extensive experience in research support, Bablo has developed strong skills in documentation, critical analysis, and knowledge management. His work plays a vital role in bridging the gap between raw data and meaningful insights, enabling researchers and stakeholders to make informed decisions.

Monika Handayani is a distinguished academic and consultant with a strong focus on sustainability reporting. She currently serves as a lecturer and senate member at Politeknik Negeri Banjarmasin, as well as an Internal Quality Assurance System Auditor. In addition, she is an Assurer for Sustainability Reporting at the National Center for Sustainability Reporting in Jakarta, specializing in the evaluation of sustainability reports for mining, oil, and gas companies across Indonesia. Her academic qualifications are extensive, including a Bachelor's degree in Economics and Accounting, a Master's degree in Governmental Management Accounting, and a Doctorate in Accounting from Universitas Brawijaya, Malang. Monika Handayani is also a certified specialist in sustainability reporting, quality management auditing, chartered accountancy, and export management, holding several prestigious certifications such as Certified Sustainability Reporting Specialist (CSRS), Certified Sustainability Reporting Assurance (CSRA), Certified Accountant (CA), and Certified International Internal Quality

Hamayun Khan is an independent researcher, award-winning author, president and founder of Collective Impact Consulting and SolaTeach.

Nuno Carlos Leitão is a professor at the Higher School of Management and Technology of Santarem. He is PhD with an Aggregation (habilitation) in Economics and is a researcher at CEFAGE, Evora University and CEsA, Lisbon University. His research fields are international economics, energy economics, resources sustainability and tourism.

Khaleda Begum Maiful is an assistant professor in the Department of Economics at the University of Chittagong (CU). Prior to joining CU, she was a research manager in the Bangladesh Foreign Trade Institute, under the Ministry of Commerce, Government of Bangladesh. With more than eight years of professional experience, she possesses a strong knowledge of research, policy analysis, and advocacy, as well as sector-wise capacity-building strategies in the area of development and international trade. As a research manager in a think tank, she was closely involved in policy advocacy for the government, analysing the trade opportunities for Bangladesh in several potential markets globally, WTO issues, WTO ministerial, bilateral, and regional trade agreements, WTO-related trade policies (TRIPS, service trade, LDC services waiver, market access, trade remedies, trade facilitation, etc.), cross-border paperless trade facilitation, WTO Trade Policy Review of different countries, trade negotiations, and so on. She has worked for several national and international organisations, including the World Bank Group (WBG), UNESCAP, UNCTAD, European Commission, DFID, SWISSCONTACT-KATALYST'S project, 'Tottho Apa' project under the Ministry of Women and Children Affairs, and so on. She has led several regional and international research projects that involved multi-sector stockholders, including leading private-sector trade bodies, marginalised groups, international donor and development agencies, government agencies, and civil societies. She has recently published a journal article on International Trade and Trade Policy Challenges in Bangladesh. She participated in more than 30 training programmes at home and abroad on WTO and trade-related issues. She holds a Diploma in Advanced Trade Policy from Trade Academy, National Board of Trade, Stockholm, Sweden.

Mohammad Rashed Hasan Polas is currently working as an Assistant Professor at Strategic Research Institute (SRI) in Asia Pacific University of Technology and Innovation (APU), Malaysia. Moreover, he is the author of several papers in Business Strategy and the Environment, Global Journal of Flexible Systems Management, Journal of Enterprising Communities, Journal of Public Affairs, International Journal of Management Practice, and Environment, Development and Sustainability and so on. He participated in several national and international conferences/seminars. He is an active editorial board member at several international reputed journals. His research interests lie in strategy, entrepreneurship, innovation, and sustainability.

Rismawati is a distinguished academic and consultant with a robust focus on sustainability reporting. She currently holds the position of lecturer and Head of the Quality Assurance Institute at Universitas Muhammadiyah Palopo, where she has been pivotal in ensuring the quality of university processes and outputs since February 2020. Additionally, she serves as an Assurer for Sustainability Reporting at the National Center for Sustainability Reporting in Jakarta, specializing in the evaluation of sustainability reports for mining companies across Indonesia. Her academic qualifications are extensive, comprising a Bachelor's degree in Economics and Accounting, a Master's degree in Accounting Science, and a Doctorate in Accounting from Universitas Brawijaya, Malang. Rismawati is also a certified specialist in sustainability reporting, risk management, and tax planning, holding several prestigious certifications including Certified Sustainability Reporting Specialist (CSRS), Certified Risk Management Practitioner (CRMP), Certified Management Accountant (CMA) and Certified Enterprise Risk Analysis (CERA). In her professional capacity, she has provided consultancy services in financial management and tax compliance for companies such as PT. Reski Barito Timur and PT. Helay Raya. Furthermore, she has authored multiple publications on Social Accounting, Sustainability Accounting, Management Accounting and CSR, contributing significantly to the academic community. Her interests in reading, writing, and travel reflect her commitment to lifelong learning and professional growth in her field.

Mallika Roy is a PhD scholar at Central Queensland University. She is an Associate Professor (study leave) at the Department of Economics, University of Chittagong, Bangladesh. Mallika graduated with Honours (Economics) and Masters' (Economics) from the University of Chittagong, followed by earning her M. Phil (Economics) from the City University of Hong Kong. She achieved the Prestigious Prime Minister Gold Medal Award Bangladesh for her scholastic academic results. She was also awarded a Hong Kong government-funded scholarship for her M. Phil study and Industry and a CQUniversity-funded Elevate scholarship, International

Excellence Award, Top up Scholarship for her PhD Program. She completed an Industry placement with Isaac Regional Council, Australia recently. Her research interests include Agricultural Economics, Supply Chain, Environmental Economics, Economic Development, and Macroeconomics. She has teaching experience of above 14 years. She successfully completed an industry placement with Isaac Regional Council, Australia, in 2025, during which she conducted a study on employee retention factors and submitted a comprehensive research report along with a policy framework. After working as a faculty member at Islamia University College for 2 years and 4 months and subsequently at BGC Trust University Bangladesh for about 1 year, she has been serving as a faculty member at the University of Chittagong for over 10 years. While working as a faculty member at the University of Chittagong, she additionally served as an adjunct faculty in multiple universities such as BGC Trust University, Premier University, Bangladesh University of Professionals (BUP), University of Science and Technology Chittagong (USTC) in Bangladesh. She worked as a research fellow and teaching assistant at the Department of Economics and Finance of the City University of Hong Kong for 2 years. She completed three research projects by UGC Bangladesh in the role of a project director. She published a good number of research papers in national, and international journals and books.

Abu Saleh Md. Sohel-Uz-Zaman earned his Ph.D. in Knowledge Management from Wuhan University of Technology in China. He also holds an MBA with a major in Management from Middlesex University in London, UK. Currently, Dr. Zaman is a Professor at the School of Business & Economics at United International University. He has previously served as the Director of the BBA program and the Director of the MBA and EMBA programs at the same university. His primary areas of interest include Human Resource Management, Strategic Management, and Knowledge Management. Dr. Zaman has authored numerous publications in both international and local journals, as well as at conferences and forums. Additionally, he has written several business cases. Before his academic career, Dr. Zaman spent nearly ten years working in an international consultancy firm. His professional experiences, combined with his academic background, have greatly enhanced his skills in professional coaching and teaching.

Eko Ganis Sukoharsono, S.E., M.Com. Hons., Ph. D. is a lecturer in accounting and sustainability at the Faculty of Economics and Business Universitas Brawijaya, Indonesia. His research interests include environmental and social accountability, sustainability accounting, and digital accounting. Drawing upon postmodern and critical traditions, he investigates how technology, ethics and culture influence accounting and organisation. Introductory chapter Prof. Sukoharsono considers, as part of the book's first chapter, elements embedded in algorithmic and AI systems that are influencing decision making-making by public and private individuals, governance formation and sustainability reporting. He has an h-index of 24 with more than 2,700 citations, and his recent publications focus on digital accountability, AI-driven governance ethics, and Pancasila-based sustainability frameworks. His intellectual gaze connects accounting, tech and culture to catalyze responsible/ human-centered innovation.

Javaid Ahmad Wagay from kashmir india is a dedicated researcher with a Master's degree in Library and Information Science from the University of Kashmir. He has also completed a Bachelor of Education (B.Ed) from the same institution. Javaid brings a diverse range of expertise to his field, including bibliometrics, scientometrics, sentiment analysis, artificial intelligence, Islamic banking, electronic resources, and cloud computing. His multidisciplinary interests and deep analytical skills make him a valuable contributor to both the academic and technological

Index

P

R

S

T

www.ingramcontent.com/pod-product-compliance
Lightning Source LLC
LaVergne TN
LVHW081539300926
849161LV00006B/1494
9798337317823